Research
Matters

A Guide to Research Writing

Second Edition

Rebecca Moore Howard
Syracuse University

Amy Rupiper Taggart
North Dakota State University

*Connect
Learn
Succeed*™

Published by McGraw-Hill, an imprint of The McGraw-Hill Companies, Inc., 1221 Avenue of the Americas, New York, NY 10020. Copyright © 2013, 2011. Printed in the United States of America. All rights reserved. No part of this publication may be reproduced or distributed in any form or by any means, or stored in a database or retrieval system, without the prior written consent of The McGraw-Hill Companies, Inc., including, but not limited to, in any network or other electronic storage or transmission, or broadcast for distance learning.

This book is printed on acid-free paper.

2 3 4 5 6 7 8 9 0 QTN/QTN 1 0 9 8 7 6 5 4 3 2

ISBN: 978-0-07-340594-0
MHID: 0-07-340594-9

Vice President Editorial: *Michael Ryan*
Publisher: *David S. Patterson*
Director of Development: *Dawn Groundwater*
Sponsoring Editor: *Nancy Huebner*
Developmental Editor: *Janice Wiggins-Clarke*
Editorial Coordinator: *Zachary Norton*
Marketing Manager: *Kevin Colleary*
Production Editor: *Melissa Williams*
Media Project Manager: *Jennifer Barrick*
Design Manager: *Jeanne Schreiber*

Cover Design: *David Carlson, Gearbox*
Interior Design: *Elise Lansdon*
Photo Research Coordinator: *Nora Agbayani*
Photo Research: *Deborah Bull*
Illustrator: *Ayelet Arbel*
Production Supervisor: *Louis Swaim*
Composition: *9.5/11 ITC Garamond Light by Thompson Type*
Printing: *45# New Era Matte Plus, Quad Graphics*

Cover image: Howard Sokol/Index Stock Imagery/Photolibrary
The credits section for this book begins on page 407 and is considered an extension of the copyright page.

Library of Congress Cataloging-in-Publication Data

Howard, Rebecca Moore.
   Research matters / Rebecca Moore Howard and Amy Rupiper Taggart. — 2nd ed.
     p. cm.
   Includes bibliographical references and index.
   ISBN-13: 978-0-07-340594-0 (alk. paper)
   ISBN-10: 0-07-340594-9 (alk. paper)
   1. English language—Rhetoric. 2. Academic writing. I. Taggart, Amy Rupiper. II. Title.
   PE1408.H68522 2013
   808'.042—dc22   2011048432

The Internet addresses listed in the text were accurate at the time of publication. The inclusion of a Web site does not indicate an endorsement by the authors or McGraw-Hill, and McGraw-Hill does not guarantee the accuracy of the information presented at these sites.

www.mhhe.com

The love, support, and patience of our families and loved ones—Tom Howard, Mike Moore, Jack Richardson, Melisa Richardson; Mark, Ella, and William Taggart—have made it possible for us to write this book. *Research Matters* is dedicated to the memory of Rebecca's sister, Sandy, and Amy's father, Glenn.

Dear Colleague:

Thank you for taking the time to consider *Research Matters, Second Edition*! You might find yourself asking, "What makes this text distinctive as a research guide?" We'll answer that question here.

Drawing on our own teaching and research, we emphasize what we believe to be central to research writing: the responsibility that comes with entering conversations, responsibility to other writers, to readers, to texts, and to self. We think of students not just as consumers of information but as potential producers of knowledge, as well.

Rebecca Moore Howard has researched and published extensively on literacy education and plagiarism. She has been driven by a concern that plagiarism circumvents the education that she regards as instrumental in individual development and essential for a democratic society. She is Professor of Writing and Rhetoric at Syracuse University.

Amy Rupiper Taggart has researched and published on teaching writing and rhetoric in college and community. Her interest in language as social action energizes and informs her teaching and research. She is Associate Professor of English and Director of First-Year Writing at North Dakota State University.

In this edition, we also marshal the knowledge generated by the Citation Project (http://site.citationproject .net/). The Citation Project is a research study that has thus far involved 22 researchers studying 174 research papers from composition classes at 16 U.S. colleges. Researchers have closely examined and documented students' use of summary, paraphrase, and quotation. They have looked at the sources students cite and compared their treatment of the material to the original material itself. The project has generated powerful knowledge for teachers and student writers.

What does it mean, then, that the 2nd edition of *Research Matters* draws heavily on these findings? It means we are able to talk to students about typical problems other students nationwide have encountered when they use sources. It means students can look into *Research Matters* to see examples of source use like those seen over and over again in the Citation Project research. It means we are able to identify ways your students can do things better. And it means you can emphasize in your teaching the primary challenges student writers nationwide seem to encounter.

To support students, we offer concise explanations of research concepts, overviews of research processes, materials that can serve as models for their work, teaching and learning activities to support their development as researchers, and resources for further information. Together, the parts of the book signal to readers that responsible writers take research seriously and have a wide range of skills and knowledge to help them do it well. Throughout, we remind readers that writing and research are lifelong endeavors, not simply assignments to be completed and forgotten.

Sincerely,

Rebecca Moore Howard and Amy Rupiper Taggart

Research Matters helps students recognize and respect their role in their own writing and research by focusing on four key areas of responsibility:

1. Responsibility to **other writers**
2. Responsibility to **audience**
3. Responsibility to **topic**
4. Responsibility to **self**

CITE LIKE AN EXPERT

Based on findings from:

The Citation Project
citationproject.net

22 researchers studying
174 researched papers from
composition classes at
16 U. S. colleges

Blending Voices in Your Text

Whenever you write from sources, you are blending the voices of your sources with each other and with your own voice. At every point in your text, your readers want to know whose voice they are "hearing." To blend voices successfully, you need to avoid patchwriting and show the beginning and end of each source use.

Some readers consider it plagiarism when a writer *patchwrites:* copying from sources, making superficial changes to its language, but not actually *paraphrasing* it, rewriting it in fresh language. Regardless of whether they classify it as plagiarism, no readers consider patchwriting good writing. The following passage from a source, and a student's first-draft writing from that source, illustrates the issue:

Passage from Source

> In the 1910s and later, as child psychology became an academic discipline, teachers increasingly looked to educational researchers rather than librarians as the central experts in children's reading.

Patchwriting

> From the 1910s on, child psychology became a discipline, and teachers more and more thought that educational researchers rather than librarians were the main experts in children's reading (248).

The patchwriting follows the original sentence, deleting a few words and substituting some others, but still depending on the source.

Writing Responsibly   Avoid Patchwriting

As you summarize, check to make sure that you are not *patchwriting*—duplicating the language of the source with minor changes. Check your language against that in your source, and revise if you have done any of the following:

- used more than a few *key terms* from the text

- presented the ideas in the *same order* as the source
- used the *same sentence structure* as the source

If you find that you are patchwriting, revise your summary using your own words.

Research Matters teaches students to recognize and respect other authors, not only by citing their work accurately but also by treating their ideas fairly.

Research Matters demonstrates that writers must be responsible to their audience by citing and integrating research clearly, allowing readers to see where their information came from and the nature of that information.

17 Citing Expertly

A citation names the source, the person or persons, with whom you are talking. Other cues you provide reveal the nature of that conversation. To cite well—to go beyond simply naming the source—is to make your conversation "transparent," to allow others to see how your ideas developed and how you are relating to others' thinking about the same issues. Your goal should be not only to credit your sources, but also to provide information about them, make obvious how and why you are using them, and explain how they relate to each other and to your thesis. This is expert *rhetorical citation*, citation that not only informs but also persuades. This chapter will help you to reveal your sources and your own stance. Also, throughout *Research Matters*, you will find two-page sections entitled Cite Like an Expert that provide you with additional information and guidance on citation.

193

Make It Your Own!

Writing
↑ Responsibly   Made-up "Evidence"

In May 2005, a stem cell expert resigned his position at Seoul National University following revelations by the journal *Nature* that his laboratory had falsified data. Hwang Woo Suk's case is not an isolated one: In 2002, for example, Bell Laboratories fired star researcher Jan Hendrik Schon for falsifying data. Commentators have noted that competition was a factor in these cases: The desire for acclaim and advancement had become more important than the desire for truth.

The highly competitive academic environment may tempt you, too, to make up "facts" to support a thesis in a paper. It is easy to alter data, invent statistics or quotations, or manipulate an image so that it "shows" what you want it to. Resist the temptation: the short-term benefits are not worth it. Not only are you likely to get caught—fabricated evidence often *sounds* fake—but you would also be sacrificing the opportunity to learn something about your topic and about the writing process and potentially influencing others through misinformation.

On the other hand, the purpose of most academic writing is not to sell products but to explore and explain ideas. Demonstrating that you have considered all sides of a thorny problem and have come to a reasonable resolution of it requires that you include counterevidence. For example, Amy Ehret offers this paragraph of counterevidence, assessing the possible shortcomings of her research:

> Limitations of this study include the small sample size ($n = 54$) with the majority of participants being white female college students. The study is not an equal representation of the university's population or the general population. There are very few native English speaking minorities present in the study. Because the sample is quite young (college students), it is difficult to generalize these findings with those from an older and more varied sample. Results containing older participants

Writing
↑ Responsibly   Keeping an Open Mind

As a writer, you also have a responsibility to avoid bias: Read sources with an open mind, use reliable sources, consider evidence that undermines your position, avoid exaggerated claims, and criticize unreasonable or poorly supported conclusions but not the people who hold them. Sound research considers all sides of an argument. Be especially careful as you evaluate sources that you immediately agree or disagree with: Just because you agree with them does not mean they are reliable sources, nor does your disagreement invalidate them.

Research Matters helps students recognize their responsibility to provide reliable information about their topic at a depth that does the topic justice.

> **Research Matters** emphasizes the responsibility of writers to themselves, to take their writing seriously and to approach writing tasks as an opportunity to learn about a topic and to expand their scope as writers.

15g Drafting

Because writing is so challenging and because so much is often riding on the success of writing projects, it is easy for other objectives (getting an A, impressing the boss, looking clever to friends, finishing the task quickly) to get in the way of fulfilling your responsibilities as a writer. At the drafting stage, ask yourself the following questions to make sure you have worked responsibly so far:

> **More about ▶▶▶**
> Introducing counter-evidence, 153, 184–86
> Citing your sources and avoiding plagiarism, 127–38

- Have I done enough research to answer my question without making too many assumptions?
- Have I acknowledged any counterevidence in my draft?
- Have I documented any sources I have referred to in my draft, whether quoted, paraphrased, summarized, or reproduced (images and other media)?
- Have I worked to fully understand each source before using it?

Sample Student Essay: First Draft

> **▶▶▶Additional** samples from Erin Buksbaum:
> Freewriting, 27–28
> Revised thesis, 153–54
> Outlines, 162–64

> **More about ▶▶▶**
> Integrating visuals, 186–87

The first draft of Erin Buksbaum's essay on social networking sites follows. Note that in this draft Buksbaum does not worry about polished writing or even perfect grammar and spelling. She knows she can make necessary alterations as she revises. For now, her focus is on getting her ideas down in a logical order and on supporting her thesis with evidence. Note, too, that Buksbaum includes a place for a screen capture from a social networking site. Although she has not selected the particular capture she will use, she wisely builds a place for this major element into her earliest draft.

> Title that
> reflects the
> research
> question

Is Social Networking a Serious Danger?

The internet has changed the way people communicate and interact with each other forever. Social networking sites let users create

Writing Responsibly **The Big Picture**

Another way to think about revising is to focus on your responsibilities to your *audience*, your *topic, other writers,* and *yourself*:

- Have you provided your *audience* with a worthwhile reading experience?
- Have you covered your *topic* fully and ethically?

- Have you represented borrowed ideas accurately and acknowledged all your *sources*, whether you have quoted, summarized, or paraphrased?
- Have you developed a voice that readers will find credible, represented your ideas clearly and powerfully, and written in a voice that reflects *your best self*?

Research Matters Makes Responsible Writing Easier!

With *Connect Composition,* course management and assessment can be easily implemented in a writing course with a wide range of tools that can all be seamlessly accessed by your local course management system.

Market-leading Integration with all Course Management Systems.

With McGraw-Hill Campus, instructors enjoy single sign-on access to *Connect Composition* through any learning management system. Seamless interoperability of all *Connect* assets allows students to access all the features and functionalities of McGraw-Hill's digital tools directly from their instructor's course management site.

The **Best** of **Both Worlds**

Outcomes Based Assessment of Writing. *Connect's* assessment tools allow instructors to provide students with the feedback they need when they need it. Pre-built, customizable grading rubrics make the set-up, management, and reporting of outcomes-based assessment efficient and professional. Finally: an affordable, easy to use, and statistically valid assessment solution—for a single course or for an entire program.

Visit Connect Composition 3.0 <http://connect.mcgraw-hill.com>

Adaptive Diagnostics develop customized learning plans to individualize instruction, practice, and assessment, meeting each student's needs in core skill areas. Students get immediate feedback on every exercise, and results are sent directly to the instructor's grade book.

Results vetted by research. McGraw-Hill's innovative series of multi-campus research studies provide evidence of improved student performance with the use of Connect, with students in high-usage groups achieving consistently better gains across multiple outcomes. Independent analysis showed that the tools within *Connect* provided a statistically valid measure for assessing these results.

For more information, visit www.mhhe.com/SCORE.

Acknowledgments

Writing *Research Matters* has been a thrilling and reciprocal learning experience. We hope readers will learn from *Research Matters* as much as we learned from the process of creating it. *Research Matters* is the product of many, many individuals' efforts beyond those of the coauthors whose names appear on the cover. We are grateful to all who have helped make *Research Matters* possible: students, editors, copyeditors, designers, and citation and documentation experts.

Students—including Erin Buksbaum, Dan Long, and Lydia Nichols from Syracuse University; Abrams Conrad from American University; Amy Ehret from Illinois State University; Heather DeGroot from James Madison University; Alicia Keene from University of Maryland; Stacy Keller from North Dakota State University; and Alea Wratten from SUNY–Geneseo—have generously provided relevant writing samples that will help other students envision good research writing. Thanks to them and to the students who also provided writing for Rebecca Moore Howard's companion handbook, *Writing Matters*. All those who contributed to the handbook also affected *Research Matters* in large and small ways.

We also want to thank the many reviewers who offered candid evaluations and suggestions for improvement. Their understanding of what works at their institutions and in their classrooms provided us with invaluable help in choosing what to include, what to leave out, and how to shape each part.

Manuscript Reviewers

Angelina College: Howard Cox, Patty Rogers
Bakersfield College: Jennifer Jett
Bluefield State College: Dana Cochran
Boston University: Matthew Parfitt

> " ...a really practical resource that is addressing the needs of contemporary college students. "
> —Moumin Quazi, *Tarleton State University*

Bowie State University: Stephanie Johnson
Capital University: Kevin Griffith

Cecil College: Craig Frischkorn
Central Oregon Community College: Cora Agatucci
Clark State Community College: Laurie Buchanan, Cecilia Kennedy
Edinboro University of Pennsylvania: Wendy Warren Austin
Edmonds Community College: Greg Van Belle
Florida State University: Deborah Coxwell-Teague
Georgia Gwinnett College: Thomas Clancy
Georgia Perimeter College: Kari Miller
Greenville Technical College: April Childress
Indian River State College: April Van Camp
Indian University-Purdue University Indianapolis: Anne C. Williams

> " ...thoroughly presents the benefits to and responsibilities of students as they pursue researched essay projects. "
> —Carol Watt, *Lane Community College*

Jones County Junior College: Cheryl Windham
Jones County Junior College: Susan Blackledge, Phillip Wedgeworth
Lane Community College: Carol Watt
Loyola University Chicago: Margaret Loweth
McHenry County Community College: Cynthia Van Sickle
Metropolitan State College of Denver: Rebecca Gorman, Jessica Parker
Metropolitan State University: Jenni Runte
Mount Hood Community College: Jonathan Morrow
North Idaho College: Amy Flint
Northern Virginia Community College—Alexandria: Brian Delaney
Northern Virginia Community College—Loudoun Campus: Arnold Bradford
Northwest Florida State College: James Suderman, Patrice Williams
Northwest Missouri State University: Robin Gallaher
Palm Beach Community College: Patricia McDonald, Vicki Scheurer
Palo Alto College: Ruth Ann Gambino, Caroline Mains, Diana Nystedt
Pioneer Pacific College: Jane Hess
Rogue Community College: Laura Hamilton
Salem State College: Rick Branscomb

San Antonio College: Alexander Bernal
Seton Hall University: Nancy Enright
South Texas Community College: Joseph Haske
Southern Illinois University–Edwardsville:
Matthew S. S. Johnson
Southwestern Illinois College: Steve Moiles
St. Clair County Community College: John Lusk
St. Johns River Community College: Melody
Hargraves, Elise McClain, Jeannine Morgan,
Rebecca Sullivan

> Innovative ideas, effective examples, and good organization . . .
> —Barbara Chambers, *Jones County Junior College*

Tarleton State University: Moumin Quazi
Tennessee State University: Samantha
Morgan-Curtis
Texas A + M University—Kingsville: Laura Wavell
University of Illinois at Urbana-Champaign:
Grace Giorgio
University of Maryland—University College:
Andrew Cavanaugh
University of Northern Iowa: Gina Burkart
University of Texas—San Antonio: Marguerite
Newcomb
University of Wisconsin at Marathon County:
Christina McCaslin
Valdosta State University: Richard Carpenter, Jane
Kinney, Chere Peguesse
Wesley College: Linda De Roche
Westminster College: Susan Gunter
Westmoreland County Community College:
Michael Hricik
Wharton County Junior College: Mary Lang,
Sharon Prince
Wharton County Junior College: Mary Lang
(design designation missing)
Wichita State University: Darren DeFrain
William Woods University: Greg Smith

Design Reviewers

Bakersfield College: Jennifer Jett
Bluefield State College: Dana Cochran
Edmonds Community College: Greg Van Belle
Georgia Perimeter College: Kari Miller
**Indian University–Purdue University
Indianapolis:** Anne C. Williams

McHenry County Community College: Cynthia
Van Sickle
Metropolitan State College of Denver: Rebecca
Gorman, Jessica Parker
North Idaho College: Amy Flint
**Northern Virginia Community College—
Loudoun Campus:** Arnold Bradford
Northwest Missouri State University: Robin
Gallaher
Rogue Community College: Laura Hamilton
South Texas Community College: Joseph Haske
Southern Illinois University–Edwardsville:
Matthew S. S. Johnson
University of Northern Iowa: Gina Burkart
University of Wisconsin at Marathon County:
Christina McCaslin
Westmoreland County Community College:
Michael Hricik
Wharton County Junior College: Mary Lang

Components of *Research Matters*

For Instructors

All of the instructor ancillaries described below, created by Andy Preslar, Lamar State College, can be found on the password-protected instructor's side of the text's Online Learning Center. Contact your local McGraw-Hill sales representative for log-in information.

Instructor's Manual

The *Instructor's Manual* provides a wide variety of tools and resources for enhancing your course instruction, including an overview of the chapter, considerations for assigning, applications for fresh-man comp and other courses, learning outcomes, strategies and tips for teaching, and exercises and activities.

Test Bank

The *Test Bank* offers multiple choice, true/false, and fill-in-the-blank questions covering key concepts in the text. These test items are available on the instructor's Online Learning Center as Microsoft

Word files and in EZ Test, a simple-to-use electronic test bank that allows instructors to edit questions and to add their own questions.

PowerPoint Slides

The PowerPoint presentations cover the key points of each chapter. The presentations serve as an organizational and a navigational tool integrated with examples and activities. Instructors can use the slides as is or modify them to meet their individual needs.

Personal Acknowledgments

Research Matters represents the efforts of a team of teachers, writers, researchers, editors, and designers, but it also reflects the family who supported us: Tom Howard, senior lecturer in University Studies at Colgate University, has worked with Rebecca Moore Howard from the beginning to the end; Mark Taggart, multimedia specialist with Left Brain Media, provided ongoing support and child care at key moments in the development of the book; Ella and William Taggart distracted Amy Rupiper Taggart from the book so that she was able to view it with fresh eyes; and Sandra Jamieson has led the Citation Project researchers to the insights about writing from sources that are part of the fiber of this book.

The entire McGraw-Hill team has provided excellent support and guidance to make *Research Matters* possible and keep it moving apace. Our thanks go to Steve Debow, President for Humanities, Social Sciences, and World Languages; Deborah Kopka, our copyeditor for the second edition; Melissa Williams, Production Editor; Dawn Groundwater, Director of Development, David Patterson, Publisher for English; and Marty Moga, Permissions Editor. Special thanks go to Janice Wiggins-Clarke, Development Editor, who gracefully kept track of tasks and schedules; and Nancy Huebner, Sponsoring Editor.

Contents

Part Two   Information Matters

Part Five   Documentation Matters

Owning Your Research

Those daring enough to climb Mount Everest, said to be the highest mountain in the world, face a perilous journey. Writers, especially those new to the process, may worry that writing a college-level research project resembles this trek: Both seem to entail long, arduous expeditions through unfamiliar, harsh terrain. Writers might also be unclear why they are making the trek—is it worth the time and energy? Good preparation, though, can fill the journey with rewards rather than anguish. As a dependable guide helps climbers stay on track, so too will this chapter and the ones that follow provide support for writing a researched document. Being clear about the goal and the rewards of the journey can make research a process of exploration and discovery rather than one of a tired retracing of steps.

1a Understanding the Benefits

Why are you making this trek? Research is taught and required throughout high school and college for a host of reasons:

- **To build knowledge.** Your research project should help you understand your topic better. Ideally, it will also help your readers come to a more nuanced understanding of the issues, ideas, and information.

More about ▶▶▶
Analysis, 18

- **To develop analytical skills.** Researchers break down information into parts that can be examined and managed; they focus on smaller pieces of large problems so that people can see them more clearly.

More about ▶▶▶
Evaluation, 20

- **To develop evaluative skills.** Each time you encounter a source, you must determine whether it is good or even the best one. This evaluative decision comes from comparison with other sources and with standards dictating what a good source is.

More about ▶▶▶
Claims and evidence,
182–84
Thesis statements,
151–53

- **To understand and practice supporting claims with evidence.** To affect other people's beliefs and actions, you must be persuasive. Few people change their minds, however, without compelling evidence. Research projects involve developing a clear claim, often in the form of a thesis statement, and making sure the information you offer supports that claim, so that your readers will agree with you or at least consider you to be reasonable.

More about ▶▶▶
Conducting research
in the disciplines,
234–38

- **To develop an understanding of academic discourse.** Members of particular disciplines and professions share some common ways of talking, thinking, writing, and acting. If you are an outsider to the group, these can seem like obstacles or unclear communication. While one research project will not teach you all of the writing techniques you need for college (these will differ from class to class and discipline to discipline), paying attention to how research is done in one context will help you determine which questions to ask when you have a research task in another context.

More about ▶▶▶
Setting a schedule,
51–52
Keeping records,
113–17
Organizing your
project, 157–62

- **To prepare for workplace and life problem solving.** Very little in the world gets done without research. As a result, very few written documents are produced without research. Yet without some careful training and practice in finding, evaluating, and using information, writers are likely to disseminate partial truths and even lies.

- **To learn about and practice project management.** Virtually all jobs, especially the professional jobs for which most college graduates prepare, involve complex projects that require pacing, prioritizing, organizing, and breaking down into tasks that can be easily completed. Research projects are similar: There are steps you must take, information to organize and track, and an end goal.

1b   Having a Sense of Purpose

Perhaps you have written research papers since you were in middle school. You might not have the most joyful relationship with what seems to be a repeat and schoolish task. Or perhaps you have not had much experience using research in your writing, and you do not yet have a clear sense of why you might do it. Beyond understanding the benefits in general for your learning and development, having a sense of the purpose for each researched writing task can really help to motivate you. Every document should accomplish a goal for someone. Sometimes the purpose is primarily educational, for you. Other times, the purpose is to propose solutions, as in the proposal genre, or to comment on some trend or issue to help readers make sense of it, as in the commentary genre. As you work, from beginning to end, try to think about who readers of your document are or should be and what your research can do for those readers.

1c   Tapping Personal and Professional Interests

A Chinese proverb says, "Instructors open the door. You enter by yourself." In a college class, research can seem like something an instructor makes you do, something that is disconnected from your life and interests. Yet most instructors hope you will be able to connect what you learn and do in school with your interests and goals. Finding ways to make connections between your research project and your interests is up to you, both in and out of school.

Recognize that you conduct research all the time

Think about the times you have had a question, ranging from one that could be answered by a single source to one for which you constantly seek more information. If you are a video gamer, you have probably done research to learn how to deal with new challenges in the game. Maybe you have just saved up enough money to buy a car and want to find a fuel-efficient, affordable, but sporty vehicle. You are motivated to find the right car and are willing to spend some time asking the right people and reading the right resources. While the experience of doing this daily research may feel less structured than your academic research, the best academic research will also come from personal motivation and may draw on a similar range of resources.

Use personal experiences as stimuli

If your family has a history of genetic diabetes, you might be more motivated than others to understand some aspect of diabetes research. A student athlete might be invested in understanding Title IX, which bans discrimination based on sex or gender in schools, including athletic activities. Think about who you are, where you come from, how you spend your time, and what forces affect you every day. In these parts of your own identity lie sources of curiosity.

Another way to define your interests is to explore what annoys, worries, or upsets you. Have you felt annoyed when talking about a particular topic with friends or family? Is there something you have read recently that excited you? Starting with an emotionally charged topic will require some care: You will need to explore the topic as a learner, rather than just looking for evidence to support what you already believe. Still, your emotions may motivate you to exert extra intellectual energy.

Start to see yourself as a professional

Professionals of all stripes conduct research, even when their titles are not "researcher." An architect planning a building researches its location, its purpose, the qualities of the materials that will be used, and traffic patterns. Corporate managers conduct research on motivating people. Doctors keep current on the latest medical research. What are your long-term goals as a professional in training? Thinking about your professional goals may suggest additional topics that will not only fulfill the assignment requirements but also help you develop professional knowledge. If you are not sure what roles research and writing play in your chosen field, conduct an informational interview with a professional working in it.

1d Finding Space in the Assignment

Sometimes your research assignment will constrain your choices. In a way, the constraint is helpful because it provides a focus. However, developing personal investment with the topic can be challenging. Think about your interests and try to connect topics you care about to the assigned one. For instance, if you are interested in music while the assigned topic is environmentalism, you could merge those interests to study musicians who take a stand regarding the environment or music industry advances with an environmental impact. Most instructors welcome initiative and creativity, as long as you find a way to connect your interest to the goals and focus of the assignment.

More about ▶▶▶
Analyzing the assignment, 48–50

1e Making Room in Your Schedule

To explore and complete your assignment well, start planning now. Find some time in your schedule that is usually available, and make that your research project time. Put it on your calendar and use it. This will help prevent procrastination and the faulty idea that the project can be completed the night before it is due. Later, when you develop your project proposal, you can break down your schedule further and get more specific about your plan. For now, at least schedule the following tasks:

More about ▶▶▶
Project proposals, 56–57
Brainstorming, 38–39
Taking notes, 113–20

- Reread the assignment.
- Brainstorm ideas (using your interest inventories and other brainstorming techniques such as freewriting and talking to peers).
- Read for discovery, to find more ideas.
- Begin a research notebook, blog, or other notes file.

Then, use the corresponding chapters in this book to complete each task.

1f Raising Questions

Perhaps the best way to own a research project is to start with authentic questions. Good research answers questions—for the writer as well as the reader. Avoid choosing a topic about which you intend to

More about ▶▶▶
Developing your research question, 35–36
Drafting research questions, 48–49

"prove" the correctness of your beliefs. Research projects are an opportunity to expand your knowledge.

After hearing on television about democratic protests in Egypt, you might be curious about what pushed people to these protests after 30 years. A question you might pursue would be, "What factors led a large portion of the population of Egypt to be willing to risk their lives for possible change?" Or you may be wondering whether such democratic protest and upheaval will be dangerous for the rest of the world and might pursue a project that reports on what political analysts have to say about impacts on broader stability.

A second way to work from questions is to think of a problem, and use the research to find a solution. This approach is especially appropriate when your assignment is to write a formal proposal, whose hallmark is a problem-solution structure. These might be campus problems: How can the campus expand its recycling program? Or they might be community problems: How can the city increase home ownership and reduce renting?

⬆ Make It **Your Own**

To get a sense of the problems that affect you directly and that might make fruitful research topics, focus in on groups with which you are involved.

- List all of the groups to which you belong, including student organizations, church groups, nonprofits at which you volunteer, and even informal groups that share common goals.
- Now choose a group and brainstorm a list of all the problems you perceive it to have, and/or consult with the group to determine what problems exist.
- Consider attending the next group meeting and asking members what kinds of information would help them solve these problems.

Think about pursuing a research project in response to one of these problems and bringing your findings to the group when you are finished. Along the way, continue to consult with group members.

Quick

Reference ➡ **Owning Your Research**

If you have just been handed a research project assignment sheet and do not yet feel invested in the project, try some of these techniques:

- Set aside an hour or two in your schedule each week for this project. Do not let other things encroach on that time.
- Think about your personal and professional goals. What information do you need to achieve those goals?
- Put a sticky note on your computer with an audience and purpose on it that can inspire and motivate you to do the research.
- Find a little corner of the assignment topic (if it is not an open topic) that corresponds

to your existing interests and goals. What kind of fusion happens when you put the topic area together with one of your interests?

- Take a potential topic, and write a couple of pages with your internal editor turned off. What do you already know? What seems to be missing in your knowledge?
- Consider fresh ways of presenting research. Would you like experience presenting research in documentary, hypertext, proposal, or another form?

1g Developing Confidence: What Do You Already Know?

Individuals sometimes procrastinate when they feel overwhelmed and believe they have nothing to say on a topic. One way to reduce the feeling of being overwhelmed is to write freely for about ten minutes on a topic, not worrying about writing coherently or cleanly, just to explore what you already know. You are not a blank slate; allow yourself to really think about what you know on the assigned topic or one you might consider as your research topic. Another benefit of this task is that you can make sure you do not rewrite things you already know as the bulk of your research project.

> *More about* ▶▶▶
> Freewriting, 37–38
> Brainstorming, 38–39

1h Presenting Your Research in an Alternate Form

Some assignments require that you present your research in traditional research essay form. However, some instructors and some assignments may be more open in terms of format and audience. Take advantage of this opportunity, particularly if you have multimedia or design skills that might make it more interesting to you to move away from the traditional academic essay form. You might feel you "own" the piece more in another medium or genre. Would your information reach a broader audience on the Web? Would the topic lend itself well to audio and visual enhancement? Think about the ways in which research

> *More about* ▶▶▶
> Designing and presenting your project, 216–229

is presented through documentary films; multimedia-enhanced websites; even print genres such as proposals, commentaries, and fact sheets. If you are already comfortable with the essay, moving into a new genre will also expand your flexibility in presenting research. Just be sure an alternate genre or approach is appropriate in your class.

A Final Thought

A then undergraduate named S. Tonia Hsieh was so curious about what made geckos stick to walls that she stuck a dead gecko to a door by just one of its toes. Then, she added a weight to the gecko. It still stuck. Her research came from a wild curiosity about what made geckos cling to surfaces. That curiosity has led through research to innovations in adhesives and other areas.

Buy into your own research. The immediate benefits go directly to you, and the long-term consequences may be even greater.

2 Reading Your Sources

Reading sources is always an interaction, much more like chemistry than it might first appear. In chemistry, one chemical reacts with another, each having an effect. Readers' experiences similarly intermingle with what is in a text, and this intermingling is an exciting part of the research process. Even when we read purely for pleasure, the experience allows for—and often demands—more than mere *comprehension,* or getting something out of a text. Active reading also means *reflection* and *interpretation,* or putting something in, as well. In college courses and beyond, reading often entails *response,* an opportunity for readers to write about the text and put themselves in conversation with it. This chapter focuses on three stages of the critical reading process: *reading to comprehend, reading to reflect,* and *reading to write.*

2a Reading to Comprehend

We constantly read texts. Some, like signs or labels, are just one- or two-word messages. Advertising slogans ("Can you hear me now? Good.") are a bit longer, and directions for assembling a shelving unit are longer still. Even longer are newspaper articles or stories in a magazine. These different types of texts all share a common goal: to communicate information quickly, simply, and clearly.

"Can you hear me now? Good."

Most texts you read in college have a different objective: to engage you in the complexities—not the simplicities—of an issue. This urge to examine complexity encourages both writers and readers to make well-informed, carefully considered judgments. *Critical reading* is more than an attitude; it is a set of skills—or a process that typically includes the following steps:

- previewing the text
- reading to get the gist
- rereading

Previewing the text

Far from adding to your reading load, *previewing* texts saves you time in the long run, allows you to read more in the time allotted, and enables you to read with greater comprehension. Before you settle down to read a text, try some of the following *prereading strategies:*

- **Read the abstract.** Many scholarly journals provide abstracts— or summaries—of their articles, either in the table of contents or at the beginning of each article. Reading the abstract can introduce you to the main ideas you will encounter in the text.

- **Read the table of contents.** When reading books, look first to the table of contents to see which chapters are likely to most directly address issues of importance to your work.

- **Read the headings.** If the text is organized with headings and subheadings, skimming these will often offer you a helpful outline.

- **Scan figures and illustrations.** Graphics might represent important ideas and can convey a complex process to you immediately.

- **Read the introduction and conclusion.** The introduction and conclusion usually contain a text's central ideas and arguments, important questions, and major discoveries.

- **Read only the first sentence of each paragraph.** Not all first sentences are topic sentences, but most introduce or summarize what a paragraph will cover.

- **Use the index.** When reading a book, consult the index to find sections where your key terms appear. (You will want to read those sections closely.)

Reading to get the gist

After using several prereading strategies, you are ready to read the entire text from beginning to end. As you do, circle words or phrases you have questions about, but press on without looking them up. If you do not understand a passage, keep moving; for now, resist rereading or taking substantial notes because you might be tempted to stop once you find a sentence that seems to support a claim you *want* to make, rather than discovering the full argument the author is making. When you have finished one read-through, put the text aside and write down what you remember, no matter how fragmentary.

More about ▶▶▶
Reading whole texts, 72–73

Rereading

Engaging with—or even just comprehending—a difficult text requires more than one reading. After you have read the entire selection from beginning to end, reread it. Retrace your steps carefully, and take time to puzzle over complexities. Look up unfamiliar words, and highlight or underline the most important, interesting, and difficult concepts. In the margins, write your questions, reactions, insights, and arguments. Connect what you read to what you know, have read, or have experienced.

More about ▶▶▶
Annotating, 13–15

Viewing visual texts to comprehend

In our information-based society, much information is communicated visually, and we strive to be savvy readers of that information. When you are reading for research projects, information graphics can be useful but sometimes perplexing sources of information. It is very easy to misread a visual display of information.

Here are some ways to approach a visual text for comprehension:

- **Determine the visual's audience, purpose, context, and author.** These contextual aspects will often help you quickly understand the text better. If you find an information graphic during a web search that is out of its original context, this process of going back to ask who produced it and why is especially important. Data on infant mortality rates produced by U.S. insurance companies as opposed to information on infant mortality gathered by the United Nations would likely have a very different focus and intent, for instance.

More about ▶▶▶
Using visuals as
support, 186–87

- **Look for keys or codes.** Labels are important to interpreting information accurately. On a chart or graph, for instance, the axes will be labeled. On a pie chart, color-coding is often used to distinguish different categories of information.

- **Pay close attention to how numbers are displayed.** To make large numbers easier to represent, information graphics sometimes use the numbers 1–100 but indicate that those numbers stand for millions or even billions.

- **Avoid relying only on the visual.** If a description or analysis accompanies the graphic, read that, too. Compare your understanding to the description.

2b Reading to Reflect

When you think about what you are reading and connect it to your prior experiences, to other readings, and to the larger world, you are practicing *reflective reading.* The text initiates a conversation in which a critical, reflective reader participates.

Keeping a reading journal

More about ▶▶▶
Taking notes, 113–25

Writing while reading helps people discover both what we know and what we want to learn more about. The latter, our curiosities, may become research topics. A great way to write reflectively is to record your intellectual and personal responses to texts in a *reading journal,* which can be paper, a computer file, blog, or even wiki you share with other readers. Articulating your responses to what you read helps build a deeper understanding and a sense of taking part in—not just taking in—your education.

Your reading journal is a good place to do any or all of the following:

- List and define specialized vocabulary in the reading.

- Summarize the main idea and supporting points in the reading.

- Respond to ideas you encounter through freewriting, clustering, or brainstorming.

- Record your own ideas in response to the reading: what you agree with, disagree with, need to learn more about, or just find interesting or important.

- Compare and connect what you have read previously to this piece.

Get into the practice of keeping bibliographic information with your journal entries so that, when you decide on a topic, you can easily go back to items you have already noted in your journal and use them as resources for the research project.

More about ▶▶▶
Summary, 16–17, 58–59
Idea-generation techniques, 23–33

More about ▶▶▶
Research logs, 24, 125
Citation, 141
Documentation, 234–38

Annotating

Like reading or keeping a journal, *annotating* (marking notes directly on a text and in its margins) is a highly individual activity. As you hone your own effective system, keep the following suggestions in mind:

- Use a highlighter or colored pen to mark important ideas. Rather than marking whole sentences, try to highlight as few words as possible, allowing the truly important points to stand out.

- Read with a pencil in hand. When you have ideas or questions, if the book is yours, write them in the margin.

- Circle or underline passages or words you have questions about or might want to respond to.

More about ▶▶▶
Choosing an organizer to fit your work style, 114–17

In addition or instead, you might want to take notes in a separate location, including page numbers and brief references for later use.

Sample annotated text

Here is how one student approached the task of annotating the text "How Hip-Hop Music Lost Its Way and Betrayed Its Fans" by Brent Staples. The annotations define unfamiliar vocabulary, note reflections, and make connections.

I loved "Just Walk on By" (same author)

There are certainly negative images out there, but there are many positive African American role models, too (including Staples).

virulent—extremely infectious or damaging. Why is rap the most "virulent" music?

Central argument—raises an important issue but over-generalizes.

"palette" compares music to painting

misogyny—hatred of women

Have things changed since then?

Too strong? Rap sometimes glamorizes, but it can raise awareness, too.

Is this logic backward? Sometimes gangsta rappers are violent, but does their music describe the violence or cause it?

The "rap community" isn't entirely gangsta rap; there are other kinds of rap/hip-hop out there.

Many people "learned" or were not involved in the violence: Kanye West, Chuck D., Public Enemy, etc.

True—recording labels are marketing an image.

Example: 50 Cent and the release/ marketing of "The Massacre"

How Hip-Hop Music Lost Its Way and Betrayed Its Fans

By BRENT STAPLES

(12 May 2005)

African-American teenagers are beset on all sides by dangerous myths about race. The most poisonous one defines middle-class normalcy and achievement as "white," while embracing violence, illiteracy and drug dealing as "authentically" black. This fiction rears its head from time to time in films and literature. But it finds its most virulent expression in rap music, which started out with a broad palette of themes but has increasingly evolved into a medium for worshiping misogyny, materialism and murder.

This dangerous narrowing of hip-hop music would be reason for concern in any case. But it is especially troubling against the backdrop of the 1990's, when rappers provoked a real-world gang war by using recordings and music videos to insult and threaten rivals. Two of the music's biggest stars—Tupac Shakur and the Notorious B.I.G.—were eventually shot to death.

People who pay only minimal attention to the rap world may have thought the killings would sober up the rap community. Not quite. The May cover of the hip-hop magazine *Vibe* was on the mark when it depicted fallen rappers standing among tombstones under the headline: "Hip-Hop Murders: Why Haven't We Learned Anything?"

The cover may have been prompted in part by a rivalry between two rappers that culminated in a shootout at a New York radio station, Hot 97, earlier this spring. The events that led up to the shooting show how recording labels now exploit violence to make and sell recordings.

At the center of that Hot 97 shootout was none other than 50 Cent, whose given name is Curtis Jackson III. Mr. Jackson is a confessed former drug dealer who seems to revel in the fact that he was shot several times while dealing in Queens. He has also made a career of "beef" recordings, in which he whips up controversy and heightens tension by insulting rival artists.

He was following this pattern in a radio interview in March when a rival showed up at the station. The story's murky, but it appears that the rival's entourage met Mr. Jackson's on the street, resulting in gunfire.

Mr. Jackson's on-air agitation was clearly timed to coincide with the release of "The Massacre," his grotesquely violent and misogynist compact disc. The CD cover depicts the artist standing before a wall adorned with weapons, pointing what appears to be a shotgun at the camera. The photographs in the liner notes depict every ghetto stereotype—the artist selling drugs, the artist in a gunfight—and includes a mock autopsy report that has been seen as a covert threat aimed at some of his critics.

The "Massacre" promotion raises the ante in a most destructive way. New artists, desperate for stardom, will say or do anything to win notice—and buzz—for their next projects. As the trend escalates, inner-city listeners who are already at risk of dying prematurely are being fed a toxic diet of rap cuts that glorify murder and make it seem perfectly normal to spend your life in prison.

Critics who have been angered by this trend have pointed at Jimmy Iovine, the music impresario whose Interscope Records reaped millions on gangster rap in the 90's. Mr. Iovine makes a convenient target as a white man who is lording over an essentially black art form. But also listed on "The Massacre" as an executive producer is the legendary rapper Dr. Dre, a black man who happens to be one of the most powerful people in the business. Dr. Dre has a unique vantage point on rap-related violence. He was co-founder of Death Row Records, an infamous California company that marketed West Coast rap in the 1990's and had a front-row seat for the feud that led to so much bloodshed back then.

The music business hopes to make a financial killing on a recently announced summer concert tour that is set to feature 50 Cent and the mega-selling rap star Eminem. But promoters will need to make heavy use of metal detectors to suppress the kind of gun-related violence that gangster artists celebrate. That this lethal genre of art has grown speaks volumes about the industry's greed and lack of self-control.

But trends like this reach a tipping point, when business as usual becomes unacceptable to the public as a whole. Judging from the rising hue and cry, hip-hop is just about there.

No concrete proof that 50 Cent planned a gun-fight to promote his album. Is the inference fair? I think so.

Is it the marketing or the art itself that is "misogynistic" and "supremely violent"? Note: Listen to this song.

In many neighborhoods, kids grow up seeing people going to prison all the time, so for them it is normal.

I wonder who these other critics are?

impresario— entertainment manager or promoter

Good example of author's point— even in the name of the record company.

A pun?

Can art be "lethal"?

tipping point— the moment when something rare becomes much more common

Hip-hop is still popular. Does he just mean against gangsta rap?

Summarizing

More about ▶▶▶
Paraphrase, 129–30
Summary, 16–17;
  58–59
Patchwriting, 119–21;
  133–34
Plagiarism, 134–35

Taking notes often involves *paraphrasing* a text, rephrasing the writer's ideas in our own words; paraphrasing pushes us to understand the specifics of what we are reading. When we *summarize,* we go a step further, presenting the main ideas in a piece in *condensed* form, a great way to reinforce and process a text. When writing a summary, you may need to use key terms from the text—calling a German Shepherd a "Central European canine bred for shepherding" is just silly—but be careful to avoid repeating the author's language and phrasing unnecessarily. Selecting a phrase here and a phrase there—a "greatest hits" approach—is a surefire way to fall into "patchwriting," a form of plagiarism.

Instead, read the text through at least twice to identify its main idea and key supporting evidence. Then write your summary, omitting less important supporting details and using language and organization that is meaningful to you (not borrowed from the source). Finally, check your summary against the text. Is it accurate? Is it brief?

If the text you are summarizing is long, consider summarizing it in sections rather than tackling the whole thing at once. It is still a good idea to complete a reading of the full text before you start, but you can write each section's summary separately.

Alea Wratten's summary of "How Hip-Hop Music Lost Its Way and Betrayed Its Fans" (p. 17) condenses the text, representing its main claims in her own words.

Quick Reference ➡ **Steps for Writing a Summary**

1. After annotating a text, put the text aside so that you are no longer looking at it.
2. On a clean sheet of paper or in a new document on your computer, try to recapitulate the main ideas from what you have just read.
3. Check the text to make sure you have conveyed the main ideas and the major supporting points without distortion or undue influence (are too many words in your summary like the language in the text?).

Writing
Responsibly   **Avoid Patchwriting**

As you summarize, check to make sure that you are not *patchwriting*—duplicating the language of the source with minor changes. Check your language against that in your source, and revise if you have done any of the following:

- used more than a few *key terms* from the text

- presented the ideas in the *same order* as the source
- used the *same sentence structure* as the source

If you find that you are patchwriting, revise your summary using your own words.

Student Summary of "How Hip-Hop Music Lost Its Way and Betrayed Its Fans"

In this essay, *New York Times* writer Brent Staples claims that both rap music and the way it is marketed perpetuate racial stereotypes and glorify violence, materialism, and sexism. Citing the example of an actual gang war in the 1990s, Staples argues that rival rappers use their music to insult each other and initiate violence. Staples worries that many inner-city kids, who already face poverty and violence on a daily basis, will buy the myth of a glamorous "gangsta rap" lifestyle and maybe even wind up in prison. He feels that white and black record producers are both to blame for the direction hip-hop has taken, and he hopes concert organizers will use security precautions to make sure that the violence they sell doesn't go beyond the lyrics or marketing materials. Staples closes the essay by saying he feels that the public will not stand for much more of this; if hip-hop continues in this vein, it will not last.

	Main claim of the original article rephrased
	Key supporting evidence
	Logic supporting evidence condensed.
	Key supporting evidence condensed.
	Extension of main claim

2c   Reading to Write

As a critical reader, you are always readying yourself for the next step: writing. Once you have identified a text's claims, you are ready to interact with them through *analysis, interpretation, synthesis,* and *critique.*

Analyzing

More about ▶▶▶
Analysis, 47–49

Critical comprehension of a text involves more than being able to repeat or even summarize it. You must be able to take the text apart, to understand how it works, even how it works on you. Critical reading requires analysis.

To *analyze* is to divide a text into its component parts, to figure out what each part means and how the parts fit together. Those "parts" may be in the text itself—its various claims and evidence, for example. Or "parts" may refer to the text and its author, topic, context, and intended audience. Finally, in the case of multimedia texts such as a documentary film, "parts" might mean the spoken language, the images, and the music. How do the separate parts of the text work together—or conflict with each other?

Rhetorical Situation

Sometimes taking apart a text like this is referred to as "rhetorical analysis" because readers are trying to understand how a text works rhetorically, or persuasively, on them and other readers. Such an analysis can empower a reader to avoid being manipulated. There are three classical types of persuasion you can look for in a text; they are often referred to as *logos* (logic), *ethos* (the credibility, authority, and character of a writer and his or her references), and *pathos* (arguments meant to sway readers' emotions). Academic writing strives to reduce appeals to emotion and draw on strong logic and evidence.

As you analyze, ask the following questions:

More about ▶▶▶
Claims, 105–06
Evidence
Counterevidence,
   183–85

- What does the *purpose* of the text seem to be?

- What major *claims*—or arguments—does the text make?

- What types of *evidence*—examples or data—does the text offer for its claims? Is the evidence based on facts; on the writer's opinion, interpretation, or logic; or on authoritative sources?

- What options does the text allow its readers? Must readers either agree or be wrong? To what extent does the text consider *alternative* or *conflicting* viewpoints?

- What *genre* is the text? How is the material in the text organized?

- What can you observe about the text's *style* and word choice? How do these make the text more or less accessible and trustworthy? Are the word choices meant to make you feel an emotional response and ignore logic or evidence?

- Who is the text's *author*? What other work has he or she done? How does this text build upon or diverge from the author's previous work?

Interpreting

After you use summary and analysis to understand the general meanings and mechanisms of a text, you can enter the text through *interpretation*. As you read, try to draw inferences about what may be below the surface of the text. Use the following questions to help guide your interpretation:

- What does the text assume to be true without actually claiming it?

- What can you infer from the text? Beyond its explicit claims, what do you derive from factors such as the author's tone and choice of words?

- Where does the text leave gaps or present contradictions? Can you explain them?

- When and where was the text written? What else was going on at that place and during that time? How does the text draw on or diverge from its historical context?

- Who published this text? Who sponsored the research? What influence might those facts have on the way the text presents information, arguments, and evidence?

- For whom was the text written, and who might be left out?

Synthesizing

Synthesis is all about putting sources (people) in conversation with one another, showing where they and you agree, disagree, and enhance each other's understanding. Reading for synthesis means thinking of the sources you read as related and talking to each other. College research assignments demand that you *synthesize*—connect what you have read to ideas in other texts or to the world around you. Throughout and after college, the techniques of synthesis will be important whenever you read—for integrating what you learn into what you already know. As you synthesize, ask the following questions:

- What else have you read or experienced that this text explains, illustrates, clarifies, complicates, or contradicts? How does this text respond to other texts?

- What claims or points in each text do you find especially compelling? How do compelling points in one text connect to ideas in others?

- What claims could these texts, taken together, provide evidence for? What purposes could they serve?

- How does considering these texts together enhance your understanding of a topic or change your thinking?

- What might others gain by seeing these texts together?

Critiquing or evaluating

A *critique* is a well-informed evaluation or review, an argument based on evidence and established criteria. Writing a highly effective research project requires that you critique sources to figure out where you stand in the midst of the arguments and which of the existing arguments are most worthy of attention.

More about ▶▶▶
Evaluating information, 100–10

Remember that writing a critical response does not necessarily involve *criticizing*. In fact, your critique may be entirely positive. The ideal critical reader approaches a text skeptically yet with an open mind.

For a successful critique, ask yourself questions like these:

- What qualifications do you have (or lack) for judging this text? What beliefs and/or prejudices do you bring to the text?

- What beliefs and/or prejudices do you detect in the text?

More about ▶▶▶
Author credibility, 102–04

- What authority or expertise does the author have regarding the topic?

- What is the intended purpose of this text? Does the work achieve it? Can you offer a critique of this purpose? An excerpt of Stacie Keller's rhetorical analysis of James Roos's "America's Musical Identify Links Jews and African Americans" on p. 22 shows a subtle positive evaluation of that article's handling of purpose.

- What kind of relationship and power dynamic does the text establish between writer and reader? How well is the relationship established, and how well does it serve the text's purpose?
- Who is the text's intended audience? What differences are there between that audience's experiences, knowledge, and culture and your own?
- Based on your analysis (or breakdown) of the text's argument, does anything seem to be missing? Is any of the evidence questionable?
- Does the text use emotion to manipulate its audience?

 Reference → **Ways of Reading Critically**

- **Analyzing:** breaking a text down into parts to study its meanings and mechanisms
- **Interpreting:** going below the surface of a text; drawing inferences about it based on contextual clues, omissions, suggestions, and assumptions

- **Synthesizing:** connecting a text to relevant ideas in other texts and personal experiences; drawing comparisons and relationships among ideas
- **Critiquing:** crafting a well-informed evaluation or review of a text through analysis, interpretation, and synthesis

 Tech

Critical Response to Digital Texts

Online texts pose significant and unique challenges for the critical reader.

- **Filter for authority.** All web pages a Google search displays may seem equally authoritative, but they are not. Some sites are set up by scholars or experts, but many others are created by children or hobbyists exploring their interests, by retailers selling a product, or by advocacy groups seeking support.

- **Filter for accuracy and appropriateness.** A website might look official and well composed but offer information that is inaccurate or inappropriate for your research purpose.
- **Filter for manipulation.** A website's design—its language, images, spoken text, and music—may exert a profound influence, discouraging readers from exercising critical judgment.

As you prepare to respond to a text, consider *your* audience. If you want your critique to resonate with people who have not read the original source, use just enough summary to help readers understand the context of your critique, as Stacie Keller does in the sample that follows. If your audience is familiar with the text, do not devote space to paraphrasing an idea; instead, refer and then respond to it.

Student Critique of the Purpose of James Roos's
"America's Musical Identity Links Jews and African Americans"

The audience's purpose in choosing to read "America's Musical Identity" may differ slightly from Roos's intended purpose. Roos's purpose is to teach others of the affinities that exist between Jews and African Americans in America's musical culture. He may not have expected his readers to take any action to change a trend. Instead, Roos simply seems to to bring awareness to the topic. This informative intent can be seen in the first paragraph. "Belatedly, people are awakening to the realization that America's cultural identity has been vitally shaped by minorities" (para 1). The key word in this sentence is "realization," which invokes a thought process rather than action. His audience, in turn, would benefit from this awareness because it provides them with some history of musical culture that they were probably oblivious of before reading the article. Also, Roos may have created an unintended result, as readers might feel moved to listen to the music of these two groups, thus increasing its sales and popularity.

→ **EXERCISE 2.1 Reading to Write**

Find an editorial on a topic that intrigues you in a newspaper, magazine, or professional blog. Read it and begin responding to it by summarizing its main claim. Then, write a page-long critical response to it. In your critique, try to make use of each of the reading-to-write techniques featured in this chapter: analysis, interpretation, and synthesis. Use the questions in each of those sections to generate your critique.

A Final Thought

As you read sources for your research project, engage actively in the conversation you "hear." What do you bring to the conversation? Who do you believe and why? What is missing in the conversation? If you comprehend the texts you encounter, you will be able to reflect on your responses to them and write in response to them.

3

Exploring and Sharpening Your Topic

Working with blunt tools is slow, tedious work. The chef with a dull knife struggles to create a beautiful product, while a sharp blade cuts easily and quickly. The work is easier and the product better. As with physical sharpening, writers need to work to sharpen their own vision of a project before they get too far into it. A blurry or dull idea makes searching for information, developing a thesis, and recognizing gaps difficult, among other challenges. Taking the time to look around, explore, and then focus your topic as tightly as possible increases the odds that you and your readers will like and learn from the finished product.

3a Exploring Research Topics

A typical first response to an academic research assignment is to choose a topic that you are already interested in or one that will be easy to research. These are legitimate considerations, but before committing yourself, be sure that enough appropriate sources are available on that "interesting" topic or that the "easy" topic will really interest your readers—and you.

Invention techniques allow you to generate several possible topics before settling on one. No single strategy works for everyone, and most writers use several methods. The following sections explain some of the more common strategies for selecting a research topic. If you have tried some of these before, experiment with the others; drawing on new visual and verbal techniques may increase your creativity. And remember that you can return to these invention techniques over and over throughout your project, whenever you get stuck, need a jump start, or simply want to rev your intellectual engine.

Maintain an interest inventory or idea journal

In the nineteenth century, the philosopher Ralph Waldo Emerson wrote his essays from ideas he had jotted down in a notebook. In the twenty-first century, writers still use paper, but they often use PDAs or weblogs to store ideas. Whatever medium you use, you may find that keeping an *interest inventory* or an *idea journal* is an effective part of the creative process.

More about ▶▶▶
Keeping a reading journal, 12–13
Keeping a research journal, 10–11

An *interest inventory* is a list of topics and subtopics that are of persistent interest to you, such as food, art, movies, or basketball. Once you've generated a list of general interests for yourself, consider putting your topics into table format with categories such as politics, technology, religion, current affairs, education, history, and culture down the side. Raise questions about the intersections of these topics. Here's what one column of a table with food as the writer's interest area might look like:

General Topic Area	Food
Politics	How does the US Food and Drug Administration (FDA) define "organic" foods?
Technology	How does seed modification constitute intellectual property that can be patented like technology?
Religion	Did Native Americans use food in spiritual ceremonies? If so, how?
Current Affairs	Genetically modified organisms (GMOs) are illegal in Europe. How does this differ from what's permissible in the United States? Why?
Education	What do nutritionists think of school food programs?
	Should schools allow beverage companies to advertise on their premises?
History	How did Europeans learn to cultivate crops in the New World?
Culture	What does America's consumption of fast food say about us as a culture?

An *idea journal* is a place for recording your thoughts about projects you are working on, discussions you have participated in, and what you have seen, heard, and read. You can use it to record quotes and your own responses to those quotes. When you take notes from sources in your idea journal, be sure to record where you found the quotes so you can keep your own ideas clearly separated from others' ideas. Like a diary, an idea journal is something to write in every day. Unlike a diary, though, it is not a record of the events of your life but a record of the events of your *mind.*

> **More about ▶▶▶**
> Avoiding accidental
>   plagiarism,
>   127–33
> Taking notes, 113-23

Not all ideas need to be noted in words. Some might be easier to capture with a sketch, a photograph, or even a sound or video recording. Ted Salizar took this photograph of a 9/11 memorial to capture his sense of sadness when visiting the site. He then included an image file in his electronic idea journal. Returning to his idea journal, he might be inspired to conduct a research project on Americans' responses to 9/11 or the role of memorials in psychological recovery.

Use the internet, the library, and classroom tools

A quick internet search can help stimulate ideas when you are faced with a new topic. Start by searching a *subject directory,* a collection of websites organized into groups by topic and arranged hierarchically from most general to most specific. (Two useful subject directories are listed in the Find Out More box on p. 26.) By clicking through a list of topics from most to least general, you can get a sense of the range of subject areas related to your topic.

> **More about ▶▶▶**
> Searching a subject
>   directory, 78–80

For very current topics, you might search a news site or find a relevant professional blog. Blogs are journals chronicling an individual's thoughts and ideas or responses to events. Specialized blogs can provide insight into what those studying your topic are thinking right now. You may need to use a specialized search engine to turn up blogs. (The Find Out More box on p. 26 lists some reliable news sites and some search engines that specialize in blogs.) Figure 3.1 shows a blog entry on Erin Buksbaum's topic, social networking sites.

> **More about ▶▶▶**
> Searching news
>   sites, 83
> Searching for blogs,
>   84

Finally, if you are writing about topics that were introduced in class, you can begin by reading (or rereading) course materials, such as your textbook, class notes, and any handouts your teacher has distributed. All can provide context or help you identify a topic that interests you.

Find Out **More . . . Internet Sources for Exploring a Topic**

Subject directories

Internet Public Library <www.ipl.org>—an academic subject directory

Yahoo! <www.yahoo.com>—a good general subject directory

Online news sources

BBC News <news.bbc.co.uk>

CNN <cnn.com>

Google News <news.google.com>

New York Times online <www.nytimes.com>

Yahoo! News <news.yahoo.com>

Weblog search engines

Blogsnow <www.blogsnow.com>

Google Blogs <blogsearch.google.com>

Technorati <www.technorati.com>

Tech

Keeping Track of Preliminary Web Searches

As you browse the internet for ideas, keep a list of "favorites" or "bookmarks," and refer to this list when you draft.

To *bookmark* a website, while looking at the site you want to record for later, go to the Bookmarks drop-down menu. Then choose "Add Bookmark" or "Bookmark This Page." Your browser may ask you whether you want to save the bookmark to a particular folder.

If you realize that you forgot to bookmark an important page, use your *browser's "history"* (a drop-down menu) to find the page again. Each browser keeps track of where you were for the past five or ten clicks.

Not working on your own computer? Instead of bookmarks, you might want to start a *blog* or a *wiki* (for a group project) where you can copy the URLs and paste them with the date you visited them and even a note about what you valued there.

You can also set up an account on a *social bookmarking service* such as *del.icio.us* or *digg,* so that your bookmarks will be accessible from any internet-connected computer.

Freewrite

Have you ever found yourself sitting in front of a blank screen, knowing you had to begin writing but just not being able to get started? When the writing must begin and you are blocked, try *freewriting:* writing the first thing that enters your mind and then continuing to write nonstop for ten to fifteen minutes (or for a set number of pages). What you write about does not matter; if you draw a blank, just write (or type) anything until something comes to you. To be useful, freewriting must be fast and spontaneous.

FIGURE 3.1 **A Blog Entry on Social Networking**

source: http://mashable.com/2009/08/13/facebook-friends-checker/

Here is a sample of freewriting for Erin Buksbaum's essay on social networking sites:

Not sure what I want to write not sure what I want to say would rather be at the gym or just catching up on sleep. Stayed up too late last night doing my MySpace page. Finally managed to get that video to play when it opens. Prob. should take down that pic of Hannah from Friday night, but it's really, really funny. Maybe she shld just put it on her page, but she hardly ever updates. I hope my mother—or Hannah's mother—doesn't look at it! OMG!

Once the time has elapsed, read through what you wrote. You might find a usable idea: Buksbaum's essay topic—social networking sites like MySpace—appears in this freewriting snippet, for example. But the exercise is also beneficial for freeing the mind and getting over writer's block.

Some writers use a variation on freewriting called *focused freewriting* to help them develop ideas. Instead of starting from the first idea to pop into their heads, they start from something specific: their general topic (if they have one), a quotation, a memory, or an image. If they stray from the topic, they just keep writing, trying to circle back to it.

Brainstorm

A prewriting strategy to help writers develop their ideas is *brainstorming* (or *listing*): writing down everything the writer can think of on a topic. Brainstorming—either alone or with friends, classmates, or colleagues—is something every writer should do all the time. It helps get ideas percolating and provides a record of that percolation, which can come in handy at the drafting stage. Here is a snippet of brainstorming for Erin Buksbaum's topic, social networking sites:

> Anyone with an email address can use a social networking site
> Lots of networking sites: Facebook, Friendster, Bebo . . .
> People post tons of pictures, not only of themselves, of friends, too
> Other things they post: name, school, job, fave bands, books, movies, etc.
> Easy for friends to stay in touch and meet friends of friends
> Easy for people to track down other people—old classmates, people with shared interests, etc.
> Do criminals take advantage of networking sites? Are people aware of this?

Cluster

Clustering (also called *mapping* and *webbing*) is a visual method for identifying and developing ideas. Because it shifts your focus from print to visual composition, clustering may spur your imagination.

Here are the three simple steps for creating a cluster:

1. Write your topic in the middle of the page, and draw a circle around it.
2. Write other ideas related to your topic around the central idea bubble, and draw a circle around each of those ideas.

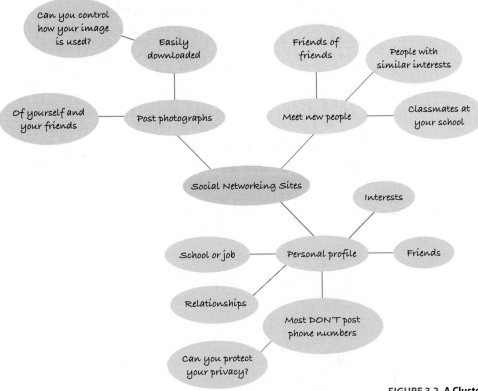

FIGURE 3.2 A Cluster Diagram

3. Draw connecting lines from the word bubbles to the central topic or to the other word bubbles to show relationships among the ideas.

When creating a cluster, keep two things in mind:

1. Keep your topic and idea notes brief—writing more than a word or two in each bubble will make the diagram difficult to read.
2. Create your cluster diagram in pencil—you will make many changes as you work. Or, put each item on a sticky note or use a free concept mapping program such as Personal Brain so you can move ideas freely within the cluster.

The cluster diagram in Figure 3.2 above was used to generate ideas for a paper on the topic "social networking sites."

Answer an expanded list of journalists' questions

Journalists' questions—who, what, when, where, why, and *how—*can not only help you generate ideas about your topic, they can also help you figure out what you need to learn. When considering a topic, ask yourself:

- **Who** are the key figures? (people)
- **What** happened, what did they accomplish, or what are the issues? (events/accomplishments/issues)
- **When** and **where** did the main events occur? (context)
- **Why** did the key figures do what they did, or why did these events transpire as they did? (reasons)
- **How** did it happen? (process)

As a college student, you will also benefit from adding two questions to the journalists' list:

- What is the **significance**?
- What are the **consequences**?

Asking the expanded list of journalists' questions for a paper on the risks of using social networking sites could generate the following questions:

- Who uses social networking sites?
- What do social networking sites allow users to do? What forms of communication do they allow?
- When did social networking sites become popular?
- Where can one find information on users of social networking sites (statistics)?
- Why do people use social networking sites? Why do they post information about themselves?
- How might social networking sites be abused?
- What social significance does the popularity of social networking sites have?
- What consequences might result from posting too much personal information?

Discuss your topics with friends and classmates

At every stage of the process, sharing ideas and writing can be useful. As you work to focus a topic, consider showing one or two peers some of your exploratory work, such as a cluster, your journalists' questions, or a brainstormed list. Ask them to pay attention to things that seem particularly interesting, ideas that still seem fuzzy, ways to sharpen those fuzzy ideas, items they might add to a cluster, and so on. Do the same for them. This mirrors productive relationships professional writers often have with other writers.

Work **Together**

Bring one version of your interest inventory to a group of two to four classmates. Make sure each person's inventory contains at least three topic possibilities beyond general categories. Sit near one another in a circle, and pass the interest inventories to the right. Spend five to seven minutes responding to the topics you see on the page. Add the following things to the topics:

- More subtopic possibilities
- Your initials next to the topic that seems most interesting and focused
- Questions for your peer about the topics represented there
- At least one research question that could be answered on the focused topic (for example, if your peer has written "student apathy" and "elections," you might develop this question: "What factors contribute to political apathy among Generation Y students?"

After the allotted time is up, pass the sheets again to the right until everyone in the group has commented on all the inventories. Return the sheets to their authors and, as a group, talk about topics you found interesting, ways to focus, and avenues to pursue next.

3b Focusing Your Topic

After you have generated some ideas, the next step is to ensure that your topic is not overly broad, too narrow, too common, or inappropriate for the occasion.

Narrowing your topic

It is typical to begin with too broad a topic. Once you have chosen a general topic, narrow it enough that you can conduct research and write about it in insightful ways, given the time you have and the length of the assignment. Narrowing means finding a viable subtopic.

Just as they can help you to explore a topic, idea-generating techniques—such as freewriting, brainstorming, and clustering—can help you narrow your topic. Consider the examples in this chapter for a reminder of how each strategy leads from general seed ideas to sprouts of more manageable and focused topics. For example, in Figure 3.2, the cluster on social networking gets increasingly specific as it moves outward from the general topic. Several steps from the center, the question "Can you protect your privacy?" emerges. That question is far more focused and closer to a final topic than "social networking" or even "personal profile." Extending an early cluster can be a way to narrow. Mixing these methods can work, too. Return to an early piece of freewriting on your topic. Find the most interesting nugget there. Then, build a cluster around that nugget idea to get increasingly specific.

More about ▶▶▶
Subject directories,
83–84

Besides traditional invention techniques, databases and subject directories are also incredibly useful resources for narrowing a topic because they organize information into topics and subtopics. For instance, if you are a business major and are trying to focus a topic related to your major but are new to the field, you might go to the Librarians' Internet Index, <www.lii.org>, starting at the home page and clicking first on Business. The page that opens lists a host of subtopics (Figure 3.3).

From this list, you might choose "Corruption & Fraud" because it sounds intriguing to you. After each subtopic, as in Figure 3.3, you will notice a number. This indicates the number of resources organized under that category. Clicking on "Corruption & Fraud" will lead you to new subtopics that will increasingly refine your focus. Figure 3.4 shows the subtopics under Corruption & Fraud in the Business category.

When your own brain is not producing sufficiently narrowed topics, using databases and subject directories can alleviate stress and lead you to subtopics you did not know existed.

More about
Effective searching,
61–62

Broadening your topic

It is rare that a topic becomes too focused and needs to be broadened. Before broadening your topic, work to make sure you have used

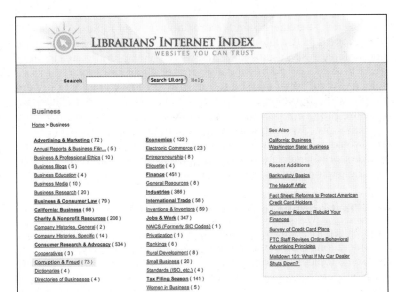

FIGURE 3.3 An Online Subject Directory, Subcategories under Business

FIGURE 3.4 Corruption & Fraud Subcategories under Business at Librarians' Internet Index good search strategies to find information on your topic. It can sometimes appear as though nothing exists on the subject because you are not looking in the right places. However, if you find yourself struggling to come up with something to say about the topic you have selected, your topic may be too narrow. If, for example, you were thinking about exploring whether social workers in your county are pressured to overreport their contact hours with Medicare patients, you may not find enough readily available material to work with. You would need to broaden your topic, perhaps to include all US social workers or a larger group, such as medical personnel (which would include doctors, nurses, and technicians).

3c   Testing Your Topic for Interest and Appropriateness

Your question might be neither too broad nor too narrow, but other considerations remain that are linked to audience and context.

Some topics (the drinking age and the death penalty, for example) have become hackneyed: It is very difficult to write something engaging on these topics. How can you ensure that your topic is interesting or not too typical or predictable? One way is to ask your teacher whether she or he frequently gets student writing on that precise topic or question. If so, try to consider another angle or a completely different topic. For example, if you have been working with the topic of gun control and you narrowed it down to the possibility of gun control legislation becoming more restrictive in the United States, your teacher may have read many researched projects on that topic. That means you will have to work harder to find something fresh to say. In such an instance, either go to another topic entirely or try more narrowing techniques, such as reading more articles on gun control and looking for specific directions gun control legislation seems to be taking or alternate systems in other countries. Then, take on that narrower and more specific aspect of the topic.

Other topics, such as hot topics in *Sports Illustrated* or *Spin,* may be new and compelling to you but may not lend themselves to the critical insight that is the objective of most academic writing. Typically, a topic is appropriate if it fits the demands of the assignment, class, and context. Academic topics tend not to be easily answerable and are relevant beyond individual interest or moment-to-moment trends. "How will Lady Gaga reinvent herself next?" does not have enduring

- **Figure out what you do not know.** Where are the gaps in your invention materials?
- **Determine what has not been said.** Is there any gap in the research conversation that you have started to notice?
- **Return to your interests.** Write down a question related to the most stimulating categories in your interest inventory, reading journal, commonplace book, or other invention materials.
- **Work from a hypothesis to a question.** If you have the sense that something might be true but you are not certain, write down the hypothesis—for example: "I think too much time spent texting might contribute to students doing poorly in school." Then, rephrase it as a question: "Is too much texting leading to kids doing poorly in school?" However, if you already are certain you have the answer to the question you are asking, you will need to develop a different question.

- **Think about scope.** Which question do you feel you could answer in the time and space of the project? If entire books (rather than chapters in books or articles) have been written in answer to the question you have now, you should probably tighten your focus further.
- **Use the keywords of your study in your question.** Make your question specific. For example, note the difference between "How can the internet be abused?" and "What are the risks of using social networking sites, and how can users avoid those risks?"
- **Determine whether the question is answerable.** Use your exploratory source searches to determine whether anyone seems to know how to answer the question.
- **Consider your readers.** If your audience is anyone other than your teacher, what do you know about them? Will your research meet their interests and needs?

relevance unless situated in a larger debate, such as one about representations of gender in popular culture.

3d Developing Your Research Question

All of this exploration should start to suggest possible questions that can drive your research. You can also use the quick reference box to make the shift from topic to question.

Since many college assignments ask you to go beyond the facts to an opinion based on knowledge and supported by information, start with a question that is difficult or impossible for you to answer definitively but that is nevertheless worth pursuing:

CONCEPTUAL QUESTION
Would writers still be motivated to write if their work were not protected by copyright laws?

Then break down the broad conceptual question into specific, focused, subquestions that you can answer through research:

SPECIFIC QUESTIONS

Why did the United States adopt international copyright regulations?

Did the adoption of copyright regulations in the United States lead to an increase in the rate of publication?

More about ▶▶▶
Drafting research,
48–49

As you've seen through Erin Buksbaum's examples, developing multiple questions on a single topic can lead you to find the one that will be the best fit for you, the project at hand, and your audience.

A Final Thought

With a question and invention materials in which you have generated keywords in hand, you are prepared to dive more deeply into your project, whether that means writing a clear project proposal or beginning your search for answers. Keep all the materials you have generated so that you can return to them as you work. They should help you to continually refine your focus as the project progresses and evolves.

4

Developing a Sense of Purpose and Context for Your Research

POOR GUY.. HE JUST GOT A 'DEAR JOHN' FAX!"

Every document—print, electronic, or even handwritten—has a function, a reason for being that suits the place and people who will use it. In addition, the type of document it is, the genre, will connect to the job it is meant to perform in the world. (Dear John letters, faxed or not, always mean a breakup!)

To work well, a document has to find an interested audience, and audiences have expectations about writing. They expect letters to come in addressed envelopes with dates, greetings, bodies, closings, and signatures. They expect newspaper articles to come with a lede (pronounced "led"), which is a short and to-the-point first paragraph that offers the main points of the story.

You might have written so many academic essays in your career as a student that you think of them as the right or only way to write, at least in school, but look around you. Wherever you are, there are texts not far away, and they are varied. Even in the subway or on a bus, you can be bombarded with advertisements, flyers, and instructions. Each document is needed or intended to do something. You may find motivation in conducting researched writing if you think of it as more than another essay written for an instructor and start to carefully differentiate what each piece of writing can do and for whom. This combination of elements—genre, audience, purpose, and context—make up the rhetorical situation of a text.

4a Recognizing Genre

In literature classes, you may have learned that poetry, drama, fiction, and nonfiction are the four major literary *genres*. However, genre extends beyond literature to types of writing as varied as letters to the editor, informed commentaries, public policy proposals, investigative reports, and instruction manuals. All genres are types of writing recognized and named by people who use them.

Often the first step to writing effectively for audiences with particular purposes and contexts in mind is to study typical documents like the ones you might produce. This kind of rhetorical analysis helps you observe how a text works. Form, format, and design may be the first things that stand out to you as distinctive to a genre of writing, but there are many aspects of the writing that become typical or expected for readers. The shifts in each of these areas are connected to audience, purpose, and context.

Form, format, and document design

More about ▶ ▶ ▶
Document design,
ch. 17

Often before you even read a document, its form and design suggest to you what it is. This is a matter of efficiency for readers, helping them to determine whether the document is what they are looking for and suggesting to them what they will find within. For instance, pamphlets are folded in a way particular to that genre and its purpose of being a handy overview. Wedding invitations use distinctive paper and font to suggest the formality and joy of the occasion. Executive summaries use bolded headings and subheadings and are clearly labeled "executive summary" at the top to help readers to quickly scan and get a sense of a larger document that follows. Look for such typical features as use of pictures and images, headings and subheadings, color or black-and-white, paragraph spacing, font size and shape changes, page sizes, and any other visual feature that readers might come to associate with the genre.

Tone or style

From whether it is acceptable or expected to use first person ("I") to how long and short sentences need to be, tone or style is linked to what and for whom you write. Many students writing college academic prose for the first year approximate the tone and style of academic writing, trying on Latinate synonyms found in their thesauruses and stringing out lengthy sentences peppered with "however" and "thus." Smartly, they have figured out that something needs to be different about their word choice and sentence structure to "fit" the academic context of college. In time, the awkwardness of the imitation tends to fall away as these writers become comfortable with the context, audience, and genre expectations. In effect, this is the process most writers go through when they are writing something new to them. As you look at samples of the type of writing you are going to produce, look at the types of word choices the writers make, the sentence lengths, and the relative casualness or formality of the tone.

Organization

When high schools teach organization, they often begin with the very simple but useful concepts of introduction, body, and conclusion. More experienced writers will begin to develop even more nuanced understandings of what goes on in typical beginnings, middles, and endings of documents. Review the organizational structures highlighted in chapter 14 (for instance, general-to-specific, problem-to-solution, and spatial organization) and consider which of these types of structures is most commonly used in the type of writing you will produce.

Evidence

There are some universals about what constitutes good evidence (such as whether the information is relevant and reliable). However, for any genre, the types of evidence expected by the audience and the ways of presenting and integrating that evidence can differ. For instance, when profiling a person to educate readers about valued leadership qualities and their applications in real-life situations, readers will likely expect and value evidence drawn from personal interviews. The first-hand relating of experience from the source her- or himself carries most weight. Conversely, in a research report about leadership trends across the nation, interview data will likely be subordinate to statistical data. Both provide important insights into the overall topic of leadership, but one genre is more humanistic and one more scientific.

More about ▶▶▶
Evaluating information, ch. 7

Some questions you can ask about evidence include these: Whose knowledge is valued in this kind of writing? Is the knowledge numerical data? Are personal experiences (yours or others') accepted evidence? Must personal experiences be paired with more formally vetted information such as research data?

Citation and documentation

More about ▶▶▶
Differing documentation and citation styles, 234–238

In school, you will learn academic styles of citation and documentation, which vary from discipline to discipline. Outside academia, too, citation can differ from context to context. Journalism, which values sources deeply and refers to them within articles, does not use works cited or references pages as we do in higher education. As you analyze samples of writing, pay attention to how writers acknowledge or give credit to their sources.

> **EXERCISE 4.1 Analyzing Models**
> Find three sample documents like the one you will compose. Using the five categories in section 4a—form, format, and document design; tone or style; organization; evidence; and citation and documentation—create a chart that analyzes what is typical across the three samples in each of these categories. There will likely be differences as well among the samples, but focus on the elements they share. So, for instance, if you are looking at three commentaries published in the *New York Times* and all three quote expert knowledge within the first two paragraphs, that is likely an expected norm for the genre in that publication. As a second step, pick out two of the patterns you have noted and write a paragraph about how each pattern makes sense, given the purpose of that kind of document.

4b Addressing Audience

Almost all writing is rooted in *connection,* moving writers and readers toward mutual understanding. For a piece of writing to be effective, then, the writer must make a careful analysis of the intended reader (or readers).

When assigned writing, the urgency to find an audience can be diminished since an instructor reads your work; you know the document will be read. The instructor is a key audience, and the one who will attend most to the learning purpose of the writing, but the instructor need not be the only audience, whether real or imagined.

Think about others, besides you, who might be interested in this topic. Consider the audience's expectations: Are you addressing a ***specialist audience***? That is, do your readers already possess a good deal of information about the topic, and are they reading your document to learn more? Or are you writing to a ***general audience,*** readers who may have a good deal of experience reading (say, they read the *New York Times,* the *Philadelphia Examiner,* and the *Manchester Guardian* online every day) but who only have a passing interest in your topic and are expecting to learn the basics? Consider, as well, their likely **demographic characteristics** such as gender, age, education level, geographical and/or religious affiliations. These considerations will have a powerful effect on the choices you make as a writer.

Writing with the following questions in mind will give your writing a focus it would not otherwise have:

- What skepticisms might audience members have toward your stance?

- What information will your audience need in order to understand and appreciate what you are saying?

- What kinds of language, examples, evidence, or reasons might be most powerful for them?

- How could you engage them best and convince them your document is worth reading?

- What genre would they be most likely to pick up and read to get this information?

- Where would they be likely to seek out the kind of information you are gathering?

Some instructors may want you to consider a different audience as the primary reader with the instructor as only a secondary reader. In this case, you will likely move away from the academic essay toward more public and professional genres. Some instructors will want you to stick more closely to academic styles and genres and thereby think of them as the first audience.

4c Writing with Purpose

Having a sense of purpose both in terms of your own learning goals and in terms the document itself may mean the difference between a seemingly empty exercise and a meaningful experience. The classical ***purposes*** for researched writing are:

- To inform
- To interpret
- To persuade
- To solve a problem

While a writer may have more than one purpose, usually one dominates and is the writer's *primary* purpose. In addition, the writer's purpose may change as the text develops. Still, as you prepare to write, you should decide on a primary purpose for it is from your purpose that all the other decisions you will make as a writer will flow.

Each of the classical purposes translates into many more specific rhetorical actions writing can take. As with audience, the more specific you are about the purpose you wish to achieve, the clearer other decisions about the writing will become. Writing a researched essay on global warming to reiterate what everyone else has said is unlikely to feel purposeful *unless* you provide an overview for readers to more quickly access the most relevant information. Convincing a skeptic that global warming really exists and that the media conversations to the contrary are about generating conflict would also give a writer a clear sense of the persuasive task at hand.

Analyzing the assignment for purpose

The details of the assignment as well as its purpose will be expressed—explicitly or implicitly—in the assignment and in the instructor's discussion of the assignment.

Analyze the language of the assignment to determine its purpose:

- Does the assignment ask you to *describe, compare, discuss, explain,* or *review* (in the sense of provide an overview)? If so, the purpose of the assignment is *informative* (or *expository*): You must use reasons and evidence (facts, statistics, examples) to explain something to your reader. Academic literature reviews, as well as both academic and professional reports *inform,* building knowledge for understanding and decision making.

- Does the assignment ask you to *analyze, interpret,* or *comment?* If so, the purpose of the assignment is *interpretive.* You must offer insight into trends or patterns you see by gathering

Reference → **Analyzing the Assignment for Purpose**

If assignment asks you to:	The purpose is:	Academic genre examples	Nonacademic genre examples
describe, compare, discuss, explain, review (that is, provide an overview)	informative (explanatory or expository)	comparison and contrast essays, literature reviews, lab reports	encyclopedia entries, newspaper or magazine reports, nonfiction books, instructions, business briefs
analyze, interpret, comment	interpretive	literary analysis, rhetorical analysis, peer review	editorials, commentaries, op-ed columns
assess, evaluate, argue, propose	argumentative or persuasive	position papers, argument essays, book reviews	legal briefs, newspaper editorials, political speeches, grant proposals, movie and other reviews

evidence, data, and expert opinion. Your goal is to persuade readers that yours is the most logical and reasonable interpretation of the situation. Academic analysis essays (sometimes requiring the application of a theoretical lens) are suited to this task, as are commentaries and op-ed pieces, among other interpretive genres.

- Does the assignment ask you to *assess, evaluate, argue* or *propose*? If so, the purpose of the assignment is *persuasive* or *argumentative*: You must make a claim with which readers may agree or disagree, and you must present reasons and evidence to support your position in an effort to persuade your readers to adopt your point of view or at least to consider it reasonable. Academic position papers commonly embody this purpose, as do reviews and proposals, both of which have academic and nonacademic applications.

4d Responding to Context

Four of the broad contexts for which you are likely to write, now and in the future, are *academic, business/professional, public,* and *personal.* Research plays a role in all of these contexts, yet each presents its own

More about ▶▶▶
Context, ch. 5

demands. For instance, research conducted in business settings often has to be both thorough and obtained as quickly as possible, but there typically are teams and resources at the researcher's disposal. In your personal life, while deadlines might not be as constraining, you may not have a team and special equipment to search for answers.

Sometimes context is hard to see when the context you typically occupy—school—becomes deeply familiar. Simultaneously, immersion in school makes it hard to envision what other contexts for writing might be like. Your instructor might work to help you occasionally break out of the academic context to write for community organizations; still, most of the writing you do in school will have school as its most immediate context. How, then, can you possibly prepare to write for anywhere but school? You will need to use a bit of imagination and investigation to understand other contexts for writing such as workplaces, the public sphere, and even other disciplines.

To give yourself a real sense of where your research might have the most impact, think about or seek out a possible publication context. Publication may not always mean places such as newspapers, magazines, and journals. Instead, anywhere that the document would find an audience would constitute "going public." What are the lengths and styles of documents used in that context? Does the publication have specific requirements for authors? Who are the audiences connected to the context?

Make It **Your Own**

After you have determined your topic and the question you are trying to answer through the research project, write a half page on your potential audience, genre, context, and purpose. Afterward, consider making a sticky note with short phrases by each of these categories (like the one on the right). Put the note on your computer to remind you of the rhetorical situation for which you are writing.

Topic: Eating disorders and their relationship to media representations of ideal beauty

Audience: Young women who consume such media

Purpose: To help them see more clearly how unrealistic and potentially damaging these images are and to be able to be critical of the media they consume

Genre: Commentary on a trend

Tone/style: Conversational but authoritative

*note to self: use lots of scholarly research about psychology and impact on health but make it accessible

A Final Thought

DaVinci's Notebook, an independent music group, produced a song in 2000 called "Title of the Song." That song parodied all of the moves of a typical boy band love song, complete with this chorus:

> Title of the song
> Naïve expression of love
> Reluctance to accept that you are gone
> Request to turn back time
> And rectify my wrongs
> Repetition of the title of the song.

While their song is meant to get a laugh, it points to both the problems and possibilities of being aware of genres and the regularity of some rhetorical situations. If treated too much like formulas, genres become canned and empty. Conversely, though, if you as a writer are aware of what genres can do, for whom, and where, you will be able to make educated choices that can make your writing more effective and provide you with an increased sense of purpose.

5

Writing a Research Proposal

A *research proposal* is a plan, one created to be read by someone other than you. It is the first formal pitch of a project. Similarly, architects' pitches come, in part, in the form of drawn plans. These plans are done with great care and attention to detail, and they take into account location and client constraints. You are the architect of your project. Careful planning at the project proposal stage can save time and energy later and offers you the opportunity to get focused feedback from your instructor and others.

5a Understanding Typical Components of a Research Proposal

Your instructor will probably define the information required for your research proposal, as it will depend in part on the assignment requirements. However, research proposals share some common features:

- Identification of the *topic* you have chosen.

- A specific *question* within the topic area that your research will answer.

- A *hypothesis,* or working thesis statement. Your research project should not begin with you thinking you already know the answer to your question. Still, you probably have some ideas about what you might find. Write up your ideas as a hypothesis you will test with your research.

- A *statement of significance.* Answer these questions: Why should anyone care about this question and topic? What is its importance?

- What you *already know.* Your existing knowledge provides a baseline for you and your instructor. It might even include experiential knowledge that has compelled you to pursue this particular topic. It will also include information you have started to gather and read for the project.

- What you *need to know.* Completing this section allows you to identify areas in which you will need to do more reading and research.

- The *methods* you will use to acquire information. Your methods for gathering and processing information should match the question you ask. That is, think about what resources will best answer the question. Will you need to look at archival materials? Survey a population? Read expert sources? Apply a theory?

- A *schedule* or *timeline* for managing the parts of the project. Break the project into bite-sized chunks, tasks that can be completed in two hours or less.

- A *working bibliography* of sources or a *literature review.* Identify the sources you may need to use (a working bibliography), or suggest how your study fits into a body of existing research (a literature review).

Other possible components of the proposal or prospectus may include:

- A specific *audience* to which you will direct the researched writing. If your instructor has not specified an audience, consider who might be most invested in the outcomes of your research.

More about ▶▶▶
Exploring research topics, 23–31
Developing a research question, 35–36

More about ▶▶▶
Audience, ch. 4
Genre, ch. 4

- A *genre* choice. In what form will you deliver the research? The answer will depend in large part on your audience and purpose.

5b   Analyzing the Rhetorical Situation

Before you can complete a research proposal, you will need to understand the assignment and its *rhetorical situation:*

- **Purpose:** what you hope to accomplish with the text
- **Audience:** who will be reading the text you produce
- **Tone:** your attitude toward your subject and audience, expressed through the words you choose
- **Context:** the setting (academic, business, personal, public) in which your text will be "consumed"
- **Genre:** the type of work you will produce—a scholarly essay for a psychology class, a formal proposal (not a project proposal but a final researched project) for a campus organization, a research report for a business

Attention to all of these issues as well as to a variety of practical factors, such as knowing the due date and length of the assignment, is essential to effective assignment analysis. Before you can write an effective project proposal, you will need to understand these factors. If you have not already read chapter 4, it will guide you through thinking about each element of your rhetorical situation.

5c   Drafting Hypotheses

To devise research *hypotheses,* turn your specific research questions into statements that express the answer you expect to find. As you conduct research, you will learn whether your hypotheses are true or false, and your thesis will grow naturally from your research hypotheses.

Your specific research questions will be most effective when you:

- Include concrete keywords that you can use in web, database, and catalog searches.
- Formulate a tentative hypothesis in response to your question, but be open to revising your response.

- Devise new questions if your research provides few appropriate sources that address your topic.

The research questions below, for Lydia Nichols's paper on underground comics, demonstrate the technique.

▶▶▶Sample student paper "Holy Underground Comix, Batman!" Lydia Nichols, 294–305

Keywords: "comics"; "graphic novels"; "underground comics." Combine with "audience"; "internet"; "market"; "artists"; "genre"; "experimentation"

Hypothesis: Characteristics of underground comics may make them unsuitable for mainstream distribution.

Research questions: What are the characteristics of mainstream comics? What are the characteristics of underground comics? What is the history of each? What is the value of each? What are audiences' responses to the characteristics of underground comics?

EXERCISE 5.1 Devising Research Questions and Hypotheses

Devise five research questions for the topics you have already begun exploring. Turn one of these research questions into a research hypothesis by providing a tentative answer to the question. You can check whether your hypothesis is well crafted to be a future thesis statement by applying the criteria in chapter 13.

5d Providing a Rationale

The project rationale provides the "so what?" of the project proposal. At each stage of your project, you should have a sense of why you are pursuing your research question and why someone other than you might be interested in reading the results of the research.

In the rationale section of your proposal, consider answering the following questions:

- What are your personal motivations for looking into this topic?

- What other groups might find the information helpful, and why?

- How will your study help to shed light on the issues? (Is this a new phenomenon worth exploration? Does the question require the insight of multiple perspectives?)

5e Establishing Methods

More about ▶▶▶
Gathering information, 60–66
Developing new information, 88–99
Archival research, 88–90
Field research, 90–98

Every research project employs methods for finding and interpreting information. Methods should not be arbitrary but should fit the question being asked. Some of the primary methods you might use for your project include:

- **Textual research.** Many questions have been answered fairly well by experts in their respective fields. It is often entirely appropriate for student researchers to rely on others' work (secondary research) as the primary evidence and answer to a research question. Your *interpretation* of that existing research is part of your contribution to answering the question.

- **Archival research.** Primary research involves searching through original documents and objects for answers. For this kind of research, you might go to an archive or a museum to study the holdings there. An example of a question well suited to archival research is "What was the nature of Jessie Redmon Fauset's working relationship with W.E.B. DuBois?" Because these two literary and socio-political thinkers worked together, many documents, such as letters and memoranda, are likely to exist from their collaborations.

- **Field research.** Through observations, interviews, questionnaires, and surveys, you can develop your own data to answer your research questions. Going into the field means drawing new information from people and places. A field researcher might ask the question "What percentage of parents in the Southside school district is satisfied with the educational system, and what are the perceived problems?"

- **Application of theory.** To understand a case, situation, artifact, or text, a researcher might use theoretical tools for interpretation. A question that might be answered through the application of feminist theory to texts, for example, would be "What do alcohol advertisements reveal about power relations between men and women?"

In the methods section of your proposal, first identify which of these methods you will use. Then be as specific as possible about the process you will use to get and interpret information. Specifying the process is especially important for field research. What questions will you include on your survey? Where do you plan to distribute it? It is appropriate to combine existing expert studies with your own archival research, field research, or application of a theory.

5f Setting a Schedule

Writing an effective and successful research project takes much more than reading a few things and sitting down to write. Complex projects like these—and many you will do in your jobs and life—require project management. To set a reasonable and complete schedule, begin by considering the practicalities:

- **When is the project due?** Knowing your project deadline is critical to good time management. Once you have determined the due date, work *backward* with a calendar to set a realistic schedule that takes into account your other responsibilities and leaves time in case you need to devise a new research question, do additional research, or revise a second (or third) time.

- **How long is the assignment?** Knowing the length requirements will give you a better idea of the scope of your project.

- **What types of research are required?** Will you be expected to do *secondary research*—gathering information from books and articles—or *primary research*—developing your own evidence through questionnaires, interviews, observation, or primary materials such as letters, memoranda, case law, or works of literature?

- **Must you turn in a portfolio with the final version of the project?** If the instructor requires you to provide a portfolio, you may be asked to include any or all of the following: your notes from the idea-generating process, your working hypothesis, your outline, your working bibliography, your research notes, your first draft, and a reflection letter. Keep copies of these if a portfolio is part of the assignment.

5g Choosing Sources Strategically

More about ▶ ▶ ▶
Gathering information, 60–66

Even at the proposal stage, you should have a sense of what has already been said about your chosen topic. Your chief concern as you begin researching will be to find enough relevant and reliable sources to answer your research questions. It is also important to ask yourself the following questions:

- Roughly how many sources do you need to consult?
- Can you rely only on websites, blogs, and other online sources, or do you need to consult books, print periodicals, and government documents? Will images, movies, or sound recordings be relevant to your research?
- Will classic authorities be useful, or should you concentrate on more recent sources?
- Are popular sources acceptable, or should you use only scholarly sources?

5h Building a Working Bibliography

More about ▶ ▶ ▶
Search strategies, 60–74

After you have determined the types of sources you might need, you are ready to begin your search. Researchers generally find it more efficient to prepare a *working bibliography,* a list of sources they may want to consult, than to identify and retrieve sources one by one. First conduct keyword searches in databases and library holdings, developing a list of *all* the promising sources on your topic. Then see how many of the sources you can find (interlibrary loan will help with sources not held by your library). Finally, preview each of the sources, to see which will best help you answer your research question(s). Starting with a working bibliography ensures that you will be using the best sources available, rather than just the first ones you could find.

Your working bibliography should include all the information you will need to locate the source and cite it in your paper. The "working" part of "working bibliography" means that you may add and subtract sources from this initial list, but it should be as comprehensive as you can make it at the proposal stage.

Tech

Citation Help

There are now free citation builders online that will significantly reduce the time you have to spend getting your citations right. The two most used are

Bibme <http://www.bibme.org/>

Easybib <http://www.easybib .com/>

But be cautious: You need to understand citation well enough to recognize which style sheet you need to use, what you need to put into the builder, and what each category of information is. Otherwise, your bibliography will be a mess. Remember that the builder is not smarter than you are. Check its work.

More about ▶▶▶
MLA style:
  In-text citations,
    243–60
  List of works cited,
    260–90
APA style:
  In-text citations,
    304–14
  Reference list,
    315–32
Chicago style:
  In-text citations,
    347–64
  List of works cited,
    367–72
CSE style:
  In-text citations,
    375–76
  Reference list,
    377–88

Noting information you will need later

Most of the information you will need to include in your working bibliography is the same for all source types and includes the following:

- Full name of author or artist
- Title and subtitle of book or article
- Publication data (such as title of journal, volume/issue number, publisher or vendor name, date of publication)
- Access information (such as catalog number or URL and date of access)

For a detailed list of the information you will need in your working bibliography, see the Quick Reference box on pp. 54–55.

More about ▶▶▶
Taking notes, 112–23

5i Annotating Your Working Bibliography

Even if your instructor does not require an annotated bibliography, annotating potential sources can save you time later (when you return to sources that looked promising or if you decide to do more research on the topic at another time). An *annotation* is typically a single paragraph that summarizes and perhaps evaluates the source. If you decide to annotate your working bibliography, place each annotation immediately following the bibliographic information for the source. Dan Long's annotated bibliography, which appears at the end of chapter 12, illustrates how useful it will be to have such information at hand when you begin drafting your research project.

More about ▶▶▶
Annotating sources,
142–43

Publication	Author	Title and Subtitle	Publication Data	Access Information
Books (printed)	– Full name of author (including editor, translator, artist, performer, director, conductor, sender of posting, etc.)	– Title and subtitle of book; edition number – If part of series, title of series, volume number and total number of volumes (if relevant)	– City (and state for less common cities) of publication – Name of publisher – Year of publication	– Call number and library where found (if you visited more than one)
Books (online)		– Same as for printed books	– Same as for printed books	– Date first accessed – Database or project name – Sponsoring organization – Date of e-publication – URL – Call number and library where found (if you visited more than one)
Articles or chapters (in printed periodical, book, or reference source)	– Same as for books	– Title and subtitle of article	– Title and sub-title of periodical – Volume and number or volume and season of publication – Page number (first–last)	
Articles (database)	– Same as for books	– Same as for printed article	– Same as for printed articles; use paragraph or section numbers if page is not provided – If published online only, day/month/year of publication	– Date first accessed – Name of online sub-scription service, URL of home page, and name of subscribing library – URL or link path for article

Publication	Author	Title and Subtitle	Publication Data	Access Information
Newspaper (printed)	– Same as for books	– Title and subtitle of article – Title of newspaper in which it appeared	– Date and edition (national edition, late edition) – Page number(s) – Section designation (if given) – City of publication (if not mentioned in newspaper title)	– Library where found (if you visited more than one)
Newspaper (online)	– Same as for books	– Same as for printed newspaper	– City of publication – Date of publication	– Date first accessed – URL of article
Web source (electronic)	– Same as for books	– Title of website; title of web page – Subject line (email message, posting) – Word or two describing source (email, online posting, blog posting) – Sponsoring organization		– Date first accessed – Date posted or last updated – URL or link path for web page; email address of moderator, if no URL
Audiovisual sources	– For creators other than author, composer, visual artist, indicate role: director, performer, producer, etc.	– Title and subtitle of work – Medium or distinguishing characteristic (DVD, videocassette, LP, map, interview, etc.)	– Studio or manufacturer – Date of release or year of creation – Location where held or performance space and city – Television or radio network that produced or broadcast it	If online: – Date first accessed – Date posted – URL or link path

Make It **Your Own**

For a research project that you are working on, create a working bibliography of at least ten sources. Choose a mix of source types, including books, scholarly articles, newspaper and magazine articles, reference works, websites, pamphlets, government publications, visuals, multimedia, and audio sources. Then locate and annotate the five most promising sources, recording complete publication information and taking preliminary notes on what the source covers and how useful it might be for your research project.

5j Developing a Literature Review

More about ▶▶▶
Synthesis, 19
Situating your re-
search in a conver-
sation, 182–90

Extended literature reviews often become part of a research project, relating the new research to what others have said about a topic, or *synthesizing* the sources. In a project proposal, a brief literature review offers readers something similar. Primarily, though, creating an overview of what you have already read about your topic indicates that you have a good enough sense of the conversation to develop an informed question. Work from your notes or annotated bibliography, and write two to three paragraphs that identify the primary strands of the discussion. Avoid just moving from author to author if you can; instead, try to group articles and arguments based on similar stances or topics. Why are these sources relevant to answering your question, and what part of the question do they not address?

5k Formatting the Project Proposal

Typically, a project proposal has a header containing standard information such as your name, the date, the instructor's name, and "Research Project Proposal." In the body of the proposal, use subheadings so that your instructor can quickly see that you have addressed all of the required areas. Finally, format the working bibliography using the appropriate style sheet (MLA, APA, *Chicago*, CSE).

Work **Together**

Before submitting your proposal, exchange it with one or more classmates. Peer review will reduce the chance that your instructor will need you to rewrite the proposal before you move on with the project. Ask your reviewers to check for the following things:

- Have you included all of the information that your instructor requested?
- Is there anything that needs clarification?
- Is your research question narrow enough to be answered in the space and time of this project?
- Can your classmates recommend any search strategies or sources to help you answer the question?

Quick Reference ➔ Checklist for Planning a Research Project

- **Analyze purpose, audience, and other requirements.** What type of research are you expected to do? Who will be reading your results? What goals do you and the audience have for the research? When is the project due, and how long should it be?
- **Choose and focus a topic.** Explore possible topics by assessing the number and types of sources available, your knowledge of the topic, your own interests, and the knowledge and interests of your audience.
- **Form research questions and develop a hypothesis.** Use the question(s) to structure your investigation and the hypothesis to focus and organize your research project.
- **Choose research methods.** Which are more appropriate to your task: primary or secondary materials? scholarly or popular sources?
- **Identify strategies for managing time, resources, and panic.** Set up a calendar, a research log and note-taking system, and a working bibliography.

A Final Thought

The planning process helps you to envision the project and the work you will need to do to answer your research questions. A good plan will reduce negative surprises and make the work much more manageable.

Reading and Summarizing the Entire Source

When working with a source, take the time to read it (all of it) and summarize it. Then when you draft your research project, blend in summary of your important sources to make your writing more informative and persuasive.

While you can also draw from sources by quoting, paraphrasing, or patchwriting, the last of these techniques is bad writing and may be considered plagiarism. Picking a quotation and pasting it into your draft is remarkably easy. Patchwriting, or changing a few words in the quotation, is equally easy and less effective. It is used extensively by unskilled writers. Instead, build the skills of paraphrase and summary.

To paraphrase, or restate a passage from the source in fresh language, you must actually understand the passage. That is even more true of summary, which restates, concisely and in fresh language, the main claims (and the most important supportive evidence of an entire source or a significant part of it.

> **More about ▶▶▶**
> Patchwriting,
> 133–134
> Paraphrase, 129–130
> Quotation, 129–130
> Summary, 129–130

Because quoting and patchwriting are so easy to do, they happen frequently in college students' writing. What also happens frequently is that the quotations and patchwriting come from the first few pages of the source—which is all the student has read. In the Citation Project study of college students' use of sources in their research papers, the majority of the citations came from the first two pages of the source. As the chart below illustrates, about 50 percent of the citations came from the first page of the source, and more than 20 percent from the second.

Are you quoting or patchwriting sentences because you don't understand them well enough to paraphrase? Are you pulling sentences from the first few pages of your source without bothering to read the whole thing? If you answered "yes" to either of these questions, you should begin pushing yourself to read the whole source so that you understand it well enough that you can summarize, in your own words, its main ideas. Push yourself toward better reading comprehension and more effective writing by using more summary when you write about sources.

Consider, for example, how little information the following passage provides about the source and its claims:

Page Cited

DATA FROM **The Citation Project**

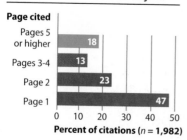

Percent of citations ($n = 1,982$)

58

First draft

Many people value their "private lives," and try to separate their private and public selves. Many are aware of being different people in the workplace, in school, on a date.	Student's voice
All this may be changing, though. "The fact that the Internet never seems to forget is threatening, at an almost existential level, our ability to control our identities; to preserve the option of reinventing ourselves and starting anew; to overcome our checkered pasts" (Rosen).	Quotation

Parenthetical note |

In this draft, readers are given no information about the source; they are only presented with this sentence from it. Does the writer understand the source, or has she simply found a "killer quote" that supports her argument? Because the writer provides the isolated quotation, it is not even clear what her claim is.

Now consider how this passage is transformed by adding summary:

Revised draft

Many people value their "private lives," and try to separate their private and public selves. Many are aware, too, of being different people in the workplace, in school, on a date.	Student's voice
All this may be changing, though. Journalist Jeffrey Rosen points out that we may no longer be in control of the multiple identities that were previously taken for granted. In our online lives, what we post on Facebook and Twitter can easily merge with what we post on a school blog, in our comments on a *New York Times* story, in our pictures on Flickr. Rosen explains that even in untagged pictures, our faces can be identified through a program called Face.com. Rosen also describes the privacy-protecting laws that are in development and the companies that offer services to clean up our online reputations. Most central to my research, though, is his explanation for this claim: "The fact that the Internet never seems to forget is threatening, at an almost existential level, our ability to control our identities; to preserve the option of reinventing ourselves and starting anew; to overcome our checkered pasts."	Signal phrase

Summary of the parts of the source relevant to the student's argument

Summary of the remainder of the source |

The writer has taken the time to read and understand the source. She is able to summarize it, showing what its main claims are. Her readers now know how the quotation supports her argument, and how it was contextualized in the source. With this summary, has explained her ideas clearly and has established a conversation between herself, her source, and her readers.

Source: Rosen, Jeffrey. "The Web Means the End of Forgetting." *New York Times* 21 July 2010. Web. 1 Feb. 2011.

Writing Responsibly: A Checklist

Audience

- ❏ Have you chosen a topic that is appropriate and interesting to your reader?

- ❏ Does your title prepare your reader for what follows?

- ❏ Does your thesis focus your reader's attention on your main point?

- ❏ Will your reader find the reasons you supply logical and compelling?

- ❏ Have you supplied enough relevant evidence to persuade your reader to accept (or at least to consider) your position?

- ❏ Will your reader find your project logically organized?

- ❏ Will your reader find your paragraphs clearly organized and tightly focused?

- ❏ Have you provided transitions to guide your reader?

- ❏ Is your project written at an appropriate level for your reader?

- ❏ Is your tone appropriate to your reader?

- ❏ Have you revised, edited, and proofread your project so that your reader will find the writing clear, correct, and powerful?

Writing Responsibly: A Checklist

Other Writers

❑ Have you given credit to those from whom you have borrowed words or ideas, whether you have summarized, paraphrased, or quoted material or whether your source is printed or online?

❑ Have you avoided patchwriting by paraphrasing borrowed material fully, putting the text into your own words and sentence structures?

❑ Have you represented the ideas of other writers accurately and fairly?

❑ Have you treated other writers respectfully, even when you disagree with them?

❑ Have you considered alternative viewpoints?

❑ Have you addressed alternative perspectives that conflict with your own position?

Topic

❑ Have you explored your topic thoroughly and creatively?

❑ Have you conducted research (when needed), using the most in-depth and reliable sources available to you?

❑ Have you provided logical reasons that support your thesis?

❑ Have you provided sufficient evidence to support your claims?

❑ Have you used visuals when they are the most effective way of presenting supporting evidence or when they provide a visual example (and only when they are appropriate to your context and genre)?

❑ Have you assessed your sources carefully and presented evidence from reliable sources?

❑ Have you represented ideas borrowed from sources accurately and fully?

Lydia Nichols

Ms. Concannon

Writing 205

6 April 2009

Holy Underground Comics, Batman! Moving Away from the Mainstream

When most people think of comic books, predictable images usually

come to mind: caped heroes, maniacal villains, deeds of incredible strength,

and other typical elements of super-powered adventures. Undeniably, characters

like Batman, Superman, and Spider-Man are the most prominent features of the

comic book landscape, in terms of both popularity and of revenue (Wright xiv).

However, there is more to comic books than superpowers and secret identities.

Underground comics (also known as *comix*), printed by small publishers or by indi-

vidual artists, are very different from what is usually exppected in the genre. While

far less well-known than their superhero counterparts, underground comics often

offer an innovative and more sophisticated alternative to mainstream titles.

Almost from the beginning, comic books were associated with superheroes.

The first comic books appeared in the early 1930s, nearly four decades after

comic strips such as *Yellow Boy* began appearing in the major newspapers. Yet

comic books did not gain widespread popularity until June of 1938, when writer

Jerry Siegel and artist Joe Shuster debuted their character Superman in *Action

Comics* #1 (Daniels 9). Superman was an immediate success, and he quickly in-

spired the creation of copycat superheroes in other comic books. The protagonists

This paper appears in full on pp. 292–303.

Audience/Topic: Nichols chooses a title that reflects her topic and draws the reader in.

Topic: Nichols uses reliable sources, including scholarly books (see list of works cited, pp. 356–57).

Audience: Nichols writes at a level appropri-ate for college-level readers, and writes clearly and correctly.

Audience: Nichols uses a transition ("Yet") to prepare readers for a contrasting idea.

Audience: Nichols chooses a topic that engages both the writer and her reader.

Audience: Nichols starts the paragraph with a topic sentence to focus the reader's attention.

Topic: Nichols provides an ac-curate summary of information borrowed from Daniels.

of these comics each had their own strengths and vulnerabilities, but the stories all shared a basic formula: individuals with extraordinary abilities battling against evil and struggling to maintain a secret identity. These superhero comics, though similar to each other, set the comic book industry on its feet, paving the way to profits and sustained success (Daniels 9). Over the decades and even today, the best-selling comics have typically been in the superhero genre.

Other writers: Nichols paraphrases fully to avoid "patchwriting."

While artists and writers over the years have certainly done inventive work in superhero comics, some similarity in mainstream titles was for many years unavoidable. This was due to the creation in 1954 of the Comics Code Authority (CCA), an organization formed by a number of the leading comic publishers to regulate the content of comics (Heller 101). It set very explicit standards, dictating what content was allowed in comic books and what content was expected. Some parts of the code are incredibly specific and controlling:

Self: Nichols writes in a voice that is true to herself and appropriate to her audience, context, and genre.

Self: Nichols has revised, edited, and proofread to make the essay the best reflection of herself that it can be.

Other writers: Nichols represents the ideas of others accurately and fairly.

> The letters of the word "crime" on a comics magazine shall never be appreciably greater in dimension than the other words contained in the title.
>
> The word "crime" shall never appear alone on a cover. . . . Restraint in the use of the word "crime" in titles or subtitles shall be exercised. (qtd. in "Good Shall Triumph over Evil")

Other writers: Nichols uses quotations as support and cites sources.

Other rules were more general—vague enough to allow the CCA a free hand in shaping content. One read, "Respect for parents, the moral code, and for honorable behavior shall be fostered" (qtd. in "Good Shall Triumph over Evil"). The CCA also regulated the presentation of criminals and criminal acts, themes of religion and race, and dialogue, especially profanity. While the CCA had no legal authority,

Self: Nichols synthesizes information from a variety of sources to provide the reader with something original.

This paper appears in full on pp. 292–303.

Yourself

- ❏ Have you used the writing assignment to learn something new and to expand your scope as a writer?

- ❏ Have you represented your ideas clearly, powerfully, and accurately?

- ❏ Have you integrated your own ideas or your own synthesis of sources to provide a text that is original and interesting?

- ❏ Have you used language inclusively, avoiding bias and representing yourself as a respectful person?

- ❏ Have you written in a voice that is true to yourself and in keeping with your context (academic, business, public, personal) and genre (college essay, PowerPoint presentation, newsletter)?

- ❏ Have you revised, edited, and proofread your project to make sure your presentation reflects the effort you have put into the writing?

- ❏ Is your project the best representation of yourself that you can make it?

6 Gathering Information

Researchers today are cursed with a wonderful gift—the internet. A simple search on *Google* or *Yahoo!* can provide ready access to a mountain of information—some excellent, much unreliable—but this mountain can collapse in an avalanche, becoming a roadblock to effective research. The inexperienced researcher, relying exclusively on online sources that do not require registration or payment for access, may miss out on important information available in books, articles, and documents that are accessible through the library, and even sources buried deeper in the Web. Experienced researchers avoid the open-source avalanche with advanced search techniques that produce a manageable number of relevant and reliable web pages. They also move beyond the open Web to the library—virtual or physical. This chapter will help you become experienced with non-internet resources.

6a Consulting a Variety of Sources

Consulting online sources alone is an alluring prospect. With the myriad of resources now available online, you might think you will never have to enter a library again. Think again. It is a rare project that does not benefit from a variety of sources:

- **Reference works** such as dictionaries, encyclopedias, biographical resources, maps, atlases, almanacs, and statistical reports offer a sound overview of your topic.

- **Books** provide in-depth analysis.

- **Scholarly articles** report the research of experts in the field.

- **Newspaper and magazine articles** offer information about recent events.

- **Pamphlets and government publications** offer information and data that may be available nowhere else.

- **Visual, multimedia, and audio sources** can enliven your research and offer new data.

- **Websites** are useful for quick answers but also often offer sound information from reliable sources.

- **Archival materials** provide insight into history and lived experiences.

- **Field research** provides data about specifically selected populations.

The ease of finding and accessing sources should take a back seat to source quality and relevance.

6b Finding Articles in Journals and Other Periodicals Using Databases and Indexes

A periodical is a publication, like a magazine, newspaper, or scholarly journal, that is issued at regular intervals—daily, weekly, monthly, quarterly. A search engine such as *Google* or *Ask* can point you to articles published online in periodicals, but many articles in academic journals are not available for free on the Web, and many magazines and newspapers require subscriptions before you can access their content. You can access a much more comprehensive listing of articles through your campus library's databases. You may need to sign in with a username and password.

Library databases are organized so that you can search for articles by author, title, subject, date, and other fields. Some databases provide only an abstract, or summary, but many provide the complete text.

Finding an appropriate database or index

Most college libraries offer a variety of databases. Most will offer an all-purpose database like *ProQuest Central, Academic Search Premier,* or *Expanded Academic ASAP,* that indexes popular newspapers and magazines and scholarly journals.

College libraries also offer a wide variety of discipline-specific databases and indexes. The University of Denver, for example, offers more than 300 online databases—from *ABELL: Annual Bibliography of English Literature and Languages* to *Worldwide Political Science Abstracts* (see Figure 6.1). Thus, the first step in finding appropriate articles for your college research project is to identify the databases and indexes that will be most appropriate for your search. Go to your library's database access page or consult with a reference librarian to find the right ones.

When searching for articles, be sure to consider the following:

- The types of periodicals the database indexes—popular periodicals, scholarly sources, or both

- The types of sources that are most appropriate for your purpose, audience, context, and genre

- The types of sources that are most appropriate to your topic

For Heather DeGroot, writing for her psychology class, *PsycINFO* (a database that indexes articles from psychology journals) was a good starting place for her periodicals search. For Lydia Nichols, researching the characteristics of underground comics, a general database (such as *Academic Search Premier*), which indexes both popular and scholarly sources, was effective.

Searching a database

Searching a database is much like using a search engine such as *Google* or *Yahoo!* You type in a search term and hit Return to generate a list of articles. Unlike a search engine, however, the database limits its search to a list of reliable publications.

More about ▶▶▶
Purpose, 37–41, 153–55
Audience, 40, 206–07
Context, 38
Genre, 38

▶▶▶ Sample student research papers
"The Power of Wardrobe," Heather De-Groot, ch. 22
"Holy Underground Comics, Batman!" Lydia Nichols, ch. 21

More about ▶▶▶
Conducting a keyword search, 77–78

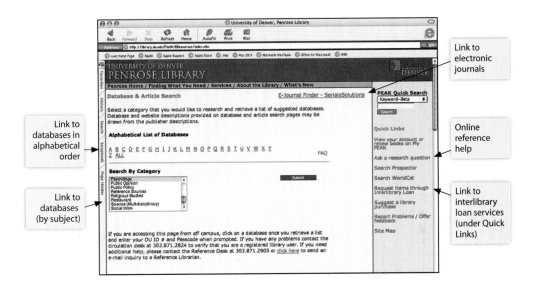

Link to electronic journals

Link to databases in alphabetical order

Link to databases (by subject)

Online reference help

Link to interlibrary loan services (under Quick Links)

FIGURE 6.1 Home and Database Access Page for the University of Denver Library

To make sure the results of a database search are relevant, narrow your search by combining search terms and using the Advanced search options the database makes available.

For example, to begin her research, Lydia Nichols might have typed "comics" in the *ProQuest* search box. Such a search would have generated a list of almost 130,000 items—far too many to be helpful. But *ProQuest* provides a variety of tools for narrowing the search (See Figure 6.2). Clicking on the Topics tab reveals a list of terms used to index subjects related to Nichols's, such as "underground comics" and "genre." A search for articles on underground comics reduces the search results (or "hits") to 287—still a long list, but much more focused. Using the Advanced tab allows her to search on multiple keywords simultaneously, narrowing the list further. Figure 6.2 shows the results for a search on both "underground comics" and "genre"; this search brought the number of sources down to a manageable 22.

Most databases allow you to search simultaneously through all the databases provided by the same vendor. If you find several databases that index periodicals on subjects that are appropriate for your research, searching them simultaneously can save you time and effort.

More about ▶ ▶ ▶
Using a metasearch engine, 79–80

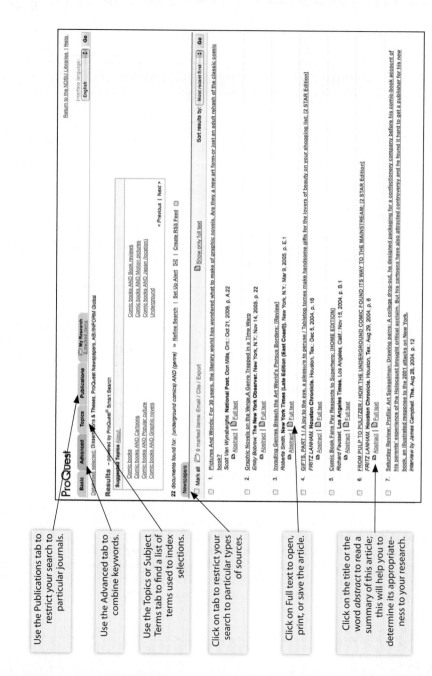

FIGURE 6.2 Search Results for "Underground Comics AND Genre"

Use the Publications tab to restrict your search to particular journals.

Use the Advanced tab to combine keywords.

Use the Topics or Subject Terms tab to find a list of terms used to index selections.

Click on tab to restrict your search to particular types of sources.

Click on Full text to open, print, or save the article.

Click on the title or the word *abstract* to read a summary of this article; this will help you to determine its appropriateness to your research.

Quick

Reference ➔ Conducting a Boolean Search

Most databases (and some search engines, like *Yahoo!*) use Boolean logic to narrow a search. Boolean logic relies on the "operators" AND, NOT, and OR (in all-capital letters) to expand or narrow a search. It also uses signs (usually parentheses) to group words into phrases and wildcard characters (* or ?) to stand in place of letters so that you can search for different forms of a word at the same time.

AND

Plagiarism AND cheating

Narrows the scope of a search by retrieving items that include both terms.

OR

Plagiarism OR cheating

Expands a search by retrieving items that include either term.

NOT

Plagiarism NOT cheating

Narrows a search by retrieving items that include one term but not the other.

NEAR   Plagiarism NEAR college

Narrows search by retrieving items with terms within a certain proximity of each other.

(/)   (plagiarism in college)
plagiarism AND (college OR education)

Groups terms into phrases, so only items that include the phrase are retrieved. Also used to group Boolean operators.

*, ?   *plagiar** to search for *plagiarism, plagiarist, plagiarize,* and *plagiary* simultaneously

Wildcard characters allow you to search for more than one version of a word at the same time by replacing the letters that are different in each word with an asterisk (*) or a question mark (?).

Finding copies of articles

Once you have generated a list of articles from your search database, you will be ready to retrieve copies of the articles. Some you can access directly from the database where you found the citation (see Figure 6.2, "Full text" links); those you can print, download to your hard drive, or email to yourself.

For some articles, however, only an abstract will be available through the database; in a few cases, only a bibliographic citation may be available. While it may be tempting to skip sources that you cannot have delivered instantly to your desktop, you may miss out on important sources of information, especially classics published before the internet revolution. To find articles you cannot link to from the database, follow these steps or consult Figure 6.3.

1. Check your library's list of electronic journals; look for a link to the list on the library's home page (Figure 6.3) or on its database access page.

More about ▶▶▶
Using a library's electronic catalog, 61–62

2. If the journal or issue you want is not available online, check the library's catalog to see if your library subscribes to the print version of the journal. It will likely be housed in one of three places: the Periodicals room, the shelves of bound periodicals, or on microform or microfiche.

3. If your library does not subscribe to the journal you need, you can request a copy through *interlibrary loan (ILL)*. Most libraries now allow you to place interlibrary loan requests directly from the library's website (see Figure 6.3). Many library sites organize ILL under "Services" links. Because it can take two weeks or more for ILL materials to arrive, be sure to start your research well in advance of the due date for your project.

Figure 6.4 (p. 68) summarizes the process of searching for periodical articles.

More about ▶▶▶
Creating a working bibliography, 52–53

▶ EXERCISE **6.1** Searching Databases

Using your research topic, search a general database (such as *ProQuest Research Library* or *Academic Search Premier*) to find citations of three or more promising articles, and add them to your working bibliography. Then perform the same search on a subject-specific database (such as ERIC, an education database). Compare the results: How many articles did each search provide? What types of sources did each search return? How many sources were the same in both searches?

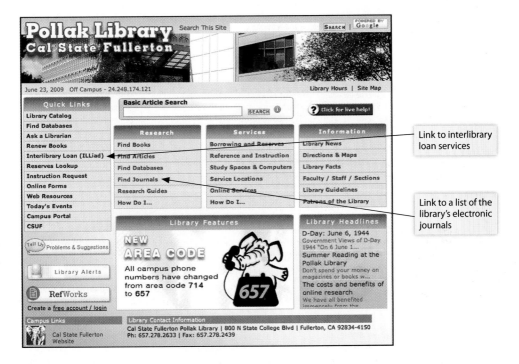

FIGURE 6.3 Link to Interlibrary Loan and Electronic Journal List on Home Page
California State University–Fullerton's library provides these links on its home page.

6c Finding Reference Works

General reference works such as dictionaries, encyclopedias, biographical sources, bibliographies, almanacs, yearbooks, and atlases can do all of the following:

- Introduce you to your topic and help you determine whether it will sustain your interest.

- Provide an overview and background information.

- Help you get a sense of subtopics you might want to explore.

Subject-specific reference works can be even more helpful. They can do the following:

- Introduce you to the main issues in a debate.

> **More about ▶▶▶**
> Specialized reference
>   works:
>   Literature, 234–37
>   Humanities,
>   234–37
>   Social sciences,
>   238–240
>   Sciences, 238–240
> Boolean operators,
>   64, 79

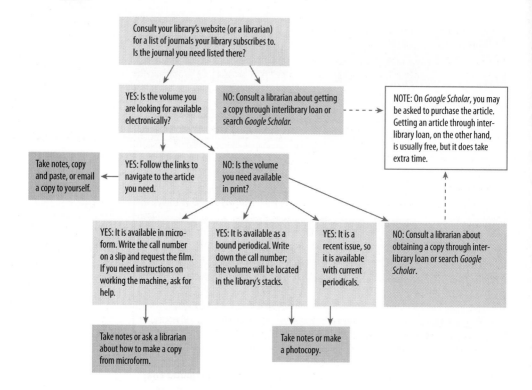

FIGURE 6.4 The Process of Finding an Article

- Provide lists of additional sources to explore.
- Help you develop your list of keywords by introducing and defining the special terminology used in the discipline.

While you will be able to link to many reference sources from your library's home page, some (especially more specialized sources) are still available only in hard copy or on CD-ROM in your college library. To find them, type the name of your subject area (for example, "American government" or "psychology"), the Boolean operator AND, and the type of source you are searching for ("dictionary" or "encyclopedia" or "bibliography") in the search box on your library's electronic catalog; then hit Return.

Because both general and subject-specific reference works provide background information to orient you to your topic, they make a useful starting point. For a college-level research project, however, reference works are only the beginning; to fulfill your responsibilities to your topic and audience, you must go beyond these sources to find books, articles, and websites that treat your topic in depth.

Dictionaries and encyclopedias

In addition to whatever online tools they may use, most writers keep a hardbound desktop dictionary at hand, to verify spellings, look up definitions, and gather additional brief information about words. An unabridged dictionary provides more—more words, more examples of usage, a more complete description of the word's roots in other languages. The most extensive unabridged dictionary is the *Oxford English Dictionary* (or *OED*), a multivolume work providing the entire history of English words and showing the ways in which their meanings have changed over time. Many academic libraries subscribe to the *OED* online.

Specialized dictionaries are written for students and scholars in specific academic fields. They often provide a comprehensive introduction to the topic as well as a list of further resources. If, for example, you want a deeper understanding of what *absolutism* means to a political scientist, you will need to turn to a source like the *Blackwell Dictionary of Political Science,* which offers a long paragraph explaining the term, followed by three recommended sources on the topic.

General encyclopedias offer a topic overview, and some include a list of further resources. Specialized encyclopedias provide more specific, detailed information than will a general encyclopedia. From reading a specialized encyclopedia on your topic, you can expect not only general information but also a sense of how scholars in the field approach the topic. You are likely, too, to find a brief bibliography of what are considered the most authoritative sources on the topic.

Writing
↑ Responsibly   Using *Wikipedia*

Wikipedia <en.wikipedia.org> is an online encyclopedia created and revised by users. Because it can be updated constantly by many people, it may be more up-to-date than other encyclopedias, but it may also be more unreliable. Approach *Wikipedia* with care, and verify the information you find there. Remember, too, that, while any general encyclopedia may provide a useful overview, it is useful only as an introduction to your topic. It is not an authoritative source for a college-level research project.

Almanacs and yearbooks

Almanacs and yearbooks are annual publications offering facts and statistics. Traditionally, almanacs and yearbooks have offered a wide variety of information, such as when each phase of the moon will occur or the time at which the sun will rise or set on a given date, the population and annual per-capita income of nations, and chronologies of events for the past year. The best-known general-purpose almanac is the *World Almanac and Book of Facts,* which has been published annually since 1923. Others, such as the *Almanac of American Politics* or the *Yearbook of Immigration Statistics,* focus on a specific topic but provide a wide body of statistical and tabular data on that topic.

Biographical reference works

Biographical resources can provide you with the facts and events of people's lives (both the famous and the fairly obscure), such as their education, their accomplishments, and their current position. These references can also help you understand the historical context in which the person lived or in which his or her works were produced. Biographical resources available to researchers are indexed in *Biography Index* and in the annual versions of *Current Biography.*

Bibliographies

Bibliographies list sources on a particular topic, providing the information you need to locate the source in your library's stacks or through interlibrary loan. They often provide an abstract or brief summary of the source—so you can tell whether it is likely to be relevant to your research.

❯ *More about* ▶▶▶
Annotation, 139–42

6d   Finding Books

While reference works can give you an overview or direct you to other sources, it is in books that you are most likely to find extensive, in-depth treatments of your topic—especially in the humanities and some social sciences. One or two well-chosen books, supplemented by journal articles and other sources, can round out your research.

Searching the library's catalog

Library catalogs, typically accessible through the library's website, index the library's holdings by author, title, and subject heading. In addition, you can now search some catalogs by keyword and call number. Because catalogs differ from library to library, check the Help or Search Tips screen before beginning a search.

- To search by *author,* most library databases ask that you enter the author's last name first.

- To search by *title,* omit the subtitle and any articles (*the, a,* or *an*) at the beginning of the title.

- To search by *subject*—the most popular search strategy—is a bit more complicated, so it is addressed in a separate section below.

Searching by subject using the Library of Congress subject headings

Typically, you will search a library's catalog much as you do a search engine or a periodical database: Type a keyword or a combination of words in the search box and hit Enter. However, whereas *Google* and other web search engines allow you to use any keyword related to your topic, library catalogs use a preset list of words and phrases to index the books in the library's collection. The terms used by your library to catalog books were devised by the Library of Congress. When searching a library's catalog by subject, use these preset headings.

More about ▶▶▶
Keyword searching, 77–79

A – General works

B – Philosophy. Psychology. Religion

C – Auxiliary sciences of history

D – History (general) and history of Europe

E – History: America

F – History: America

G – Geography. Anthropology. Recreation

H – Social sciences

J – Political science

K – Law

L – Education

M – Music and books on music

N – Fine arts

P – Language and literature

Q – Science

R – Medicine

S – Agriculture
T – Technology
U – Military science
V – Naval science
Z – Bibliography. Library science. Information resources (general)

The letter at the left (from A to Z) is the first letter in the call number your library assigns to every item in its collection. Because libraries organize books according to call numbers, you can consult a map of your library to find out where the books beginning with each letter are shelved.

There are three ways to look for your topic in the subject listing:

1. Consult the classification outline in the series of big red books aptly titled *Library of Congress Subject Headings* (or *LCSH* for short) shelved in the reference section of the library.
2. Find this list of topics online at the Library of Congress's website <www.loc.gov/catdir/cpso/lcco/lcco.html>.
3. Go to a catalog entry for a book on your topic that you have already identified as relevant. The book's record will list the subject headings used (see Figure 6.5). Clicking on them will bring you to a list of related subject headings and to other books catalogued using the same terms.

Browsing the stacks or the catalog

Many researchers enjoy browsing library stacks to find books. Since books on a topic all share the first part of a call number, they are shelved close together. Wandering your library's stacks may lead to interesting discoveries.

Another approach that is useful is to browse the online catalog by call number. Once you have identified a book appropriate for your topic, look at its call number. Some library catalogs allow you to click on the call number to see other related items. Others require you to conduct a new search by call number.

6e Finding Government Publications and Other Documents

Government agencies, businesses, nonprofit groups, and libraries provide rich resources, including statistical data, annual reports, archives of records, and documents from the past.

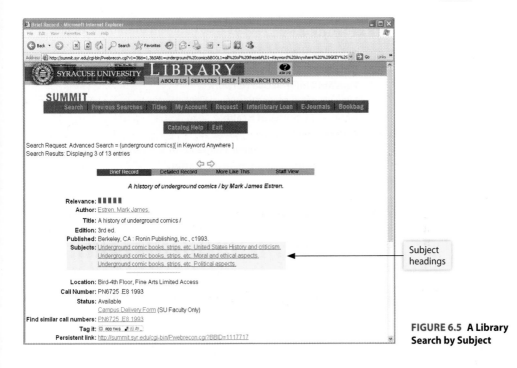

FIGURE 6.5 A Library Search by Subject

Finding government publications

If you are researching a social, legal, or political issue or need up-to-date statistics about almost any group, you may find valuable information in government publications. U.S. government publications include information from all three branches of the government—executive, legislative, and judicial. More than 300,000 government documents are available, free of charge online. To find them, conduct an advanced web search limited to the domain .gov or search library databases such as *CQ* (for *Congressional Quarterly*) *Electronic Library* and *Lexis/Nexis Congressional*. A list of useful websites for federal, state, local, and foreign government documents appears in the Quick Reference box on p. 74. You can also visit one of the 1,250 libraries that act as depositories for government documents. (To find a depository library in your area, visit <www.gpoaccess.gov/libraries.html>.)

Quick **Reference** → **Accessing Government Documents Online**

European Union

FedStats

FedWorld Information Network

Library of Congress: Thomas

National Institutes of Health

Northwestern University Library

Organization for Economic Cooperation and Development

State and Local Government on the Net

USA.Gov

US Census Bureau

US Government Printing Office

United Nations

6f Finding Sources in Special Collections: Rare Books, Manuscripts, and Archives

More about ▶▶▶
Doing primary re-
search on original
documents, 88–90

Many libraries house collections of rare books, manuscripts, and archives. Rare-book collections can include a variety of texts, such as Bibles printed during the early days of the printing press, original documents from the Revolutionary or Civil War period, and first editions of books by writers such as T. S. Eliot and Jack Kerouac. Manuscript collections may include letters by politicians or works by writers in their own hand. Archives include documents, records, and memorabilia that preserve the historical record of an institution or an event. Harvard College and the *New York Times,* for example, both have archives that preserve their history.

To find such sources, search your library's catalog and the internet using your keywords plus the words "rare book," "manuscript," or "digital archive." Pertinent items from special collections can enliven your understanding of your topic and enhance your appreciation of its social or historical significance.

6g Finding Multimedia Sources

Photographs, graphs, charts, and drawings have long been a staple of research papers in disciplines such as art history, film studies, history, geography, geology, political science, psychology, and sociology. With research in all disciplines now being shared through multimedia presentations and websites, the demand for multimedia resources has also grown. Many library catalogs list not only books but also audiocassettes, films, manuscripts, maps, musical scores, slides, and sound and video recordings. Look for a drop-down menu from which you can select the type of resource you need. (This menu may be labeled "Record type," "Material," or "Format.") Additional multimedia resources can be located through search engines that index non-HTML files such as *Google, AllTheWeb,* and *AltaVista* Advanced searches.

In addition to finding multimedia materials in a library's collection or online, you can also create your own graphics (tables, charts, and graphs) by putting data from a government website, an almanac, a yearbook, or your own research into a spreadsheet program.

More about ▶▶▶
Creating graphics, 219–20
Using visuals as support, 186–87
Formatting papers, 286–90, 332–34, 366–73, 389–90

⬆ Make It **Your Own**

For a research topic for this or another class, create a working bibliography with ten sources, one from each of the following categories: scholarly journals, popular periodicals, books, government documents, subject-specific reference works, and media sources. See p. 52 for what to include in a working bibliography.

A Final Thought

It is easy to feel overwhelmed by an avalanche of internet-accessible information, but there are many rewards in searching the library. Both the library's web portal (its home page and website) and its physical location offer trustworthy resources. And do not forget the librarians, who are often the best guides through an effective research process.

7

Meeting the Challenges of Online Research

Jorge Luis Borges, an Argentinean writer, describes in "The Library of Babel" a library so vast it contains all possible information, even every variation of mistake. All answers might be found there, if only one knew how to search this library. Readers today often think Borges anticipated the internet's vast reaches and the challenges of finding the best information it contains. The more the Web proliferates, the more skills and knowledge it demands of those who come looking. Understanding the ways search engines work and the organization of the Web can help make the difference between an online search that turns up lots of junk and one that quickly leads to reliable answers.

7a   Web and Database Searches: Developing Search Strategies

To find information on the Web, researchers typically begin with a search engine, like *Google* or *Yahoo!* Search engines scan billions of Web pages for whatever words the user enters and return links in order of relevance, as determined by the search engine's criteria. (*Google,* for example, ranks its results based on the number of other pages that link to that site, as well as advertising, while a *Yahoo!* search ranks results in part on the number of times a search term turns up.) The results retrieved can differ based on the criteria the search engine uses to rank relevance, as well as on the web pages it indexes. For that reason, it is a good idea to run a search on multiple engines. A list of popular search engines appears in the Quick Reference box below.

Before using a search engine or web directory for the first time, read about how it works. Look for links (often at the bottom of the page) called "About" or "Help" to find answers to frequently asked questions (FAQs) or advice about how best to conduct a search on that site. Look, too, for advanced search options; these will help you focus your search.

Using keywords

The most common way to begin a web search is with a simple keyword search. A search on *Google* for the word "robotics," for example, yields the results shown in Figure 7.1.

This kind of searching is very easy, and it yields plenty of results—in this case, more than 19.4 million of them. How helpful are these search results? Not very. Too much data has been delivered.

A better way to begin is to create a list of search terms for your topic and then to use them to search the Web systematically. Since

---

Quick Reference → **Popular Search Engines and Web Directories**

Alta Vista	**Go.com**
Ask	**Gigablast**
Bing	**Google**
Dmoz	**HotBot**
Excite	**Yahoo!**

Search term

Number of hits

Advertisements

URL for website

FIGURE 7.1 A Simple Keyword Search on *Google*

More about ▶▶▶
Library electronic
catalogs, 70–73
Library periodicals
databases, 61–66

search engines—unlike your library's electronic catalog or the periodicals databases your library subscribes to—do not use a systematic list of terms, you must rely on your ingenuity to come up with a list of effective keywords. Here are some suggestions for making an effective list:

More about ▶▶▶
Generating ideas,
23–30

1. Begin by reviewing whatever prewriting you have already completed, underlining the distinctive nouns you find there (including names, titles, acronyms) and compiling these nouns into a list.
2. Next, add variant spellings ("Beijing" for "Peking," for example) and synonyms (such as "generalization" for "stereotype"). A thesaurus can help you find alternatives.

3. Browse the results of your early searches to find additional keywords. A "robotics" search turns up information on military uses, jet propulsion, and robotics research labs, for instance.

4. As you read about your topic, add possible keywords to your list.

More about ▶▶▶
Keeping a research journal, 12–13
Planning, 56
Drafting, 170–80
Revising, 203–12

Keep your list of keywords in your research journal so that you can track terms (and combinations) as you use them. Then throughout the research, drafting, and revising stages of your project, conduct new keyword searches to flesh out areas of your paper as your ideas develop.

Using search engine math and Boolean searches

After finely tuning your keywords, use combining and limiting strategies to increase search effectiveness. Boolean searches use the primary search terms AND, OR, and NOT for combining and limiting. Search engines sometimes recognize these terms, but many also use symbol operators (+, -, " ", *), sometimes called search engine "math."

More about ▶▶▶
Boolean searching, 63

With search engine math, a long series of terms can be effectively combined for a search. To find out who originated thought on robotics, you might conduct the following search: +robotics +inventor +origin* (the asterisk allows the engine to find all variations of the word: *origin, original, originals, originate, originated*). To search for how the military is involved in developing and using robotics, you might use the following string: +robotics +military -training. From this search you could limit the results once you found the area of military robotics you were interested in: +robotics +military +vehicles. Be sure to check

Quick Reference ➡ Search Engine Math

Operator	Function	Example
+	Always include	+robotics
-	Do not include	-lab
" "	Look for the phrase exactly as typed	"robotics lab"
*	Search for words with this root and various endings	Robot*

which search strategies the search engine you are using recognizes before you enter either Boolean terms or search engine math.

Using advanced search options

Another method for refining searches is using advanced search screens built into the search engines and directories (Figure 7.2). Advanced searches allow you to search for results only in languages that you can read, desired file types (*Word,* rich text, PDF, or *Excel*), pages that have been updated recently, and sites that are published in noncommercial domains (sites with URLs, or addresses, that end in *.org, .gov,* or *.edu,* rather than *.com*) and other options.

Notice that the Advanced Search page allows you to add ("with **all** of the words") and subtract ("**without** the words") terms much as you can with search engine math. Going directly to the Advanced Search

Search for an exact phrase.

Eliminate irrelevant items.

Narrow results to sites in English or other languages.

Limit results to specific file types such as .pdf.

Limit results to specific domains such as *.edu* and *.org.*

Narrow results to recently updated pages.

FIGURE 7.2 An Advanced *Google* Search

Quick Reference ➡ **Metasearch Engines**

Copernic Agent	Search.com
Dogpile	Surf Wax
Info.com	Webcrawler
Ixquick	Yippy!
MetaCrawler	

page when you conduct online research can save you some time reviewing how the engine works.

Using metasearch engines

You may have a favorite search engine, one that you go to automatically when you have a question. But because search engines index different web pages and use different methods to rank sites, using more than one engine increases your odds of finding useful resources. To search multiple sites simultaneously, use a *metasearch engine* that sends your keyword search out to several search engines, returning the top results from each with duplicate entries deleted. Entering "underground comics" and "history" into the metasearch engine *Dogpile,* for example, produced a manageable thirty "hits," many of them quite promising.

However, if your topic is obscure, you may find that searching a few comprehensive search engines, such as *Ask, Google,* and *Yahoo!,* one by one is more effective because metasearch engines only turn up the "top" results.

Searching the invisible Web

A wide variety of information sources exist on the Web but are not routinely turned up by a keyword search on a search engine. These gaps in web searches occur because of the inability of some search engines to find the following:

- Data within a database
- Files that are dynamically created in response to a user typing a keyword into a search box
- Files that require a password or login information

- Files that are not in HTML format (like blogs and news feeds, which are usually in XML format)
- File names (URLs) that contain question marks
- Image, sound, and video files

Because these kinds of sites are not always flagged by search engines, they make up what is sometimes called the invisible (or dark) Web. Finding information on the invisible Web requires the use not just of simple searches on search engines but the use of databases, subject directories, and search engines that go beyond HTML files.

More about ▶▶▶
Devising a topic, 23–31
Narrowing a topic, 32–34
Expanding a topic, 35

Using subject directories

Subject directories list websites by topic and are often annotated. Their organization—from general to specific—can provide an effective overview of a topic and can help you discover, narrow, or expand your topic. The annotations provide information about a site before you navigate to it.

Two types of subject directories are available: commercial directories and academic ones. Commercial directories rarely scrutinize their listings as carefully as the academic directories do, and because they cater to a general audience, they do not emphasize academic topics or links. Academic directories, on the other hand, offer a smaller number of links, but the links are evaluated carefully and the categories are chosen to be of use to an academic audience. So, while commercial directories like *Yahoo!* <dir.yahoo.com> and *About.com* <www.about.com> can be useful for helping you devise a topic, use an academic directory, such as the ones in the Quick Reference box below, to locate useful sources.

NOTE Most subject directories today emphasize keyword searching but still list websites by category.

Quick **Reference** ➡ **Academic Subject Directories**

Academic Info
BUBL LINK
INFOMINE

The Internet Public Library (ipl2)
Librarians' Index to the Internet

→ Tech

Using *Google Scholar*

Google Scholar <scholar.google.com> allows users to search the Web exclusively for scholarly materials—articles in academic journals, theses, books, and abstracts.

Pros

- *Google Scholar* can help you locate material that you would otherwise need both your library's catalog and its subscription databases to find.
- It may link to your own library's digital holdings (see the preferences settings in *Google Scholar*).
- It indicates how many online sites have cited the source and provides links to those citations; a source heavily cited in scholarly journals is likely to be reputable.

Cons

- *Google* does not define "scholarly," so your instructor may not consider some listed works authoritative.
- You may be shifted to sites where you will be asked to pay for full-text versions of the text. (Check your library's holdings or interlibrary loan before paying.)
- Recent sources are often not included, or they appear at the end of the list. (You can include a date range in Advanced Scholar Search.)
- Bibliographic data cannot be imported to bibliographic software such as *Endnote, Refworks,* or *Bibliomaker.*

> *More about* ▶▶▶
> Evaluating sources, 100–11
> Interlibrary loan, 65

→ EXERCISE 7.1 Conducting a Keyword Search

Using one of the search engines listed on p. 77, conduct a keyword search on your topic. Follow these steps in your search:

1. Compile a list of keywords for your topic.
2. Enter a single keyword, and conduct a simple search.
3. Enter two or more keywords with Boolean operators or search engine math to conduct a more complex search.
4. Use Advanced Search options to limit your results to items posted after 2002 with a noncommercial domain.

How do the results differ at each step in terms of effectiveness, efficiency, and accuracy in coming up with relevant information? Which step returns sites that are most useful in academic research?

> **EXERCISE 7.2 Conducting a Search on an Academic Subject Directory**
>
> Using the keywords you generated for Exercise 7.1, conduct a search using one of the subject directories listed in the Quick Reference box above. Write a paragraph comparing the results from the subject directory with those you generated in Exercise 7.1.

7b Finding Other Electronic Sources

In addition to conventional websites, a variety of other electronic sources, including weblogs ("blogs"), discussion lists, and news alerts, can offer insight into your topic.

Finding blogs

More about ▶▶▶
Evaluating reliability
of a blog, 107–09
Citing a blog,
  MLA style, 270–71
  APA style, 330
  Chicago style, 362
  CSE style, 387

Individuals increasingly maintain weblogs in which they write informally about their hobbies, interests, and special areas of knowledge. For this reason, blogs have become an important source for news, in politics as well as in academic disciplines.

To find a blog on your topic, try visiting a search engine that seeks out blogs. The Quick Reference box below offers multiple blog search engines you can try.

CAUTION Not all blogs are reliable; they can be generated by anyone. Evaluate them carefully before using the information they provide.

Finding discussion lists

Discussion lists—including email discussion lists and newsgroups—allow people with common interests to carry on electronic discussions. *Email discussion lists* allow members of a group to send email messages to all other subscribers. *Newsgroups* are web-based bulletin

Quick Reference ➡ Blog Search Engines

Blogarama	**Eatonweb Portal**
Blogdigger	**GlobeofBlogs**
Bloglines	**Google Blogs**
Blogsearch	**Readablog**
Blogstreet	**Technorati**

› **Quick Reference** ➔ **Discussion List Catalog Sites**

CataList   **Usenet**
Deja.com   **Yahoo!**

boards on which members can read or respond to postings. Both email discussion lists and newsgroups require participants to subscribe.

To find an email discussion list or a newsgroup pertinent to your topic, enter your search terms in one of the email discussion list or group catalog sites listed in the Quick Reference box above.

You can also enter your keyword plus "email discussion list" or "newsgroup" in a search engine that finds dynamic websites. You will have the best results if you begin with very general keywords. As with weblogs, always keep in mind that the information you gain from discussion groups will have to be verified, and write down the information you will need later for citing any post you refer to as a source. One benefit of seeking information through discussion lists is that, when the list is associated with a professional organization, you may be able to ask a direct question of a pool of experts.

> ***More about ▶▶▶***
> Search engines
>   that find dynamic
>   websites, 77
> Citing email discussion lists, newsgroups, and
>   chat rooms,
>   MLA style, 270
>   APA style, 330
>   *Chicago* style, 362
>   CSE style, 383

Using news alerts

News alerts help you track media coverage of current events and are an invaluable resource for research. To register for news alerts, go to *Google* <www.google.com/newsalerts> or a news outlet such as *CNN* <www.cnn.com/profile/> and register for the service. You will then receive daily email updates on the topics you have chosen.

Finding online reference works

Online resources are easily updatable and often quite searchable. Thus, online reference works can be good places to start a search, particularly when you do not know much about your subject. Some, such as the *Encyclopedia Britannica,* are available online to all users. Others, such as the *Oxford English Dictionary* (*OED*), require a subscription for access.

Subject librarians at your school may have filtered the Web for the best reference works in their areas, and the library may even have a subscription to give you access to restricted works. Check your library website for "subject librarians" or "research guides." From these locations on the library website, you will be able to choose subject areas

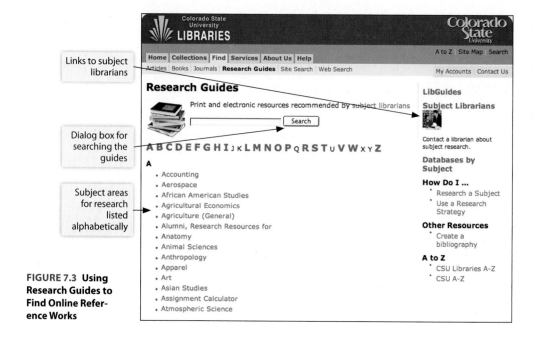

Links to subject librarians

Dialog box for searching the guides

Subject areas for research listed alphabetically

FIGURE 7.3 Using Research Guides to Find Online Reference Works

in which you are interested (Figure 7.3). The lists created by your school's research librarians will include a range of resource types including online reference works.

Find Out **More ... Online Government Statistics**

Much of the statistical data found in yearbooks and almanacs can be accessed online from the following government agencies:

Bureau of Economic Analysis

Central Intelligence Agency (CIA)

USA.gov

US Census Bureau

US Department of Justice

Some almanacs and yearbooks, too, are now available online. Check your library's catalog or its list of databases.

7c Finding Multimedia Sources Online

Photographs, graphs, charts, and drawings have long been a staple of research papers in disciplines such as art history, film studies, history, geography, geology, political science, psychology, and sociology. With research in all disciplines now being shared through multimedia presentations and websites, the demand for multimedia resources has also grown.

More about ▶▶▶
Finding multimedia
sources in the
library, 74

There are many impressive and reliable online sources for visual and other media: The Berkeley Digital Library, for example, offers an invaluable source on Goldman, *Emma Goldman: A Guide to Her Life and Documentary Sources*. And multimedia sites abound: The Library of Congress, for example, maintains a useful hypermedia archive of William Blake's works.

Besides the video clips you can find on *YouTube* and *Hulu,* you may also find appropriate multimedia resources online at the sites hosted by the organizations listed in the Quick Reference box below.

In addition to finding multimedia materials in a library's collection or online, you can create your own graphics (tables, charts, and graphs) by putting data from a government website, an almanac, a yearbook, or your own research into a spreadsheet program to create a table, chart, or graph.

More about ▶▶▶
Using visuals as sup-
port, 186–87
Formatting papers,
286–90, 332–34,
366–73, 389–90

A Final Thought

The Web does not have to be an impenetrable Library of Babel. Nor should you approach it as though everything you find when you search is true and reliable. With the right search tools and techniques, however, research online can be rewarding.

Quick Reference ➡ **Multimedia Resources**

Academy of American Poets
American Rhetoric: The Power of Oratory in the United States
Library of Congress
National Aeronautics and Space Administration (NASA)
National Park Service
New York Public Library
Perry-Castañeda Library Map Collection, University of Texas
Smithsonian Institution

8

Developing New Information

This ancient Egyptian wall painting depicts smiths refining ore to produce gold. Like these goldsmiths, writers engaged in primary research produce valuable nuggets of information from firsthand research in archives and databases as well as by conducting interviews, observational studies, and surveys. Developing new information can also feel like discovering new worlds, richly rewarding and exciting.

8a Using Archives and Primary Information

One mode of primary research is the study of primary documents. This research may include analyzing any of the following:

- A novel, story, play, or poem for a literature class

Quick

Reference ➔ **Primary Sources versus Secondary Sources**

Primary Sources	Secondary Sources
Eyewitness accounts of events, experiments, or studies; information that has not been interpreted by other researchers ("raw" data)	Works that interpret firsthand accounts, raw data, or art and other media

Examples	**Examples**
■ The data recorded in a laboratory notebook ■ A work of literature or art ■ A letter home from a soldier about a battle in which she or he has fought	■ A laboratory report that analyzes the data from an experiment ■ An interpretation of a work of literature or art ■ A historian's analysis of a battle based on soldiers' letters, the general's battle plans, and other sources

- A famous speech for a political science or speech class

- A historical document, such as the Magna Carta or the Emancipation Proclamation, for a history class

- A painting, sculpture, or drawing for an art history class

- A radio show, television show, or advertisement for a media studies class

> **More about ▶▶▶**
> Evaluating visual sources, 110–12
> Using visuals as support, 186–87

You may also gather information from archives or special collections, which may include any of the following:

- Written records, such as diaries and letters.

- Statistical data, such as the average SAT score of college applicants in the United States. This information might be collected by the US Census Bureau or the National Center for Education Statistics.

- Survey archives that record, for example, the popularity ratings of politicians. This type of information is collected by organizations such as Gallup and CNN.

Worthwhile research on primary documents requires:

- Perseverance—you may need to take several trips to the archive if the materials have not been digitized and cannot be removed

- Creative analysis to make sense of the information

More about ▶▶▶
Evaluating for reliability, 102–03

- Comparison of data from different sources to reach a reliable conclusion

Contacting the archive

Archives have many rules to protect documents and monitor access. To use your time efficiently, find out before you visit how the archive operates:

- Where is the facility, and what are its operating hours?
- Can you make an appointment with an archivist or librarian to get advice on finding information about your topic?
- Are the materials you want to examine restricted? Do you need to request materials in advance or get special permission or a letter of introduction from a professor?
- Will you need to bring money (for a locker, to make photocopies), and can you get change if you need it?
- What will you be able to bring into the archive to take notes (for example, a laptop? a pencil, notepad, etc.)

In short, seek guidance from the archive or special collections personnel and from any online guidelines.

Many archives and special collections now offer electronic catalogs online. Take advantage and search such catalogs before your visit. This will help you determine which artifacts you want to examine, saving you time when you get there. Increasingly, collections even digitize materials so you can study them online, making archival research easier than it has ever been.

8b Conducting Interviews

While much information can be acquired by studying documents, interviews can sometimes be the only way to get the "inside scoop." You can draw on expert information differently in an interview than through reading articles: Interviews let you shape the questions and follow up the responses.

Selecting an interview type

Interviews take three primary forms: informal, semistructured, and structured. An *informal interview* involves a very casual question-and-answer structure and may be conducted early in the research process

> ### Find Out **More . . . Multimedia Materials in Online Archives and Special Collections**
>
> Multimedia archives such as those listed here contain maps, photographs, recorded speeches, music, videos, and even scanned documents:
>
> African Studies Center, University of Pennsylvania
>
> Kennedy Space Center's Media Gallery
>
> Library of Congress
> > Moving Image Collection
> >
> > Rare Books and Special Collections
> >
> > Recorded Sound Reference Center
>
> Miller Center of Public Affairs, University of Virginia, Scripps Library and Multimedia Archive
>
> The Newberry Library, Chicago
>
> Smithsonian Institution

to get a general idea about a topic. A *semistructured interview* involves prepared questions in a preplanned order from which you might deviate slightly as you respond to the interviewee. Semistructured interviews allow you to follow an idea and ask for more information, even skipping or adding a question when it seems appropriate. Finally, a *structured interview* is similar to a survey or questionnaire; you would use it to interview more than one person in a standard way, always asking the questions in the same way and in the same order.

Media such as email, instant messaging, and even the telephone extend your range of possible interviewees, but face-to-face interviews give you an opportunity to "read" the other person's body language—facial expressions and gestures. Still, conducting interviews online offers benefits of its own: a written record of responses and time for your interviewee to consider each response.

If you choose an email interview, consider offering the option of a phone or in-person interview if the interviewee prefers it, as writing answers will probably demand more of the respondent's time.

Choosing and contacting interviewees

When looking for an expert to interview, start with your college campus and local community: Are there instructors or local professionals with special expertise in your subject? Many organizations can connect you to experts who work or volunteer for the group, and government employees may provide insight into the workings of their departments. When researching cultural or historical events, consider interviewing participants—the attorneys in a legal case, your soldier-cousin for her experience in Iraq, and so forth.

Writing
↑ Responsibly   **Conducting Interviews Fairly**

When interviewing an expert to gather information, be fair to the interviewee:

- Ask about available times, and work around the interviewee's schedule.
- Show up for the interview on time and prepared.
- Ask for information that you need the interviewer to provide, not for information you can easily gather on your own.
- Tell the interviewee at the outset how you plan to use the information

you gather, and get his or her written consent.

- Ask permission to record the interview.
- Stay within the allotted time.
- Confirm any quotations you may want to use.
- Offer the interviewee an opportunity to review your notes or your draft document. (You need not change your notes or document in response, but you should acknowledge to your reader(s) any difference of opinion.)

Preparing for the interview

Your interview will be only as good as the preparation you put into it:

- Consider your purpose, and shape your questions accordingly.

- Conduct background research on the topic and on the person you want to interview.

- Contact the potential interviewee, letting the subject know who you are, what you are researching, why you selected her or him, and the date by which you will need responses.

- Develop preliminary questions. Avoid asking yes/no, either/or questions (often called "closed" questions). Instead of asking, "Is the president of the student senate doing a good job?" (a closed question), ask "How would you rate the job the president of the student senate is doing and why?" (an open question). Open questions prompt more than a "yes" or "no" response from your interviewee.

- Have your teacher, a writing center consultant, or a classmate review your questions. Ask reviewers to add any they feel are missing, suggest a more logical order, remove any that are beyond the scope of your study, or reword any that are too narrow or too vague.

Conducting the interview

A good semistructured interview (the type you are most likely to conduct) is like a good conversation. There should be some give-and-take, and your questions should lead the interviewee to elaborate. The following guidelines will help you to conduct an effective interview:

- Remind the interviewee of the purpose of the interview and the way you plan to use the information you receive.

- Have the interviewee sign your informed consent form. (See Figure 8.1 on p. 94 for a model.)

- Put the interviewee at ease by leading off with some easy questions and assuring the subject that you are interested in his or her perspective.

- Use your prepared questions, but also listen for surprise responses and ask follow-up questions. Those surprises may shed new light and become central to your research project.

- Affirm the interviewee's responses. Nodding, maintaining eye contact, even occasionally saying "uh-huh" or "that's interesting" can encourage an interviewee to say more.

- Take extensive notes or make a recording (with permission) so that you can represent the interview faithfully when you are ready to write.

- Ask the interviewee to repeat important points if you are not recording, so that you can document them accurately.

Wrapping up and processing the information

The interview is not complete when you leave the interviewee. There is still much to be done:

- Send a thank-you note within twenty-four hours of your interview acknowledging your gratitude for the interviewee's time, offering to provide a copy of your research project when it is completed, and repeating your contact information.

- Make a transcript of the interview to which you can refer as you write up your results, and send a copy to your interviewee for comment or confirmation. (You are not obliged to accept the interviewee's revisions, but you may gain deeper insight by considering his or her comments.)

Consent for Using Interview Results

I am conducting this interview for my _____ course on _____ topic. I believe your knowledge and expertise will shed important light on the topic; therefore, I request the right to use your responses to my interview questions as a component of my research, which is part of my academic scholarship. Please consider signing the following statement, indicating that you give me consent to use these responses:

I agree to allow _____ to use my responses as part of his or her academic scholarship. I understand that I may be quoted at length and carefully paraphrased.

Name (please print):

_____

Address:

_____

_____

Signature:

_____

Date:

_____

FIGURE 8.1 Interview Consent Form

- Ask any additional questions, or request clarification of earlier responses, via email or phone.
- Send the interviewee a copy of your finished project.

8c Making Observations

Observational studies allow researchers to pay attention to people's activities and behaviors in action. Observation is a central research technique in the social sciences, such as sociology, psychology, anthroplogy, and education, but can also be used to answer questions related to such diverse fields as business, politics, and even architecutre.

> **Hypothesis** A tentative explanation for a phenomenon

Preparing to observe

To prepare for observation-based research, consider the following:

- **Your purpose.** What do you hope to learn? Write down a hypothesis before you begin your observations. Plan to refine it as your observations progress.

- **Your role.** Will you participate in the group or observe it from outside? Consider how your experiences and perspectives will affect your observations. Take steps to minimize bias.

- **Your methods.** Establish categories or a plan for tracking the observations you expect, and adjust them in response to your actual observations. Take notes diligently—do not trust your memory.

The plan that follows shows how one student prepared to observe a computer gaming party to learn about the ways games bring people together and the kinds of behaviors associated with group gaming.

Preparing to Observe Student Gaming and Group Behavior

Purpose	Discover the way games can bring people together by observing gamers in action.
Hypothesis	Games bring people together through socializing, problem solving, and the building of common experiences and languages.
Role	Participate (participant researcher role) to experience what goes on in the networked environment as well as in the room itself.
Methods	Categories: socializing in pairs or small groups, group-specific language, problem solving, other.*

*Use the "other" category to note things that do not seem to fit my predetermined categories. Afterward, build one or two new categories based on what shows up in the "other" column.

For observations of organized groups, ask permission from the group's leader (e.g., the pastor of a church congregation or the president of a student organization), and let the leader decide whether the larger group should be informed. For unorganized groups (users of your dorm's laundry room or patrons of a game arcade, for example), inform the manager of the facility, and reveal your purpose to patrons when asked directly.

Conducting an observation

While conducting an observation, avoid disrupting the normal flow of activity as much as possible. This is true even when you are a participant observer. Drawing attention to the fact that you are conducting research can cause the people you are observing to behave differently. We might call it the Big Brother factor: If people know they are being observed, they are likely to be guarded or on their best behavior, and neither is good for researching real life. How, then, can you reduce your impact on the research environment?

- Sit out of others' line of sight.

- Try to blend in. Find out, for instance, how people will be dressed and dress similarly. If laptops are not common in the situation you are observing, avoid using one for note taking (even though doing so can be very handy).

Processing the information

More about ▶▶▶
Interpreting, analyzing, and evaluating information, 100–10

The hard work of observation often occurs after the observation is over. You need to decide how to interpret, analyze, and evaluate what you saw.

- Review the notes you made, developing new categories for any actions that do not fit neatly into your preestablished scheme. Consider any patterns that emerged within your observation data: What kinds of things occurred repeatedly and similarly? What seemed surprising?

- Write some reflections on what you are seeing in the data. What is the significance of the patterns? Do they reinforce, enhance, or change your hypothesis?

- Compare the information you found to existing research. Has other research confirmed what you saw? Is what you saw different from other researchers' observations?

Writing
↑ Responsibly **Avoiding Bias When Conducting Surveys**

To avoid bias when developing and conducting surveys:

- Frame your questions carefully to avoid leading respondents. Asking "Don't you think we should have a new parking lot?" prompts respondents to agree.
- Select a representative sample of the population you are studying, not just those who are easy to locate or who you believe will support your hypothesis.
- Draw only the conclusions that the data you collect support.
- Alert your readers to the limitations of your research: Be candid about what your research does and does not demonstrate.

8d Developing and Conducting Surveys

Surveys collect information from people about their beliefs, experiences, opinions, and behaviors. Designing surveys that fairly and accurately represent a population is an advanced technical skill: Arlene Fink's guide to conducting surveys—*The Survey Kit,* 2nd ed. (2003)—for example, is a ten-volume work. Most surveys conducted for a college research project cannot meet the high standards of statistical accuracy, but if designed with care, they can provide tentative insights into local situations.

Preparing to survey

When developing a survey, consider these issues:

- **Your purpose.** What do you hope to learn from your survey? Write down a hypothesis before you design your survey.

- **Your target population.** What group will you try to reach, and how will you contact them? Strive to include a broad and representative range of respondents.

- **Your survey.** What type of questions will you ask, how many questions will you include, and how will you administer the survey? Most surveys provide a fixed number of responses (as in a multiple-choice test) because it is easier to administer and analyze surveys of this type, but be sure that your answer options are fair and offer an adequate range of responses.

Because respondents are not likely to spend more than a few minutes answering questions, surveys should be brief: Two pages is a reasonable limit.

The table below shows an example of one student's preparation for a survey to study student gaming and group behavior:

Preparing to Survey: Student Gaming and Group Behavior

Purpose	To determine whether gaming affects students' schoolwork or is a higher priority to some students than homework.
Hypothesis	A minority of students spend significant amounts of time (more than ten hours) gaming each week, and those students are more likely to be doing badly in school than are those who do not play games as frequently. I suspect the type of games students play also matters.
Target Population	All college students

Sample Questions	• How much time each week do you spend playing computer or video games (including card games, Wii, online games, etc.)?
	 • Which type of game do you play most frequently?
	    • Shooter games
	    • Exercise games
	    • Card games
	    • Immersive world games
	    • Other (write in type) _____
	 • What is your GPA?
	 • How many hours a week do you typically spend doing homework?

Distributing and collecting surveys

There are several things to keep in mind about distributing and collecting surveys:

- The more surveys you distribute and collect, the more confident you can be about your findings.

- Distribute your surveys to maximize representation of your target population. To answer a question about the general student population, for example, look for a location nearly *all* students use, such as the Union. Alternatively, use a resource such as Survey Monkey to create your survey online; then distribute the survey link via email to a campus list. Get permission from the list manager.

- Make it clear that the survey will be anonymous; if paper, consider providing a box into which respondents can drop the survey. Again, online survey services make it easy to maintain anonymity.

Processing the information

Responses to many survey questions can be tabulated as percentages: What percentage of those surveyed answered in a specific way? If you have included an open question or two in your survey, you will have to analyze the responses for patterns. As with other kinds of research, it is useful to verify your findings against those of other sources.

⬆ Make It **Your Own**

Return to your research question(s). Write down potential sources of new information to answer your question: surveys, observations, archives, or other uninterpreted data. After generating at least two viable possibilities, write a paragraph on what you might expect to learn from these sources.

A Final Thought

Developing new information can be an exciting and rewarding experience. You may find that, in its archives, your school has documents that give you insight into your grandparents' and great-grandparents' lives. Interviews allow you to access expert knowledge firsthand. Observing can give you a clearer idea of people's actions and interactions. Surveys can produce timely information that is focused on your question. Building these kinds of hands-on research skills will help to develop your critical mind.

9 Evaluating Information

You hear a politician speak about getting the national budget back under control, indicating that his plan reduces the deficit and "does not cut Medicaid," while the opposition's budget "commits seniors to bureaucratically rationed health care." Can you take these statements at face value? The answer is no.* The official might be overstating the potential of his plan and misrepresenting the potential of other plans to "win" at the polls.

*FactCheck.org assessed the truthfulness of an advertisement on this theme sponsored by the Democratic Congressional Campaign Committee.

If you rely on sound bites, you might be misled into throwing your support behind a candidate whose platform you do not support. Worse, you could pass along this misinformation, undermining your own credibility. Whether in your personal life, your professional life, or your academic life, critically assessing sources of information is a crucial skill.

Evaluating sources means assessing how *relevant,* or useful, a source is to your research; determining the source's *reliability*—how much you can trust it; and checking *logic,* the ways the authors build an argument.

9a Evaluating Relevance

When considering a potential source, first consider its relevance: Does the source offer information that could enrich your understanding of your topic, provide background information or evidence for your claims, or suggest alternative perspectives? Before reading the entire text, determine its relevance by *previewing* it:

❯ *More about* ▶▶▶
Previewing, 10–11

- **Read the title and subtitle.** These elements can often give you a sense of the contents.

- **Check the publication date.** Recently published works are most likely to be of the greatest relevance, as they will probably provide the most up-to-date information. Be alert, though, for classics; they contain information or ideas on which researchers still rely. Classics will be cited frequently by other reliable sources, and your instructor can help you identify them.

- **Read the abstract, foreword, introduction, or lead (first paragraph in a newspaper article).** These sections usually provide a summary, an overview, or key facts detailed in the source.

- **Read the headings and subheadings.** These elements provide an outline of the work.

- **Scan figures and illustrations.** Visuals might signal important ideas and explain complex processes.

- **Read the conclusion.** The conclusion—the last few paragraphs in a journal or magazine article or in the final chapter of a book—often reiterates the central idea and argument, important questions, and major findings.

- **Consult the index.** If the potential source is a book with an index, check it for key terms in your research.

Writing
↑ Responsibly   **Keeping an Open Mind**

As a researcher, you have a responsibility to avoid bias: Read sources with an open mind, use reliable sources, consider evidence that undermines your position, avoid exaggerated claims and logical fallacies, and criticize unreasonable or poorly supported conclusions but not the people who hold them. Sound research considers all sides of an argument, especially those that challenge the position the researcher holds.

9b **Evaluating Reliability**

Judging reliability is not a simple yes-or-no litmus test. Instead, rate the source on a variety of criteria. The more criteria on which you can rate the source highly, the more reliable it is likely to be:

- **Is the source scholarly or popular?** Scholarly texts are written by subject matter experts for academic journals and presses as a contribution to knowledge, and they are reviewed by other experts before being published. Many databases will allow you to check a box to find only peer-reviewed articles. Articles in magazines and books published by the popular press are commercial; they were selected by an editor who believes an audience will buy the material. Popular sources are not reviewed by experts and thus are generally less reliable. The Quick Reference chart on page 103 details many of the markers distinguishing scholarly from popular texts.

- **Is the author an expert on the topic?** Does the author have special knowledge of or experience with the subject? You can answer this question by reading about the author in a biographical note or a biographical reference work, finding other works the author has published, considering the author's academic background, and determining whether the author has been cited in the footnotes or bibliographies of other reliable sources.

- **Does the source seem objective?** Does the author use an objective tone, make reasonable claims supported by logical reasons and solid evidence, recognize alternative perspectives, and treat opponents with respect? Or does the author use emotionally loaded language, make exaggerated claims,

Quick

Reference ➡ Scholarly versus Popular Periodicals

Scholarly Articles	Popular Articles
■ Are written by scholars, specialists, researchers	■ Are written by journalists or professional writers
■ Use technical terminology	■ Avoid technical terminology
■ Tend to be long	■ Tend to be brief
■ Include citations in the text and a list of references	■ Do not include citations or a list of references
■ Are reviewed by other scholars before publication	■ May be fact-checked but not reviewed by experts
■ Acknowledge any conflicts of interest (such as research support from a pharmaceutical company)	■ Are unlikely to acknowledge conflicts of interest
■ Generally look serious; unlikely to include color photographs, but may include charts, graphs, and tables	■ Are often published on glossy paper with color photographs
■ Published by professional organizations	■ Are published by commercial companies

or support those claims with faulty logic and questionable or scanty evidence?

■ **Does the author or publisher have a vested interest?**
Consider whether or how the author stands to benefit from the work. Most authors will benefit in some way: through sales of the book or through prestige in publishing. In addition, is the author promoting a product or process from which she or

Clicking on "Cited References" will call up this article's bibliography.

Clicking on "Times Cited in this Database" will call up a list of other articles that cite this one as a source.

FIGURE 9.1 Determining Reliability by Assessing Citations Both the number of times an article has been cited and the citations in the article itself are useful ways of determining an article's reliability.

he will benefit financially? Will the author or publisher gain adherents to a political position? Check the author's or publisher's website for biographical information, advertisements, and a mission statement to see whether one of these items reveals an agenda.

More about ▶▶▶
Citing sources:
  MLA style, 243–59
  APA style, 305–15
  Chicago style,
    348–66
  CSE style, 375–388
Choosing a citation
  style, 235

- **Does the text cite its sources?** Most scholarly articles and books and some popular books include a bibliography, and some journal databases list the articles' sources in the citation. Reputable newspapers and magazines check a writer's sources, though those sources are often identified only as a "White House source" or a "source close to the investigation."

- **Do other scholars cite the text?** Also important is the number of times a source has been cited by other scholarly works (Figure 9.1). Some journal databases indicate the number of times an article has been cited by other articles indexed by that database. Citation indexes, such as *Web of Science* and *Google Scholar,* also provide this information.

- **How did you find the source?** Sources located through your college library are more likely to be reliable than sources located through a *Google* search because library sources are selected in consultation with subject matter experts, in response to reviews, or after considering where the source was published. A source published solely on the Web (unless in a scholarly journal published online) is not likely to have been subjected to the same level of scrutiny.

More about ▶▶▶
Choosing research sources strategically, 52

- **Is the source well written and edited?** Has the writer approached the task with a sense of responsibility, writing, organizing, editing, and proofreading the material carefully?

More about ▶▶▶
Editing and proofreading, 203–15
Designing, 216–33

9c Evaluating Logic: Claims, Grounds, and Warrants

The philosopher Stephen Toulmin says that people make *claims* (main points or theses); we support our claims with *grounds,* or evidence; and we tie the grounds to the claims with *warrants,* or assumptions. When analyzing an argument, begin by assessing the strength of the main claim. Claims of fact are nearly indisputable. Claims of opinion and belief can be supported by compelling evidence. Claims of superstition or prejudice, however, are founded on false assumptions and misinformation. Some may be obviously flawed. Others require closer examination of the evidence presented. Is it a claim of *fact, opinion,* or *belief*? Or is it simply a *superstition* or *prejudice*?

Next, evaluate the grounds, or evidence, supplied to support the claim. Writers use various types of evidence to support their claims. Some types of evidence—like stories—are *qualitative,* using examples to show relationships and patterns; other types of evidence—like statistics—are *quantitative,* using empirical data and numbers to show how many and to what extent. Regardless of its type, good evidence must be all of the following:

- **Accurate.** *Is the evidence true?* If evidence is exaggerated, distorted, or just plain false, it is inaccurate.

- **Reliable.** *How consistently does the evidence support the claim?* If the evidence supports the claim only in certain circumstances, it may be unreliable.

- **Balanced.** *Does the evidence represent all credible angles of the issue?* The principle of balance in evidence suggests that a writer weigh all of the alternatives and give them equal consideration.

- **Sufficient.** *Has enough evidence been gathered to support the claim?* Scanty evidence does not prove an argument.

- **Relevant.** *Does the evidence have logical connections to the claim?* If the evidence proves something different than the claim—if the evidence and claim do not match—then the evidence is irrelevant.

- **Untainted by stakeholders' investments.** *Who are the stakeholders, and how did they influence the process or result?* If the author, publisher, or other stakeholders are biased, the evidence may skew the argument.

As you read a text critically, also look for the underlying warrants, or assumptions, unstated claims for which no evidence is offered. If the argument is to succeed, what must both writer and audience agree is true? Identifying a text's assumptions will help you decide whether you agree with its claims; it will also help you identify the writer's audience. When Martin Luther King, Jr., said, "The nations of Asia and Africa are moving with jetlike speed toward gaining political independence, but we still creep at horse-and-buggy pace toward gaining a cup of coffee at a lunch counter," he relied on the assumption that American progress should not lag behind that of Africa and Asia. Is this assumption *correct?* That depends on whether you share it; Dr. King knew that most people in his audience—U.S. citizens—would. An African or Asian audience, on the other hand, might be less likely to share this assumption about American progress.

▲ Make It **Your Own**

Using the criteria in the section above (summarized in the Quick Reference box at the end of the chapter), write an evaluative paragraph for each of three print sources that are in your working bibliography or that you plan to consult for a research project.

9d Evaluating Online Texts: Websites, Blogs, Wikis, and Web Forums

Anyone can create a website, post a blog, or contribute to an open wiki. This freedom makes the Web exciting, and it also requires researchers to evaluate online sources with special care. In addition to the general criteria listed in this chapter for evaluating sources, consider these other factors when evaluating websites: URL, site sponsor, whether the site is open or moderated, and number of links to the site.

> *More about ▶▶▶*
> Meeting the challenges of online research, 76–87

URL

A site's URL (short for *uniform resource locator,* its Web address) appears at the top of the browser window. Every item on the Web has a URL, and all URLs end with an extension that indicates the site type. The most common URL extensions are these:

- **.com** (commercial): sites sponsored by businesses.

- **.edu** (educational): sites sponsored by colleges and universities, including administration, faculty, and students. Note that U.S. primary and secondary schools typically have *.k12* in their URLs and end in *.us*.

- **.gov** (government): sites sponsored by a branch of federal, state, or local government.

- **.net** (network): typically, sites sponsored by businesses selling internet infrastructure services (such as internet service providers), but this extension is also sometimes chosen by businesses that want to appear technologically sophisticated.

- **.org** (organization): usually sites sponsored by nonprofit groups (though sometimes the nonprofit status of these groups may be questionable).

 Tech

Identifying Personal Websites

A URL that includes a personal name (jsmith) plus a tilde (~) or a percent sign (%) or words like "users" or "members" indicates that the site is likely to be *personal* (not sponsored by a larger organization). Before using information from a personal site, investigate the author's credentials carefully.

Sites sponsored by educational, governmental, and most nonprofit organizations are likely to be reliable, but your evaluation of websites should not end with their URLs. Businesses usually offer information intended to sell products or services, yet commercial sites can nevertheless be highly informative. A site ending in *.edu* may just as easily have been constructed and posted by a student as by a faculty or staff member, and much of the information posted on university websites is designed to entice new students (which is a type of advertising). Although not trying to sell a product, nonprofit organizations are usually seeking support. And government sites, while usually highly reliable, are unlikely to publish information that would undermine the administration's agenda. Carefully scrutinize the reliability of information from all sites (and, indeed, all texts).

Site sponsor

As with any publication, the credentials of a website's creator are an important factor in assessing reliability. You may be able to research the owner of a blog, the contributors to an email discussion list, or visitors to a chat room, and you can *lurk* (read online discussions without contributing) to get a sense of the quality of a discussion. But websites frequently lack a single author. Instead, they have *sponsors*—corporations, agencies, and organizations that are responsible for creating and posting the site's content. To determine who sponsors a site, navigate to the home page, link to pages called About Us or Contact Us, or click on the website's logo. If the website yields little information, try conducting a web search on the site's title. If the site is secretive about its sponsor, be especially wary of its content.

Open or moderated

The reliability of online discussion forums and wikis depends in large part on their contributors. Open sources (those to which anyone can contribute) should be screened carefully; nonexpert enthusiasts can post inaccurate information, and people can deliberately insert distorted "truths." For example, in January 2006 *Wikipedia* had to block certain web addresses on Capitol Hill to keep congressional staffers from altering—and falsifying—the biographies of their bosses or their bosses' political opponents.

While Wikipedia has since bolstered its community-based systems for reducing error, wikis and web forums in which prospective contributors are screened by the site's owner, or *moderator*, are more likely to be reliable. The wiki *Encyclopedia of Life*, for example, promises to provide reliable information because it will be created and moderated by a consortium of highly regarded scientific institutions. Some scholars are even writing wiki textbooks to which they invite other experts to contribute.

Type "link:[URL]" in search box (note that there is no space between the colon after *link* and the URL)

Number of sites that link to <owl.english.purdue.edu>

Page 1 of sites that link to <owl.english.purdue.edu> (note other reliable *.edu* sites)

FIGURE 9.2 Weighing Source Reliability Use the number of links to a page to assess reliability.

Links

An additional step in assessing the reliability of a website or blog is to determine the number and type of sites that link to it. From the *Google* search page, you can determine the number of times a site has been linked to and review the linked sites: Type "link:" followed by the URL in the search box, and click on "Search" or hit Return (Figure 9.2). Popularity does *not* guarantee reliability—the site may be fun to read or authored by a celebrity—but when coupled with other criteria, it can be one indication of reliability.

EXERCISE **9.1** Evaluating Web Pages

Using the criteria discussed on pp. 107–109, write a paragraph or two evaluating the two web pages on p. 110. Which would be the more reliable source on plagiarism, and why?

9e Evaluating Visual Sources

More about ▶▶▶
Evaluating visuals,
186–87

Visual texts, such as information graphics (tables, graphs, flowcharts), photographs, drawings, maps, and even video, convey their messages powerfully yet sometimes so subtly that uncritical viewers may accept their claims without even realizing that a claim is being made. The image of a hungry child, for example, has long been a staple of humanitarian fund-raising. One hungry child looking at you plaintively can be far more persuasive than whole paragraphs of logical claims and evidence. As with printed texts, researchers need to evaluate visual texts carefully.

To determine relevance and reliability, ask these questions:

- What purpose(s) does the image serve? Is it to entertain, to inform, or to persuade?

- What is the overall message the visual sends?

- Who is the item's intended audience?

- How authoritative is the source in which the visual appears?

- On what date was the visual created?

- What are the credentials of the visual's creator?

- How accurate are the title, headings, labels, and any other text that appears with the visual? How does the text influence how you "read" the visual? How relevant is the visual to the accompanying text?

- What is in the foreground and background, and what is your eye drawn to?

- To what social, ethnic, or national groups do the subjects belong, and is this relevant?

- What emotions does the visual depict? What emotions does it elicit from you or other viewers?

- Has the visual been manipulated or cropped to omit or distort information (Figure 9.3)?

For graphics, also consider the following:

- What do the data represent?

- What relationships does the graphic show?

- How up-to-date is the information in the graphic?

- Are the data complete? Are there any gaps in years covered or groups represented?

- Are the data presented fairly?

- Is the source of the data unbiased?

- How were the data gathered? If there is no explanation of the data-gathering process, question the information further.

FIGURE 9.3 President Franklin D. Roosevelt in a Wheelchair, 1945 Although many Americans knew that President Roosevelt had been partially paralyzed by polio, only two photographs were taken of the President in a wheelchair. Were photographers protecting FDR's privacy or suppressing important information? FDR at Hilltop Cottage, in Hyde Park, NY, Franklin D. Roosevelt Presidential Library and Museum

A Final Thought

In school and in life you will be expected to be able to critically filter sources, to not take them at face value. Without skills in this area, you risk being manipulated and misinformed at precisely those moments when you wish to be most in control. The flip side of this coin is that you will also want to be able to evaluate your own claims, evidence, and other rhetorical moves so that you can responsibly offer information to *your* readers.

Quick Reference ➡ **Judging Reliability**

All Sources

Scholarly work. Was the source published in a scholarly journal or book or in a popular magazine, newspaper, or book?

Expertise. Is the author an authority on the subject?

Objectivity. Do tone, logic, quality of the evidence, and coverage of the opposition suggest that the source is unbiased?

Citations. Does the text cite sources, and is it cited by others?

Scrutiny. Did someone else subject the text to scrutiny before you saw it? For example, was it selected by the library, reviewed by another scholar, or fact-checked for accuracy?

Presentation. Is the text clearly written, well organized, and carefully edited and proofread?

Logic. Does the evidence match the claims, and is the evidence reliable?

Web Sources

URL extension. Does the main portion of the URL end in *.edu* or *.org,* suggesting a noncommercial purpose, or does it end with *.com* or *.net,* suggesting a commercial purpose?

Site sponsor. Is the site's host identified? Does the host promote a specific viewpoint or position?

Number of links or hits. Is the source visited often and frequently linked to other reputable sources?

Visual Sources

Graphics. Is the graphic based on recent data with no groups/years omitted and not misleadingly drawn?

Photographs. Is the image accurate and not misleadingly presented?

10

Taking Notes and Keeping Records

A stunning innovation, cuneiform, the world's first written symbol system, was used by the Sumerians primarily to keep records. This ancient civilization pressed its symbols into clay, allowing some of its records to survive for 5,000 years or more. The ability to keep records was so valuable it transformed cultures.

Web 2.0 technologies, which allow us to collect, sort, organize, comment on, and share sources and notes all in online environments, make note taking and record keeping fast, flexible, and portable. Without careful note-taking practices, however, web technologies can lead writers to lose track of where they found information, making it difficult not to plagiarize or patchwrite. Good notes and records provide an intellectual trail; they allow you to put your reading into context; they give you opportunities to step away from the information and return to it with fresh eyes. Perhaps your records will not survive for 5,000 years, but they should last through the duration of your project and beyond.

Tech

Filing with Folders and Subfolders

If you typically save everything as a separate file with no folders, use this research project as a motivator to try folders. Here is a sample saving strategy:

- Start with a folder titled something like your project title: Obscenity_Defs.
- Create subfolders: Notes, Outlines, Drafts.

- Save files with the date they were last altered (Obscenity_ Defs_Outline 080711) as part of the title so that you can keep a record of your changes.
- Each time you reopen the file, save it with an updated file name.

10a Choosing an Organizer to Fit Your Work Style

Note taking can be done on note cards, in computer files, or on weblogs or wikis, but the method you choose will depend on the project and your own work patterns.

Taking notes on index cards

Do you enjoy the tactile feel of pen and paper? Do you like to spread things out in front of you to see what you have to work with? While they are harder to back up and therefore easier to misplace, note cards may fit your work style best.

Taking notes on a computer

Increasingly, writers do most of their work directly on a computer because typing is faster than handwriting and the text is easy to copy, move, reorganize, and save. You can even save your notes in outline order to create a skeleton of your essay.

If you maintain your notes on a computer, always make a backup in a separate place: on another computer, on a thumb drive, on an iPod, or even printed out. Finally, notes on a computer are useful only if you can find them. When taking notes on a computer, decide where your notes will "live," and name files in a way that will be meaningful to you later (see the Tech box above for guidance).

A *double-entry journal* uses two columns for two different types of entries, inviting writers to engage in critical reading. Insert a two-column table into your word-processed file to create the side-by-side structure. You can divide reading responses into any of the following categories:

More about ▶▶▶
Keeping a reading
journal, 12–13
Freewriting to
explore a research
topic, 26–28
Summarizing, 16–17,
58–59, 118–120,
190–92

- A record of new vocabulary
- A summary of main points
- Freewriting on the topic
- Your responses to the text

The following student's double-entry journal response refers to Wray Herbert's "Why Uncertainty May Be Bad for Your Health" (*Newsweek*, 19 Sept. 2006).

Vocabulary

<u>deep-seated</u> (par. 3) – firmly established, rooted, ingrained. [Always thought this was "deep-seeded" – never saw it written down before.]

<u>qualifiers</u> (par. 5) – words that modify or specify the meaning of other words. [Par. 8 uses the examples "possibly" and "likely."]

<u>untoward</u> (par. 5) – unfortunate, hard to control. [Also means "improper," but that doesn't seem to fit in this context.]

<u>euphemisms</u> (par. 5) – indirect, innocuous terms or phrases used instead of direct ones to avoid seeming harsh or offensive. [Example: "She's in a better place." Yet, when used in talking to patients and their families, euphemisms may cause more damage in the long run! Sometimes direct is better.]

<u>unambiguous</u> (par. 7) – without uncertainty, clear, straightforward. [I guessed what this meant from context and the word "ambiguous," then looked it up to double-check.]

<u>nebulous</u> (par. 8) – indistinct, vague. [<u>Qualifiers</u> and <u>euphemisms</u> are also nebulous. There are many precise kinds of "uncertainty."]

Response

- The opening story (a meteorologist predicting a "chance" of rain while it pours outside) made me laugh. It was a great way to introduce a key point: Language can often confuse what we mean instead of making it clearer. Herbert shifts the tone and raises the stakes effectively when he points out that doctors use these same inexact phrases—like "possible" or "unlikely"—to refer to patients' conditions and chances of recovery. That's not just annoying, like an imprecise weather report; that's someone's life. (pars. 1–3)

- What does "possibly" mean? The insomnia/deafness test and the estimated percentages (10%–100%) support a "severity bias," another misleading factor. The results of Bonnefon's study are good evidence for Wray's point: that under-informed patients can suffer severe distress by assuming their situation is more dire or less severe than it actually is. (pars. 6–7)

- Wray makes a case for more specificity when doctors talk to patients. I agree 100%. (pars. 8–9)

- This relates to my research question about patients' responsibilities in their own health care because it suggests patients should be asking questions and demanding more precision in the doctors' language.

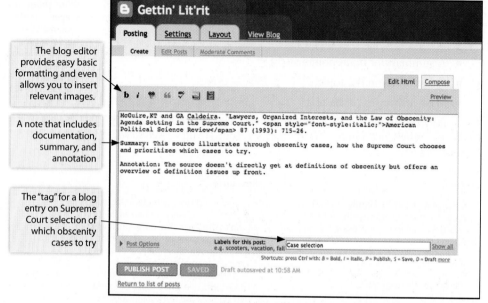

The blog editor provides easy basic formatting and even allows you to insert relevant images.

A note that includes documentation, summary, and annotation

The "tag" for a blog entry on Supreme Court selection of which obscenity cases to try

FIGURE 10.1 Sample Research Blog Entry This entry is for a project on arts, obscenity, and the First Amendment.

Taking notes in a weblog

Much like a journal, a *blog* (short for *weblog*) is a website created by an individual or group to chronicle thoughts and collect sources. When you take notes in a blog, you can create an entry for each source, insert links to online texts, and sort sources by category ("tagging") (Figure 10.1).

Taking notes on a wiki

A *wiki* is an online collaborative environment that typically mimics word processing. Wikis are best for collaborative research projects because multiple users can make changes to them, but they can also be very useful to the independent writer because they are accessible through the Web.

As with a blog, you will need to do a little advance setup to use a wiki for your note taking. *Google Documents* <www.docs.google

.com>, *wikispaces* <www.wikispaces.com>, and *Wetpaint* <www
.wetpaint.com> offer free wiki services.

10b Keeping the Trail: Your Search Notes

Because few researchers find what they are looking for with their very
first search, keeping track of search terms and location can save time.
Such a chart would *not* include content notes, but only information on
the search: search date, search location (the database, search engine,
catalog), search terms and strategies (including search engine math
and Boolean operators), and general notes on what you have found.
Then, if you are not finding the information you need, show your
search record to a librarian. He or she can help you quickly develop
more effective strategies.

10c Determining what to Include in Research Notes

Research note taking involves the following activities:

More about ▶▶▶
Annotating your
  working bibliogra-
  phy, 53–55
Writing an anno-
  tated bibliography,
  139–49
Quoting, paraphras-
  ing, and summariz-
  ing, 190–92
Sample annotated
  bibliography,
  143–46

- Annotating sources
- Summarizing sources accurately and without patchwriting
- Paraphrasing sources accurately and without patchwriting
- Recording quotations that you may want to use later
- Analyzing sources by dividing them into their component
  parts
- Interpreting the meaning of sources
- Synthesizing information from one source with information
  from other sources
- Critiquing, or evaluating, sources
- Recording source information, including the page number on
  which the noted material appears

10d Taking Content Notes

When taking content notes, you have to decide two things:

1. What is worth recording?
2. How should I record the information: as a summary, a direct
   quotation, or a paraphrase?

What is worth recording?

More about ▶▶▶
Evaluating information, 100–12

Decide what is worth recording based on the principles you would use for overall evaluation of a source, including relevance to your topic, accuracy, reliability, balance, and bias. Be selective; recording anything and everything can lead to accumulation of useless data. Ask yourself this question: What are the main points you need to convey to get your argument across without suppressing critical portions of the conversation? Being selective is far easier if you quickly read whole sources first and then return to take careful notes the second time through.

Summarize, paraphrase, or quote?

More about ▶▶▶
Synthesis, 19–20

More about ▶▶▶
Documenting sources:
MLA, 241–303
APA, 304–46
Chicago, 347–74
CSE, 375–91

When to summarize You should *summarize* a source when you want to convey its basic argument to your audience in an abbreviated form, omitting specific details and examples. Work to use summary frequently; it is the most sophisticated way to represent a source because it takes into account the entire argument. You will typically *synthesize* these summaries with your argument, comparing and contrasting them.

Quick Reference ➡ What to Include in Your Research Notes

Bibliographic Information (Documentation)
- **Books:** author(s), title and subtitle, edition, publisher, place and date of publication, and page numbers.
- **Articles:** author(s); title of article; title of periodical; volume and number of issue; date of publication; page numbers; if accessed through a database, name of library, name of subscription database (e.g., *EBSCO* or *ProQuest*), and date of access.
- **Website:** name of organization sponsoring site, title of web page, author's name, date updated, and date of access.

Summary
A brief restatement capturing the gist of the source's main argument. Use fresh words (except key terms).

Paraphrase
A restatement at approximately the same length of a source's main points and examples. Use fresh words (except key terms).

Quotations
An exact (word-for-word) restatement of a passage from a source (useful for capturing an idea expressed with special complexity, verve, or power); enclose it in quotation marks or use a block indent.

Commentary
Your analysis, interpretation, or critique of the source or your synthesis of ideas from the source with your own ideas or ideas from other sources.

When to paraphrase You should paraphrase portions of your sources when you want to do the following:

- Understand the logic of complex passages (paraphrasing information helps you understand it)
- Mention examples and details from the source so that readers can better follow your generalizations

When to quote You should *quote* from sources under the following circumstances:

- When your source uses particularly vivid or engaging language
- When you want to reproduce a subtle idea that might be difficult to paraphrase or summarize without distortion
- When your source uses specialized language that is difficult to paraphrase (but resist quoting just because you do not yet understand the material)
- When you want to *analyze* the specific language used in the source
- When you are working with primary sources, such as interviews and surveys that you have conducted

More about ▶▶▶
Analysis, 18–19

More about ▶▶▶
Conducting interviews, 90–94
Surveying, 97–99
Primary versus secondary sources, 89

10e   Taking Notes to Avoid Plagiarizing and Patchwriting

Inadvertent plagiarism is a growing problem for researchers because cutting and pasting material from online sources into notes is so easy. It is easy to lose track of which material has been borrowed, and it is easy to lose track of which material came from which source. Resist the urge to cut and paste your notes; take the time to summarize, paraphrase, and selectively quote at the notes stage.

Summarizing

To achieve the best results in your summaries, follow this process:

1. Annotate the source and then close the book.
2. On a clean sheet of paper (or a new document on your computer), try to repeat the main ideas of the source.
3. Check the text to make sure you have conveyed the main idea and the major supporting points without distortion and without recycling the source's words.

More about ▶▶▶
Summarizing, 16–17, 58–59, 118–120, 190–92

Check your summary carefully and revise as necessary. Summaries, too, should convey the main idea of the source, not merely identify the topic. The note below illustrates this problem, and the second example shows a solution.

Note (Summary that Merely Identifies Topic)

> DuBois
>
> In "The Hampton Idea," a 1906 speech, W. E. B. DuBois explains how African Americans should be educated and talks about the Tuskegee model.

The verbs in the draft note are neutral and do not convey DuBois's argument.

Solution

> DuBois
>
> In "The Hampton Idea," an essay from a 1906 speech, W. E. B. DuBois argues that college education for African Americans should not just be ~~explains how African Americans should be educated and argues against~~
> ^
> vocational but should instead prepare teachers, thinkers, and leaders. ~~the Tuskegee model.~~
> ^

Verbs lead into claims.

Note does not just list topics but states claim as well.

Paraphrasing

More about ▶▶▶
Avoiding patchwriting, 17
Defining patchwriting, 128
Drafting to avoid plagiarism and patchwriting, 133–34
Paraphrasing, 190–92

Writers who are inexperienced with paraphrasing often *patchwrite:* They replace some key terms with synonyms, delete a few words, or alter the grammar slightly, but they do not put the passage fully into fresh words and sentences. Some people consider patchwriting a form of plagiarism, and nobody considers it good writing.

To paraphrase without patchwriting, follow these steps:

1. Read the source until you feel you understand it. Make sure you think about the overall meaning of the passage. Figure out whether there are any key terms that should be retained in your paraphrase. You may put quotation marks around these.
2. Close the book and walk away. Do something else for a few minutes or a few hours.

3. Come back to your desk and write what you remember. If you cannot remember anything, repeat steps 1 and 2.

4. Check your paraphrase against the source to make sure you have correctly represented what it says. If you have closely retained any of the source language or even its sentence structures, either copy it exactly and include quotation marks, or repeat steps 1 and 2.

When your paraphrase is complete, check to be sure that you have done *all* of the following:

- Quoted key terms exactly, placing them in quotation marks the first time you use them but not thereafter.

- Used synonyms rather than the source language for the remainder of your paraphrase.

- Freely rearranged the ideas of the source so that they make sense in your own text. For example, if the author presents a cause and its effects, you might present the effects first and the causes second.

- Provided transition words to clarify relationships among ideas.

- Used different sentence structures from those in the original passage. If you find yourself mirroring the source's sentence structure, try dividing or combining sentences or varying their length and structure to alter their rhythm.

- Omitted details that are not relevant to *your* main point. Make sure, though, that your deletions do not alter or distort the meaning of the source text.

> **More about ▶▶▶**
> Reading and sum-
> marizing your
> entire source, 9–10

The following example illustrates techniques for revising passages to avoid patchwriting:

Passage from Source

Until recently, the Church was one of the least studied aspects of the Cuban revolution, almost as if it were a voiceless part of Cuban society, an institution and faith that had little impact on the course of events." —Super, John C. "Interpretations of Church and State in Cuba, 1959–1961." *The Catholic Historical Review* 89.3 (2003): 511–29. Print.

The following first-draft paraphrase contains patchwriting: Despite some minor changes in word order and some synonym substitutions, the paraphrase follows the original, phrase by phrase. Even with a citation, this would be a misuse of the source.

Note (with Patchwriting)

> Super 511
>
> The Catholic Church until recently was not much studied as an aspect of the Cuban revolution. It was as if the Church was voiceless in Cuban culture, as if it had little influence on events.

Note (Revised to Avoid Patchwriting)

> Super 511
>
> *Scholarship on the Cuban revolution is only beginning*
> ~~The Catholic Church until recently was not much studied as an aspect~~
> ^
> *to recognize the influential role of the Church.*
> ~~of the Cuban revolution. It was as if the Church was voiceless in~~
> ^
> ~~Cuban culture, as if it had little influence on events.~~

The revised note still retains a version of a word from the source: "influence" has been changed to "influential." And, of course, the identifying terms "Cuban revolution" and "Church" are in both the original passage and the revised note. But the passage no longer draws heavily on the source's sentence structure, organization, or word choices.

→ EXERCISE 10.1 Recognizing Patchwriting

Study the following source text, as well as the first draft of a paraphrase that follows. Identify the ways in which the draft is patchwriting rather than paraphrasing. Then revise the note, correcting the patchwriting.

PASSAGE FROM SOURCE

Washington has posed a special problem for Wikipedia, which is monitored by 800 to 1,000 active editor-volunteers. In the recent flare-up, a community of Wikipedia editors read a story in the *Lowell Sun* newspaper in which staffers for [Representative Marty] Meehan acknowledged replacing an entry on him [in Wikipedia] with more flattering verbiage. That prompted last week's Capitol Hill Wikipedia blackout; all computers connected to servers at the House of Representatives, identified by a numerical Web address, were denied access. —Yuki Noguchi, "On Capitol Hill, Playing WikiPolitics." *Washington Post* 4 Feb. 2006: A1. Print.

DRAFT NOTE

> Noguchi A1
>
> Wikipedia and its active editor-volunteers have a special problem with Washington. Recently the editors read a *Lowell Sun* newspaper story about Meehan's staffers having acknowledged that they had replaced an entry on him with more flattering words. That resulted in last week's Wikipedia blackout on Capitol Hill computers, which were denied access.

Quoting

A *quotation* is someone else's words transcribed exactly, with quotation marks or block indention (for long quotes) to signal that it is from a source. When taking notes, copy quotations exactly, word for word, and check them against the source. To avoid any confusion later (Are those my words or the source's?) put quotation marks around each selection that you copy. In your writing project, you can—and should—adjust quotations when writing your paper, but you must use ellipses for signaling cuts and brackets for indicating words you have added or changed. But in your notes, the quotation should appear exactly as it did in the source.

When working with primary sources such as interviews and surveys that you have conducted, you are likely to use quotations extensively. In contrast, secondary sources such as newspaper articles and scholarly books are already quoting, summarizing, and paraphrasing their sources, so you should limit the number of direct quotations you copy from them.

More about ▶▶▶
Primary versus secondary sources, 89

More about ▶▶▶
Using quotation
marks, 195, 215
Quoting, 190–92
Reading your
sources, 9–22

If you find that you are copying a lot of quotations and paraphrasing or summarizing very little, it could be that you do not fully understand what you are reading. Try the following:

- Read the source again.

- Look up words you do not understand.

- Consult reference sources that can provide background knowledge.

- Discuss the source with your instructor, classmates, or friends.

The following reading notes on Claudia Milne's article "On the Grounds of the Fresh Water Pond: The Free-Black Community at Five Points, 1810–1834" in the *International Journal of Historical Archaeology* (June 2002) correctly use quotation marks to signal material taken word for word from the source. Yet they also signal that the note taker does not fully understand what he is writing about.

Draft

Milne 140

The "free-black community . . . of Five Points" is not reflected in "the areas of Block 160 that were excavated." "All that survived . . . were the remains of their ancestors interred in the mostly forgotten burying ground, a few intriguing and unusual items discarded in the defunct privies and cisterns, and a handful of church addresses." But "it is probable that many members of this community remained in the neighborhood, living 'off-the-grid.' . . ."

These notes are merely a string of quotations, sewn together with a few of the note taker's own words. A research paper based on these notes would similarly be a mosaic of quotation, difficult to read and lacking the researcher's critical judgment. The following revision is better:

Revision

> Milne 140
>
> Very few items belonging to members of the African American population in Five Points have been excavated, most likely because members of this community were not part of mainstream society, not because they had all moved away.

Quick **Reference** ➡ **Avoiding Common Errors in Note Taking**

Some of the most common errors note takers make include the following. As you take notes, ask yourself:

- Have I avoided reading the whole source and instead grabbed any quote that looked like it might fit my argument?
- Have I cut and pasted chunks of what should be quoted materials without using quotation marks?
- Have I taken a note without a page number (print sources) or enough information to find the internet source again quickly (precise URL and/or full title of the page where I found the information)?
- Have I taken a note that looks like a paraphrase or a summary but that only changes a word here or there and does not exactly and carefully quote the source?
- Have I indicated the topic in my note without recording the source's argument or main point?

10f Using Analysis, Interpretation, Synthesis, and Critique in Your Notes

In addition to recording information from sources, the note-taking stage is also the time to start analyzing, interpreting, synthesizing, and critiquing what you read. The following note for Lydia Nichols's research project provides a summary of the source while also including her own assessment of it.

▶▶▶Student sample research projects: "Holy Underground Comics, Batman!" Lydia Nichols, 291–303 "The Power of Wardrobe," Heather DeGroot, 335–46

Sample Summary Note with Writer's Assessment

Heller

Summary that includes analysis and interpretation

Critique

Synthesis

Provides a history of *Zap* comics from the first issue by Robert Crumb in 1968 to the most recent issue in 1994. Describes *Zap* as founding the underground "comix" movement in reaction to the superhero comics that adhered to the 1950s Comics Code and spurred on by late 1960s cultural challenges to the status quo, but doesn't go into detail or identify any comics it inspired. Identifies artists who joined forces with Crumb, and highlights their contributions. Discusses censorship battle over *Zap* #4, which was accused of violating community standards of decency. But not sure what happened: Bookstore owner was fined, but article doesn't indicate what other legal troubles it caused. Later issues continued to be sexually explicit, but they also satirized contemporary mores and included "comic documentary" similar to comic books published during World War II. Article provides a good overview of the history of *Zap* comics (including showing all 14 covers); it assumes that readers will already know a good deal about the history of comics. "Good Shall Triumph" and "Comic Book Code" provide more info about the Comics Code Authority, but I would like to know more about early examples of documentary comics. Heller is obviously a fan of *Zap* comics (I read online that he was an art director at the *NY Times*) but I would like to know more about what motivated Crumb and the others to rebel.

A Final Thought

In many ways it is easier than ever to keep good records while doing research. Cell phones allow writers to text a note to their email accounts when they do not have the relevant research folder in their bags. Wikis allow collaborative groups to share and keep track of notes that they update collectively. Databases allow users to save citations to folders and email citations and whole documents to themselves. Databases even generate perfectly formatted citations in virtually any discipline's style. Yet all of these good tools are only as effective as their users. Develop a note and record-keeping system that works for you and with your technological strengths and weaknesses.

11

Citing Your Sources and Avoiding Plagiarism

Louis Bloomfield

Ibrahim al-Marashi

Plagiarism makes news. In 2001, physics professor Louis Bloomfield (University of Virginia) accused more than a hundred students of plagiarism. Many were found guilty and expelled from the university.[1]

In January 2008, Mounir Errami and Harold Garner (University of Texas, Southwestern Medical Center) published a report in the journal *Nature* on duplicate articles in the *Medline* database. They tested a portion of the abstracts in *Medline* using text-matching software, coming up with some 420 potential duplicates. Of these, 73 were written by different authors, leading them to suspect plagiarism. They worry that the publication of plagiarized drug-safety studies can give practitioners a false sense of the safety or efficacy of the drugs tested.[2]

In 2003 the British government "borrowed" information from Ibrahim al Marashi's doctoral thesis to make its case for war against Iraq—without citing Ibrahim al-Marashi, the author of the

Harold Garner

1. Hansen, Brian. "Combating Plagiarism: The Issues." *CQ Researcher* 13.32 (19 Sept. 2003): 775–96. Print.
2. Errami, Mounir, and Harold Garner. "Commentary: A Tale of Two Citations." *Nature* 451 (2008): 397–99. Web. 30 March 2009.

thesis.[3] The appropriation made big news and undermined the British government's credibility.

Plagiarism involves the presentation of another person's work—a paper or story, a photograph or graphic, a speech or song, a web page or email message—without indicating that it came from a source. Buying or borrowing a paper is plagiarism. So is using a sentence from a source and not putting it in quotation marks.

More about ▶▶▶
Taking notes to
avoid plagiarism
and patchwriting,
119–125

Also be alert to the possibility of *patchwriting,* copying and only partially changing the language of a source. The National Council of Writing Program Administrators defines patchwriting as a misuse of sources. Sometimes, though, instructors and college policies categorize it as plagiarism. In either case, patchwriting is not good writing. It often results not from an intention to present another's words and ideas as one's own but, rather, from inaccurate note taking, misunderstanding the source, incorrect use of or omitting quotation marks, or incomplete paraphrasing.

Inform yourself in detail about what your instructor and your college (or your employer) define as ethical writing; although everyone rejects plagiarism, the definition of what constitutes plagiarism can vary subtly from one discipline or profession to another. Still, following the guidelines for writing described in this chapter (and throughout this book), you can be confident that the work you produce represents its sources responsibly.

11a Developing Responsibility: Why Use Sources Carefully?

Never has it been more important to think of writing in terms of *responsibilities*. Part of your responsibility as a writer is to your audience and your topic. You owe it to your audience to offer a complete, accurate representation of your material.

You have responsibilities to yourself as well. You may have come to college to obtain a credential that will get you a job. If, however, you arrive at that position without the skills you need, you will not last long in the job. You have the responsibility to acquire not just a credential but also an education. You owe that to yourself.

---

3. Hinsliff, Gaby, Martin Bright, Peter Beaumont, and Ed Vulliamy. "First Casualties in the Propaganda Firefight." *Observer.* Guardian News and Media, 9 Feb. 2003. Web. 26 June 2009. "The Plagiarism Plague." *BBC News.* BBC, 7 Feb. 2003. Web. 26 June 2009.

You also have a responsibility to other writers. In college and the workplace, you will typically work from texts that others have written, whether they are business reports, websites, or scholarly articles. You owe it to these other writers to acknowledge the contributions they have made to your thinking on your topic.

The practice of acknowledging sources has another benefit: It places you *in conversation* with your sources. Although avoiding plagiarism is a compelling reason for citing sources, this other reason is more important: When you acknowledge sources, you position yourself, not as a copier or an amateur, but as a scholar, a thinker, a member of a community of people interested in this topic. You gain credibility.

Make It **Your Own**

Write three to five paragraphs describing and reflecting on your attempts to write responsibly and ethically. What is most difficult for you about using sources? What do you worry about the most? How might you address your concerns?

11b   Understanding What You *Must* Cite: Summaries, Paraphrases, Quotations, *Un*common Knowledge

You must document summaries, paraphrases, quotations, and information that nonexperts are unlikely to know.

- **Summaries and paraphrases.** A summary conveys entire arguments or main ideas in fewer words, while a paraphrase restates only a section or portion of an argument and may be roughly equivalent in length. Both require the writer to use fresh language. Cite all sources used, even when you are not quoting. As with quotations, cite the author and page number in the text, and include full source information in your list of works cited, reference list, or bibliography.

MLA Style Example

> The University of Missouri is one example of universities whose opening was delayed for lack of adequate funding (Williams 191).

More about ▶▶▶
Using quotation marks, 123–25, 195
Citing sources:
MLA style, 241–303
APA style, 304–46
Chicago style, 347–74
CSE style, 375–91

More about ▶▶▶
Summarizing, 16–17, 58–59, 118–120, 190–92
Paraphrasing, 120–22, 190–92

Paraphrase

In-text citation (author's last name and page reference in parentheses)

> Works Cited
>
> Williams, Jeffrey J. "The Post-Welfare State University." *American Literary History* 18.1 (Spring 2006): 190–216. Print.

- **Quotations.** A *quotation* is an exact transcription of someone else's words, with quotation marks for short quotes or block indentation for extended passages to signal that the language is from another source. Name the author either in a signal phrase (*Jones argues*) or in a parenthetical citation, and include the page number. (In some styles, you may include this information in a footnote or endnote.) Then document the source in your list of works cited, reference list, or bibliography.

More about
Signal phrases,
194–96
Integrating quotations, 190–92

Chicago **Style Example**

Signal phrase

Quotations in quotation marks

In-text citation (page reference in parentheses)

> Williams describes as "distinctly American" the decision not to have national oversight over the state universities that emerged in the nineteenth century: "George Washington had proposed a national university in 1790 . . . but the idea languished in part because of lack of federal funds and in part because it went against the American idea of states' rights" (191).

Documentation (complete source information in a list at the end of the paper)

> Bibliography
>
> Williams, Jeffrey J. "The Post-Welfare State University." *American Literary History* 18, no. 1 (2006): 190–216.

- **Ideas and information that are *not* common knowledge.** Whenever you provide information from a source that is *not* common knowledge, acknowledge that source in your text and provide full source information in your list of works cited, reference list, or bibliography. If you are in doubt about what is considered common knowledge, see the list on pp. 131–32 and check with your instructor. Remember that an interview with an expert needs to be cited just as much as information found in an article or a book does.

APA Style Example

When a college has an honor code, its faculty are more likely to regard cheating as a serious matter (McCabe, Butterfield, and Treviño, 2003, p. 391).

Summary

In-text citation (authors' last names—not mentioned in text—and page reference in parentheses)

References

McCabe, D. L., Butterfield, K. D., & Treviño, L. K. (2003). Faculty and academic integrity: The influence of current honor codes and past honor code experiences. *Research in Higher Education, 44*(3), 367–385.

11c Knowing What You *Need Not* Cite: Common Knowledge (Facts, Dates, Events, Cultural Knowledge)

You need not acknowledge your source for common knowledge (unless the information is included in a quotation). *Common knowledge* is general information that is available in a number of different sources and that is considered factual and incontestable (such as the height of the Empire State Building or the characteristic markings of the red wolf).

Whether an idea is widely known and accepted depends on who your readers are. Experts in the field may be aggravated by unnecessary and distracting citations to what they consider common knowledge. On the other hand, your instructor may assign a high priority to source citation and may be concerned about absence of a citation for material that is new to you (however well known it may be to experts in the field).

Here are more examples:

Facts

- On average, the earth is about 93 million miles from the sun.
- Labor organizer "Mother" Jones worked on behalf of the United Mine Workers of America.

Dates

- The spring equinox occurred on March 20 in 2011.

- U.S. women won the right to vote on August 26, 1920, when the Nineteenth Amendment was passed.

Events

- Francis Crick, James Watson, and Maurice Wilkins are credited with discovering the structure of DNA.

- The Stonewall Rebellion occurred in a Greenwich Village bar in New York City, when its gay patrons violently resisted a police raid.

Cultural Knowledge

- The composer Wolfgang Amadeus Mozart was a child prodigy.

- Elvis Presley made the song "Hound Dog" a smash hit, although he did not write it.

Writing
Responsibly   **Visuals and Common Knowledge**

Images, including maps, are not considered common knowledge. You may know that the capital of Nebraska is Lincoln, but if you include a map of Nebraska (that you did not draw) in a paper, you must credit the creator of that map, even if you downloaded it from a website. Unless you made the image yourself, you must credit the sources of all images that you talk about or reproduce in your project.

Even if you are learning such information for the first time, you do not need to cite your source. Everything else, though, should be cited in the text of your project and documented in a footnote or in your bibliography, reference list, or list of works cited.

> *More about*
> Using visuals as
> support, 186–87

11d   Understanding Why There Are So Many Ways to Cite

As you go about your research, you may find one source that puts page numbers in parentheses at the end of a sentence while another seems to have no page numbers in the text. The former is probably an academic source using MLA style, while the latter might be an article from a newspaper. When you download PDF articles from a scholarly database, too, you will find a range of citation and documentation styles.

These differences reflect a range of disciplinary and professional values. While in the sciences the date is one of the most important pieces of information a reader needs to know about a source (because

> *More about* ▶▶▶
> Conducting
> research in the
> disciplines,
> 234–40

timely information is key in these fields), in the humanities the date is far less important because old information is often just as credible as new.

Each of these documentation styles is summarized in this book, but you should consult the style manual itself—your college library is likely to have copies in its reference collection—for more examples or to cite types of sources not included here.

Once you know which documentation style sheet to follow, do not forget to convert citations you find from their found form to the right form for the style sheet you are following. The entry in the first example appears as formatted in *EBSCO*'s search results list; this is what it would look like if you simply copied and pasted it from the list. While it includes all of the information necessary to find the source again, it needs to be altered significantly to conform to APA documentation style.

More about ▶▶▶
MLA style, 241–303
APA style, 304–46
Chicago style, 347–74
CSE style, 375–91

Found Bibliographic Entry

Visual hallucinations in schizophrenia: Confusion between imagination and perception. Brébion, Gildas; Ohlsen, Ruth I.; Pilowsky, Lyn S.; Neuropsychology, Vol 22(3), May 2008. pp. 383-389. [Journal Article]

Revised Bibliographic Entry

References [APA style—see chapter 20]
Brébion, G., Ohlsen, R. I., & Pilowsky, L. S. (2008). Visual hallucinations in schizophrenia: Confusion between imagination and perception. *Neuropsychology, 22*, 383–389.

11e Drafting to Avoid Plagiarizing and Patchwriting

From notes to first drafts, many of the techniques for avoiding plagiarizing and patchwriting are similar. If you have taken effective notes with attention to how each source might be useful to your study and with care to preserve quotations where appropriate and alter them fully where useful, you should have little trouble avoiding plagiarism.

More about ▶▶▶
Taking notes, 113–126
Drafting, 170–181

However, all writers make mistakes sometimes. As a result, it is a good idea to do some double-checking when you get to the drafting stage.

To continue best practices for using sources at the drafting stage, take the same care as you move your notes into the document that you took when you made them initially:

- If you have a quotation in your note, include the quotation marks in your draft.

- Always include page numbers for quotations and paraphrases.

- As you integrate sources into your draft, transfer the documentation information immediately into your list of works cited, reference list, or bibliography. One approach is to use a page break (Insert, Page Break) to separate the documentation from the draft text.

- Avoid warping the source to fit your purposes. Capture and preserve primary claims and then situate your ideas in relation to other arguments.

- Paraphrase and adapt information carefully from a note to your draft, to make everything in your final document coherent. This may mean that, after you have altered your paraphrase, you will need to return to the original source to make sure the source language has not slipped back in.

- Each time you integrate a note from a source, look at the balance between source information and your interpretation and contextualization of that information. Did you *talk about* the source as much as you *quoted it?* Maintaining balance helps prevent source misuse.

- If you feel overwhelmed by drafting *and* paying close attention to citation and documentation, build in a separate stage—an evening, perhaps—when you can check all of your citations as part of your editing and proofreading process.

> **More about** ▶▶▶
> Proofreading,
> 214–15

- As part of this proofreading, read through your draft aloud. Anything that feels strange coming out of your mouth might signal that you have adopted the form or language of a source. If you do not find instances of plagiarism or patchwriting, you may at least identify awkward sentences that would be better if rewritten.

11f **Getting Permissions**

Plagiarism and copyright violation are two separate things. Plagiarism is a matter of local customs and guidelines. Each college, for example, writes its own plagiarism policy and sets its own penalties for violation of that policy. Plagiarism is concerned with *acknowledgment* of the sources for ideas or language.

Copyright law, in contrast, is unconcerned with source acknowledgment. Instead, it focuses on source *use* and authors' *permissions*. When a writer takes a substantial portion of another writer's text, acknowledging the source is not enough: The writer must obtain the original author's permission, often in exchange for payment.

As a student, your use of sources is covered under the *fair use* provision of copyright law. Your use of source material for educational purposes—for your own education—cannot violate copyright. If, however, you publish your work for others to read (and a web page is a publication), your text is no longer exclusively for educational purposes, so you have to think not only about avoiding plagiarism but also about observing copyright law. In this situation, you need to ask for permission to use images, music, and video, and any text that is more extensive than a short quotation.

When you publish work on a website or elsewhere that contains chunks of text longer than a quotation or when you use images, audio, or video that you did not create, you need to seek permission to use those items or find items that are part of the *cultural commons,* a resource free for anyone to use within reasonable guidelines. To gain permission, you will want to write a letter or an email to the copyright owner that includes the following information:

- A specific reference to the work that you would like to use: "I am writing to request use of your photo 'Afghan hound,' which appears on the Pet Planet website in a research report on dog training."

- A clear statement of how you will use this work (Will it be published on a website? In a research proposal sent to a particular audience?): "This report is primarily for educational purposes and will be published on my student website."

- A statement regarding whether you will profit from using this material (for a student these occasions are rare, and copyright owners are much more likely to grant rights to use when there is no profit involved): "Because I am completing this report for a research writing course, I will not profit in any way from using your photo, and my website should not compete in any way with your pet resource."

- How long the item will be public, and to how broad an audience: "I do not anticipate keeping the website active beyond 2011, when I will complete my undergraduate course work. The audience for this work will be my instructor and anyone who happens to find my site."

- The date by which you need a response: "The project completion date is October 30; therefore, I appreciate in advance your quick response to my query." It would not be reasonable to make a request such as this with less than a week remaining in your project cycle. If your time is this tight, you will need to instead seek a free resource.

- Your contact information.

Do your best to determine the copyright owner based on what you can find on the source itself. It is also a good idea to pursue more than one option simultaneously, as permissions often take time to acquire.

11g Collaborating and Source Citation

More about ▶▶▶
Collaboration, 180–81

Collaboration adds new dimensions to source use and citation. Many effective groups initially divide the labor and then work in the drafting and revising stages to create a unified document. What this means is that, somewhere in the process, you or one of your teammates could introduce a plagiarized bit of writing. As with any plagiarism or unethical source use, this could come from inaccurate notes, a misunderstanding of citation standards, or a deliberate misrepresentation of work. As a team, you will probably all share equal responsibility for a piece of collaboratively written work handed in.

How, then, can you make sure that what you sign your name to embodies responsible citation and documentation practices? You may be tempted to block off chunks of the work and then not touch something someone else drafted, to keep the work effectively singular, planning an "I-never-touched-that-part" defense. The danger is

Quick

Reference ➡ **Avoiding Plagiarism**

- Have you used another person's work (part of a text, an image, a media resource) without indicating that it came from a source?
- Have you used a string of the same words as your source without enclosing them in quotation marks and including the proper in-text citation, as well as an entry for the source in your list of works cited, reference list, or bibliography?
- Have you used even one word that is distinctive and central to someone else's argument without using quotation marks, in-text citation, and an entry in your list of works cited, reference list, or bibliography?
- Have you paraphrased (put into your own words) a sentence without including a citation and documentation?

- Have you summarized a key idea without including citation and documentation?
- Have you patchwritten—that is, altered a word or phrase in what would otherwise be a quotation rather than quoting it directly or paraphrasing it more fully?
- Does your list of works cited, reference list, or bibliography contain an entry for every source you quote, paraphrase, summarize, or reproduce (images, etc.) in your project?
- Do you cite all kinds of sources, from interviews to surveys, from photographs to book chapters?

that, if the goal is to create a coherent document, the work may not read fluidly. Instead, use good project management, note-taking, and editing strategies *as a team:*

- Make sure all members of the team keep copies of sources they have used.

- Plan in advance as a team the form you want notes and materials to be in, and ask that teammates follow the outlined procedures.

- Read closely for anything that seems suspicious in the final draft. Does a passage sound too technical to have been written by one of your partners? Are there any uncited data? This close reading should be a part of your copyediting process.

- Assign a member of the team to be a quotation and citation checker. Provide that person with copies of all cited sources.

→ EXERCISE 11.1 Plagiarism and Source Use

After reading this chapter, test your knowledge using one of the many online quizzes on source use and plagiarism. Here are two possibilities:

- "How to Recognize Plagiarism," Indiana University's School of Education
  This quiz uses APA style, which is primarily used by the social sciences, as its base style sheet.

- "Plagiarism Quiz Flash File," Empire State College
  This quiz tests your knowledge of common plagiarism scenarios.

About which aspects of plagiarism and source use were you still unclear? Write down any questions that taking the quiz raised, and direct them to your instructor. This will help to ensure that you understand what is expected in terms of citation.

A Final Thought

In "The Day the Violence Died," an episode of *The Simpsons*, Bart and Lisa discover their favorite cartoon, "Itchy and Scratchy," was an idea stolen from its rightful originator. The real creator, having lost all benefits of his good idea, ends up on the street, and is forced ultimately to sue for his idea. While failing to cite your sources may not leave authors on the street or you in a courtroom, not citing can hurt your credibility and the effectiveness of your document, not to mention possibly leading to more extreme outcomes such as punishment in school and your professional life. Instead, develop your skills of source integration; it is likely you would want other writers to do the same for you.

12

Writing an Annotated Bibliography

Annotated Bibliography of Writings in Feminism and Aesthetics

JOSHUA SHAW

This is a selective annotated bibliogra[phy]
thetics from 1990 to 2003. It is inte[nded]
by Linda Krumholz and Estella Laut[er]

Annotated Bibliography on Musician Wellness

COMPILED AND ANNOTATED BY LINDA COCKEY WITH KATHRYN KALMANSON

The items marked with this symbol can be ordered via the MTNA website through our affiliation with Amazon.com. Go to www.mtna.org and choose Member Services from the Membership option in the main menu bar for more information.

Introduction
The annual Annotated Bibliography on Musician Wellness has been researched and compiled annually for

more than 15 years now, first for the National Keyboard Pedagogy Conference and the last 10 years for MTNA. The publication of new wellness resources for musicians is currently slowing down a bit; therefore, this year's review will also devote a portion to discussing and recapitulating the most useful resources out there for the purpose of giving readers a list of what they might really utilize and want to own in their own personal libraries. New updates will also be included as

issues. Topics include prevention of medical problems, medication, performance anxiety, performance preparation, healthy practicing techniques, learning theories and physiological and psychological issues related to overall musicianship.

Update
Smith, Brenda, and Robert T. Sataloff. (2006) *Choral Pedagogy, 2nd edition.* Plural Publishing, 5521 Ruffin Rd., San Diego, CA 92123;

Have you ever had a great conversation in which you really debated ideas? Research conversations can be like that. Kenneth Burke, something of a Renaissance thinker, said the research conversation is like a parlor where lots of people are talking and we, as researchers, enter in.[1] We need to listen to the people already talking before we can catch the drift of the conversation and consider joining in ourselves. Our own thinking will be affected by those who preceded us. And after we

---

1. Burke, Kenneth. *The Philosophy of Literary Form.* Berkeley: U of California P, 1941. 110–11. Print.

contribute to the conversation, that conversation will also be affected by us, so we should participate with care. The annotated bibliography allows researchers to listen carefully and start testing ideas before they contribute to the conversation surrounding a topic.

12a Understanding the Annotated Bibliography

An annotated bibliography provides brief summaries of selected sources on a research topic, with the sources arranged in alphabetical order. It can also include your evaluations of and responses to these sources. Annotated bibliographies are common college assignments, and they can be freestanding published works (journal articles or even books) because they are very useful to readers who want a quick understanding of a research conversation. The images that open this chapter illustrate two such publications.

One of the greatest benefits of preparing an annotated bibliography is processing your sources so you can represent them ethically and effectively. Preparing an annotated bibliography helps you consider these issues: Who are the key thinkers on the topic? What are their basic stances? Who is in conversation with whom?

Other benefits include:

More about ▶▶▶
Summary, 16–17,
58–59, 118–120,
129, 190–92
Synthesis, 19–20,
125–26, 188–190

- Slowing down your reading process enough that you do not miss anything important in your sources.

- Giving you practice with summary, a difficult and important writing technique.

- Placing you and your ideas among the other thinkers and writers on the topic without demanding that you immediately synthesize all of the information.

- Allowing an instructor or other readers to help you identify gaps in the research.

Students who write annotated bibliographies sometimes initially feel that they are labor-intensive, but when they begin to write their research projects (from essays to commentaries to proposals), they remark how much easier the projects are to write after having prepared an annotated bibliography. Even when an annotated bibliography is not part of the assignment, you may find it useful to write one to build comprehension and develop a stance.

12b Preparing the Citation

Each entry in the annotated bibliography begins with full source information, presented as if it were in a list of works cited or a reference list at the end of a researched essay. (*Note:* The examples in this chapter follow Modern Language Association [MLA] style; for other documentation styles, see chapters 21–24.)

> Hudson-Williams, Harri Llwyd. "Political Speeches in Athens." *Classical*
>
> *Quarterly* ns 1 (1951): 68–73. Print.

The entries are arranged in alphabetical order by author. If any entries do not have an author, use the first word (except *a, an,* or *the*) of the title to determine the alphabetical location of the entry.

More about ▶▶▶
Acknowledging
  sources, 127–138
Preparing an MLA-
  style list of works
  cited, 241–303
Preparing an APA-
  style reference list,
  304–46
Creating *Chicago*-
  style notes and
  bibliography
  entries, 347–74
Preparing a CSE-
  style reference list,
  375–91

Writing Responsibly Dealing with Abstracts

Many published texts begin with a one-paragraph abstract of the source. Source abstracts can also be found in many databases, such as *ProQuest* and *EBSCO*. When you are assigned to write an annotated bibliography, you are expected to read the sources and write your own summaries. Copying abstracts that others have written and representing them as your own work is plagiarism. Even paraphrasing the abstracts that others have written is unacceptable, especially if it means that you have not read the sources yourself.

But how do you avoid being overly influenced by abstracts? One option is to put them out of sight where they cannot tempt you. A better option is to read them; they are extremely useful in helping you anticipate what you will read in the article. Read the abstract, and then read the article, taking notes that you can use to write your annotation. To ensure that you use your own language in your annotation, try not to return to the abstract again, except after drafting your annotation, and include the following elements:

- The main claim in the first sentence or two
- All major subpoints (but not specific examples)
- Enough logical guidance that a reader can understand the connections between the main argument and those key subpoints you have included
- Almost no quotations, with the exception of a short phrase or two that are key to the argument and not easily paraphrased

12c Writing the Annotation

More about ▶▶▶
Summary, 16–17,
58–59, 118–120,
129, 190–92
Avoiding patchwriting in your summary, 17

Each citation is followed by an annotation that summarizes the source. Usually these annotations are two to five sentences long.

Sometimes this *abstract*—this very condensed summary of the source—is introduced by a sentence or two that offers information about or evaluation of the author or the publisher. You can see this approach in the selection from Dan Long's annotated bibliography at the end of this chapter.

More about ▶▶▶
Evaluation and
critique, 20–22,
187–88

Annotated bibliographies that precede other researched writing will typically also include an evaluation, from one sentence in length, as in Dan Long's sample in this chapter, to a full paragraph. In the evaluative portion of the annotation, you begin to work out your argument and each source's role in it. Evaluate the strengths, weaknesses, and stance of the source in general (but avoid including any worthless sources). What makes the source credible? What does the source assume its readers will agree with? What does it leave out? Does it agree, disagree, or modify any of the other sources? Also discuss how you plan to use the source in your written project.

12d Formatting the Annotated Bibliography

Your annotated bibliography should include your name, a title, a brief explanation of why you have read these sources, full bibliographic information for each source, and annotations for each source. Unless your instructor gives you different instructions, follow the format and layout of Dan Long's annotated bibliography in section 12e.

12e Sample Student Annotated Bibliography (in MLA Style)

Following is a selection of four entries from Dan Long's annotated bibliography, which originally contained ten entries.

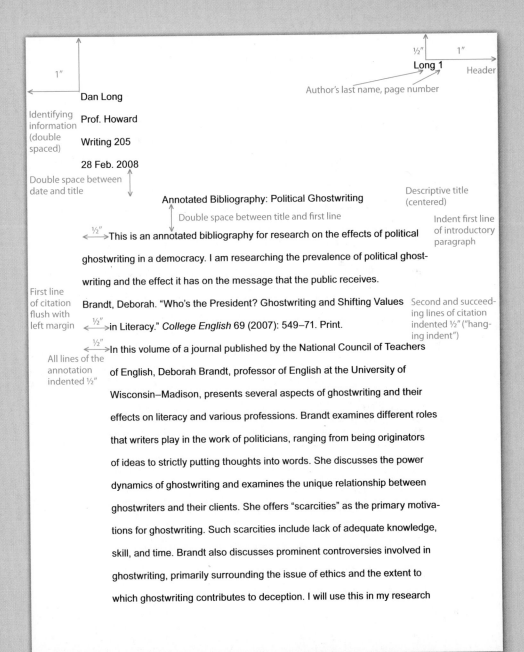

1″

½″　1″

Header

Author's last name, page number

Dan Long

Identifying information (double spaced)

Prof. Howard

Writing 205

28 Feb. 2008

Double space between date and title

Annotated Bibliography: Political Ghostwriting

Descriptive title (centered)

Double space between title and first line

Indent first line of introductory paragraph

½″ This is an annotated bibliography for research on the effects of political

ghostwriting in a democracy. I am researching the prevalence of political ghost-

writing and the effect it has on the message that the public receives.

First line of citation flush with left margin

Brandt, Deborah. "Who's the President? Ghostwriting and Shifting Values

Second and succeeding lines of citation indented ½″ ("hanging indent")

½″ in Literacy." *College English* 69 (2007): 549–71. Print.

½″ In this volume of a journal published by the National Council of Teachers

All lines of the annotation indented ½″

of English, Deborah Brandt, professor of English at the University of

Wisconsin–Madison, presents several aspects of ghostwriting and their

effects on literacy and various professions. Brandt examines different roles

that writers play in the work of politicians, ranging from being originators

of ideas to strictly putting thoughts into words. She discusses the power

dynamics of ghostwriting and examines the unique relationship between

ghostwriters and their clients. She offers "scarcities" as the primary motiva-

tions for ghostwriting. Such scarcities include lack of adequate knowledge,

skill, and time. Brandt also discusses prominent controversies involved in

ghostwriting, primarily surrounding the issue of ethics and the extent to

which ghostwriting contributes to deception. I will use this in my research

143

as a scholarly evaluation of the ethics and a controversy surrounding ghost-writing's effect on various professions.

Dille, Brian. "The Prepared and Spontaneous Remarks of Presidents Reagan and Bush: A Validity Comparison for At-a-Distance Measurements." *Political Psychology* 21 (2000): 573–85. Print.

Brian Dille's research is focused on how differences between prepared and spontaneous remarks reflect psychological characteristics. His primary hypothesis is that the psychological scores for spontaneous remarks would be significantly different from the scores of prepared remarks. He tested his hypothesis on prepared and spontaneous remarks from President Reagan and President Bush. His findings showed that there was a significant difference between prepared and unprepared speech in relation to the respective presidents' operational code and policy implementation. There was a difference in the measurement of conceptual complexity in the speeches for President Reagan, which could reflect slightly different ideologies between President Reagan and his writers. Dillie's study will provide me quantitative evidence for discrepancies between ideologies reflected by prepared speeches and spontaneous speeches.

Hudson-Williams, Harri Llwyd. "Political Speeches in Athens." *Classical Quarterly* ns 1 (1951): 68–73. Print.

In this volume of the peer-reviewed *Classical Quarterly*, Harri Llwyd Hudson-Williams of the University of Liverpool focuses on written speeches in ancient Greece. Hudson-Williams uses the work of Alsidamas and Isocrates to analyze the role of written speech as opposed to extempore speech in Greece. The philosophers viewed written speeches as a necessary evil but held reservations against their role in politics. In ancient Greece it was common for legal and forensic speeches to be written, but political speeches were primarily spontaneous. Many felt that specific preparation of political speeches interfered with truth. The philosophers largely felt that it was acceptable to outline specific points and arguments before the speech but that the delivery of the speech should be extempore. Hudson-Williams effectively addresses ancient philosophical thought about speechwriting but could have elaborated further on its role in Greek politics. I will use this in my research as a source of philosophical thinking on the ethics of political speechwriting. It will be particularly useful as an indication of how famous philosophers viewed the role of political speechwriting in society.

Hult, Karen, and Charles Walcott. "Policymakers and Wordsmiths: Writing for the President under Johnson and Nixon." *Polity* 30 (1998): 465–87. Print.
This article addresses the increasing gap between administrative policies and written presidential statements, and the beginning of contemporary political ghostwriting starting with the Lyndon Johnson and Richard Nixon presidential administrations. Hult and Walcott find that speechwriters are aloof from policymakers and don't have enough knowledge about specific policies to effectively write about them. Due to both an increased demand for writers and disorder within President Johnson's administration, speechwriters became less specialized and wrote about many different topics. Nixon

established an Office of Speechwriting and Research in his first term, effectively expanding the number of writers and their duties. His writers were often invited to policy meetings, but only to become more in-tune with how the policymakers thought of ideas. In Nixon's abbreviated second term, writers didn't have as much guidance and became further separated from the ideas behind the policies about which they were writing. This study will be useful in my research because it gives me a transition from a time when writers were well connected with politicians to a time when they were disconnected. It gives me reasons for the shift and how it has affected political ghostwriting.

Quick

Reference → **What to Include in Your Annotated Bibliography**

1. A title indicating the topic of the annotated bibliography
2. A one-paragraph introduction to the topic
3. The source citation in the appropriate documentation style (MLA, APA, *Chicago*, CSE) for your class, discipline, or task
4. A summary of the source, representing its main argument in new language, usually one paragraph long
5. Often, an evaluation of or response to the source, indicating how reliable you think the source is and/or how you will use it in your research project

A Final Thought

Responsible communicators listen carefully so they do not misunderstand or misrepresent what others have said and so they do not sound uninformed when they contribute. The same is true when the communication is written. Writers can learn from those who have written before them, and they too, can add to the discussion. An annotated bibliography is one of the best tools for sorting out and comprehending the conversation you hope to enter.

Explaining Your Choice of Sources

One of the differences between experienced and inexperienced academic writers is how much they talk *about* their sources. As college writing teachers involved in the Citation Project read and analyzed research papers from U.S. colleges, they became concerned about how few of the student papers talked about their sources. Most just pulled out information—usually a "word bite" of only a sentence or two—from sources, as if all the sources were alike. Except for the citations, the sources were invisible to the reader. The following example shows the result:

First draft

Student's voice	Hostility toward women can be seen in the ancient West. Stevenson observes, "Livy's underlying message, it would seem, is that Roman men have to regulate public contributions by prominent women, and not accept female advice too easily, without prolonged consideration" (189).
Signal phrase	
Quotation	

The material from the Stevenson source is accurately quoted and cited. But who is Stevenson? Where did this source come from? Why did the writer choose it? Why should the writer's audience respect what this source says? What else did the source have to say; what was the *context* in which this quotation appeared?

Revised draft

Student's voice	Hostility toward women can be seen even in the ancient West. Tom Stevenson, a classics scholar at the University of Queensland, writes in the scholarly journal *Classical World* that the Roman historian Livy described women who supported their menfolks' success, which might seem to be a compliment to the women. But notice that the women aren't having their own successes. To make matters worse, all of Livy's women are either described too briefly, or they are flawed. Even as Stevenson provides this analysis, he also cautions against being too simplistic about Livy's portrayal of women; some of their faults were because their men were flawed. Still, Stevenson concludes, "Livy's underlying message, it
Signal phrase	
Credentials of author and publisher	
Summary of source	
Counterevidence	
Quotation	

> would seem, is that Roman men have to regulate public contributions by prominent women, and not accept female advice too easily, without prolonged consideration" (189).

Now the material from the source is not only accurately quoted and cited, but the author's credentials and the authority of the place where his article is published have been established, along with a description of his argument.

Sometimes the reason you choose a source is not because it is published in a scholarly journal but because of your favorable analysis of the source's argument or information. In these cases, too, you should let your audience know why you have chosen the source:

> One good way to understand the treatment of women in contemporary society is to consult newsmedia. They aren't reports of research written by experts, but they are sources that reflect and shape popular opinion. *Time* magazine publishes an article on date rape because they believe it is an issue that readers will or should care about. They also report on current events. So it is *Time* that reports on a Congressional bill intended to reduce sexual violence in colleges. Why is the bill needed? "One in five college women will be the victim of a sexual assault (and 6% of men)" (Webley).

Information about why the writer chose this source

Summary of some information in the source

Student's voice

Quotation

Sources:

Stevenson, Tom. "Women of Early Rome as *Exempla* in Livy, *AB Urbe Condita*, Book 1." *Classical World* 104.2 (Winter 2011): 175–89.

Webley, Kayla. "It's Not Just Yale: Are Colleges Doing Enough to Combat Sexual Violence?" *Time* Apr. 18, 2011. Web. 18 Apr. 2011.

13

Writing and Refining Your Thesis

More about ▶▶▶
Exploring topics, 23–31
Developing your research question, 35–36
Drafting research questions and hypotheses, 48–49

Answering research questions is like blazing trails in the wilderness. It can be hard work, can surprise you, and can lead you places you have never been. Typically, when the trail is completed, at its head stands a signpost that signals what to expect and the direction the trail takes. Through the written product of your research, then, you invite readers to travel with you along the intellectual trails you have blazed, and the signpost is the thesis statement.

A *thesis statement* is one or two sentences indicating the main idea of your paper, the idea that each body paragraph and all the reasons and evidence in those body paragraphs support. Your thesis should grow out of your research question and hypothesis (or hypotheses), revised in light of what you learned through the research process. A good thesis interests readers, gives them a clear sense of what will follow, and is well supported. The path to the conclusion will be clear of obstacles because you, as the writer, have thought through what your readers will need to believe your main claim.

13a Drafting a Thesis Statement

A well-crafted thesis statement should do all of the following:

- **Answer a research question**. For instance, the question "What impacts does coal have on the environment?" might be answered with "Soft coal's primary impact is on water quality."

- **Make an assertion**, or claim, that you will explain in the essay. "I will talk about global warming" does not express a claim, while "Citizens should be more aware of soft (bituminous) coal's impact on water quality and what they can do to lobby against its use" makes a strong claim.

- **Reflect your findings** by forecasting what you learned through your research. The soft coal thesis statement above lets readers know they will learn about *impact* and *lobbying*.

- **Express your purpose.** You need not say specifically, "I will persuade" or "I will inform," but your purpose should be clear nonetheless. For example, the writer of the earlier thesis about soft coal seeks to persuade readers. If, instead, the writer's purpose were to inform, the thesis could be rewritten in this way: "Soft (bituminous) coal is a major contributor to water pollution in the United States."

- **Convey your point of view.** You can, of course, agree with one or more of your sources, but always try to add your perspective on that position. Otherwise, why should someone read your paper instead of one of the sources you consulted?

- **Use concrete language.** Weed out vague words such as *good* and *interesting*.

- **Suggest the topic's significance or relevance.** For example, the thesis on soft coal suggests the environment is an issue critical to American citizens becaause it impacts their water supply.

- **Achieve a balanced and reasonable tone.** Extreme positions can be difficult to support and can alienate readers. Considering counterarguments can help you achieve a reasonable tone.

More about ▶▶▶
Analyzing the
assignment for
purpose, 42–43

- **Fit the assignment and genre.** Do you need to propose a plan for change? Comment on a trend? Analyze a situation? Persuade someone to change his or her mind on a subject? Go back to the assignment to make sure your thesis suits both its rhetorical and learning goals.

Lydia Nichols's research question, hypothesis, and thesis statement for her student research essay on underground comics illustrate the process of developing a thesis statement:

▶▶▶Sample student
paper:
    "Holy Under-
    ground Comics,
    Batman! Moving
    Away from the
    Mainstream" by
    Lydia Nichols,
    335–346

Purpose is both infor-
mative and persuasive:
compares types of
comics (informative) to
convince readers that
underground comics
are more innovative
and sophisticated
(persuasive)

Research question: What are the characteristics of underground comics?

❶ _____

Hypothesis: The characteristics of underground comics are a

❷ _____

focus on topics that challenge social mores, an author or author

❸ _____

team that has creative control, and an adult readership.

Thesis: While far less well-known than their superhero counterparts, underground comics offer an innovative and sophisticated alternative to mainstream titles.

Hypothesis
answers resea[rch]
question by lis[t-]
ing three disti[n-]
guishing traits

Thesis places
underground
comics in con-
text familiar to
readers

Thesis trans-
forms specifics
into a broader,
more engagin[g]
claim

The thesis statement grows out of the hypothesis, but it is broader: It offers to explain how underground comics differ from mainstream comics, but it leaves the exact ways in which they differ for the body of the essay. The thesis conveys the essay's dual purpose—it uses comparison to persuade readers that underground comics are more innovative and sophisticated than their superhero cousins—and it clearly announces the position the writer is taking.

⬆ Make It **Your Own**

For a research paper that you are working on, draft (or revise) a thesis statement. Does the thesis statement concisely assert your central idea? Does it convey your purpose? Be sure to refer to the criteria for an effective thesis statement on pp. 150–52.

Writing Responsibly

Acknowledging Counterevidence

While sorting your notes, be sure to retain *counterevidence—evidence* that *undermines* your claims. Do not suppress this counterevidence. Instead, revise your thesis or supporting reasons with it in mind, or acknowledge the counterevidence and explain why the support for believing your thesis is more convincing than the challenges to it. Your readers will appreciate your presentation of multiple perspectives.

13b Refining Your Thesis

Most writers revise their thesis statement repeatedly as they draft, sharpening it so that it reflects their developing ideas. In the section that follows, look carefully at how Erin Buksbaum's and Tom Hackman's thesis statements evolved from dull and general to interesting and specific.

More about ▶▶▶
Reasons and evidence, 183–86

Purpose: Informative

The thesis of an informative document makes a claim of fact—a claim about something that can be verified—and the balance of the document provides the verification. To be engaging, an informative thesis must make a claim of fact that is not yet widely known to or accepted by the audience.

More about ▶▶▶
Purpose in the project proposal, 46–57

Draft Thesis

This paper is about using social networking sites.

This draft thesis statement makes a claim of fact, but it is far too general, doing nothing more than identifying the paper's general topic.

Revision 1

While social networking sites allow for new forms of social communication, they can also be dangerous.

This thesis statement is more specific but still too general: Because it does not specify the types of dangers social networking sites represent, it commits the writer to discussing *all* the ways in which social networking sites can be dangerous (physically, psychologically, financially; for users, families and friends of users, companies).

Revision 2

While social networking sites allow for new forms of communication, they also open new avenues for privacy violations.

This thesis statement narrows the scope: The writer is responsible only for reporting on privacy violations. Because the thesis covers a current topic about which many students know far more than their instructors, it is also likely to spark the instructor's interest.

Purpose: Argumentative/Persuasive

More about ▶▶▶
Positioning your argument in relation to others, 101–02

A persuasive thesis must make a claim of judgment rather than a claim of fact. It must offer an opinion, a provisional judgment, that is not widely shared and that can be explained with reasons and evidence.

Draft Thesis

There are many types of plagiarism.

This is a simple claim of fact; it is insufficient for a text with a persuasive purpose.

Revision 1

Plagiarism has many motivations, which, I believe, makes a single punishment inappropriate.

This draft makes a claim of judgment, but the first half of the statement remains overly general (it would take many pages to discuss the motivations of *all* writers), and it announces a claim ("I believe"), that is unnecessary.

Revision 2

Reducing the incidence of plagiarism among college students will be difficult without understanding its causes. This requires going beyond the simplistic explanations that are frequently offered.

The thesis now focuses on a much smaller group (college students), and it no longer unnecessarily announces its claim.

Although you can revise your thesis statement at any stage of the writing process, you are most likely to revise it at two points:

1. After collecting and processing your information
2. After writing your first draft and beginning your revisions

Quick

Use this checklist as you revise and refine your thesis statement to make it as strong as possible. The goal is to check off each item in the checklist. Before you revise, ask an outside reader to check off the items he or she feels your thesis satisfies.

Does the thesis:

- ☐ answer your research question?
- ☐ make a debatable claim, one with which some readers might disagree until convinced otherwise?
- ☐ express the main topic by using the key terms of your study?
- ☐ use precise terms instead of broad and general ones?
- ☐ emerge logically from your research findings?
- ☐ express your take on the topic, rather than simply repeating what one of your sources has said?
- ☐ take a balanced and reasonable stance, not overstating the case? (Watch for "all," "never," "always," and other absolutes, and revise where the absolute is unsupportable.)
- ☐ suggest the significance or relevance of the topic?
- ☐ make your purpose (to inform, persuade, analyze, or interpret) clear?
- ☐ excite and engage your thinking?

Work **Together** ⬅

Using your thesis statement, pair up with a classmate to debate your claims. One person should play the role of the investigative reporter and the other, the role of the researcher defending his or her research. The reporter should try to poke holes in the researcher's argument by asking probing questions. Then, switch roles. After each round, take a few moments to jot down information you need to find that will strengthen your argument, and note ways you need to refine your claim. Which questions did your partner ask that you could not answer adequately?

A Final Thought

How well your readers comprehend your central claim depends on the clarity and strength of your thesis statement. All other parts of your writing hinge on these one or two sentences, supporting, enhancing, and elaborating on the thesis. From the reader's perspective, the thesis offers a sense of what is to come. From the writer's perspective, a strong thesis is about getting your voice heard. It should be neither a shout nor a whisper. Your audience should know what your primary claim is and why they, too, should believe as you do on the topic.

14 Organizing Your Project

Home improvement shows often depict organization as a way to improve the look and feel of household spaces. Messy, disorganized rooms are almost unlivable and unusable. Writing benefits similarly from attention to its structure and order. Most documents need attention to organization both *before* and *after* drafting. Organizing beforehand makes drafting easier and more effective. Reviewing the structure after you have written a draft can show you where you need more support, whether the document is logically organized, and whether any of the evidence you have included is irrelevant.

More about ▶▶▶
Reorganizing a draft, 206–07

14a Reviewing Your Prewriting

Start organizing by reviewing all the preparatory writing you have done: your research log, any freewriting, brainstormed

> **More about ▶▶▶**
> Keeping a journal
> or blog, 12–13,
> 24–25, 116
> Freewriting, 26–28
> Brainstorming, 28
> Clustering, 28–29
> Hypothesis develop-
> ment, 48–49
> Thesis statements,
> 151–53

lists, clusters in progress, and so on. Your materials should be fresh in your mind as you outline and draft.

Ask yourself whether reading through all of your prewriting has given you any new insight into your topic. If so, adjust your thesis statement. Then write your preliminary thesis statement at the top of a new electronic document or a clean sheet of paper. If you are working as a team, you might want to make a new wiki page. Below the thesis statement, list all the ideas that might be relevant to it.

14b Grouping Your Ideas

> **▶▶▶Student**
> sample essay by Erin
> Buksbaum:
> Early draft, "Is Social
>   Networking a
>   Serious Danger?"
>   178–80

Read through your list of ideas. How are they related? For instance, Erin Buksbaum noticed three different types of subtopic groupings she could use for her notes on social networking: positive aspects versus dangers, profiles and photos, and violations and dangers.

There are many grouping methods that will help you get closer to an outline of your project. If you are working with an electronic document, you can cut and paste your ideas into logical groups using *subheadings* (these subheadings might be functional parts of the final document or might disappear altogether as you write) or display all related ideas in the *same font color*. If you have been using a blog and tagging your entries, the *tags* serve as functioning groups you can refine. If you are working with pen and paper, you can highlight related ideas with the *same color highlighting marker* or write each group of ideas on a *separate sheet* of paper. If you favor note cards, you can create *piles* that represent each subtopic or potential section of your research project. You might also want to create a *cluster diagram* or table based on your subtopics or sections.

Do you have an item that does not seem to fit your categories? Anything that must be forced into a group either might not be relevant or might reveal information you still need to gather.

14c Arranging Your Ideas from General to Specific

Within each grouping, arrange ideas from most general to most specific. Grouping general and specific ideas can help you determine whether you have enough specific reasons, evidence, and examples for each major point.

A *tree diagram* can help. To create a tree diagram, place the most general information at the top and increasingly specific information on branches below. The tree diagram in Figure 14.1 shows the preliminary organization for Erin Buksbaum's essay.

FIGURE 14.1 Tree Diagram A tree diagram can help you organize your thoughts before you begin writing.

14d Considering Your Project's Overall Shape

The typical academic research essay has three basic parts: introduction, body, and conclusion. In its simplest form, the essay has a "five-paragraph" structure: one paragraph for the introduction, three for the body, and one for the conclusion. Of course, college writing seldom takes such a tidy form. Instead, it is more likely to unfold as described below.

Introduction

The introduction is typically brief: one to three paragraphs, depending on the length of the project. Often, the thesis statement appears in the introduction, where it can shape the reader's expectations, but it may also appear in the conclusion as the answer to a question or problem posed in the introduction. What goes into the introduction depends on the document's purpose, audience, context, and genre. In most cases, though, the introduction should do the following:

- Identify the topic

- Entice readers to read on

- Provide a thesis statement or a research question

- Prepare readers for what follows, in some cases by forecasting the project's main points

> *More about* ▸▸▸
> Conducting research in the disciplines, 234–40

> *More about* ▸▸▸
> Drafting the introduction, 174–75
> Revising the introduction, 204–05

Body

More about ▶▶▶
Developing paragraphs, 175
Reasons and evidence, 183–86
Counterevidence, 153, 184–86
Providing evidence to support claims, 184

The body is the longest portion of a text, with its length depending on the complexity of the ideas being expressed and the quantity of support needed to convince the audience. Each paragraph in the body should make one point, expressed in a topic sentence; the body paragraphs should supply reasons and evidence supporting the topic sentence; and each topic sentence should support the thesis.

The one major deviation from this pattern is the introduction of *counterevidence*—alternative points of view on your topic. Introduce counterevidence either early or at the very end of the body, explaining why the evidence you present is more compelling.

Conclusion

More about ▶▶▶
Drafting the conclusion, 176–77

Like the introduction, the conclusion is usually rather brief (one to three paragraphs, depending on the length of the project). Just as the introduction should entice readers, so the conclusion should convince them that they have spent their time well. An effective conclusion might do one of the following:

- Point to further avenues for research

- Offer a personal reflection

- Explain why readers should follow your recommendations

- Suggest the broader significance of your findings

An effective conclusion should not introduce reasons to doubt your argument, nor should it offer new supporting material or repeat your thesis word for word ("In my paper, I have shown . . .").

14e Choosing an Organizational Strategy

Once you have collected and organized your notes, choose an organizational pattern that best fits your thesis and supporting materials. Some organizational patterns include the following:

- **General-to-specific/specific-to-general order.** Probably the most common organizational scheme for academic essays begins with a general statement—the thesis—and then proceeds to the body of the essay, where specific reasons and evidence are provided. With indifferent or even hostile readers, consider reversing this order: Begin with something specific—an engaging anecdote, some dramatic statistics, a provocative illustration—that will gain your audience's interest, attention, or sympathy, and then move on to the general conclusion.

- **Familiar-to-unfamiliar/unfamiliar-to-familiar order.** If you are writing for an audience likely to balk when faced with new ideas, especially ones that challenge their beliefs, lead with what you believe your readers already know and accept, and move gradually toward what they do not. To startle your readers into seeing a familiar issue in a new light, use unfamiliar-to-familiar order: Begin with surprising issues or information, and then move on to familiar ground.

- **Problem-to-solution organization.** Much research is aimed at solving problems. Such projects typically begin by defining the problem and offering an informed rationale for a particular solution. This structure is typical of the proposal genre.

- **Cause-and-effect organization.** Research often helps us to understand how things came to occur and what the impacts of those causes have been. Historians are often interested in what led people to war, for instance.

- **Climactic organization.** You may choose to organize your body paragraphs from least to most exciting. You might even save your thesis until the conclusion.

- **Chronological organization.** Use *chronological* (or *time*) order to tell a story (*narrative*) or explain a process (*process analysis*). For instance, to explain how to snowboard, you might start with how to strap on the board, move on to how to adopt the right position when you first start down the hill, and conclude with how to get up after you fall.

- **Spatial organization.** When your findings are descriptive, organize spatially, from left to right, inside to outside, top to bottom. To describe the sedimentary layers in a mountainside for an assignment in your geology course, for example, you might begin your description with the top layer and move downward into the earth. This structure is best suited to observation-based field research.

Make It **Your Own**

Revisit a research project you wrote recently. What organizational strategy or strategies did you use? What organizational changes would you make now? Why?

14f Choosing an Outlining Technique

Outlines, whether "scratch" or formal, not only guide you as you draft, but also allow you to experiment with ways to sequence your supporting paragraphs. Perhaps most importantly, they allow you to check whether all your evidence really supports your thesis.

An informal (scratch) outline

▶▶▶Student sample essay by Erin Buksbaum: Early draft, "Is Social Networking a Serious Danger?" 178–80

An *informal*, or *scratch, outline* is simply a list of ideas in the order you want to present them. You can jot down your ideas in words, phrases, complete sentences, even pictures—whatever jogs your memory about what to put next. You can present the ideas in a simple series, or you can cluster them in groups—introduction, body, conclusion. Below is a sample scratch outline for Erin Buksbaum's essay on social networking sites.

Intro:

Social networking sites = new pathways of communication.

Benefits: Way to communicate with friends, make new friends, promote movies, shows, bands.

Thesis: While social networking sites allow for exciting new forms of communication, they also open new avenues for privacy violations and even danger.

Body:

Background: User profiles and the kind of information/ elements they include, how information is accessed

Dangers: Pictures—some inappropriate or misused (ruin reputation, lose jobs); Profiles—information available too widely (teachers, parents, criminals, perverts), lying about who you are

Conclusion:

Be cautious; don't post info you wouldn't want to see in the newspaper.

A formal outline (topic or sentence)

A *formal outline* uses roman numerals (I, II, III), capital letters (A, B, C), arabic numerals (1, 2, 3), lowercase letters (a, b, c), and indentions of five spaces (or half an inch) to indicate level of generality, with roman numeral headings being the most general to lowercase letters the most specific. Each level of your outline should include at least two entries. Each subsidiary point must support the idea at the level above it, and each heading must unify the subsidiary points in the level below. To use a simple example, if the first-level heading is *I. Types of Cheese,* the next-level headings could be

    A. Muenster

    B. Swiss

    C. Cheddar

They should not be

    A. Methods of Making Cheese

    B. Aging the Cheese

    C. Using the Right Feed Grain

because all the headings at each level must be *parallel,* or follow the same pattern. Thus, the sequence

    A. Muenster

    B. Swiss

    C. Cheddar

is fine (all are adjectives describing a type of cheese), whereas the sequence

    A. Methods of Making Cheese

    B. Aging the Cheese

    C. Using the Right Feed Grain

is not. (You would have to change *Methods of Making Cheese* to *Making the Cheese* to make the first heading parallel with the others.)

The examples above are from a *topic outline:* They use words and phrases to indicate the ideas to be discussed. Some writers prefer to create a *sentence outline* because it provides a starting point from which to draft. Compare the first section of a topic outline and a sentence outline for Erin Buksbaum's essay:

Thesis: While social networking sites allow for exciting new forms of communication, they also open new avenues for privacy violations and other social dangers.

Topic Outline

I. User profiles

    A. Typical components

        1. Basic personal information: name, age, school

        2. Favorite music, movies, books

        3. Animations, videos, Flash movies, banners

    B. Dangers they create

        1. Make personal info available to anyone with an account

        2. Children may post details that make them easy to find and harm

Sentence Outline

I. The center of the social networking experience is the user's profile.

    A. These profiles can be thought of as personalized web pages.

        1. Profiles usually include basic personal information such as a user's name, age, and school.

        2. Most users also post lists of their favorite books, bands, and songs.

        3. More sophisticated users post animations, videos, and Flash movies.

    B. While it sounds like harmless fun, what people post in their profiles can be extremely dangerous.

        1. User profiles allow any other member of the social network to learn personal details about that user.

        2. Many children may foolishly post details that make it easy for others to track them down offline.

Though Buksbaum has not referred directly to sources in these outlines, when drafting you should cite any sources to which you refer within your outline, not only when you include a full quotation but also when you paraphrase an idea.

A storyboard or a site map

For a multimedia research project or if you are a visual thinker, you will want a more visual kind of outline such as a storyboard or a site map. *Storyboards* are analogous to cartoon frames. Each square of the storyboard usually has both a visual and a textual component, and the storyboard moves from the beginning to the end of the project. This

Website on Implications of Plato's *Phaedrus* for Modern Writers, Site Map

Sample Storyboard: *PowerPoint* Video on Underground Comics (first four frames)

Home: Brief introduction to what *Phaedrus* is, when it was written, **why we should care today (thesis)**, navigation bar on top

Plato feared writing technologies and was wrong

Plato was wary of rhetoric and was right

Defending writing and memory, also draw on Ong

Defending writing as alive, also draw on Barthes

Rhetoric as manipulation?

Ads, include images and video with my and expert analysis

Political campaigns, include images and video with my and expert analysis

First few shots should be of "predicable images": Superman, the Joker, Spidey swinging from a web, possibly swelling dramatic music to enhance the "feel." Voice-over argument about how most people associate the predictable with comic books.

Contrast with images from underground comics to give viewers a sense of the difference. Music with a more mundane feel. Briefly suggest these are sophisticated alternatives offering a different viewpoint.

Cut to image of people shopping in a comic book store, panning shot of the diverse people in the store. The wide range of possibilities in comic books will appeal to a wider audience.

Shift to historical backdrop of evolution of comic books: 1938 Superman's debut. Use a transition that looks "vintage"— perhaps like the title before a newsreel?

FIGURE 14.2 Site Map and Storyboard A site map can help you visualize the organization of research presented across multiple web pages. A storyboard establishes a sequence of "shots."

allows you to employ visual and verbal evidence where appropriate. A *site map* is an outline of a website or hyperlinked project, allowing you to indicate the relationships among pages. Figure 14.2 shows a sample site map of a research project on Plato's *Phaedrus* and a storyboard of a multimedia project on underground comics.

14g Checking Your Outline for Unity and Coherence

Once you have completed your outline, review it critically for unity and coherence. You have achieved *unity* when all the supporting paragraphs are relevant to the thesis and all the examples, reasons, and evidence are relevant to the main idea of the supporting paragraph.

> *More about* ▶▶▶
> Developing paragraphs, 175

You have achieved *coherence* when the supporting paragraphs, with all their reasons, evidence, and examples, are organized logically, so that readers can move from idea to idea without having to pause to consider the relationships among the parts.

When reviewing your outline, ask yourself the following questions:

- Are all the reasons, evidence, and examples relevant to the main idea?

- Do all the ideas reinforce the thesis statement?

- Are all the ideas organized logically?

- What is the connection between consecutive points? (This connection will become your transition when you begin drafting.)

EXERCISE **14.1** Outlining Formally

Using your own research findings, create a formal topic outline.

Work **Together**

Exchange your project outline with a classmate, and assess your classmate's outline for unity and coherence. Explain your observations to your classmate. Then, using the useful ideas you gained from your classmate's response to your outline, revise it.

Quick Reference ➡ Getting Organized

- Review your prewriting for patterns.
- Group your ideas logically.
- Arrange your ideas from general to specific.
- Consider your project's overall shape (introduction, body, conclusion).
- Choose an organizational strategy.
- Choose an outlining technique and develop the outline.
- Check your outline for unity and coherence.

A Final Thought

The classic Tetris video game is all about seeing how visual objects fit together, planning quickly and effectively as one plays. While it is very satisfying to see pieces lock into place with no gaps in between, one of the great challenges of the game is having to plan, organize, and execute virtually all at once. Fortunately, most researched writing does not have to proceed that way; writers get the opportunity to make plan through a proposal, sketch the plan more specifically through outlining, and return and revise the organization throughout the drafting and revising stages. And seeing claims and evidence lock into place to build knowledge and inform and persuade an audience of readers can be much more satisfying than the fleeting pleasure of virtual block stacking.

Choosing and Unpacking Complex Sources

College writers in a hurry may choose too many short, simple sources that can be read quickly. The following graph shows the length of source being cited in the citations that appear in the research papers analyzed in the Citation Project:

This graph shows that many of the students writing these papers often chose to work from the shortest possible sources. Yet as the Citation Project researchers (all of whom are college composition instructors) read and analyzed these papers, they were impressed with how much the quality of the paper was affected by the complexity of its sources. The papers working primarily from short, simple sources were neither as interesting nor as impressive as the ones that used complex, extensive sources. The reasons are obvious: short sources can provide only very basic data. Writers relying on short sources do not have much to say. What they write tends to be simplistic and awkward.

Extensive sources, in contrast, explore the complexities of and debates about their topic. Such sources give writers—and the writers' audience—things to think about and talk about. They provide research *material*. In your own researched writing, look for extensive sources that explain the complexities and debates on the topic, not just ones that provide basic facts.

Then share your reading of these sources with your audience. Consider the following sample:

Length of Source Cited
DATA FROM **The Citation Project**

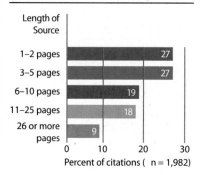

Percent of citations (n = 1,982)

First draft

Student's voice	Every time you go to the doctor, you should be aware of the risks of unnecessary medical testing. A doctor from San Francisco says, "[M]ost experts agree that overuse needs to be curbed. If it isn't, we could face a future public health problem of rising cancer rates, thanks to our medical overzealousness" (Parikh).
Signal phrase	
Quotation	
Parenthetical note	

The writer offers a quotation that supports her argument, and she has cited the quotation correctly. She has also provided some information about the writer of the source. However, because this quotation stands alone, readers of this student's paper may think that the source made this statement as a simple directive: *overuse of CT scans should stop.* In fact, the source offered a detailed review of the reasons for overusing CT scans, as well as a thoughtful set of recommendations.

Such information deserves to be represented; readers deserve to know the whole picture that the source offers. Consider how much more interesting, informative, and persuasive the passage becomes when it acknowledges the source's argument:

Revised draft

Every time you go to the doctor, you should be aware of the risks of unnecessary medical testing. A doctor from San Francisco says that CT scans are a dangerously overused test, putting children in particular at risk for cancer. "[M]ost experts agree that overuse needs to be curbed. If it isn't, we could face a future public health problem of rising cancer rates, thanks to our medical overzealousness." Dr. Parikh notes, though, that the test is quick and easy. Moreover, television medical shows give people a general awareness of tests like the CT scan, and thus patients may demand it even when it isn't medically necessary. Doctors, too, have a reason for overusing the test: it is financially profitable. In addition to recommending that the test be administered less often, Parikh advocates adjusting the radiation dose when the CT scan is administered to children.	Student's voice — Signal phrase — Summary that clarifies the argument of the source — Quotation — Signal phrase — Summary of the source's complex treatment of the topic — Signal phrase

Paying attention to the complexity of the argument in the source and incorporating that complexity into your paper increases the sophistication of your own writing. It can also save you from misrepresenting the source; notice that in the first draft above, it sounds as if the doctor quoted is talking about all medical testing, when in fact Parikh is talking about a specific test, the CT scan.

Source: Parikh, Rahul. "How TV Illustrates a Disturbing Medical Trend." *Salon.com* 18 Apr. 2011. Web. 18 Apr. 2011.

15 Drafting Your Project

Before producing a new line of clothing or an automobile, designers sketch the product, drafting and arranging the shapes before dressing them in colors and textures. Writers, too, begin with a draft: They sketch their ideas in words and arrange them in topics, sentences, and paragraphs. Both artists and writers sometimes erase initial ideas, reconceive preliminary thoughts, and revise early efforts. That first sketch is an important step forward to a satisfying finished work.

15a Preparing to Draft

When it is time to draft, setting aside some time and finding a place where you can concentrate are essential. Even in the best circumstances, you may encounter writer's block, but by using the appropriate techniques, you will be able to get past it.

Getting ready

Ideally, reserve a substantial block of time for writing your first draft. How you define *substantial* depends on how long or complex your essay will be: An hour or two might be enough for a first draft of a three- to five-page essay; a longer text will probably require more time. If you are unable to set aside a large block of time, work in smaller segments over several days. Do not delay starting just because you can cobble together only a half hour at a time.

Next, consider what place is best for you. For some this means a study carrel in the library; for others, it is a table for one at a noisy street-side café. Whatever your preference, focus on the task at hand by turning off your cell phone and exiting from instant messenger, email, and your internet browser. It is a common misconception that people can multitask effectively.

Starting to write

Gene Fowler, a newspaper columnist, novelist, and screenwriter, once said that "[w]riting is easy: All you do is sit staring at a blank sheet of paper until drops of blood form on your forehead." Fortunately, there are techniques to help you avoid writing trauma. After reviewing your predrafting and revising materials, try one of the following drafting methods (or a combination of them):

- **Method 1: Fill in your outline.** Save your outline file with a new name. Then, use your outline as scaffolding, filling it in and fleshing it out until it becomes a first draft.

- **Method 2: Start anywhere.** Instead of beginning at the beginning, start writing whatever parts of the essay you feel confident about—an engaging example or a descriptive passage in support of one of your ideas, even just a sentence or phrase that captures a relevant thought. Continue writing out-of-order thoughts until you can begin stitching them together, filling in the gaps.

- **Method 3: Write straight from your brain.** Place your thesis statement at the top of a sheet of paper or the beginning of a computer file, and then just start writing. This may produce a very brief, general first draft, but it will be one that speaks your message. You can supplement later.

Make It **Your Own**

For a paper that you are working on, produce a first draft using one of the methods of drafting described on p. 171.

If you still get stuck, try one of these methods for alleviating writer's block:

More about ▶▶▶
Idea-generating
techniques, 23–33

- **Write something else.** Write a journal or blog entry about the problems you are having with the paper. Write about another topic you know well or care passionately about. Just the act of writing can help unblock you.

- **Write a message to yourself.** For some writers, the idea of an audience can be inhibiting, so try writing a note to yourself: "What I want to say is . . . ," and then finish the sentence.

- **Talk.** Tell a tutor, instructor, classmate, or family member what your paper will be about. Get your listener to take notes as you talk. Then use those notes as a starting point for writing.

- **Use technology.** Instead of talking with someone face-to-face, use Web communication tools such as email, *Twitter*, or *Facebook*. Explain your topic to jump-start your writing.

- **Return to research.** Perhaps you are stuck because you do not yet know enough to continue writing. If this is the case, do some more research, but be alert for when you *do* know enough to return to writing.

➤ Tech

Protecting Your Work

Because terrible things often happen to computer files, it is important to take these steps:

- **Save early and often.** Adjust your computer to save your file automatically every five or ten minutes. Also, each time you pause, manually save your file.

- **Save your file in multiple locations.** After each writing session, burn your file to a CD or DVD; save it on a USB flash drive, your school's network drive, or a web-based

backup service; or send a copy to your email account.

- **Do not delete.** When you reject something you have written, do not delete it. Instead, cut and paste it to a file for discards. You may want to restore something later that you cut.

- **Use your word processor's Undo function.** If you delete a paragraph by mistake or make a change you do not like, use "Undo" to go back a step.

- **Change your situation.** Switch the medium—from pencil and paper to word processing, or vice versa—or change the setting in which you are writing by shutting off (or turning on) some background music or by moving from a study carrel to a table in the cafeteria.

Whatever method of drafting you choose, do not worry about the language you use to present your ideas. You can smooth out the kinks later, when you revise, edit, and proofread.

More about ▶▶▶
Revising, editing, and proofreading, 203–15

15b Developing a Title

A project title might at first seem like an afterthought or unimportant because it is so small. For some writers, though, developing a good title can help focus the drafting and remind them of their thesis.

To develop a draft title, return to your thesis and the key terms you used to search for information. Using your list of the terms, develop multiple possible titles, playing with word combinations until you have something you believe suggests your main point and might catch a reader's attention. Remember that titles are the first clue readers have about your text and may encourage them to read on—or may confuse or turn them off. These approaches can help you write a good title:

- Ask a question to which your reader will want to learn the answer. For example, Erin Buksbaum titled her first draft "Is Social Networking a Serious Danger?"

- Create a two-part title divided by a semicolon or other punctuation. You might make half the title funny or playful and the other half more serious and directly expressive of your main point. For example, Lydia Nichols titled her project "Holy Underground Comics, Batman! Moving Away from the Mainstream." Heather DeGroot used this structure to create a serious two-part title: "The Power of Wardrobe: Male Stereotype Influences."

- Create a descriptive one-part title. For example, an alternate title for Heather DeGroot's project might be "Wardrobe's Influence on Male Stereotypes."

- Avoid uninspiring or overly general titles such as "Essay 1" or "Global Warming."

15c Drafting the Introduction

Introductory paragraphs shape readers' attitudes toward the rest of the text. Yet writers often have a hard time producing these paragraphs. Many find it helpful to draft the body of the essay before tackling the introduction.

More about ▶▶▶
Writing and refining
your thesis, 150–56

Whether you write the introduction first or last, keep in mind that it should prepare readers for what follows. In many cases, this means including the thesis. A common placement for the thesis statement is at the end of the introduction—this is the *funnel* introduction. For a traditional funnel introduction, move from broad issues related to your topic toward your main claim. Be cautious you do not begin too broadly, however, as this can lead to a stale "in the world today" introduction.

General issues

Specific thesis

Another possibility is to hold the thesis until the end of the essay so that the essay leads readers inductively from evidence to main claim. Regardless of whether you include your thesis in the introduction, hold it until your conclusion, or (in genres such as the memoir or profile) merely imply your main idea; your introduction should convey your stance, establish your purpose, and engage readers.

One or more of the following strategies can help you write an effective introduction:

- Begin with a vivid quotation, a compelling question, or some interesting data.

- Start with an engaging—and relevant—anecdote.

- Offer a surprising but apt definition of a key term.

- Provide needed (not obvious) background information.

- State a commonly held belief and then challenge it.

- Explain what interesting, conflicting, difficult, or misunderstood territory the document will explore.

In the introductory paragraph that follows, the writer uses several effective strategies: She begins with a question that challenges the audience to examine some common assumptions about the topic. Then she provides background information that her readers may lack. She concludes with a thesis statement that explains why reading her text should be important to the audience.

Opening question

Many people enjoy sitting down to a nice seafood dinner, but how many of those people actually stop to think about where the fish on their plate came from? With many species of wild fish disappearing because of overfishing, increasingly the answer will be a fish farm. But while fish farming can help to supply the demand, it can threaten the environment and cause problems with wild fish. It can also threaten the health of consumers by increasing the risk of disease and increasing the quantity of antibiotics consumed. In fact, as a careful and conscientious consumer, you would do well to learn the risks involved in buying and eating farm-raised fish before one winds up on your dinner plate.

> Answer that provides background information

> Thesis

> —Adrianne Anderson, Texas Christian University, "Aquaculture: Booming Business Fraught with Controversy"

Although brief texts may require only a one-paragraph introduction, longer texts often need more than one paragraph. While there are no hard-and-fast rules about the length of an introduction, it should be in proportion to the text's length.

15d Developing Paragraphs

As you draft, you will develop paragraphs that are structured like mini-essays. While at first you should concentrate on getting ideas written, ultimately each paragraph should be an organic part of the whole text. A paragraph will be effective when it is all of the following:

- **Relevant.** It should support the main idea of the paper (your *thesis*) and, when possible, remind readers of what that thesis is.

- **Unified.** It should have a clear point (*topic*) and include only material that explains that point.

- **Coherent.** It should include connections that make relationships among sentences clear to readers.

- **Well developed.** It should supply the information your readers need to be persuaded of your point.

- **Connected.** It should begin and end in a way that shows readers its relationship to the paragraphs that precede and follow it.

- **Interesting.** It should make your readers want to read on.

> *More about* ▶▶▶
> Supporting your
> claims, 182–87

15e Connecting Paragraphs

Coherent paragraphs provide guideposts that point readers from one sentence to the next. These *transitional words and phrases* alert readers to the significance of what you are saying and point up the relationships among your ideas. Make sure you choose the appropriate transition for the job (a number of transitions appear in the Quick Reference box below), and vary your selection to avoid ineffective repetition. In addition, you can connect paragraphs by repeating words and phrases strategically, creating parallel sentence structures, and carefully using pronouns and synonyms to refer back to words and ideas.

15f Drafting the Conclusion

Specifics

Broader implications

The shape of the conclusion is often what might be called an *inverted funnel:* starting out specific and then broadening out.

The purpose of the conclusion is to provide readers with a sense of closure and also a sense that reading the text was worthwhile. To achieve closure and convey the importance of the research, try one or more of these strategies:

- Refer to the anecdote, question, or quotation with which you began.
- Summarize your findings (in long or technical projects).
- Discuss how your thinking has changed.

Quick **Reference** → **Sample Transitional Expressions**

To add to an idea: again, also, and then, besides, further, furthermore, in addition, incidentally, likewise, moreover, next, still, too

To compare: alike, in the same way, like, likewise, resembling, similarly

To concede: certainly, granted, of course

To conclude: finally, in brief, in conclusion, in other words, in short, in sum, in summary, that is, to summarize

To contrast: after all, although, and yet, but, conversely, despite, difference, dissimilar, even so, even though, granted, however, in contrast, in spite of, instead, nevertheless, nonetheless, notwithstanding, on the contrary, on the other hand, otherwise, regardless, still, though, unlike, while this may be true, yet

To emphasize: after all, certainly, clearly, even, indeed, in fact, in other words, in truth, it is true, moreover, of course, undoubtedly

To indicate cause or effect: accordingly, as a result, because, consequently, hence, since, then, therefore, thus

To offer an example: as an example, for example, for instance, in other words, namely, that is, thus, to exemplify, to illustrate, specifically

- Suggest a possible solution (or solutions) to the problems raised in the text.
- Indicate additional research that needs to be conducted.
- Suggest what the reader can do.
- Leave readers with a vivid image, quotation, or anecdote.

The concluding paragraph that follows provides an example of an effective introduction.

> The farmers of nineteenth-century America could afford to do here what they had not dared to do in the Old World: hope. This hope—for greater economic security, for more opportunity for themselves, their children, and their grandchildren—is the optimism and idealism that has carried our country forward and that, indeed, still carries us forward. Although the American dream has evolved across the centuries, it survives today and is a cornerstone of American philosophy. It is what underlies our Constitution and our laws, and it is a testimony to the vision of the farmers who founded this nation.

Makes reader feel time reading was well spent by showing importance of American dream

Restates thesis (American dream = hope for greater security, opportunity)

Achieves closure by referring to introduction with mention of American dream

> —Leonard Lin, University of Southern California, "The Middle Class Farmers and the American Philosophy"

Quick **Reference** ➜ **Five Don'ts for Conclusions**

1. **Do not offer additional support for your thesis in your conclusion.** Such conclusions undermine the feeling of closure and leave readers wanting and expecting more.
2. **Do not end with a generality or a cliché.** Almost nothing will undermine the readers' sense that they have spent their time well than ending with something trite.
3. **Do not apologize for the shortcomings of your paper.** Such an ending will leave readers feeling they have wasted their time. If your paper is truly bad, you should have revised your draft, not passed it on to readers; if it is not, you have nothing to apologize for.

4. **Do not repeat your introduction.** It may be useful to recur to the anecdote or statistics with which you began, but a mere rehash of your introduction or word-for-word repetition of your thesis will not work. Your readers will not want to read the same text a second time.
5. **Do not announce what your essay has done or shown ("In my paper, I have shown . . .").** In a long or complicated text, a summary can be useful to readers, but your readers will be reminded of what your text has done when they read your summary; there is no need to announce it.

15g Drafting Responsibly

Because writing is so challenging and because so much is often riding on the success of writing projects, it is easy for other objectives (getting an A, impressing the boss, looking clever to friends, finishing the task quickly) to get in the way of fulfilling your responsibilities as a writer. At the drafting stage, ask yourself the following questions to make sure you have worked responsibly so far:

> **More about ▶▶▶**
> Introducing counter-
> evidence, 153,
> 184–86
> Citing your sources
> and avoiding pla-
> giarism, 127–38

- Have I done enough research to answer my question without making too many assumptions?

- Have I acknowledged any counterevidence in my draft?

- Have I documented any sources I have referred to in my draft, whether quoted, paraphrased, summarized, or reproduced (images and other media)?

- Have I worked to fully understand each source before using it?

Sample Student Essay: First Draft

> **▶▶▶Additional**
> samples from Erin
> Buksbaum:
> Freewriting, 27–28
> Revised thesis,
> 153–54
> Outlines, 162–64

> **More about ▶▶▶**
> Integrating visuals,
> 186–87

The first draft of Erin Buksbaum's essay on social networking sites follows. Note that in this draft Buksbaum does not worry about polished writing or even perfect grammar and spelling. She knows she can make necessary alterations as she revises. For now, her focus is on getting her ideas down in a logical order and on supporting her thesis with evidence. Note, too, that Buksbaum includes a place for a screen capture from a social networking site. Although she has not selected the particular capture she will use, she wisely builds a place for this major element into her earliest draft.

> Title that
> reflects the
> research
> question

> Funnel
> introduction:
> moves from
> general to
> specific

Is Social Networking a Serious Danger?

The internet has changed the way people communicate and interact with each other forever. Social networking sites let users create a personalized web profile, meet new people with common interests, organize clubs, plan gatherings, promote bands or movies—the possibilities for communication are nearly endless. But there are risks involved. The immediate access of these sites is easily exploited. (Remember the teenage girl who killed herself because of a mean message from a boy she liked—really from a friend's mom?) While social networking sites allow for exciting new forms of communication, they also open new avenues for privacy violations and other social mischief.

Draft thesis

The center of the social networking experience is the user's profile. The user's profile can be thought of as personalized web pages. Profiles usually include basic personal information such as a user's name, age, current school, and Zodiac sign. They also usually include lists of the user's "favorites": favorite books, songs, bands, and movies. More sophisticated users also post animations, videos, and Flash movies on their profiles. People really push the technical envelope in their profiles, and it's very impressive.

Paragraph topic: profiles

[INSERT SCREENCAPTURE HERE.]

While it sounds like harmless fun, what people post in their profiles can be extremely dangerous. User profiles allow any other member of the social network to learn personal details of that user. In other words: If you have a profile, anyone else in the network can see what you are like. That's fine for users who are experienced using the internet, and know to keep certain key details hidden. However, many children post details that make it easy for others to track them down offline. Considering how open a site like MySpace.com is, this is a serious problem.

Paragraph topic: profile dangers

Photographs are another key feature of social networking sites. Photographs are an extremely popular element in most user profiles. The internet is a visual medium, after all. Hence, most profiles include many, many pictures. Usually, users post photographs of themselves,

Paragraph topic: photographs

Paragraph
focus: user
interaction

their friends, or their pets. But the prevalence of photographs creates its own set of problems. Children may see images that are not appropriate for their age group. Also, photographs can be easily downloaded and hence easily misused. When you post your face on the internet, you lose all control over what happens to it.

Perhaps the most powerful part of social networking sites, though, is their capacity for user interaction. Using a "Search" feature, you can find a user who likes the same band, or who lives in the same area, or who is the same age. Then you can send them a message or post a note on their profile. It's that easy. But while most users are just looking for new friends, some might have darker purposes. Criminals like stalkers and pedophiles have been known to use social networking sites to track down targets.

Conclusion
that features
general
warning and
actions for
the reader to
take

There is no way to reverse the internet revolution, even if we wanted to. MySpace, Facebook, and other such sites are here to stay. So, users need to be careful. A good rule of thumb is to never post something online you wouldn't want to appear in a major newspaper. While you might not realize it, the internet offers that level of access to the outside world. While social networking sites offer exciting new paths of communication between people the world over, these new rewards also come with new risks.

> **More about** ▶▶▶
Developing topics
  collaboratively, 31
Using wikis to take
  notes, 116–17
Collaboration and
  source citation,
  136–38
Outlining collabora-
  tively, 166

15h Drafting Collaboratively

Drafting collaboratively can be a difficult process to manage, but it can also be rewarding and creative. The following principles will help keep the experience a positive one:

- If possible, limit group size to three or four participants. Smaller groups can reach the "critical mass" needed for creativity without as many management difficulties (such as finding a time to meet) that larger groups face.

- Each member of the group should have an opportunity to contribute to the draft. Make an effort to restrain overbearing members and to encourage reluctant participants.

- Treat everyone's writing (and the writers themselves) respectfully. Some group members may be more skilled than others, but insightful ideas can be coaxed from initially unimpressive material.

More about ▶▶▶
Revising and editing with others, 211–14

- Make sure everyone has a copy of the latest draft, the current schedule, and a to-do list following each session.

A Final Thought

All writers, even professionals, write first drafts that do not quite come together. Recognizing this fact and continuing to write in spite of a first draft's shortcomings can prepare you to identify what is valuable when you revise and edit.

16 Entering Conversations and Supporting Your Claims

People often speak of "proving" an argument they are making: "I need evidence to prove my thesis." You may already have written an argument to prove a belief you held. Most of the research assignments you receive in college, however, have a different objective: They are intended to help you *explore a topic* and then, based on what you learn, *make a claim*. In this model of forming an argument, you do not know what your claim is until you have studied the evidence.

Writers of the first type of argument look for and present only evidence that supports their claim. This model is familiar in advertising, politics, and propaganda. Writers of the second type of argument include both evidence and counterevidence. Exploring their topics means including all perspectives and then explaining why, despite mixed evidence, their claim is believable. In this model, writers are not solely persuaders but are also participants in a conversation. They explore with others—with their sources and their audience—the issues and possible answers surrounding their topics.

More about ▶▶▶
Exploring your topic, 23–31
Evidence, 39–40
Counterevidence, 153, 184–86

16a Explaining and Supporting Your Ideas: Reasons and Evidence

If popes or presidents say something is true, many people believe them, even if they offer no explanation, because people trust these speakers. Popes and presidents (and many others as well) carry great authority among large groups of people.

Your authority is probably much more limited. Your friends, family, and co-workers may respect you and consider you very knowledgeable, but even they may want some explanation for what you claim is true. Even presidents and popes provide evidence for their claims when they want to be especially persuasive.

Such explanations are at the heart of researched arguments. It is not enough to say that something is true; you must also explain its truth to your readers by offering *reasons* and *evidence*.

Offering reasons for your thesis

Why do you believe your thesis and the other claims you make in your researched writing? You may not be able to answer this question easily; it may require reflection. Write down your reasons as you think of them. Make as long a list as possible, even if you think some of your answers are trivial. "I believe we should invest more money in diabetes research because my uncle has been diagnosed with the disease" may not be very persuasive to others, but it is to you. You may be able to use it as an illustration or anecdote in your paper.

More about ▶▶▶
Thesis, 150–56

Providing evidence to support your claims

To support your thesis, you will also need to supply evidence that will make your claims persuasive to others. Here are some of the most common types of evidence:

- Facts
- Statistics
- Expert testimony
- Observations

- Examples
- Case studies
- Anecdotes
- Textual passages

More about ▶▶▶
Analyzing the rhe-
torical situation, 48

▶▶▶ Samples from
Erin Buksbaum:
Freewriting, 27–28
Revised thesis,
153–54
Outlines, 162–64
First draft, 178–80

More about ▶▶▶
Writing in the
social, natural, and
physical sciences,
238–40
Writing in the hu-
manities, 234–37

Tailor the type of evidence you offer to the reasons you supply, as well as to the rhetorical situation (purpose, audience, context, and genre) of the text you are writing. The outline for Erin Buksbaum's essay in chapter 14, for example, indicates that while social networking sites have a lot of enjoyable components, they also carry with them some significant risks for users. By highlighting the issue of risk, Buksbaum takes into consideration the possibility that her audience might also use *Facebook* and be unaware of the dangers.

In support of her claim, Buksbaum includes a discussion of user profiles, the central component of social networking sites like *MySpace,* and how these profiles open the door for privacy violations. She first provides facts about what profiles commonly reveal, later noting that criminals have often used social networking sites to identify potential victims. As evidence, she cites the existence of *MyCrimeSpace. com,* a website dedicated to documenting crimes that involve social networking sites.

Content and genre matter. In a laboratory report for a science class, you are likely to use evidence from your own observations, as well as the observations others have made in their research. In a paper for an economics course, you will probably use statistics, as well as expert testimony, examples, and case studies to show relationships among economic forces.

Incorporating the counterevidence to your claims

More about ▶▶▶
Counterevidence,
153, 184–86

Advertising almost always suppresses counterevidence. Shampoo ads, for example, tell you the benefits of the product but not its shortcomings. The shampoo may eliminate dandruff, but it may also make your hair dry and brittle. In recent years, government regulations and public pressure have brought counterevidence into ads for potentially dangerous products such as tobacco and alcohol.

Writing Responsibly   Made-up "Evidence"

In May 2005, a stem cell expert resigned his position at Seoul National University following revelations by the journal *Nature* that his laboratory had falsified data. Hwang Woo Suk's case is not an isolated one: In 2002, for example, Bell Laboratories fired star researcher Jan Hendrik Schon for falsifying data. Commentators have noted that competition was a factor in these cases: The desire for acclaim and advancement had become more important than the desire for truth.

The highly competitive academic environment may tempt you, too, to make up "facts" to support a thesis in a paper. It is easy to alter data, invent statistics or quotations, or manipulate an image so that it "shows" what you want it to. Resist the temptation: the short-term benefits are not worth it. Not only are you likely to get caught—fabricated evidence often *sounds* fake—but you would also be sacrificing the opportunity to learn something about your topic and about the writing process and potentially influencing others through misinformation.

On the other hand, the purpose of most academic writing is not to sell products but to explore and explain ideas. Demonstrating that you have considered all sides of a thorny problem and have come to a reasonable resolution of it requires that you include counterevidence. For example, Amy Ehret offers this paragraph of counterevidence, assessing the possible shortcomings of her research:

> Limitations of this study include the small sample size ($n = 54$) with the majority of participants being white female college students. The study is not an equal representation of the university's population or the general population. There are very few native English speaking minorities present in the study. Because the sample is quite young (college students), it is difficult to generalize these findings with those from an older and more varied sample. Results containing older participants may be dramatically different from those of this study. In general, students may have more experience and access to computers and internet-related activities.
>
> —Amy Ehret, Illinois State University, "Navigational Layout and User Preferences in Internet Privacy Notice Design"

Do not worry that your counterevidence will overwhelm your evidence. You can deal with that concern in two ways. First, be sure that you not only offer both evidence and counterevidence but also explain why you believe the evidence to be more persuasive than the counterevidence. You need not give counterevidence the same amount of space as evidence within the project.

More about ▶▶▶
Organizing your
project, 157–69

Second, think about the organization of your material. If you place counterevidence at the end of your project, that is what your audience will have in mind as they reflect on what you have written. Instead, you might place the counterevidence toward the beginning of the project. At the beginning, it follows your introduction, which identifies your topic and suggests the position you are taking on that topic (your thesis). Immediately after the introduction, acknowledge that there are other perspectives on this topic that the audience should take into account. Then explain the counterevidence. Finally, say that you nevertheless believe your thesis because . . .—and begin to present your evidence.

More about ▶▶▶
Designing your
project, 216–29

16b Using Visuals as Support

Visuals can offer crucial support in college research projects as examples, explanations of processes, or displays of factual or statistical data. Remember that in academic writing, all visuals must contribute to your argument, not merely ornament the text.

Quick Reference ➡ **Matching Visual Evidence to Claims**

- **Tables** are most effective at displaying large amounts of data that readers may want to examine in detail.
- **Pie charts** convey divisions in a single entity that add up to 100 percent.
- **Bar graphs** compare two or more variables.
- **Line graphs** show changes among variables over time.
- **Diagrams** help readers visualize something difficult to describe in words.
- **Maps** represent geographic locations and spatial data.
- **Drawings** can capture a setting, and they can portray your idea of possible scenarios.
- **Cartoons** can simplify a concept or can critique a person or situation.
- **Photographs** can offer concrete illustrations, provide readers with a reference point, or show change over time.

- **Screenshots** can offer illustrations of electronic resources such as websites and software.
- **Movie stills** can capture a moment for discussion and analysis, offer a concrete example, or, in a series, show a process.

If you are using multiple media to present your research, the types of illustrations you can use expand to include the following:

- **Animations** can bring your graphics to life.
- **Video clips** can illustrate a process, offer an example, or document a performance.
- **Sound files** can make musical notation come alive, provide an example in an analysis, or document a performance.

Information graphics, such as *tables, bar graphs, pie charts, line graphs, flowcharts, timelines,* and *maps,* convey complex data efficiently. Information and concepts that require long passages of text to explain can often be conveyed quickly through information graphics. Other types of visuals—such as *drawings, cartoons, photographs, screenshots,* and *movie stills*—capture and evoke emotion, image, and relationship. For instance, a project on body language and presidential speeches might benefit from photos illustrating the differences in body language between presidents delivering bad news and presidents offering strategic plans. Use the Quick Reference box on p. 186 to determine which kinds of visuals might enhance your project.

Writing ↑ Responsibly   Exploitative Images

When using images in your academic work, refrain from including images that may be seen as emotionally manipulative of the reader, as well as those that might be emotionally exploitative of those whom they depict. As you review the images you have selected, think about whether they respectfully depict their subjects and how those subjects might feel about the use of the images.

→ EXERCISE **16.1** Thinking about Visuals as Evidence

For your research project, gather or create at least two possible visuals. What kinds of evidence does each visual provide?

16c   Weaving It All Together like an Expert

When you have figured out your thesis, reasons, and evidence, you still have the challenge of weaving everything together. Evaluation, analysis, and synthesis are the tools you will need for that job.

Evaluating

Evaluation is your own assessment of a source—its credibility and relevance to your research. Evaluation involves identifying and judging the credibility of the author or authors, identifying and examining who published the source, and assessing how much of the source is pertinent to your research. Are you drawing only from a small portion of the source, or is the entire source relevant? It is all right to draw on sources in which only small passages are pertinent to your research. But you also want sources that centrally address what you are investigating; otherwise, your research becomes a collection of "sound bites"—tiny snippets—on your topic. Your readers, too, will want to know whether you (and your text) are in a substantial conversation

> **More about ▶▶▶**
> Evaluating sources,
> 20–22
> Evaluating information, 100–12

with a source or whether you are drawing on only a small portion of that source.

Analyzing

More about ▶▶▶
Analyzing sources,
20–22

Analysis is your dissection of a text into its component parts and interpretation of its meaning. Analyze your sources carefully, figuring out what they are saying, how they support their position, and whether their position is reasonable. Be alert for logical fallacies. Think, too, about how much a source is in conversation with other sources. Does the author seem well read on the topic?

Synthesizing ideas and information

More about ▶▶▶
Synthesizing
sources, 19–20

Synthesis is the integration of the ideas you have gleaned from sources with your own insights or with ideas from other sources. As you conduct research, you may notice that information in one source supports ideas in another source. You may also recognize areas of agreement (or disagreement) among sources and draw conclusions of your own about which sources are more persuasive, and why. This is synthesis, and it is the crucial step in moving from simply reciting other writers' ideas to writing a research project.

▶▶▶Sample student
research project:
"Holy Underground
Comics, Batman!"
by Lydia Nichols,
291–303

When Lydia Nichols wrote her research paper comparing conventional comics with underground comics, she found the Comic Book Code in one source, and examples of comics that adhered to the code or that suffered as a result of the code in others. In the paragraph below, she weaves together evidence from two sources with her own ideas to support her claim:

Nichols's claim

Signal phrase (identifies credentials)

Supporting evidence (paraphrase)

Underground artists not only push the envelope in terms of content—they also employ innovative and experimental visual devices, earning critical praise for breaking away from traditional comic layouts in favor of more experimental, cinematic perspectives. Artists such as Daniel Clowes have suggested that in some senses, comic art can be more evocative than film, especially in the use of nonlinear storytelling techniques (Hignite 18). *New York Times* columnist John Hodgman agrees: Discussing a moment of existential crisis in Kevin Huizenga's *Ganges #1,* he writes, "I have never seen any film . . . that gets at that frozen moment when we suddenly feel our mortality, when God is seen or denied, as effectively as a comic panel" ("Comics Chronicle"). Artist Chris Ware manipulates the borders and frames in his comics so extensively that even reading his works can feel like an art to be mastered (see Fig. 5). The demands his comics place on the reader create a powerful interactive dynamic between viewer and artist, one that is rarely found outside of a museum—and even more rarely in the pages of superhero titles.

Source citation

Signal phrase (identifies credentials)

Signal phrase (quote introduction and paraphrase)

Supporting evidence (quotation)

Supporting evidence (analysis of illustration)

Supporting evidence (illustration)

Fig. 5. Cover from Chris Ware's *Jimmy Corrigan: The Smartest Kid on Earth* (New York: Pantheon, 2000). Critically acclaimed *Jimmy Corrigan* comics experiment boldly with visual storytelling techniques, pushing the genre's limitations and making the reader work to achieve understanding.

Figure number

Figure title (including source information)

Figure caption

When synthesizing sources, ask yourself what your sources have in common and how they differ, using your thesis as a lens. Pay attention, too, to your reactions to your sources: Your prior reading and knowledge are an integral part of the equation. Synthesis is a process of connecting the dots: establishing connections among the sources you have consulted and placing them in conversation with each other and with your own thoughts.

16d Quoting, Paraphrasing, and Summarizing

More about ▶▶▶
Quoting, paraphrasing, or summarizing, 118–19

So your paper will not seem like a series of quotations strung together with a few words of your own, use quotations sparingly. Instead, put borrowed ideas into your own words by either paraphrasing or summarizing, and use quotations only when the language is particularly vivid or technical, when you want to borrow the authority of the writer, or when you are analyzing the language of the source.

Notice that in the sample paragraph on p. 189, Lydia Nichols uses a combination of quotation, paraphrase, and her own ideas. She *quotes* Hodgman because the passage is especially vivid. She *paraphrases* Hignite because she wants to borrow his argument and reasons and because it is easier to incorporate the information after she has put it into her own words. Had she wanted to briefly relate another source's argument, she would have used *summary*.

Integrating quotations

On the rare occasions when you quote directly from your sources, integrate the quote so it reads seamlessly. In some cases, material you want to quote may contain information that is irrelevant to your project. In the example on p. 189, Nichols omits a few words from the Hodgman quotation because they do not help her make her point. She uses ellipses to signal where the deletion occurred. As long as the meaning is not significantly changed, writers may do any of the following to fit the borrowed material more fluidly into their prose:

- Add or change words for clarity
- Change capitalization
- Change grammar
- Remove nonessential words
- Indicate by inserting "sic" that the original writer made a mistake

All changes, with the exception of replacing words with ellipses, should be placed in square brackets.

The example below shows a responsible alteration:

Quotation integrated into student text

Certain portions of the code were incredibly specific and controlling, such as the rule that forbade "[t]he letters of the word 'crime' on a comics magazine . . . [to] be appreciably greater in dimension than the other words contained in the title" (qtd. in "Good Shall Triumph over Evil").

Original quotation

"The letters of the word 'crime' on a comics magazine shall never be appreciably greater in dimension than the other words contained in the title."

▶▶▶ Sample student research project: "Holy Underground Comics, Batman!" by Lydia Nichols, 291–303

In this passage, Nichols changes a capital letter to a lowercase one, adds a word ("[to]"), and omits a couple of words ("shall never"), but the overall meaning of the passage remains the same.

Imagine, however, that Nichols had made these changes instead:

Quotation integrated into student text

Certain portions of the code allowed some flexibility. Consider, for example, the rule that allowed "[t]he letters of the word 'crime' on a comics magazine . . . [to] be appreciably greater in dimension than the other words contained in the title" (qtd. in "Good Shall Triumph over Evil").

Original quotation

"The letters of the word 'crime' on a comics magazine shall never be appreciably greater in dimension than the other words contained in the title."

Clearly this alteration of the quotation is *not* acceptable because it completely changes the meaning by leaving out the word "never."

⟶ EXERCISE 16.2 Integrating Quotations

Read the passage below. Then, in the following quotations, circle the numbers of those that alter the quotation fairly, and cross through the numbers of those that change the meaning of the quotation.

> Paul Revere was half French and half English, and always entirely American. He was second-generation American on one side, and old-stock American on the other, and cherished both beginnings. He was the product of a Puritan City on a Hill and a lusty, brawling Atlantic seaport, both in the same American town. He thought of himself as an

artisan and a gentleman without the slightest sense of contradiction—a new American attitude toward class.

—David Hackett Fischer, *Paul Revere's Ride*
(New York: Oxford, 1994, p. 5)

1. Because Revere was "half French and half English," he was troubled, asserts Fischer, by being born an American.
2. Fischer comments that Revere "was the product of [both] a Puritan City on a Hill and a lusty, brawling Atlantic seaport."
3. Although "[h]e thought of himself as an artisan," explains Fischer, Revere aspired to the status of gentleman.
4. Fischer points out that Revere embodied "a new American attitude toward class."
5. Being "second-generation American on one side" was not sufficient for most old-stock Americans to trust Revere's loyalty, suggests Fischer.

Make It **Your Own**

For a research paper you are drafting, show how you have integrated supporting evidence from sources by listing:

1. Three different sentences in which you identify source authors in a signal phrase
2. Three sentences in which you contextualize source information
3. Three sentences in which you incorporate quotations fairly by adding, deleting, or changing words

As you look at your results, think about whether you need to change or vary your methods for integrating information drawn from sources.

A Final Thought

This chapter began with the notion that research writers should be open to hearing what sources on their topics have to say—that the conversation is worth having. Through signaling, citing, quoting, synthesizing, and documenting, you can ethically depict this conversation and situate yourself within it. By relating traces of the conversation you have had with your sources, you can create a sophisticated, readable document that readers are likely to trust.

17 Citing Expertly

A citation names the source, the person or persons, with whom you are talking. Other cues you provide reveal the nature of that conversation. To cite well—to go beyond simply naming the source—is to make your conversation "transparent," to allow others to see how your ideas developed and how you are relating to others' thinking about the same issues. Your goal should be not only to credit your sources, but also to provide information about them, make obvious how and why you are using them, and explain how they relate to each other and to your thesis. This is expert *rhetorical citation*, citation that not only informs but also persuades. This chapter will help you to reveal your sources and your own stance. Also, throughout *Research Matters*, you will find two-page sections entitled Cite Like an Expert that provide you with additional information and guidance on citation.

193

17a Integrating Source Material

Your most basic task is to let your readers know whenever your text is drawing on sources. *Citation,* whether through parenthetical notes, signal phrases, or a combination of the two, accomplishes that task.

Parenthetical notes

You can cite your sources by using the author's last name and relevant page number(s) in a parenthetical note. Place that note at the end of the material from your source:

> "His name was Mark Zuckerberg, he was a sophomore, and although
>
> Eduardo had spent a fair amount of time at various Epsilon Pi events
>
> with him, along with at least one prepunch Phoenix event that Eduardo
>
> could remember, he still barely knew the kid" **(Mezrich 15)**.
>
> parenthetical note

When you are paraphrasing or summarizing material, you can also use parenthetical citation to acknowledge that your material comes from a source:

See also Cite Like an Expert: Reading and Summarizing the Entire Source in Part 1.

> Who wouldn't envy the genius and wealth of the person who invented
>
> *Facebook*? But who wouldn't pity a person who has no close friends?
>
> Mark Zuckerberg may have great wealth, but he has few confidantes
> parenthetical note
> (Denby 98).

Signal phrases

To incorporate borrowed material smoothly into your prose, introduce it with a signal phrase. A signal phrase couples an identification (usually the name) of the writer from whom you are borrowing with a verb that conveys your sense of the writer's intent. (A list of sample signal verbs appears in the Quick Reference box on p. 196.)

In choosing your signal verb, consider the attitude or position of the writer you are quoting. Is the writer making a claim? Is she or he agreeing or disagreeing, or even conceding a point? Or is the writer's position neutral? In most cases, you will probably choose a neutral verb, such as "writes," "says," or "comments."

Where possible, go beyond the neutral verbs to indicate the writer's attitude:

Oscar Wilde quipped, "A poet can survive everything but a misprint."

For the quotation above, "quipped" (which means "uttered a witty remark") is clearly appropriate, given the cleverness of the sentence quoted. "Snarled," on the other hand, would not be appropriate: Although Wilde's quip may have an edge to it, few would agree that the comment conveys the anger or viciousness associated with the verb "snarl." In your choice of verbs for your signal phrases, avoid ascribing intentions to a writer that cannot clearly be inferred from the text. To maintain your reader's interest, vary the signal words you use. You may also vary your placement of the signal phrase:

See also Cite Like an Expert: Choosing and Unpacking Complex Sources in Part 3.

E. M. Forster asked, "How do I know what I think until I see what I say?"

"How do I know what I think," E. M. Forster asked, "until I see what I say?"

"How do I know what I think until I see what I say?" E. M. Forster asked.

When the material from your source is a quotation, it is easy for readers to see where the source material begins; the quotation marks accomplish that task. When you are paraphrasing or summarizing the source, however, the beginning of the source material is not as clear. *Signal phrases* help solve the problem; you can place a signal phrase at the beginning of the source material and a parenthetical note at the end. In the following example, it is clear that the first sentence is the writer's statement of her own ideas, the second is a paraphrase from the Denby source, and the third is a quotation from Denby:

Who wouldn't envy the genius and wealth of the person who invented

Facebook? But who wouldn't pity a person who has no close friends?
    signal phrase
David Denby describes Mark Zuckerberg as having great wealth, but he

has few confidantes. "*The Social Network* is shrewdly perceptive about

such things as class, manners, ethics, and the emptying out of self that
       parenthetical note
accompanies a genius's absorption in his work" (98).

Notice that when the author's name is included in the signal phrase, you do not need to include it in the parenthetical reference.

Quick Reference ➡ Signal Verbs

Neutral signal verbs		Signal verbs that indicate:		
		Claim/Argument		**Concession**
analyzes	introduces	argues	finds	acknowledges
comments	notes	asserts	holds	admits
compares	observes	believes	maintains	concedes
concludes	records	charges	points out	grants
contrasts	remarks	claims	proposes	
describes	reports	confirms	recommends	
discusses	says	contends	suggests	
explains	shows	demonstrates		
focuses on	states			
illustrates	thinks			
indicates	writes	**Agreement**	**Disagreement**	
		agrees	complains	questions
		concurs	contradicts	refutes
		confirms	criticizes	rejects
		supports	denies	warns
			disagrees	

Writers in literature and the other humanities generally use present tense verbs in signal phrases; writers in the sciences use the present or past tense, depending on the context.

> **More about ▶▶▶**
> Conducting research
> in the disciplines,
> 234–40

Unpaginated source material

Many of the sources that writers use are accessed electronically and are unpaginated. When no page number is available, include only the author's last name in the parenthetical note:

> "Facebook, which surpassed MySpace in 2008 as the largest social-networking site, now has nearly 500 million members, or 22 percent of all Internet users, who spend more than 500 billion minutes a month on the site" (Rosen)

When you are quoting from the source, the quotation marks show where the source use begins and ends.

When you are paraphrasing or summarizing from an electronic source, however, you must work subtly with the material to show your readers where the source use begins and ends. Usually you can accomplish this by using the author's name in the parenthetical note, and describing the author in a signal phrase:

> signal phrase
> A writer for the *New York Times* explains how damaging *Facebook*
> parenthetical note
> material can be when one searches for a job (Rosen).

17b   Representing Your Voice

Just as important as signaling your sources is the need to signal your own voice. Your readers want to know clearly when it is *you* talking. In the following example it is not clear where the writer stops drawing from the Rosen source and begins to state his own ideas:

> signal phrase
> Rosen explains, "Seventy percent of U.S. recruiters report that they have ejected candidates because of information found online, like photos and discussion-board conversations and membership in controversial groups." With 500 million people on *Facebook,* the dangers are widespread. It is ironic that this phenomenon of personal data revealed to the world was begun by a person who himself had poor social skills.

See also Cite Like an Expert: Blending Voices In Your Text in Part 4.

The use of a signal phrase with a parenthetical note shows the boundaries of the information from Rosen:

> signal phrase
> A writer for the *New York Times* explains, "Seventy percent of
>
> U.S. recruiters report that they have rejected candidates because
>
> of information found online, like photos and discussion-board
>
> conversations and membership in controversial groups." With 500 million
>
> parenthetical note
> people on *Facebook,* the dangers are widespread (Rosen). It is ironic
>
> that this phenomenon of personal data revealed to the world was begun
>
> by a person who himself had poor social skills.

The final sentence in this passage is an interesting one, and the writer would want his readers to know that it is his own insight. That could be accomplished with phrases such as *I believe* or *in my opinion:*

A writer for the *New York Times* explains, "Seventy percent of U.S. recruiters report that they have rejected candidates because of information found online, like photos and discussion-board conversations and membership in controversial groups." With 500 million people on *Facebook,* the dangers are widespread (Rosen). I think it is ironic that this phenomenon of personal data revealed to the world was begun by a person who himself had poor social skills.

writer's own voice

There are more sophisticated ways to accomplish the task. You might, for example, refer to your research rather than yourself.

A writer for the *New York Times* explains, "Seventy percent of U.S. recruiters report that they have rejected candidates because of information found online, like photos and discussion-board conversations and membership in controversial groups." With 500 million people on *Facebook,* the dangers are widespread (Rosen). After reading all these sources about the founding of *Facebook* and the privacy issues raised by social networking sites, I find it ironic that this phenomenon of personal data revealed to the world was begun by a person who himself had poor social skills.

writer's own voice

Or you might speak in the first person plural, drawing your reader into the argument:

A writer for the *New York Times* explains, "Seventy percent of

U.S. recruiters report that they have rejected candidates because

of information found online, like photos and discussion-board

conversations and membership in controversial groups." With 500 million

writer's own voice

people on *Facebook,* the dangers are widespread (Rosen). We cannot

escape the irony that this phenomenon of personal data revealed to the

world was begun by a person who himself had poor social skills.

You could also comment upon the source or its information:

A writer for the *New York Times* explains, "Seventy percent of U.S.

recruiters report that they have rejected candidates because of

information found online, like photos and discussion-board conversations

and membership in controversial groups." With 500 million people on

writer's own voice

Facebook, the dangers are widespread (Rosen). Such information

suggests an irony: this phenomenon of personal data revealed to the

world was begun by a person who himself had poor social skills.

17c Providing Context

Readers appreciate knowing not only when you are talking and when your sources are, but also *who* your sources are and why you chose them. Rhetorical citations can provide this information smoothly: You can integrate into the citation information about why you chose the source, what kind of source it is, when the source was published, and what its argument was.

See also Cite Like an Expert: Explaining Your Choice of Sources in Part 2.

Explaining your choice of source

Unless your readers are familiar with your sources, they may have no reason to respect them and thus no reason to believe your claims. You can fix this problem with rhetorical citations that not only name your source but also indicate why the source is authoritative. In the following example, the writer establishes that the source is thorough in its treatment of the topic:

> evaluation of the source
> Gary Wolf provides a wide-ranging overview of our motivations for gathering and sharing data about ourselves, offering examples like this: "*Foursquare,* a geo-tracking application with about one million users, keeps a running tally of how many times players 'check in' at every locale, automatically building a detailed diary of movements and habits; many users publish these data widely."

The selection below acknowledges the shortcomings of the source and also asserts its usefulness:

> evaluation of the source
> Mezrich has made a fiction of Zuckerberg's rise, while claiming he is sticking as closely as possible to reality. Yet his fiction is worth reading; it shows how people perceive Harvard and its geniuses: "There was something playful about those eyes—but that was where any sense of natural emotion or readability ended. His narrow face was otherwise devoid of any expression at all. And his posture, his general aura—the way he seemed closed in on himself, even while engaged in a group dynamic, even here, in the safety of his own fraternity—was almost painfully awkward" (15).

Identifying the type of source

Is your source a newspaper column? Blog? Scholarly article? The differences among types of sources are important. If you want up-to-the-minute information, a newspaper or blog is likely to have it. If you want carefully researched, accurate information, a scholarly journal article is a good choice. Your readers want this information, too, and you can provide it in a rhetorical citation:

> information about source and author
>
> Writing in the *New York Times*, journalist Gary Wolf provides a wide-ranging overview of our motivations for gathering and sharing data about ourselves, offering examples like this: "*Foursquare,* a geo-tracking application with about one million users, keeps a running tally of how many times players 'check in' at every locale, automatically building a detailed diary of movements and habits; many users publish these data widely."

Identifying the date of publication

For many topics, the date of publication is important. The number of *Foursquare* users, for example, changes constantly. The date on which such data are published helps readers know how up-to-date the numbers are:

> information about source   signal phrase
>
> In a 2010 article in the *New York Times,* journalist Gary Wolf says, "*Foursquare,* a geo-tracking application with about one million users, keeps a running tally of how many times players 'check in' at every locale, automatically building a detailed diary of movements and habits; many users publish these data widely."

For the most successful, persuasive writing from sources, you need to read the sources, rather than just pulling sentences from them. That allows you not only to position the quotation, paraphrase, or summary in your text, but also to indicate how it functioned in your source text. Build brief source summary into rhetorical citation:

signal phrase

In a 2010 article in the *New York Times,* journalist Gary Wolf provides a summary of the source wide-ranging overview of our motivations for gathering and sharing data about ourselves, offering examples like this: "*Foursquare,* a geo-tracking application with about one million users, keeps a running tally of how many times players 'check in' at every locale, automatically building a detailed diary of movements and habits; many users publish these data widely."

Citation is not only ethical but rhetorical; it not only safeguards you from charges of plagiarism, but it also creates a sophisticated, readable document that readers are likely to trust.

 ## Make It **Your Own**

Using your draft in progress, either on paper with five different colored highlighting markers or on screen using the highlighter tool in your word processing program, highlight the different rhetorical moves you are using in different colors:

- Parenthetical notes that are the *only* acknowledgment of the source in the sentence (that is, any sentences that do not have signal phrases or other cues outside the parenthetical note)
- Signal phrases
- Phrases that you feel clearly signal a shift to your voice
- References to context: explaining your choice of source, the type of source, and the date of publication

When you have completed the highlighting, look back to see which types of signals you are missing or using least. In the sections where you seem to have the least transparency regarding sources, revise to include some of these conversational cues.

A Final Thought

"Show your work" is something you hear in math but rarely when you are writing, yet it might apply just as well here. Show your readers that you understand whole sources and that you are not just grabbing sound bites. Make it clear when you are talking and when you are using sources to make a point.

18

Revising, Editing, and Proofreading

As writers chisel meaning from their first words and sentences, they erase and redraw parts of the broad outline, carve out details to craft meaning, and refine their workmanship by sanding down rough edges. Only through revising, editing, and proofreading carefully can a writer transform a rough-hewn draft into a polished work.

REVISING GLOBALLY: LEARNING TO RE-SEE

Revising globally means looking at the big picture to address issues such as purpose, audience, context, genre, and ethical responsibilities. The first step toward assessing these aspects of your writing is to gain perspective by distancing yourself from your work.

Quick Reference → Revising Globally

	Focus (topic/thesis/purpose)	Audience
Introduction	Does my introduction identify my topic? Does it indicate my purpose and attitude toward my topic? Does it convey my main claim or research question?	Does my introduction provide needed background information? Will my readers find my introduction engaging or compelling?
Body Paragraphs	Is each body paragraph relevant to my thesis? Is the evidence in each paragraph relevant to the paragraph's topic?	Will my readers need more (or less) information? Will my readers be receptive, or, if not, how can I win them over? Is my language at the right level and tone?
Conclusion	Does my conclusion make my topic's importance clear? Does my thesis statement appear in my conclusion if it is *not* in the introduction?	Does my conclusion give readers something to think about or supply a necessary summary? Does my conclusion provide readers with a satisfying feeling of completion?

18a Gaining Perspective

Writers feel a sense of ownership toward the texts they compose. Ownership helps writers develop a commitment to the ideas they express. But during revision, too much ownership can keep a writer from making necessary changes. To gain objectivity in your writing, draw on techniques like these:

- **Allow time between drafts.** A few days or even a few hours between drafts can give you perspective.

- **Clear your mind.** If you cannot allow much time between completing your first draft and beginning to revise, do something to clear your mind—go for a run, play a quick game, or read something unrelated to your topic.

- **Learn from other readers.** Having others read and react to your draft will give you a sense of what your text is (and is not) communicating.

	Organization (cohesion/unity)	**Development (reasons/support)**
Introduction	Is my thesis statement or research question placed so that readers will recognize it? Does my introduction prepare readers for what follows?	Does my introduction hint at the reasons I will offer to support my thesis?
Body Paragraphs	Does my organizational pattern suit my reasons and evidence? Does each paragraph lead logically to the next? Have I provided logical transitions between paragraphs?	Are the reasons and evidence I supply relevant? Do I provide enough evidence? Is the evidence compelling? Do I credit my sources?
Conclusion	Is my conclusion logically organized? Do all the sentences fit together and support the topic sentence? Does my conclusion grow logically out of my introduction and body paragraphs?	Do I avoid introducing new supporting evidence in my conclusion?

- **Learn from helping other writers.** Most tutors and teachers will tell you that they learn as much from the coaching experience as do the people whom they coach.

- **Listen to your draft being read aloud.** Every time you or your reader stumbles or has to reread a passage, mark the spot. Then, figure out what caused the interruption, and revise accordingly.

- **Reverse-outline your draft.** Locate the main idea and key supporting points of each drafted paragraph and arrange them into an outline. If any sections seem unconnected to the thesis or to the sections before or after, reorganize.

- **Compare texts in the target context and genre.** When writing in an unfamiliar context or genre, reading professional texts can help you see what does and does not work in your own writing.

> *More about* ▶▶▶
> Organizing your
>   project, 157–169
> Genre, 38–40
> Context, 43–45

18b Revising Your Draft

Once you have gained some perspective, you are ready to start revising. Work through each paragraph considering issues of *focus, audience, organization,* and *development.* Be sure to read through to the end before making any changes, and remember to revise before editing. Avoid the temptation to look at your spelling, grammar, and mechanics before adding, cutting, reorganizing, and making other big-picture, or global, changes.

Focus: Is your thesis the consistent focus of your draft, and does your draft fulfill your purpose and assignment?

> **More about ▶▶▶**
> Drafting a thesis,
> 151–53
> Refining your thesis,
> 153–56

After rereading your text, make sure that the points you make support your thesis. Because writers often discover and develop their ideas as they draft, the draft thesis may not describe the project's real main idea (often, the true thesis appears in the conclusion of the first draft). This might mean you should adjust your reasons and evidence to your thesis. More frequently it means you should revise your thesis to match the reasons and evidence you offer in your draft.

When revising, make sure, too, that your draft fulfills the assignment. If you were asked to analyze a work of literature, check to see that you have not merely summarized it; if you were instructed to argue for or against corporal punishment in elementary school, be sure you have adopted a clear position and not merely repeated the arguments on both sides.

Audience: Is your draft appropriate for your readers?

> **More about**
> Audience, 40–41
> Reasons and evidence, 183–86

> **More about ▶▶▶**
> Drafting the introduction, 174–75
> Developing paragraphs, 175
> Transitioning within and between paragraphs, 175–76
> Drafting the conclusion, 176–77

Consider how your readers will react to your text. Will they be receptive to your topic and your approach to it? If not, how can you win them over?

Think about your *introduction.* Will it draw your readers into your text? Next, consider the *reasons* and *evidence* you supply in your body paragraphs. Are they likely to persuade your readers, given their background, interest level, and attitude toward your topic? Is the *language* appropriate to your audience? An academic or business audience will expect a more formal tone but will not need you to define specialized terms; a general audience, however, may be more engaged by a casual tone and may need specialized terms clearly defined. Finally, consider your *conclusion.* A conclusion should leave readers with a feeling of closure. For a long or complex text, readers may need you to summarize your findings in your concluding paragraphs. If you want your readers to take action, offer them a plan.

Organization: Is your draft coherent and unified?

Rereading your text may have alerted you to problems with organization. When revising, make sure that your essay is both unified and coherent. In a *unified* essay, all the paragraphs support the thesis, and all the details in each paragraph support the paragraph's main idea. When revising, be prepared to delete ideas, facts, and even whole paragraphs—no matter how much you like them—if they do not support your thesis.

> **More about ▶▶▶**
> Unity and coherence, 165–67
> Transitions, 175–76

In a *coherent* essay, the relationship among the paragraphs is clear and logical. A text may lack coherence because the writer has not included transitional words and phrases that signal the relationships among ideas. Other texts lack coherence because the writer has omitted a step in the argument. Be sure to clarify the relationships among your paragraphs by adding or changing transitions, by tightening the logic of your argument, or both.

Development: Did you explore and support your ideas fully?

In rereading your text, you may have had concerns about the reasons or evidence you offered in support of your thesis. Perhaps you noticed that one of your reasons was weak or irrelevant, that you did not offer enough reasons, that the evidence you supplied was overly general, or that you just did not supply enough evidence. If you need more or better reasons or more relevant, more specific evidence, or just more evidence, go back to the idea-generating stage or return to the library to do additional research.

> **More about ▶▶▶**
> Relevance, 101
> Generating ideas, 23–30
> Developing paragraphs, 175
> Finding information, 60–75, 76–87

You may find it possible to revise for focus, audience, organization, and development simultaneously. Most writers, though, focus on only one issue at a time.

18c Reconsidering Your Title

Once you have revised your draft globally, revisit your title. If your thesis has changed, you will probably need to change your title. In most college projects, your title should accurately reflect not only the

> **More about ▶▶▶**
> Developing a title, 173

topic, but also your approach to the topic and possibly your main claim:

- The Power of Wardrobe: An Analysis of Male Stereotype Influences
- Transcending Stereotypes in Hurston's *Their Eyes Were Watching God*
- Holy Underground Comics, Batman! Moving Away from the Mainstream
- My View from the Sidelines: A Close Reading of Gary Snyder's "Front Lines"

Here are additional tests of a title's effectiveness:

- Would you pick up this piece and read it based on its title?
- Can someone else anticipate what you will argue by reading the title? The closer the reader can come to identifying your argument based on your title, the more effective the title. Also, will readers find the title interesting?

↑ Make It **Your Own**

Revise a current draft or past writing assignment considering the global issues outlined in the Quick Reference box on p. 204.

REVISING LOCALLY: EDITING WORDS AND SENTENCES

Revise locally to make sure that your words and sentences convey your meaning and that together they create a persona (the writer's personality conveyed through tone and style) that is appropriate for your purpose, audience, context, and genre.

18d Choosing Your Words with Care

When revising, reconsider your word choices. Each word should reflect your intended meaning (the right *denotation*). In a project on graphic novels, for instance, "comics" would not be accurate and specific enough to discuss the subgenre of the graphic novel, and "picture books" would be inaccurate and misleading. Readers may sometimes guess your intent, but you cannot count on it, and you should not expect them to be charitable.

In addition to denotations, words carry emotional associations, or *connotations,* that color meaning and indicate the writer's attitude. Be particularly careful with words describing groups (religious, ethnic, gender, age, sexual orientation). For example, while it may be acceptable among your friends to refer to young women as "girls" or "ladies," many women find these terms condescending. It is also inappropriate to refer to experts by their first name. Use their full names instead: Martin Luther King, Jr., instead of "Martin." Because word connotations reveal biases, writers must choose their words carefully to avoid alienating their readers.

Finally, there are three basic formality levels: formal, mid-level, and informal. Formal style is that of professionals communicating in the highly specific language of their work. Mid-level formality signals professionalism without being inaccessible; some specialized jargon might be used but usually is defined. Finally, informal style is accessible to everyone. The appropriate level of formality depends on audience, context, and genre: Academic research essays typically aim for mid-level formality, while a public commentary might adopt a less formal tone, even employing slang when it helps to make a point. One of the questions to ask your instructor or to note in any models is whether it is appropriate to speak in the first ("I") or third ("this project," "the research") person.

18e Crafting Grammatically Correct, Varied, and Concise Sentences

When revising, reconsider the structure of your sentences:

1. Are they grammatically correct?
2. Are they varied in length and structure, and do they emphasize the most important information?
3. Are they as concise as they can be without sacrificing meaning or affecting style?

Writing grammatically correct sentences

In most contexts (academic and business, in particular), readers expect sentences to be formed according to the conventions of English grammar. Nongrammatical sentences may confuse, distract, or even annoy readers, so it is important to edit your prose to conform to standard written English. Handbooks and online resources can help you with editing for correctness.

Writing varied sentences

Once you are sure that your sentences are clear and correct, shape them to reflect your emphases. A good way to begin editing for style is to read your draft aloud—or better still, get a friend to read it to you. Listen to the rhythm of your sentences. Do they all sound alike? If so, your sentences probably use the same sentence structure, begin the same way, or are the same length.

To correct this problem, consider the information in your sentences. Combine related information in a single sentence, putting the most important information in the independent clause and additional information in the subordinate or dependent clause (created by using such connectors as *while, because, since, when,* and *although*). If the information is of equal weight, use compound sentence structure (connected by *and, or, nor, for, yet, but,* or *so*) to emphasize this balance. Where appropriate, use questions, commands, and exclamations for variety or emphasis.

Writing concise sentences

In addition to writing varied sentences, work to eliminate clutter. Try these strategies to revise for wordiness:

- Eliminate empty expressions (*to all intents and purposes*), intensifiers (*actually*), roundabout expressions (*due to the fact that*), and redundancies (*future plans*).

- Eliminate ineffective repetition (*Global warming threatens the world's ~~aquatic~~ fisheries.*).

- Favor the active voice (*The ~~destruction of~~ the town ~~by the tornado was complete~~.*). _{tornado completely destroyed}

Writing concisely for the Web is particularly important because most users prefer pages that are easy to scan.

You may be tempted to pad a paper that is not long enough, but doing so will make it harder for your audience to finish. Instead of adding "fluff," expand your piece by searching out additional relevant information and fully explaining the significance of your evidence.

Find Out **More . . . Revising Globally and Locally**

For a different view of the revision process, visit one or more of the following sites:

Attending to Grammar, Dartmouth College

Revision: Cultivating a Critical Eye, Dartmouth College

Steps for Revising Your Paper, The OWL at Purdue

Making a personalized editing checklist

Writers make a variety of mistakes, so a personalized editing checklist can come in handy. To create one, try the following:

1. Review the last five texts that you have written, looking for errors and less-than-effective choices.
2. List the issues you found (or that your instructor marked).
3. Reorganize the list, arranging items from most to least frequent mistake.

The next time you have to produce a document, use the top five items on the list to guide your local revision. Over time, you are likely to find that you make fewer of these errors and can focus on some of your less common mistakes.

↑ Make It **Your Own**

Create your own personalized editing checklist. Then, revise a writing project, focusing on your words and sentences.

REVISING WITH OTHERS

Writers can be touchy. We pour ourselves into our texts and worry that others might not understand or appreciate what we have written. Little wonder, then, that we often feel defensive when others read our work. Yet paradoxically, getting feedback from a real, live audience is one of the best ways to make sure readers will understand your writing, be convinced by your evidence, be persuaded by your conclusion, and form a high opinion of you as a responsible, authoritative writer.

More about ▶▶▶
Audience, 40–41

18f Receiving Feedback

Whether in a business or academic context, the roles of writer and respondent carry their own responsibilities.

Understanding the writer's role

When readers respond to your text, adopt a stance that is both engaged and receptive:

- **Talk, or write in the margins.** Explain orally—or, even better, in writing, directly on your text—what you are trying to accomplish in this project and what you would like help with.

- **Listen.** As others respond to your draft, listen instead of arguing, defending, or dismissing. If readers seem clueless or careless, figure out how you can revise the text so that even a clueless or careless reader can understand what you are trying to say.

- **Question.** If your readers are not addressing your concerns or are speaking in generalities, ask them to point to specific passages. Ask yourself what underlying issue they are trying to get at. Do not settle for a disappointing response.

- **Write.** Take notes as your readers talk. What they say may be vivid at the time, but you may be surprised by how quickly you forget the details.

- **Evaluate.** You are the person who must make the final decision about your writing. Be open to advice, but consider whether there may be a better way of solving the problem.

Understanding the reader's role

As a respondent, keep the following guidelines in mind:

- **Stay positive.** Tell the writer what is working well, along with what could be improved (Figure 18.1).

- **Talk to the writer.** Listen and respond to the writer's concerns, whether replying face-to-face or electronically.

- **Look at the big picture, but be specific.** Focus on what the writer is trying to achieve, and help her or him think

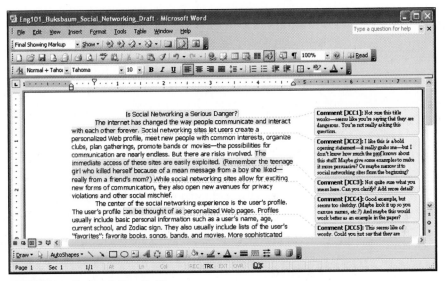

FIGURE 18.1 Electronic Peer Review
If you are reviewing a peer's work electronically, remember that there is a person on the receiving end of your comments. Keep them positive, helpful, and friendly, and link them to something specific in the text, as Buksbaum's respondent has done using the Comment feature.

about alternative strategies for achieving those ends. Back up general comments by pointing to specific passages in the text and explaining as best you can why they do or do not work for you.

- **Be a reader and a fellow writer—not a teacher, editor, or critic.** Your job is not to judge the text or rewrite it, but to provide the writer with one reader's responses to it and offer suggestions for improvements.

EXERCISE 18.1 Practicing Feedback

Read Erin Buksbaum's first draft in Chapter 15. Before class, write two paragraphs of response to Buksbaum, using the questions in the Quick Reference box on pp. 204–05. Then, as a whole class, discuss how to make the draft better.

Work **Together**

In groups of three or four, read through a group member's draft and use the questions in the Quick Reference box on pp. 204–05. Discuss how the writer could improve the draft globally. Save editing comments for a later stage.

Make It **Your Own**

Using comments you received from a respondent, revise your draft. After completing the process, write a paragraph discussing which suggestions made the biggest difference in your revision, and why. If you did not find the review process helpful, what might you and the reader have done to make it more productive?

PROOFREADING

When you revise and edit, you concentrate on your ideas and how you have expressed them. When you proofread, you pull back from the content to concentrate on finding and correcting errors.

To proofread effectively, print out your draft, and read the hard copy sentence by sentence from the bottom up. (This will keep you from focusing on the meaning.) Placing a ruler under each line as you read it will help you catch even more errors. Mark your corrections on the printout as you read, enter them one by one, and then check

Writing **Responsibly**   Beware Spelling Checkers!

While spell-check software can be very helpful in catching typos, it cannot distinguish between homonyms (*they're, there, their; it's, its*) or other frequently confused words (*lay, lie; affect, effect*). Spelling checkers may even lead you astray, suggesting words that are close to the word you mistyped (*defiant* for the misspelled *definate*) but worlds away from the word you intended (*definite*). Do not merely run your computer's spell-check software; also use a dictionary, and proofread your text carefully yourself. Only you know what you *meant* to say!

Quick **Reference** ➔ **A Checklist for Proofreading**

Spelling

- Spell-check your project using your word processing software.
- Read through the text carefully, looking for misused words.
- Check for words you frequently confuse or misspell.

Punctuation

- Check punctuation, especially use of the comma and the apostrophe.
- Double-check that all quotations have opening and closing quotation marks and that end punctuation is correctly placed (end-punctuation placement may depend on the style guide you are using).

- Check for punctuation errors you commonly make.

Documentation

- Check that you have included in-text citations where needed (for summaries, paraphrases, quotations, or ideas you have borrowed).
- Check in-text citations against the list of works cited, reference list, or bibliography to ensure that you have included entries for all citations.
- Double-check the format of all entries in the list of works cited/reference list/ bibliography against models from the style guide you are using.

More about ▶▶▶
Style guides:
MLA, 241–303
APA, 304–46
Chicago, 347–74
CSE, 375–91

to make sure that you have made each correction without introducing additional errors.

A Final Thought

Taking the time to revise, edit, and proofread as three separate activities will allow you to be responsible to your readers, the topic itself, the writers of your sources, and your own writer's persona. Readers will see the traces of this work. Like good craftsmanship in other fields, the best writing happens over time with continued attention to detail.

19 Designing and Presenting Your Project

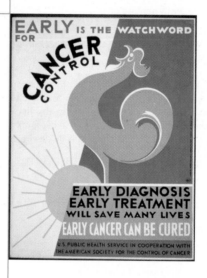

Posters like this one from 1938 rely on striking visual design for impact and meaning. To convey the idea that cancer treatment rests on early detection, its creators used strong color *contrast* to make the black text of "cancer control" stand out against its white background and the contrast of straight and curved text to add emphasis. They used *proximity* and the *repetition* of curves to pull the image of the rooster (the "early bird"), the idea of cancer control, and the positive symbol of the sun together. They used *alignment* to draw readers' eyes down the angled line, and *repetition* of the word "early" to drive home the main point of the poster. According to renowned graphic designer Robin Williams, these four principles—proximity, alignment, repetition, and contrast—are the pillars on which good design rests.

19a Understanding Design Principles: Proximity, Alignment, Repetition, and Contrast

Williams explains how the four principles of design work:

- **Proximity** (nearness or grouping) suggests that content is related; lack of proximity (distance) suggests that content is unrelated.

Find Out **More . . . Robin Williams on Design**

For more design advice, as well as before and after makeovers for newsletters, brochures, flyers, websites, and other media, see Williams's

Robin Williams Design Workshop, 2nd ed. (with John Tollett) (Berkeley, CA: Peachpit, 2006)

Two earlier books by Williams may also prove helpful:

The Non-Designer's Design Book, 3rd ed. (Berkeley: Peachpit, 2008)

The Non-Designer's Web Book, 3rd ed. (with John Tollett) (Berkeley: Peachpit, 2005)

- **Alignment,** the arrangement of objects in a straight line (vertical, horizontal, or diagonal), creates invisible lines of connection. Centered alignment feels more conservative than left or right alignment, even dull.

- **Repetition** of a design element lends unity (oneness).

- **Contrast** among design elements calls attention through difference, highlighting one element among others.

Effective design exemplifies the four principles, directing readers to the most important information and highlighting relationships among the elements on the page or screen. The web page in Figure 19.1 uses Williams's design principles to highlight important elements and link related content.

19b Planning Your Design Project

Before applying the four principles of design to your project, analyze and organize your information.

Purpose, audience, tone, context, and genre

Begin planning the design of your project by carefully considering purpose, audience, tone context, and genre:

- **Purpose.** How can you reflect your purpose (to inform, persuade, interpret, or analyze) in your design?

- **Audience.** Who is your audience, what kind of expectations do they bring with them, and what kind of relationship do you have (or want to have) with them? Will they be drawn to

More about ▶ ▶ ▶
Purpose, audience, tone, context, and genre, 37–45

FIGURE 19.1 A Web Page from the Boston Public Library's Website

a conservative academic design; a bolder, more artistic design; or something else entirely?

- **Tone.** What kind of attitude do you want your design to convey? Seriousness? Playfulness? Professionalism?

- **Context.** In what context (academic, business, public) or setting (over the internet, in person) will your project be "consumed," and how will this affect its design?

- **Genre.** What category does your project fall into: Is it a résumé or a business letter? an essay or a lab report? a newsletter, brochure, flyer, or website? What design conventions are associated with that genre?

Organization

More about ▶▶▶
Organizing, 157–69
Claims and evidence,
182–86

Determine how the pieces of your information relate to one another:

- What information is most (and least) important?

- Is the information evidence, or does it represent the main claim?

- How can the information be grouped?

19c   Applying the Principles of Design

Once you have analyzed and organized your information, you are ready to begin designing the project.

Creating an overall impression

Consider the overall impression you want to give the reader: Should the design be conservative or trendy? serious or playful? contemporary or classic? Your answers will affect your choice of colors, fonts, and visuals.

More about ▶▶▶
Storyboards and site maps, 164–65

Creating the layout

Next consider your project's overall *layout,* the visual arrangement of text and images. Use proximity, alignment, repetition, and contrast to make the relationships among the elements clear. Keep your layout simple, and use it to direct the reader's eye to the most important pieces of information. Create white space around elements you wish to emphasize. Making a sketch, or *mock-up,* of your layout (such as the one in Figure 19.2 for a flyer) can help you decide where to place elements on the page.

Designing the document

Now you are ready to create the actual document with a cohesive and attractive design.

Fonts Word processors give writers a wide range of fonts (or typefaces) to choose from. Selections range from **Arial** and `Courier` to Palatino and **Verdana**, with many choices in between. Serif fonts (fonts with a little tail on the ends of letters, such as `Courier` and Palatino) are easier to read when printed on paper, while sans serif fonts (fonts with no letter tails or tops, such as **Arial** and **Verdana**) are easier to read on-screen. Decorative fonts (such as **Jazz LET** and Marker Felt) should be used very sparingly for

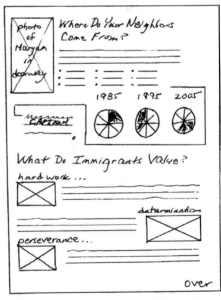

FIGURE 19.2 Sketch for Front of Flyer on Immigrants The persuasive purpose of this flyer is evident in its invitation to view immigrants as neighbors. The three subheadings in the second section emphasize that immigrants and citizens share the same values.

Serif fonts	Have curled or flat tops and bottoms of letters. Use for long sections of print text.	Times New Roman Book Antiqua
Sans serif fonts	Have no curls, tops, or bottoms to finish the letters. Use for online texts.	Helvetica Arial
Decorative fonts	Evoke a distinctive style. Use sparingly for emphasis.	BANK GOTHIC *Cracked*

dramatic effect. All-capital letters should almost never be used because they look like yelling on the page.

In addition to selecting a font family, you can choose from a variety of styles, including **boldface,** *italics,* underlining, or **color**. Use color or boldface for emphasis and contrast, but do so consistently and sparingly: The more these emphasis styles are used, the less effective they are. Since italics and underlining often have specific meanings, use them only when required.

Choose an easy-to-read font, especially in the *body* (the main text) of your project. A 10- or 12-point type is legible for most readers. Print out a page of text to check the size: 10-point type in one font may look larger than 12-point in another.

Choose fonts to add contrast or, through repetition, to group items. If you choose a serif font for most of your text, call attention to headings by using a sans serif font (or the serif font in bold, a different color, and/or a larger size) for them. In multimedia, Web, or other public writing, create more contrasts than for an academic essay.

Especially in headings, your fonts can contribute to the overall impression you are trying to create. A typeface such as 𝔒𝔩𝔡 𝔈𝔫𝔤𝔩𝔦𝔰𝔥, for example, might be appropriate in a poster announcing the first meeting of the Shakespeare Society. But for a document that is mainly text, legibility is more important than drama. More than a few words in a decorative font like *Edwardian Script* or **Haettenschweiler** will be hard to read.

White Space   White space is the portion of a page or screen with no text or images—it does not literally have to be white. The margins at the top, bottom, left, and right of this page provide white space, as does the extra space before a paragraph or around a heading or a visual. Extra white space above or around text or a visual can group elements into sections (Figure 19.3). Using the same amount of white space around all headings of the same level or visuals of the same type lends consistency to your layout; adding extra white space lends emphasis through contrast.

Ample white space makes a page inviting and easy to read (Figure 19.4). Without it, the page looks crowded and confusing.

Lists   Another strategy for grouping related items (and for adding white space) is to use lists (see Figure 19.4). List entries should be written succinctly so that readers can skim them for information. When creating lists, remember to:

- Keep list items parallel (all phrases or all sentences).

- Limit the number of items in the list.

- Begin list items with a dot, diamond, square, or number, and align all items.

- Use numbered lists to indicate steps in a process and bulleted lists to group related pieces of information.

Lists are common in business writing but should be used sparingly in most academic writing.

Color   Color, through contrast, calls the reader's attention to what is important in the text. Headings, bullets or numbers in lists, boxes,

Writing Responsibly

Selecting Fonts with Readers in Mind

Not all readers have perfect vision. If your audience includes members over forty (or under twelve), use a font size of at least 12 points to make the reading experience easier and more pleasant. If individuals with visual impairments will make up a portion of your audience, increase your font size even more.

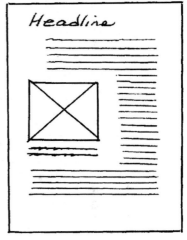

FIGURE 19.3 Using White Space to Group Elements   Adding white space above a heading or around a figure and its caption groups them into a unit for readers.

FIGURE 19.4 Use of Color and White Space in Web Pages The *C-Span* web page (*right*) is crowded with information, so the designer has used headings, colored panels, and appropriate white space to group information
and make the page easier to navigate. The web page from the Museum of Contemporary Art (*left*) contains far
less text, so the designer has used headings and white space to group information and make the page attractive
(crucial given the sponsoring organization's mission). Both pages make use of lists and columns, common design
features of website home pages, to organize information.

charts, graphs, and illustrations often appear in color so that readers
will notice them. But use color judiciously:

- **Use a limited color palette.** Too many colors displayed
  together create a hodgepodge effect.

- **Use complementary colors.** Analogous colors, those adjacent to each other on the color wheel (Figure 19.5), create a
  harmonious look. Complementary colors, those opposite each
  other on the color wheel, contrast with each other, each making the other color look brighter.

- **Use legible colors and color combinations.** Make sure
  colors contrast enough with their background that they are
  legible—yellow type on a white background may sound attractive but is hard to read.

- **Use appropriate colors.** Colors and combinations of colors
  carry associations: pastels for new babies, bright yellow and
  black for warnings, green for nature. Warm colors, such as
  red and orange, are seen as more aggressive than cool colors,

such as green and blue, which are considered calming. Choose colors that reinforce your topic and purpose.

- **Use colors consistently.** Use the same color to group items of the same type. For example, set all headings of the same level in the same color, and use the same background color for boxes of the same type.

Headings Headings and subheadings make long documents easier to read. They can help readers find information quickly and comprehend a text's structure at a glance. The principles of repetition and contrast are crucial for the design of headings:

- Set all headings that are at the same level in the same font, style, and color; and position each level the same way on the page:

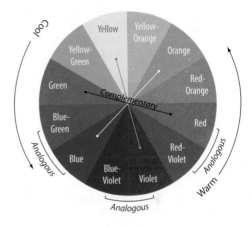

FIGURE 19.5 The Color Wheel Colors on opposite sides of the wheel are complementary; colors next to each other are analogous. Source: <http://wgu.educommons.net/liberal-arts/visual-and-performing-arts-after-11-30-2007/color-wheel/image_view_fullscreen>.)

First-level heading

Second-level heading

Third-level heading

More about ▶▶▶
Headings, 163–64

- Use the same grammatical structure for all headings of the same level. For example, use all *-ing phrases* (Containing the Economic Downturn, Bailing Out Wall Street) or all *noun phrases* (Economic Downturn, Wall Street Bailout).

Headers and Footers Headers and footers are located at the top and bottom of a page, respectively. They are set off from the main text by white space and/or a rule (see the example on p. 229 in Figure 19.7) and include information that is repeated from page to page, such as the author's last name, the page number, and sometimes a portion of the title or chapter information. This repeated information is particularly important for navigating long documents.

Text Boxes Text boxes can hold pull quotations, sidebars, and explanations of images. *Pull quotations* are key quotations from the document text itself, "pulled" out and made larger so that readers scanning the document can get a sense of the main argument before reading the text. *Sidebars* add related information alongside a text. Text boxes are also helpful for *image annotation,* drawing attention to parts of an image for analysis or illustration.

Alignment, Justification, and Columns You can choose from left, right, and centered *alignment* for different parts of your document. Centered text sends a conservative message. Left-aligned text (in which the left margin is straight while the right margin is uneven, or unjustified) is typical in academic projects and for large segments of text. Aligning text at the right draws attention to it. *Justification* (addition of space between words to create text with even right- and left-hand margins) gives text a boxy, solid feel but is not recommended by most style guides for academic writing. You can also use *columns* to create a more journalistic feel and increase the white space on a page for readability.

LEFT ALIGNED

The quick, brown fox jumped over the lazy dog.

RIGHT ALIGNED

The quick, brown fox jumped over the lazy dog.

CENTERED

The quick, brown fox jumped over the lazy dog.

JUSTIFIED

The quick, brown fox jumped over the lazy dog. The quick, brown fox jumped over the lazy dog. The quick, brown fox jumped over the lazy dog. The quick, brown fox jumped over the lazy dog. The quick, brown fox jumped over the lazy dog.

TWO COLUMNS

The quick, brown fox jumped over the lazy dog. The quick, brown fox jumped over the lazy dog. The quick, brown fox jumped over the lazy dog. The quick, brown fox jumped over the lazy dog. The quick, brown fox jumped over the lazy dog. The quick, brown fox jumped over the lazy dog. The quick, brown fox jumped over the lazy dog. The quick, brown fox jumped over the lazy dog.

FIGURE 19.6 Use of Lines (Rules) and Borders *CNN.com* uses a thick red masthead that works like a dividing line, repeated consistently on each page of the site. Subtle grey borders segment the page into units.

Lines and Borders Lines, or rules, and borders can be used to define document sections (through proximity); draw attention to what is above, below, or beside them (through contrast); provide a repeating feature (for continuity); and create clear vertical or horizontal alignment (Figure 19.6).

Visuals Because visuals are the first thing readers notice when they look at a text, they are integral to documents such as websites, newsletters, brochures, and flyers that must catch the eye of potential readers. Ideally, any visuals you include in a document should be arresting. But this does not mean that you should choose images just because they will capture a reader's attention. To be effective, images must be compelling and expand readers' understanding of your text.

Choose the types of visuals that will be appropriate for your text:

- **Images.** Photographs, sketches, drawings, and screenshots of websites (among other images) can be used to depict or

> **More about ▶▶▶**
> Evaluating visual
>   sources, 110–12
> Visuals and common
>   knowledge, 132
> Using visuals as support, 186–87

explain an event or a process, illustrate a concept, summarize a discussion, or analyze for deeper understanding. In some writing contexts, you can use images to reinforce or even to make an argument. But in most academic and business contexts, you should avoid using images to persuade without making your argument explicit in your text.

- **Graphics.** Tables, bar graphs, pie charts, timelines, and maps (among other graphics) are useful in all contexts and genres as tools for making large amounts of data readily accessible to readers. Be sure to avoid graphics that will mislead your readers.

Position visuals as close as possible to, but *after,* the text discussion of them. In academic and business writing, include a reference to each figure or table in your text, numbered in order of appearance (Figure 1, Table 2, for example). Provide a title (for tables) or a caption (for figures) that identifies the image and, when possible, adds relevant information that is not included in the text. Place the caption adjacent to the visual: For tables, place the title immediately above the visual; for figures, place captions immediately below or beside the image. Identify the source of any visual you did not create yourself.

EXERCISE **19.1** Learning Design from Models

Find a document you think is in the spirit of the project you are writing, with a similar audience, context, purpose, and genre. Analyze its layout and design, answering these questions:

- What overall impression does the document give (for example, trendy, conservative, playful, serious)?

- What kind of font variation is there?

- How are white space, lists, color, headings, and text boxes used to create proximity, alignment, repetition, and contrast?

- What kinds of visuals does the document include, and how do they function: Do they, for example, reinforce product identity, provide an example, offer additional information, further the argument, or demonstrate a process?

Finally, consider the overall effect of the document. Did your assessment of its purpose, audience, context, and genre change as you studied it more closely?

➤ Tech

Inserting Images and Text Boxes

To insert an image into a word-processed document, click on the image file on your desktop and drag it to the document. Or in your word processing program, you can choose "Insert" and then "Picture" from the drop-down menu. Then, choose "Clip Art" to select from your word processor's stock art or "From File" to select an image from your hard drive. Finally, if you want to adjust the size of the image, click on it, then click on a corner, hold down the mouse, and drag to resize.

To insert a text box, follow a similar procedure: Choose "Insert" and then "Text Box." Then click in your text where you would like to place the text box. An outlined box will appear. Click inside the box to place your cursor and start typing.

To insert an image into a web page, place the image file in your server folder. Then insert the tag <img src = "*"> in your document. Replace the asterisk with the file name of your image, including its file extension (e.g., *jpg, gif,* or *tif*).

19d   Designing an Academic Research Essay

Printed academic writing is typically designed conservatively, and you can use your style guide's instructions on formatting. Typical design features for academic writing include:

More about ▶▶▶
Formatting a paper
in MLA style,
286–91
Sample paper
formatted in MLA
style, 292–302
Formatting a pa-
per in APA style,
332–34
Sample paper
formatted in APA
style, 335–46
Formatting a paper
in *Chicago* style,
366–67
Sample paper for-
matted in *Chicago*
style, 368–74
Formatting a pa-
per in CSE style,
389–90
Sample paper
formatted in CSE
style, 391

- 12-point font for paragraph text

- 1-inch margins

- Either a cover page or a header on page one indicating title, author, and contextual information such as course and date

- Headers after page one showing author's last name and the page number (sometimes the page number appears in a footer instead)

- Boldface type for subheadings

- Figures for visual illustration of concepts and information discussed in the text

Successful academic writing sometimes deviates from these design norms. Lindsay Bohl's essay, published in the *Vanderbilt Undergraduate Research Journal* (Figure 19.7), illustrates the use of columns, boldface, and lines (rules) for clean, readable, and scholarly design.

Ask your instructor which style guide is appropriate for your assignment and course, and whether alternative designs, formats, genres, and media are acceptable for your research project.

Quick Reference ➡ **Checklist for Good Design**

Use these guidelines to determine whether you have achieved a good design for your document:

- Is my color scheme consistent and harmonious?
- Have I thought about the meanings of my color choices? Do they match and enhance the meaning of my text?
- Have I provided enough white space for my readers' eyes to rest, and have I placed it where it will draw attention to important information?
- Have I avoided using too many different fonts?
- Are the fonts I have chosen readable?

- Have I created a consistent pattern among my headings and subheadings?
- Have I chosen images and graphics that add value, not just visual impact?
- Have I aligned like items consistently?
- Have I avoided using all capital letters, except in one- or two-word instances?
- Have I created enough contrast to lead readers through my text?
- Do my choices convey the tone I need to achieve, whether playful, professional, serious, or other?

HUMANITIES AND SOCIAL SCIENCES

Courting the Youth Vote in 2008: The Obama Effect ◄————

Lindsay Bohl   College of Arts and Science, Vanderbilt University

> Boldfacing and a larger font size emphasize the title.

This paper examines a few of the numerous factors that may have led to increased youth turn-out in the 2008 Election. First, theories of voter behavior and turnout are related to courting the youth vote. Several variables that are perceived to affect youth turnout such as party polarization, perceived candidate difference, voter registration, effective campaigning and mobilization, and use of the Internet, are examined. Over the past 40 years, presidential elections have failed to engage the majority of young citizens (ages 18-29) to the point that they became inclined to not participate. This trend of low youth voter turnout began to reverse starting in 2000 Election and the youth turnout reached its peak in 2008. While both short and long-term factors played a sig-nificant role in recent elections, high turnout among youth voters in 2008 can be largely attributed to the Obama candidacy and campaign, which mobilized young citizens in unprecedented ways.

> Boldfacing, larger margins, and a single column set off the abstract.

The youth population is frequently the most underrepresented group in the American Electorate. Every four years, despite hopes of youth activists, this demographic continues to disappoint, allowing older generations to make up a disproportionately large amount of the electorate. Prior to November of 2008, turnout among eligible voters aged 18-24 had not exceeded 50% since 1972 in comparison to participation among the general electorate, which typically exceeds 60%. (CIRCLE, 2008). The lack of political engagement among young citizens can be attributed to a variety of factors such as a lack of political knowledge or efficacy, a lack of interest in politics, and the failure of the candidates to effec-tively engage the youth.

By 1996, some researchers suggested that "the youth do not view voting as a civic duty, do not see politics as personally relevant, do not identify with political parties, do not like the candidates, and use work as school as excuses" to avoid voting (Bystrom, 2007). Finally, after years of discouraging results, youth turnout rates increased significantly across the country in the 2004 Presidential Election (CIRCLE 2004), and the data from 2008 shows substantial youth participation and a reversal of generations of political apathy. In January of 2008, Time Magazine declared 2008 "The Year of the Youth Vote" and judging by the results of the 2008 Presidential Election, they appear to have been correct. The Center for Information and Research on Civic Learning and Engagement (CIRCLE) estimates that about 23 million young voters participated in the 2008 Election, an increase of at least four to five percentage points from 2004 (CIRLE, 2008). The numbers in 2008 are equiva-

lent to about 52-53% of eligible youth. According to Heather Smith, the Executive Director of *Rock the Vote*, "Young voters have dispelled the notion of an apathetic generation and proved the pundits, reporters and political parties wrong by voting in record numbers"(Borenstein, 2008). This signifi-cant turn of events begs the question, what made the youth turnout in record numbers in 2008?

Increased youth turnout can be credited to a variety of factors surrounding the 2008 Elec-tion. The increased civic and political activism of the millennial generation is the result of registra-tion and mobilization activities sponsored by both partisan and non-partisan organizations, campaign tactics that targeted young voters, and even the historic candidacy of President Barack Obama. The assertion that Barack Obama inspired young citizens to vote appears to be backed by the fact that the youth favored the Democratic candidate, Obama over John McCain, by more than a 2:1 ratio. In this paper, I will use a variety of scholarly and popular sources to examine why the youth turned out to vote on November 4th, 2008. I will begin by examining different theories of voting behavior and turnout. Next, I will use these theories to explain the different factors that may have produced high turnout in 2008. Additionally, I will analyze why Barack Obama's candidacy and campaign were so effective in mobilizing the youth vote. While there is little conclusive data about why the youth turned out in such high levels, the results seem to indicate that Barack Obama and his remarkable campaign organization played a significant role in motivating young citizens to get out the vote.

> Two columns with full justification increase readability of dense text.

> Line (rule) divides footer from text.

> Footer provides journal information and page number.

FIGURE 19.7 First Page of a Research Essay Designed for an Undergraduate Journal

19e Presenting Your Research

Research is often transmitted in more than one form; in print and then verbally before a live audience, as a podcast, or in another multi-media format. Translating your research from written to oral presenta-tion means adjusting for a new audience, context, purpose, and genre, and it may alter your tone. Translation also often requires drawing on your design skills.

Quick Reference ➡ **Overcoming Presentation Anxiety**

Rehearsing in front of a live audience of friends or family is a good way to overcome stage fright. These techniques may also help:

- Work hard on your presentation (especially your introduction) so that you can have well-founded confidence in yourself and your material.
- Envision success. Picture yourself calm and relaxed at the podium. Imagine your sense of accomplishment when the presentation is over.
- Get a good night's sleep the night before, and eat something an hour or two before the presentation.

- Take several slow, deep breaths, or tighten and relax your muscles just before you take the podium.
- Ignore your racing heart or clammy hands. Instead, use the adrenaline surge to fill your presentation with energy.
- Focus on your message. Conveying excitement about what you have to say will draw the audience into your presentation.
- Accept the fact that you may stumble, and be prepared to go on.

Organizing your presentation

People have more trouble understanding and retaining ideas presented orally than they do ideas presented in writing. To help your audience hold your main points in memory while your presentation unfolds, you will need to organize your talk carefully.

Introduction During your brief introduction (10–15 percent of your presentation), try to accomplish the following three things:

1. **Get your audience to relate to your topic.** An engaging anecdote, startling statistics, or an apt quotation are all good opening gambits.
2. **Establish your credentials.** Why should the audience listen to you? What special expertise do you offer? Knowledge, experience, or the research you have conducted all give you special expertise.
3. **Briefly summarize your main points.** Let listeners know in advance what they should be listening for.

Body The body (75–85 percent of your presentation) should develop the points you previewed in your introduction. Ideally, present only three to five main supporting points, regardless of the length of your presentation. The audience might have trouble keeping track of more than that.

Conclusion Keep your conclusion brief (5–10 percent of your presentation). Use it to reinforce the main point of your presentation. This can mean repeating your main idea and key supporting points for listeners to take away with them. But it can also mean reiterating your main point with a brief but powerful statement or quotation or returning to the anecdote, example, or statistics you opened with.

Creating visual, audio, and multimedia aids

When using visual or multimedia aids during a presentation, make sure of the following:

- You use only relevant visual and multimedia aids.
- You explain each aid clearly and succinctly.
- You are selective, limiting the number of aids so that the audience pays attention to you rather than to them.
- You speak to your audience, not to your visual aids.

Designing your visual, audio, and multimedia aids well is essential to a successful presentation:

- Keep your aids simple: Audience members should be able to absorb their contents quickly and then return their attention to you.
- Be sure your aids are clearly visible, audible, and legible from all parts of the space in which you are speaking.
- Use simple fonts that are large enough to be read easily.
- Choose a limited number of colors, and use them consistently to highlight key points.
- Keep the contrast between background and foreground sharp: A light background with dark type works best in a well-lit room; a dark background with light type works best in a dark room.

➤ **Tech**

Ten Steps to Using Software Effectively

1. **Review your outline to determine where slides would enhance your presentation.** Do not overwhelm your presentation by creating a slide for every moment.

2. **Create a title slide.** Begin with a slide that includes the title of your presentation, your name, and any other useful identifying information.

3. **Use templates and slide layouts to create a uniform design, but vary slide content.** In general, slides are most effective when the text component is brief (the audience should be listening to you, not reading your slides) and the other components (images, sound clips, etc.) are varied.

4. **Add blank slides.** Blank slides let you display a blank screen when you move on to a part of your presentation that is not illustrated.

5. **Make sure your slides are visually pleasing.** Keep slides uncluttered (use only a few fonts; limit text to what the audience can take in quickly), balanced, consistently designed, and with few animations.

6. **Proofread your slides carefully.** Check for both clarity and correctness.

7. **Learn your software commands so that you can move smoothly through your presentation.** Keystroke commands allow you to advance or return to slides, use the animation effects, and end the slide show.

8. **Practice your presentation in advance.** Use animations to bring information forward. Do not continue to display a slide after you have moved on to the next topic.

9. **Check the equipment; make sure it will function properly in the presentation space.** Make sure, for example, that the cord linking your computer to the projector is long enough, that you have needed extension cords, and that you know how to lower the lights and can cover the windows to darken the room.

10. **Be prepared to give your presentation *without your slide show*.** If the power fails or your computer dies, you should be able to go on with the show.

A Final Thought

Skill in design and presenting comes from attention and practice. Pay attention to the good designs you encounter as you read. Notice the contrasting colors on covers as you browse the magazine rack. Observe how elements align—vertically, horizontally, and diagonally—on flyers and brochures. Become aware of repeated features in your textbooks. Notice how authors in various contexts group and divide information with white space, columns, boxes, lines, and borders. Pay attention to effective presenters, too: How do they open, hold their audience's attention, use graphics and media, pace their presentations, and close? Apply these good design and presentation strategies to your own work.

Blending Voices in Your Text

Whenever you write from sources, you are blending the voices of your sources with each other and with your own voice. At every point in your text, your readers want to know whose voice they are "hearing." To blend voices successfully, you need to avoid patchwriting and show the beginning and end of each source use.

Some readers consider it plagiarism when a writer *patchwrites:* copying from sources, making superficial changes to its language, but not actually *paraphrasing* it, rewriting it in fresh language. Regardless of whether they classify it as plagiarism, no readers consider patchwriting good writing. The following passage from a source, and a student's first-draft writing from that source, illustrates the issue:

Passage from Source

> In the 1910s and later, as child psychology became an academic discipline, teachers increasingly looked to educational researchers rather than librarians as the central experts in children's reading.

Patchwriting

> From the 1910s on, child psychology became a discipline, and teachers more and more thought that educational researchers rather than librarians were the main experts in children's reading (248).

The patchwriting follows the original sentence, deleting a few words and substituting some others, but still depending on the source.

Paraphrase

> The academic discipline of child psychology, which emerged in the early twentieth century, looked to researchers for expertise about children's reading. Librarians were no longer the primary authority on the topic (248).

The paraphrase appropriately uses keywords such as discipline and child psychology, but it otherwise uses fresh language and fresh sentences to restate the source.

Being able to write true paraphrase is an advanced skill, and inexperienced college writers may struggle to do it. The chart below shows how sources were being used in the citations from papers written in composition classes at 16 different U.S. colleges and universities:

Ideally, 0% of these citations would have been for patchwriting, and a far greater number would have been for paraphrase or summary of the source. In your own writing, aim for paraphrase, with 0% patchwriting. The more you practice paraphrase, the easier it will be to do.

When you quote, it is easy for your readers to see where you are using sources; the quotation marks do that work. With summary and paraphrase, though, you need to show where your source use begins and ends. Using a signal phrase at the beginning of the source use and a parenthetical citation at the end is a standard way to make this happen. If your source use is lengthy, you can also occasionally mention the source or the author within your source use, just to remind your reader that they are reading your summary or paraphrase of a source:

Students' Use of Sources
DATA FROM **The Citation Project**

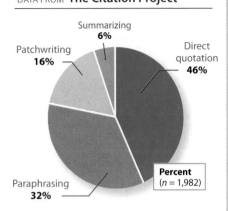

Summarizing
6%

Patchwriting
16%

Direct quotation
46%

Paraphrasing
32%

Percent
($n = 1,982$)

Marking where the source use begins and ends

> McDowell explains that the academic discipline of child psychology, which emerged in the early twentieth century, looked to researchers for expertise about children's reading. Librarians were no longer the primary authority on the topic. Both librarians and child psychologists were interested in children's reading patterns, but for different reasons. The librarians, McDowell says, wanted to understand what sorts of texts would interest children so they could get them into the library. Child psychologists, in contrast, wanted to understand the children themselves. Both groups collected information about children's reading, but they did it in different ways. The librarians observed children's reading and reported on their observations, while the child psychologists conducted scientific research (248-249).

Signal phrase at beginning of source use

Paraphrase of a sentence from the source

Signal phrase within the source use

Summary of two pages in the source

Parenthetical note at end of source use

Source: McDowell, Kathleen. "Toward a History of Children as Readers, 1890–1930." *Book History* 12 (2009): 240–265.

20

Conducting Research in the Disciplines

To understand the range of animal behaviors, characteristics, and relationships, scientists have divided the animal kingdom into groups: kingdom, phylum, class, order, family, genus, species. Academic studies, too, are classified into groups, or *disciplines:* communities of scholars who share a subject, approaches, and resources (types of evidence) for answering questions. The traditional disciplines are the humanities, the social sciences, the physical and natural sciences, and mathematics. (The Quick Reference box on p. 237 identifies the subject matter, approaches, and usual style guide for each of these disciplines.)

Success in college requires that you understand the approach, the tools used to conduct research and answer questions, the language, and the formats that are specific to the disciplines in which you take classes.

20a Conducting Research and Writing in the Humanities

> *More about* ▶▶▶
> Archival research, 74

> *More about* ▶▶▶
> Interpretation, 19
> Analysis, 18–19
> Synthesis, 19–20
> Critique, 20–22

The *humanities* focus on the meaning and value of human experience by studying *texts* (including works of literature, art, and music; films; philosophical works; historical artifacts, documents, and events; speeches; and so on), and asking how these texts are created and used. Students in the humanities read not just to comprehend but also to *engage with* texts: to ask difficult questions about them and to explore a range of possible answers.

Quick

Reference ➡ **The Liberal Arts Disciplines**

Discipline	Humanities	Social Sciences	Natural Sciences and Mathematics
Areas of study within the discipline	Art history, history, languages, literature, philosophy, religion, theater	Anthropology, communications, economics, geography, political science, psychology, sociology	Astronomy, biology, chemistry, geology, physics; algebra, calculus, geometry
Subject matter	Works of art, music, literature; cultural phenomena; abstract ideas	Human behavior (individual and group)	Natural phenomena
Primary sources	A painting or sculpture; a poem, novel, or play; manuscripts and diaries; legal cases and government documents	Data from observational studies, surveys, or interviews	Data from laboratory and field research
Secondary sources	Books or articles about a primary source	Books or articles describing primary research	Books or articles describing primary research
Typical assignments	Interpretation, analysis, and critique	Reports on field and experimental research; reviews and analyses of such research	Reports on experimental and field research; reviews and analyses of such research
Style guide	**Literature and languages:** *MLA Handbook for Writers of Research Papers*, 7th ed. **Other subjects:** *Chicago Manual of Style*, 16th ed.; *A Manual for Writers of Research Papers, Theses, and Dissertations*, 7th ed.	**Psychology and communications:** *Publication Manual of the American Psychological Association*, 6th ed. **Other subjects:** *Style Manual for Political Science* (American Political Science Association); *ASA (American Sociological Association) Style Guide*, 2nd ed.; *Chicago Manual of Style*, 16th ed.	**General:** *Scientific Style and Format: The CSE (Council of Science Editors) Manual for Authors, Editors, and Publishers*, 7th ed. **Specific fields:** *AMA (American Medical Association) Manual of Style*, 10th ed.; *IAU (International Astronomers Union) Style Manual*; *Mathematics into Type*, updated ed.

More about ▶▶▶
Documentation:
 MLA style, 241–86
 APA style, 304–32
 Chicago style,
  347–66
 CSE style, 375–88
Formatting:
 MLA style, 286–90
 APA style, 332–34
 Chicago style,
  366–67
 CSE style, 389–90

Artist Keith Haring creates one of his iconic paintings.

Adopting the approaches of the humanities

More about ▶▶▶
Primary versus sec-
 ondary sources, 89
Developing new
 information, 88–99

In most humanities courses, you are likely to be required to study *primary sources.* For instance, in art history, a painting (such as an image of St. Cecilia) or a video of an artist such as Keith Haring (above) at work would be considered primary sources.

More about ▶▶▶
Scholarly and popu-
 lar sources, 61–62
Finding reference
 works, 67–70

You will also draw on *secondary sources* to find out what others have said about the work or to learn about a critical framework that can provide the scaffolding for your interpretation. Of those secondary sources, *scholarly works,* like peer-reviewed articles in a scholarly journal or books published by a university press, are likely to be deemed more reliable by your instructor than are more accessible *popular sources,* like magazine or newspaper articles. You may also draw on *specialized reference works* to get an overview of your topic.

Using the language of the humanities

Learning the language of a discipline (both the vocabulary and the way words are used) is crucial to academic success. When writing in the humanities, pay particular attention to these issues:

- **Past versus present tense.** Writers in the humanities use the past tense to discuss real events that have happened and the present tense for the work being studied, elements or events within the work being studied, or the ideas of other scholars.

- **First person** (*I, we*) **versus third person** (*he, she, they, it*). Choose first- or third-person pronoun according to your emphasis: Is the focus your own argument (first person) or the evidence on which your argument is based (third person)? Personal pronoun usage also varies in humanities disciplines; ask your instructor about the preferred style, or read samples of writing from the discipline to figure out current practice.

- **Active versus passive voice.** Writers in the humanities usually choose the active voice because it produces clearer, concise writing.

  ACTIVE VOICE   Jonas Salk invented the vaccine for polio in 1955.

  PASSIVE VOICE   The vaccine for polio was invented in 1955.

  The first provides more information than the second, clearly indicating who did what. Of course, some circumstances may require the passive voice, as when the "who" is unknown or when you want to emphasize the action rather than the actor.

Writing assignments in the humanities

Assignments in the humanities frequently call on students to include the following:

- **Summary/description.** An interpretive analysis, critique, review, or bibliographic essay often includes a summary or description of the text, event, or object being discussed.

- **Synthesis.** A synthesis connects one text to another, explaining how the works relate and what new understandings might be derived from their combination. Frequently, writing in the humanities begins with a review of other works (a literature review).

- **Interpretation.** Writers in the humanities are usually expected to offer their own interpretation of primary texts, explaining what meaning they found in the text and what features of the text prompted their interpretation.

- **Evaluation.** An evaluation involves judging a text's quality or plausibility, offering a rationale for the judgment, and considering possible objections.

> *More about* ▶▶▶
Summary, 16–17, 58–59, 118–20, 129, 190–92
Synthesis, 19–20
Analysis, 18–19
Interpretation, 19
Evaluation and critique, 20–22
Literature review, 56
Primary sources, 88–90

20b Conducting Research and Writing in the Social, Physical, and Natural Sciences

Social scientists focus on the behavior of people, whereas physical and natural scientists focus on the natural world. Social scientists share with physical and natural scientists a reliance on the scientific method.

More about ▶▶▶
Developing new information, 88–99
Developing hypotheses, 48–49

Adopting the approaches of the social, physical, and natural sciences

The search for verifiable evidence anchors the writing produced by all scientists. Verifiable evidence comes from *empirical research:* experiments, observations, surveys, questionnaires, and interviews.

To conduct empirical research, social, physical, and natural scientists first develop *hypotheses*—predictions that can be proved true or false—and then they test these hypotheses. A hypothesis that successfully explains or predicts other phenomena and that is consistently confirmed by research becomes a *theory.*

Using the language of the social, physical, and natural sciences

Pay particular attention to these language issues when writing in the social, physical, and natural sciences:

Quick Reference ➡ The Scientific Method

Four major elements comprise the scientific method:

- **Descriptions** identify the object of study by systematically observing, measuring, and quantifying, while keeping careful records in a laboratory notebook.
- **Hypotheses** offer a prediction or explanation about the object of study. A hypothesis should be "elegant": clear, simple, and based on established facts.
- **Experiments** test the accuracy of a hypothesis by explaining, step by step, how an experiment was conducted, so that others who repeat the experiment can obtain identical results.
- **Theories** draw on hypotheses and experiments to explain the behavior of the object of a study.

- **Specialized terminology.** Even at the introductory level, learn the specialized terminology you encounter in textbooks and class, and use it with precision.

- **Third person and passive voice.** Since (in principle) the individual conducting the research is unimportant, writing in the sciences uses the third person and passive voice to describe how research was conducted. Some social scientists use the first person (*I, we*) when discussing observations they made as a participant or the conclusions they drew from their research. Check with your instructor about what is customary in your discipline and writing situation.

- **Past versus present tense.** Use the past tense to discuss methods, and the present tense to discuss implications.

Writing assignments in the social, physical, and natural sciences

The most common types of writing projects in the social, physical, and natural sciences include the following:

More about ▶▶▶
Summary, 16–17, 58–59, 118–20, 129, 190–92
Analysis, 18–19
Evaluating sources and information, 100–12
Synthesis, 19–20
Literature review, 56

- **Literature reviews** summarize research on a specific topic, analyze and evaluate the sources and the research on which these studies were based, and synthesize sources to develop a thorough understanding of the topic.

- **Research or laboratory notebooks** record in precise detail (1) the materials you used, in the order you used them; (2) a chronological list of the procedures you followed; and (3) your results (raw data, clearly labeled and logically organized), including any graphs or calculations you made.

- **Research or laboratory reports** provide a detailed description of your research, including your methods, your results, and the conclusions you drew from those results.

Unlike a humanities research paper, a research or laboratory report in the social, physical, or natural sciences usually follows this format in this order:

Title Page The title page should include the following information: title of the report, instructor, date of submission, author of the report, and author's affiliation.

Abstract A brief (150-word) summary of the report, the abstract may include a one-sentence summary of the most important points in each section of the report.

Introduction The report introduction should provide necessary background, such as a brief review of other, closely related studies; indicate your purpose in conducting the research; and introduce the limits of your research.

Methods The methods section should provide information about participants and describe how you collected information and recorded data, with enough detail that others could repeat your study or experiment.

More about ▶▶▶
Matching visual evidence to claims, 186
Integrating visuals, 186–87

Results The results section should provide details of your outcome. Use information graphics to convey results succinctly.

Discussion The discussion section offers readers an interpretation of your results, showing how the data you collected support or disprove your hypothesis, recognizing the limitations of your data, and relating your results to those of earlier researchers.

Conclusions The conclusions section summarizes your findings and explains the implications of your research.

More about ▶▶▶
Creating an APA-style reference list, 317–33
Creating a CSE-style reference list, 379–90

References Unless your instructor specifies otherwise, use American Psychological Association (APA) style in the social sciences and Council of Science Editors (CSE) style for the physical and natural sciences.

Appendices Place in an appendix any figures, tables, photographs, or other materials that amplify but do not directly support the discussion. Appendices should be mentioned in the main body of your text so that readers know to consult them. Each appendix should have a succinct, descriptive title, such as "Appendix C: Interview Questions."

A Final Thought

College-level discourse can seem mysterious and complicated. Part of the mystery is that researched writing in college is simply not all the same. From discipline to discipline, differing practices have arisen to deal with studying and talking about different kinds of problems. To dispel the mystery, pay attention, ask questions, and observe patterns in the disciplines.

21 Documenting Sources: MLA Style

> **More about ▶▶▶**
> Popular academic styles per discipline, 237
> APA style, 308–50
> *Chicago* style, 349–76
> CSE style, 377–93

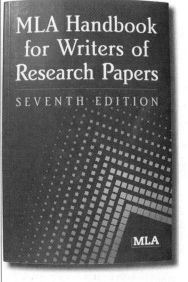

MLA Handbook for Writers of Research Papers

SEVENTH EDITION

MLA

Developed by the Modern Language Association (MLA), MLA style guidelines are used by many researchers in the humanities—especially in languages and literature—to cite and document sources and to format papers in a uniform way. The MLA requires that sources be acknowledged in two ways:

- **Citation:** Provide an in-text citation for each source used in the body of your project.

- **Documentation:** Provide a list of all works cited at the project's end.

Writing Responsibly   Citing and Documenting Sources

When you cite and document sources, you acknowledge any material that you have borrowed from a source, and you join the conversation on your topic by adding your own interpretation. Simultaneously, you give interested readers (including your instructor) a way to join the conversation: Accurate entries in the text and list of works cited allow your audience to find and read your sources so that they can evaluate your interpretation and learn more about the subject themselves. Accurate entries also demonstrate the care with which you have written your research project, which reinforces your credibility, or *ethos*.

Quick Reference ➡ **General Principles of In-Text Citation**

- Cite not only direct quotations but also paraphrases, summaries, and information gathered from a source.
- In most cases, include the author's surname and a page reference. You may place the name(s) in a signal phrase or a parenthetical note; the page reference should appear in parentheses.
- A signal phrase makes it easier to integrate borrowed information or the author's credentials into your own prose. A parenthetical citation is appropriate when establishing facts or citing more than one source for a piece of information.
- For one-page and unpaginated sources (such as websites), provide only the author's name.
- For two or more sources by the same author, include the title—either a complete title in the text or an abbreviated title in the parenthetical note.

Quick Reference ➡ **MLA-Style In-Text Citations**

21a Creating MLA-Style In-Text Citations

In-text citations appear in the body of your paper. They mark each use you make of a source, regardless of whether you are quoting, paraphrasing, summarizing, or drawing ideas from it. They also alert readers to a shift between *your* ideas and those borrowed.

More about ▶▶▶
What you must cite,
    129–31
What you need not
    cite, 131–32
Signal phrases,
    194–95
Signal verbs, 196
Parenthetical notes,
    194

You can cite a source in your text by using a signal phrase and page reference (in parentheses) or a parenthetical note:

- **Signal phrase.** Include the author's name (often just the surname) and an appropriate verb in your sentence before the borrowed material, and put the page number(s) in parentheses after the borrowed material.

  While encouraging writers to use figurative language, journalist

  signal phrase
  Constance Hale cautions that "a metaphor has the shelf life of a fresh

  page no.
  vegetable" (224), illustrating the warning with her own lively metaphor.

  Using a signal phrase allows you to integrate the borrowed material into your sentence, to put the source in context by adding your own interpretation, and to describe the qualifications of the source author or publisher. For these reasons, most summaries, paraphrases, and quotations should be introduced by a signal phrase.

- **Parenthetical note.** Include in parentheses the author's surname plus the page number(s) from which the borrowed material comes:

  While figurative language can make a passage come alive, be aware

  parenthetical note
  that metaphors have "the shelf life of a fresh vegetable" (Hale 224).

  Parenthetical notes are most appropriate when you are citing more than one source, when you are establishing facts, or when the author is not relevant to the point you are making.

NOTE The works-cited entry is the same whether you use a signal phrase or a parenthetical note:

author   title   publication info.   medium
Hale, Constance. *Sin and Syntax*. New York: Broadway, 2001. Print.

1. Include enough information to lead readers to the source in the list of works cited.

Whether you are using a signal phrase or a parenthetical note, in-text citations should provide enough information for readers to locate the source in your *list of works cited*. In most cases, providing the author's surname and a page reference is enough. Occasionally, however, you need to provide more information:

Example 6, 250–51

- If you cite more than one source by the same author, mention the title of the work in the text or include a shortened form of the title in the in-text citation. (You may also want to mention the title of the work, if it is relevant to the point you are making.)

Example 7, 251

- If you refer to sources by two different authors who have the same surname, mention the authors' first names in the text, or include the authors' first initials in the in-text citation.

Example 16a, 257

Occasionally, you may need to include less information. For example, you would omit a page number when you are summarizing an entire source, when your source is just one page long, or when your source, such as a web page, is not paginated.

2. Place in-text citations to avoid distracting readers and to show them where borrowed material starts and stops.

When you incorporate a quotation, paraphrase, summary, or idea from a source into your own text, carefully consider the placement of the in-text citation, keeping the following goals in mind:

- To make clear exactly which material is drawn from the source
- To avoid distracting your reader

→ Tech

Page References and Web Pages

Despite the term *web page*, most websites do not have page numbers in the sense that printed books do. Your browser may number the pages when you print a web page from a website, but this numbering appears only on your printed copy. Different computers and printers break pages differently, so your printed page 5 might be someone else's page 4 or 6. For this reason, citations of most web pages include only the author's name. If a website numbers its paragraphs, provide that information instead of a page reference.

Signal Phrase When using a signal phrase, bookend the borrowed information: Insert the author's name *before,* and the page number *after,* the cited material.

> Daniels, who has written several books about DC Comics' creations, notes that underground comic artists are not controlled by corporate interests that discourage "daring" material that might not sell (165).

Parenthetical Note When using a parenthetical note, place the note at a natural pause—at the end of a phrase, clause, or sentence—right after the borrowed material and before any punctuation.

Following a sentence

> Underground comic artists are not controlled by corporate interests that discourage "daring" material (Daniels 165).

Following a clause

> Other common themes of underground comics include sex and sexual identity, politics, and social issues (Daniels 165), as shown in Robert Crumb's *Snarf* comics.

Following a phrase

> The themes of underground comics, such as sex and sexual identity, politics, and social issues (Daniels 165), are all demonstrated in Robert Crumb's *Snarf* comics.

Block Quotations When the text you are quoting takes up more than four lines of your project, indent the borrowed material as a block by indenting one inch from the left margin, and place the parenthetical

More about ▶▶▶
Block quotations, 118, 123

note one space *after* the closing punctuation mark. No quotation marks should be used when indenting quoted material as a block.

Example

signal phrase

Howard and Kennedy assert that parents and school officials tend to ignore hazing until an incident becomes public knowledge. They describe a concrete incident that demonstrates their claims:

←—1"—→In general, the Bredvik school community (parents, teachers, coaches, and students) condoned or ignored behaviors that could be called "hazing" or "sexual harassment." However, when the incident was formally brought to the attention of the larger, public audience of the community, a conflict erupted in the community over how to frame, understand, and react to the event. (347–48)

3. Adjust in-text citations to match your sources.

The exact form of an in-text citation depends on the source. Is there one author? Are there several authors or no authors? Is the source paginated? Is the source a novel, a story in an anthology, or a PowerPoint presentation? The examples below cover the most common source types. (A list of in-text citation examples in MLA style appears on the following pages.) For more unusual sources, study the general principles as outlined here and in the *MLA Handbook for Writers of Research Papers,* 7th ed. (available in any library), and adapt them to your special circumstances.

MLA In-Text
Citations

1. One author

1. One author
2. Two or three authors
3. More than three authors

a. Signal phrase

Cahill cautions responsible historians against disparaging the Middle Ages; medieval Europe's reputation as a time of darkness, ignorance,

page no.

and blind faith is "largely (if not wholly) undeserved" (310).

b. Parenthetical note

> The Middle Ages are often unjustly characterized as a time of darkness,
>
> ignorance, and blind faith (Cahill 310).

2. Two or three authors Include the surnames of all the authors in your signal phrase or parenthetical note; use *and*, not an ampersand (&), in the parenthetical note.

> To write successfully about their families, authors must have motives—
> and perspective—beyond merely exposing secret histories (Miller and
> Paola 72).

3. More than three authors For sources with more than three authors, you may either list each author by surname (follow the order in the text) or insert the abbreviation *et al.* following the first author's surname.

NOTE *al.* is an abbreviation, so it requires a period; *et* is a complete word, so it does not. There should be no punctuation between the author's name and *et al.*

> all authors in signal phrase
> Visonà, Poynor, Cole, Harris, Abiodun, and Blier stress that symbols
>
> used in African art are not intended to be iconic but instead to suggest a
>
> wide variety of meanings; the authors liken this complexity to "a
>
> telephone line that carries multiple messages simultaneously" (19).

> Symbols used in African art are not intended to be iconic; rather, the
>
> artist's goal is to suggest a complex range of meanings to different
> 1st author + et al.
> viewers (Visonà et al. 19).

MLA In-Text Citations

1. One author
2. **Two or three authors**
3. **More than three authors**
4. Group, government, or corporate author
5. Unnamed author

et al. Abbreviation of the Latin phrase *et alii,* "and others."

Whichever you choose, do the same in your list of works cited.

4. Group, government, or corporate author When a government agency, corporation, or other organization is listed as the author, use that organization's name in your in-text citation. The MLA suggests incorporating names into your sentence in a signal phrase to avoid long parenthetical notes.

> government agency as author
> The Federal Emergency Management Agency indicates that Kansas
>
> City is located in a region of frequent and intense tornadic activity (4).

MLA In-Text Citations

2. Two or three authors
3. More than three authors
4. **Group, government, or corporate author**
5. **Unnamed author**
6. **Two or more sources by the same author**
7. Two or more authors with the same surname
8. Entire source

If a parenthetical note makes more sense in the context, use common abbreviations ("U.S." for *United States,* "Corp." for *Corporation*) to shorten the name where you can.

5. Unnamed author If the author is unnamed and the work is alphabetized by title in the list of works cited, use the title in your in-text citation. Abbreviate long titles in parenthetical citations.

> One nineteenth-century children's book vows that "when examined
>
> by the microscope, the flea is a pleasant object," and the author's
>
> vivid description of this sight—a body "curiously adorned with a suit of
>
> polished armor, neatly jointed, and beset with a great number of sharp
>
> pins almost like the quills of a porcupine"—may win readers' curiosity, if
>
> title
> not their sympathy (*Insects* 8).

If you do abbreviate the title, start your abbreviation with the word by which the title will be alphabetized in your list of works cited. Only if the author is listed specifically as "Anonymous" should you use that designation.

6. Two or more sources by the same author When you draw on two or more sources by the same author, differentiate between these sources by including titles.

> book title
>
> In her book *Nickel and Dimed,* social critic Barbara Ehrenreich
>
> demonstrates that people could not live on the then-current minimum
>
> blog entry title
>
> wage (60). Perhaps, as she notes in her blog entry "'Values' Voters
>
> Raise Minimum Wages," people will be a little better able to hold their
>
> own in the six states (Arizona, Colorado, Montana, Missouri, Nevada,
>
> Ohio) that have recently raised their minimum wage.

Use the full title in signal phrases, and abbreviate it in parenthetical
citations ("'Values' Voters").

7. Two or more authors with the same surname When you cite sources
by two different authors with the same surname, differentiate them by
including their first names (the first time you mention them in a signal
phrase) or by including their first initials (in a parenthetical reference
or subsequent text references).

> Including citations is important not only because they give credit but
>
> also because they "organize a field of inquiry, create order, and allow for
>
> accountability" (S. Rose 243). This concern for acknowledging original
>
> sources dates back to the early eighteenth century: Joseph Addison
>
> was one of the first to argue for "the superiority of original to imitative
>
> composition" (M. Rose 114).

8. Entire source (including a one-page source) Mention an entire
source—whether it is a film or a website, a book or an article, a painting or a graphic novel—in your text using the information that begins
the entry in your list of works cited.

> The film *The Lady Eve* asks whether love is possible without trust.

MLA In-Text
Citations

5. Unnamed
   author
6. Two or more
   sources by the
   same author
7. **Two or more
   authors with
   the same
   surname**
8. **Entire source**
9. Selection from
   an anthology
10. Multivolume
    source

MLA In-Text Citations

9. Selection from an anthology If your source is a work included in an anthology, reader, or other collection, your citation should name the author of your source—not the editor of the anthology. In the example below, Faulkner is the author of the selection "A Rose for Emily," a story that appears in a literature anthology edited by Robert DiYanni.

> Southern fiction often explores the marked curiosity that women of
>
> author of story
> stature and mystery inspire in their communities. Faulkner's "A Rose for
>
> Emily," for example, describes the title character as "a tradition, a duty,
>
> and a care; a sort of hereditary obligation upon the town . . ." (79).

10. Multivolume source If you use information from more than one volume of a multivolume work, your in-text citation must indicate both the volume and page from which you are borrowing. (This information can be omitted if you use only one volume of the work; your works-cited entry will indicate which volume you used.)

> author
> Tarbell writes that in 1847 Abraham Lincoln was a popular man of
>
> "simple, sincere friendliness" who was an enthusiastic—though
>
> vol. no. pg. no.
> awkward—bowler (1: 210).

The words *volume* and *page* (or their abbreviations) are not used.

11. Literary source Because many classics of literature—novels, poems, plays—are published in a variety of editions (printed and digital) with pagination that varies widely, your citation should provide your readers with the information they will need to find the passage, regardless of which edition they are reading.

a. Novel Include the chapter number (with the abbreviation *ch.*) after the page number (or location reference for digital books) from your edition:

> Joyce shows his protagonist's dissatisfaction with family, faith, and
>
> country through the adolescent Stephen Daedalus's first dinner at
>
> the adult table, an evening filled with political and religious discord
>
> pg. no. ch. no.
> (274; ch. 1).

Use arabic (*2, 9, 103*), not roman (*ii, ix, ciii*), numerals, regardless of what your source uses.

If the novel has chapters grouped into parts or books, include both the part or book number and the chapter number, using the appropriate abbreviation (*pt.* for *part* or *bk.* for *book*).

> Even though New York society declares the Countess Olenska beyond
>
> her prime, Newland Archer sees in her a "mysterious authority of
>
> beauty" (Wharton 58; bk. 1, ch. 8).

MLA In-Text Citations

9. Selection from an anthology
10. Multivolume source
11. **Literary source**
12. Sacred text
13. Motion picture, television or radio broadcast

b. Play When citing plays, use act, scene, and line numbers (in that order), not page numbers or location numbers (used in digital editions). Do not label the parts. Instead, separate them with periods.

> When the ghost of Hamlet's father cries, "Adieu, adieu, adieu!
>
> remember me," Hamlet wonders if he must "remember" his father
>
> through vengeance (1.5.91).

Use arabic (*1, 5, 91*), not roman (*i, v, xci*), numerals for act, scene, and line numbers, and omit spaces after periods between numbers.

c. Poem For poetry, use line numbers, rather than page or location numbers. With the first reference to line numbers, use the word *line* or *lines;* omit it thereafter.

In Audre Lorde's poem "Hanging Fire," her fourteen-year-old frets,

1st ref.
"What if I die / before morning" (lines 7–8), making me remember my

own teenage worries of just a few years ago. Each of the three stanzas

later refs.
ends with "and momma's in the bedroom / with the door closed" (9–10,

20–21, 32–33), bringing me back to my "now": I am that mother who

does not understand.

Audre Lorde, "Hanging Fire." *The Collected Poems of Audre Lorde.* Copyright © 1978 by Audre Lorde. Used by permission of W. W. Norton & Company, Inc. This selection may not be reproduced, stored in a retrieval system, or transmitted in any form or by any means without the prior written permission of the publisher.

MLA In-Text Citations

10. Multivolume source

11. Literary source

12. Sacred text

13. Motion picture, television or radio broadcast

14. Indirect source

For long poems that are divided into sections (books, parts, numbered stanzas), provide that information as well, omitting the section type (such as *book* or *part*) and separating the section number from the line number(s) with a period.

David Mason's *Ludlow* (2007) begins with a description that captures

Luisa's life:

Down below

the mesa, smells of cooking rose from shacks

in rows, and there Luisa scrubbed the pot

as if she were some miner's wife and not

sec.
a sapper's daughter, scrawny, barely twelve. (1.5–8)

lines

Use Arabic (*1, 5, 8*), not Roman (*i, v, viii*), numerals, and omit spaces

12. Sacred text Cite sacred texts (such as the Bhagavad-Gita, the Talmud, the Qur'an, and the Bible) not by page number but by book title (abbreviated in parenthetical notes), chapter number, and verse number(s); and separate each section with a period. Do not italicize book titles or put them in quotation marks, and do not italicize the name of the sacred text, unless you are referring to a specific edition.

sacred text
In the Bible's timeless love poetry, the female speaker concludes her

description of her lover with this proclamation: "This is my beloved

                                                    book   ch.verse
and this is my friend, / O daughters of Jerusalem" (Song Sol. 5.16).

No spaces

specific edition
The *New Oxford Annotated Bible* offers a moving translation of the

                                            book
timeless love poetry in the Song of Solomon. The female speaker

concludes her description of her lover with this proclamation: "This is

                                                    ch.verse
my beloved and this is my friend, / O daughters of Jerusalem" (5.16).

MLA In-Text
Citations

11. Literary source
12. Sacred text
**13. Motion picture,
   television or
   radio broadcast**
14. Indirect source
15. Dictionary or
   encyclopedia
   entry

13. Motion picture, television or radio broadcast The information you include in an in-text citation for a motion picture or for a television or radio broadcast depends on what you are emphasizing in your project. When you are emphasizing the work itself, use the title; when you are emphasizing the director's work, use the director's name; when you are emphasizing an actor's work, use the actor's name. Start your works cited entry with whatever you have used in your in-text citation.

title
While The Lady Eve is full of slapstick humor, it is mainly remembered

for its snappy dialogue, at once witty and suggestive.

actor's name
Barbara Stanwyck's portrayal of Jean Harrington is at once sexy and

wholesome.

14. Indirect source When you can, avoid quoting from a secondhand source. When you cannot use the original source, mention the name of the person you are quoting in your sentence. In your parenthetical note, include *qtd. in* (for *quoted in*) plus the name of the author of the source in which you found the quotation.

> Handel's stock among opera-goers rose considerably over the course
>
> author quoted
> of the twentieth century. In 1912, an English music critic, H. C. Colles,
>
> maintained that "it would be difficult, if not impossible, to make any one
>
> source of quotation
> of Handel's operas tolerable to a modern audience" (qtd. in Orrey 62).
>
> Today, however, Handel's operas are performed around the world.

In your list of works cited, include the *indirect* source (*Orrey*), not the source being quoted (*H. C. Colles*).

15. Dictionary or encyclopedia entry In the citation of a dictionary or encyclopedia entry, omit the page number on which you found the item. For a dictionary entry, place the defined word in quotation marks, followed by the abbreviation *def.* Follow this with the letter or number of the definition you wish to reference.

> Another definition of *honest* is "respectable" ("Honest," def. 6), but what,
>
> if anything, does truth have to do with respectability?

In the parenthetical note for an encyclopedia entry, include the entry's full title in quotation marks.

> The study of ethics is not limited to philosophers, as its "all-embracing
>
> practical nature" makes it an applicable or even necessary course of
>
> study in a wide variety of disciplines, from biology to business ("Ethics").

If you are citing two entries with the same name from different reference sources, add an abbreviated form of the reference work's title to each entry.

> While the word *ethics* is commonly understood to mean "moral
>
> principles" ("Ethics," def. 4, *Random House Webster's*), to philosophers
>
> it is "the evaluation of human conduct" ("Ethics," *Philosophical Dict.*).

16. Website or other electronic source Cite electronic sources such as websites, online articles, e-books, and emails as you would print sources, even though many of these sources do not use page numbers.

More about ▶▶▶
Evaluating online texts, 107–09

a. Without page, paragraph, screen, or slide numbers Unless there is another numbering system at work (such as numbered paragraphs, screens, or slides), cite the author without a page reference.

> When first published in 1986, Alan Moore's *Watchmen* revolutionized
>
> the comic book; today, even its harshest critics acknowledge the
>
> *author only*
> book's landmark status (Shone).

MLA In-Text
Citations

You may credit your source more elegantly by mentioning the author in a signal phrase and omitting the parenthetical citation altogether.

> *signal phrase*
> Reading Alan Moore's *Watchmen* in 2005, critic Tom Shone found it
>
> "underwhelming," but he admitted that in 1986, the comic book was
>
> "unquestionably a landmark work."

b. With paragraph, screen, or slide numbers If an electronic source numbers its paragraphs, screens, or slides, you can reference these numbers as you would pages (with an appropriate identifying abbreviation—*par.* or *pars., screen* or *screens, slide* or *slides*).

The internet has also become an outlet for direct distribution through artist websites, making independent titles not only more accessible to consumers but also more affordable for individual artists to produce and market (Fenty, Houp, and Taylor, par. 1).

c. In a PDF file Online documents offered as a PDF (portable document format) file include all the elements of the printed document, including the page number. Since pages are fixed, you can and should cite page numbers.

17. Personal communication As with other unpaginated sources, when citing information from a letter, email message, interview, or other personal communication, you should include the author's name in a signal phrase or parenthetical citation. Also indicate the type of source you are citing.

Many people have asked why teachers cannot do more to prevent
source type
school shootings; in an email to this author, one instructor responds: "As creative writing teachers untrained in psychology, can we really determine from a student's poetry whether he or she is emotionally
author of email
disturbed—even a threat to others?" (Fox).

More about ▶▶▶
Using visuals as support, 186–87

18. Table, chart, or figure If a copy of the visual you are discussing is *not* included in your project, include relevant information in the text, and include an entry in your list of works cited.

. . . There is no experience quite like standing in front of a full-size painting by Jackson Pollock; they have an irresistible sense of movement to them, the particular quality of which is unique to his work. This is especially evident in *One Number 31, 1950,* which currently hangs on the fourth floor of New York's Museum of Modern Art. . . .

If a copy of the visual *is* included in your project, reference it in your text and include the source information in a table's source note (see Figure 21.1) or in a figure's caption (see the figure on p. 297 in the model student project at the end of this chapter).

19. Government document Because government documents are alphabetized in the list of works cited by the name of the nation that produced them, mention the country as well as the agency in your text.

TABLE 1	THE DEMISE OF THE THREE-DECKER NOVEL
Year	**No. of 3-deckers published**
1894	184
1895	52
1896	—
1897	4
1898	0

Source: Information from John Feather, *A History of British Publishing* (Clarendon: Crown Helm, 1988), quoted in Kelly J. Mays

FIGURE 21.1 Table in MLA Style

Just as the nation was entering World War II, the United States War Department published a book outlining what it had learned about reading aerial photographs.

20. Legal source Laws, acts, and legal cases are typically referred to by name either in your sentence or in a parenthetical citation. Laws and acts are neither italicized nor enclosed in quotation marks.

In 2008 the U.S. Congress passed the Combat Bonus Act.

Legal cases are italicized in your text, but not in the list of works cited.

In 1963 the Supreme Court ruled that poor defendants should receive legal representation, even if they could not pay for it themselves (*Gideon v. Wainright*).

21. Multiple sources in one sentence When you use different information from multiple sources within a single sentence, give separate citations in the appropriate place.

MLA In-Text Citations

17. Personal communication
18. Table, chart, or figure
19. Government document
20. Legal source
21. Multiple sources in one sentence
22. Multiple sources in one citation

MLA In-Text Citations

Other common themes of underground comics include sex and sexual identity, politics, and social issues (Daniels 165), as shown in Crumb's work, which is well known for its satirical approach to countercultural topics (Heller 101–02).

Quick Reference ➡ A List of MLA-Style Works-Cited Examples

22. Multiple sources in one citation When you draw information from more than one source, follow the borrowed material with a list of all relevant sources, separated by semicolons.

MLA In-Text Citations

20. Legal source
21. Multiple sources in one sentence
22. Multiple sources in one citation

> Jamestown was once described as a failed colony populated by failed colonists, but new findings suggest that the colonists were resourceful survivors (Howard; Lepore 43).

Entire source—no page reference

MLA Works-
Cited Entries

1. One author
2. Two or three
   authors
3. More than three
   authors

▶▶▶Annotated
visual of where to
find author, title,
publication, and
other information,
on foldout following
p. 393.

21b Preparing an MLA-Style List of Works Cited

The list of works cited, which comes at the end of your research project, includes information about the sources you have cited in your
text. (A bibliography that includes sources you read but did not cite
in your research project is called a *list of works consulted*.) Your list of
works cited provides readers with the information they need for locat-
ing the material you used in your project. The format of each entry
depends in part on the type of source it is.

Books—Printed and Electronic

In a printed book, most or all of the information you need for creating
an entry in the list of works cited appears on the title and copyright
pages. In an online or e-book, print and electronic publication information often appears at the top or bottom of the first page or is available through a link.

1. One author
a. Printed The basic entry for a printed book looks like this:

> Author's surname, First name. *Title: Subtitle.* Place of publication: Publisher
>
> (shortened), date of publication. Medium of publication.

Here is an example of an actual entry in the list of works cited:

> author   title   publication information medium
> Morrison, Toni. *A Mercy.* New York: Knopf, 2008. Print.
>   place   pub.   date

b. Database Some books are available in online, full-text archives, or
databases, such as *Bartleby.com.* When you are documenting a book
you accessed through a database, add the name of the database and
change the medium of publication from *Print* to *Web.* Also, add the
date (day, month, year) on which you accessed the work.

> Wharton, Edith. *The Age of Innocence.* New York: Appleton, 1920.
>   database   date accessed
>   *Bartleby.com.* Web. 5 July 2007.
>   medium

c. E-book The citation for an electronic version of a book is the same as
for a printed book except that the medium of publication changes from
Print to the specific type of e-book file you read: Gemstar e-book file,
Microsoft Reader e-book file, Kindle e-book file, and so on.

Morrison, Toni. *A Mercy*. New York: Knopf, 2008. Kindle e-book file.

2. Two or three authors List authors in the order in which they appear on the title page. Only the first author should be listed with surname first.

author 1   author 2
Miller, Brenda, and Suzanne Paola. *Tell It Slant*. New York: McGraw,

   2004. Print.

author 1   author 2   author 3
Fleming, Robert L., Jr., Dorje Tsering, and Liu Wulin. *Across the Tibetan*

   Plateau: Ecosystems, Wildlife, and Conservation. New York: Norton,

   2008. Print.

3. More than three authors Either list all the authors, or just list the first and add *et al.* Whichever you choose, do the same in your in-text citation.

More about ▶▶▶
et al., 249

Visonà, Monica Blackmun, et al. *A History of Art in Africa*. New York:

   Abrams, 2001. Print.

Visonà, Monica Blackmun, Robin Poynor, Herbert M. Cole, Michael D.

   Harris, Rowland Abiodun, and Suzanne Preston Blier. *A History of*

   Art in Africa. New York: Abrams, 2001. Print.

4. Unnamed (anonymous) author Start the entry with the title.

title
Terrorist Hunter: The Extraordinary Story of a Woman Who Went

   Undercover to Infiltrate the Radical Islamic Groups Operating in

   America. New York: Ecco-HarperCollins, 2003. Print.

Alphabetize the entry in your list of works cited using the first significant word of the title (not *a, an,* or *the*). Only if the author is listed specifically as "Anonymous" should you use that designation.

Anonymous. *Go Ask Alice*. Englewood Cliffs: Prentice, 1971. Print.

5. Author using a pen name (pseudonym) If the author is using a pen name (or *pseudonym*), document the source using the author's pen

MLA Works-
Cited Entries

1. One author
2. Two or three authors
3. More than three authors
4. Unnamed (anonymous) author
5. Author using a pen name
6. Two or more works by the same author
7. Group or corporate author

name, and insert the author's actual name in brackets following the pseudonym.

> Keene, Carolyn [Edward Stratemeyer]. *The Secret of the Old Clock*. New
>
> York: Grosset, 1930.

6. Two or more works by the same author Alphabetize the entries by the first important word in each title. Supply the author's name only with the first entry. For subsequent works, replace the author's name with three hyphens.

> Chabon, Michael. *The Final Solution: A Story of Detection*. New York:
>
> Fourth Estate, 2004. Print.
>
> ---. *The Yiddish Policeman's Union: A Novel*. New York: HarperCollins,
>
> 2007. Print.

7. Group or corporate author Treat the sponsoring organization as the author.

> corporate author
> Blackfoot Gallery Committee. *The Story of the Blackfoot People:*
>
> *Nitsitapiisinni*. Richmond Hill: Firefly, 2002. Print.

8. Edited book or anthology (printed or online) When citing the book as a whole, treat the editor as the author and insert the abbreviation *ed.* (or *eds.* if there is more than one editor) after the name.

> Furman, Laura, ed. *The O. Henry Prize Stories: The Best Stories of the*
>
> *Year*. New York: Anchor, 2008. Print.
>
> Delbanco, Nicholas, and Alan Cheuse, eds. *Literature: Craft and Voice*.
>
> New York: McGraw, 2009. Print.

9. Author and editor or translator List the author first. After the title, include the abbreviation *Ed.* or *Trans.* (as appropriate) before the editor's or translator's name. If the book was accessed online, add the information shown in item 1b–c.

Larsson, Asa. *Sun Storm.* Trans. Marlaine Delargy. New York: Delacorte.

2006. Print.

NOTE When the abbreviation appears before the editor's or translator's name, it means *edited by* or *translated by,* so use the same abbreviation whether there is one editor or translator or many. When the abbreviation *ed.* appears after the name, it means *editor,* so add an *s* (*eds.*) if more than one editor is listed. The abbreviation *Trans.* does not change.

Larsson, Asa. *Sun Storm.* Trans. Marlaine Delargy. New York: Delacorte,

2006. Print.

10. One or more selections from an edited book or anthology If you are citing a selection from an edited book or anthology, start the entry with the selection's author and title. Include the page numbers for the entire selection (even if you used only part).

      author   title (selection)
Faulkner, William. "A Rose for Emily." *Literature: Reading Fiction, Poetry,*

and Drama. Ed. Robert DiYanni. 6th ed. New York: McGraw, 2009.

  pages
79–84. Print.

When documenting a longer work, such as a novel or a play, that is included in the anthology or selection, italicize the work's title.

           title (selection)
Ives, David. *Sure Thing. Literature: Reading Fiction, Poetry, and Drama.* . . .

If you are citing more than one selection in the anthology or collection, include an entry for the collection as a whole.

DiYanni, Robert D., ed. *Literature: Reading Fiction, Poetry, and Drama.*

6th ed. New York: McGraw, 2009. Print.

Then, for each selection you use, include the author and title of the selection, followed by the surname of the editor and the page numbers of the selection.

Faulkner, William. "A Rose for Emily." DiYanni. 79–84. Print.

For a scholarly article included in an edited book, list the article's original publication information first, the abbreviation *Rpt. in* for *reprinted in,* and then the publication information for the anthology.

Example 24 (a–c), 271

original publication info.
Stock, A. G. "Yeats and Achebe." *Journal of Commonwealth Literature*
reprint publication info.
5 (1968): 105–11. Rpt. in *Things Fall Apart.* By Chinua Achebe.

Ed. Francis Abiola Irele. New York: Norton, 2008. 271–77. Print.

11. Edition other than the first Insert the edition number (*2nd ed., 3rd ed.*) or edition name (*Rev. ed.* for "revised edition") before the publication information. The edition number or name should appear on the title page.

Rosebury, Brian. *Tolkien: A Literary Phenomenon.* 2nd ed. New York:

Palgrave, 2004. Print.

12. Imprint (division) of a larger publishing company Name both the imprint and publisher, separating them with a hyphen.

Betcherman, Lita-Rose. *Court Lady and Country Wife: Two Noble*

Sisters in Seventeenth-Century England. New York:
imprint   publisher
Morrow-HarperCollins, 2005. Print.

13. Introduction, preface, foreword, or afterword Begin with the name of the person who wrote this section of the text. Then provide a descriptive label (such as *Introduction* or *Preface*), the title of the book, and the name of the book's author. (If the author of the section and the author of the book are the same, use only the author's surname after the title.) Include the page numbers for the section.

author of intro.   label   title of book
Barrett, Michèle. Introduction. *The Origin of the Family, Private Property*
author of book
and the State. By Friedrich Engels. New York: Penguin, 1986.

7–30. Print.

If this section has a title, include it before the descriptive label.

MLA Works-
Cited Entries

9. Author and editor or translator

10. One or more selections from an edited book or anthology

11. **Edition other than the first**

12. **Imprint (division) of a larger publishing company**

13. **Introduction, preface, foreword, or afterword**

14. Entry in a reference work

15. Multivolume work

afterword's title

Burton, Larry W. "Countering the Naysayers: Independent Writing

Programs as Successful Experiments in American Education."
label
Afterword. *A Field of Dreams: Independent Writing Programs and the*

Future of Composition Studies. Ed. Peggy O'Neill, Angela Crow, and

Larry W. Burton. Logan: Utah State UP, 2002. 295–300. Print.

14. Entry in a reference work Format an entry in a dictionary or encyclopedia as you would a selection from an edited book or anthology. For signed articles, include the author's name. (Articles in reference works often carry the author's initials only, so you may need to cross-reference the initials with a list of contributors in the front or back of the book.) If an article is unsigned, begin with its title.

a. Printed For familiar reference works, omit publication information other than the edition and year of publication. If the entries are arranged alphabetically, omit a page reference.

"Culture." *Oxford English Dictionary.* Compact 2nd ed. 1991. Print.

Green, Michael. "Cultural Studies." *A Dictionary of Cultural and Critical*

Theory. Cambridge: Blackwell, 1996. Print.

b. Online For online reference works, add the site's sponsor, change the medium of publication to *Web,* and add the date you accessed the site.

sponsor
"Culture." *Merriam-Webster Online Dictionary.* Merriam-Webster Online,
medium access date
2008. Web. 1 Dec. 2008.

c. CD-ROM or DVD-ROM Although CD-ROMs and DVD-ROMs have largely been replaced by the internet, you may still need to use them. If the CD-ROM or DVD-ROM is published in versions rather than editions, use the abbreviation *Vers.* and include the version number after the title or editor's name. Change the medium of publication to *CD-ROM* or *DVD-ROM.*

Cooley, Marianne. "Alphabet." *World Book Multimedia Encyclopedia.*
version   medium
Vers. 6.0.2. Chicago: World Book, 2002. CD-ROM.

Example 10, 265

15. Multivolume work

a. Multiple volumes Indicate the total number of volumes, followed by the abbreviation *vols.*, and indicate the span of years in which the volumes were published. Specify the volume from which you borrowed a particular passage or idea in your text citation.

> no. of vols.
> Tarbell, Ida M. *The Life of Abraham Lincoln.* 2 vols. New York: Lincoln
>   pub. date
> Memorial Association, 1895–1900. Print.

b. One volume If you used only one volume, include the number of the volume you used before the publication information, and give only the publication date of that volume.

> vol. used
> Tarbell, Ida M. *The Life of Abraham Lincoln.* Vol. 1. New York: Lincoln
>   pub. date
> Memorial Association, 1895. Print.

16. Book in a series If the book you are citing is part of a series, the series title will usually be noted on the book's title page or on the page before the title page. Insert the series title (with no quotation marks or italics) after the medium of publication. If books in the series are numbered, include the number following the series title.

> Todorov, Tzvetan. *Mikhail Bakhtin: The Dialogical Principle.* Trans. Wlad
>   series title
>   Godzich. Minneapolis: U Minnesota P, 1995. Print. Theory and
>   no.
>   Hist. of Lit. 13.

17. Republished book If a book has been republished, its original date of publication will appear on the book's copyright page. If the original publication date may be of interest to your readers, include it before publication information for the version you consulted. If the book was edited or an introduction was added, include that information before the republication information.

>   orig.
>   pub. date   editors
>   Burroughs, William S. Naked Lunch. 1959. Ed. James Grauerholz and
>   repub. info.
>   Barry Miles. New York: Grove, 2001. Print.

18. Title within a title Omit italics from any title that would normally be italicized when it falls within the main title of a book.

book title   title within title

Blamires, Harry. *The New Bloomsbury Book: A Guide Through* Ulysses.

    3rd ed. London: Routledge, 2006. Print.

If the title within the title appears in quotation marks, retain the quotation marks and italicize both titles.

19. Sacred text Italicize the title only when you are documenting a particular edition. Editors' and translators' names usually follow the title.

The New Oxford Annotated Bible. Ed. Michael D. Coogan, Marc Z. Brettler,

    Carol A. Newsom, and Pheme Perkins. Augmented 3rd ed. New

    York: Oxford UP, 2007. Print. Rev. Standard Vers. with Apocrypha.

The Holy Qur'an. Ed. and trans. Abdullah Yusuf Ali. 10th ed. Beltsville:

    Amana, 1997. Print.

20. Missing publication information Replace missing information with an appropriate abbreviation, such as *n.d.* for *no date* or *n.p.* for *no publisher* or *no place of publication.* (The letter *n* is capitalized following a period and lowercased after a comma.)

Barrett, Edgar, ed. *Football West Virginia 1960.* N.p.: West Virginia U,

    n.d. Print.

21. Pamphlet, brochure, or press release Follow the format for book entries. For a press release, include day and month of publication, if available.

Family Teams Key to March for Babies. Fargo: March of Dimes, 17 Jan.

    2008. Print.

If the item was emailed or published online, document it as you would a book published online.

MLA Works-Cited Entries

16. Book in a series
17. Republished book
18. **Title within a title**
19. **Sacred text**
20. **Missing publication information**
21. **Pamphlet, brochure, or press release**
22. Conference proceedings
23. Dissertation

Examples 1–7, 246–51

Example 1, 246

22. Conference proceedings Include the name of the conference, the sponsoring organization, and the date and location of the conference, if that information is not already included in the publication's title.

Bizzell, Patricia, ed. *Proceedings of the Rhetoric Society of America:* [sponsor]

Rhetorical Agencas: Political, Ethical, Spiritual. 28–31 May 2004, [title (conference)] [date]

U of Texas—Austin. Mahwah: Erlbaum, 2005. Print. [location]

Example 47, 283

For a paper delivered at a conference, follow the format for a lecture.

23. Dissertation Include the abbreviation *Diss.,* the school to which the dissertation was submitted (abbreviate *University* to *U*), and the year it was submitted. For published dissertations, set the title in italics.

Agopsowicz, William Joseph. *In Praise of Fantasy: A Study of the*

Nineteenth Century American Short Story (Poe, Hawthorne, Irving,

Melville, Bierce, James). Diss. Arizona State U, 1992. Ann Arbor:

UMI, 1992. Print.

For unpublished dissertations, put the title in quotation marks.

Brommer, Stephanie. "We Walk with Them: South Asian Women's

Organizations in Northern California Confront Domestic

Abuse." Diss. U of California–Santa Barbara, 2004. Print. [diss. submission info]

MLA Works-Cited Entries

20. Missing publication information
21. Pamphlet, brochure, or press release
22. Conference proceedings
23. Dissertation
24. Article in a scholarly journal
25. Article in a magazine

Periodicals—Printed and Electronic

A periodical is a publication issued at regular intervals—newspapers are typically published every day, magazines every week or month, and scholarly journals four times a year. Most researchers today find articles in periodicals by searching their library's *databases,* online indexes that provide citation information as well as an abstract (or summary) and sometimes an electronic copy of the article itself, in either PDF or HTML format. (A PDF file shows the article more or less as it would have appeared in print; an HTML file includes the text of the article but not the illustrations or formatting of the print version.) For all periodicals, include not only the title of the article (in quotation marks) but also the title of the periodical (in italics). The other publication information you include depends on the type of periodical you are documenting.

24. Article in a scholarly journal The information you need to create an entry for a printed journal article is on the cover or in the table of contents of the journal and the first and last page of the article. For articles downloaded from a database, the information you need appears on the screen listing the articles that fit your search terms and on the first and last page of the article. For articles downloaded from a database, the information you need appears on the screen listing the articles that fit your search terms, on the first and last page of the file you download, or in the full record for the article you select. For articles that appear in journals published solely online, you may find the information you need on the website's home page, in the journal's table of contents, or on the first screen of the article. Access dates for database and online articles should come from your notes.

a. Printed The basic entry for an article in a printed journal looks like this:

> Surname, First name. "Article Title." *Journal Title* volume.issue (year):
>
> pages. Medium of publication.

Here is an example of an actual entry:

> authors   article title
> Cantor, Nancy, and Steve Schomberg. "What We Want Students to Learn:
>   subtitle
> Cultivating Playfulness and Responsibility in a Liberal Education."
>   journal
>   title   issue yr.   pgs. medium
> *Change* 34.6 (2002): 47–49. Print.
>   vol.

b. Accessed through a database When you document an article from a scholarly journal that you accessed through an online database, add the name of the database (in italics), change the medium of publication to *Web,* and add the date (day, month, year) on which you accessed the work at the end of your entry.

▶▶▶Annotated visual of where to find author, title, publication, and other information, on foldout following p. 393

MLA Works-Cited Entries

Cantor, Nancy, and Steve Schomberg. "What We Want Students to

Learn: Cultivating Playfulness and Responsibility in a Liberal

Education." *Change* 34.6 (2002): 47–49. *Academic Search*
database

Premier. Web. 2 Dec. 2008 3 Mar. 2010.
medium   access date

c. Online

To document an online journal article, follow the model for a printed journal article, change the medium to *Web,* and add the date on which you accessed the article. Although many journals that are published only online do not provide all the information that is available for printed journals, your entry should include as much of that information as possible. If the article you are documenting omits page numbers, use *n. pag.* in their place. Include the article's URL only if readers will not be able to find the article by searching for the author or title. (The parts that are different from a printed journal article are highlighted below.)

Lohnes, Sarah, and Charles Kinzer. "Questioning Assumptions about

Students' Expectations for Technology in College Classrooms."

Innovate 3.5 (2007): n. pag. Web. 28 June 2007.
medium   access date

25. Article in a magazine (weekly, monthly)

a. Printed Provide the issue's publication date (month and year; or day, month, and year) and the page range for the article, but not the magazine's volume or issue number, even when they are available.

Samuels, David. "Shooting Britney." *Atlantic Monthly* Apr. 2008: 36–51.
pub. date   pgs.

Print.

Borowitz, Andy. "Not Your Father's Taliban." *New Yorker* 8 Mar. 2010: 31.

Print.

If the article appears on nonconsecutive pages (the first part appears on p. 2 but the rest of the article is continued on p. 10), include a plus sign after the first page number (*2+*).

b. Accessed through a database

Samuels, David. "Shooting Britney." *Atlantic Monthly* Apr. 2008:
      database   medium access date
    36–51. *Academic Search Premier.* Web. 25 Apr. 2008.

c. Online Very few online magazines include page or paragraph numbers; use *n. pag.* instead.

                                            pgs. medium

Stevenson, Seth. "Ads We Hate." *Slate* 26 Dec. 2006: n. pag. Web.
   access date
   3 Jan. 2007.

If you are documenting the online edition of a print magazine, provide the site name (usually a variation on the print title, such as *Progressive .org* or *Vanity Fair Online*), the publisher of the site, the publication date, and the date you accessed the material.

                                    site name

Carr, Nicholas. "Is Google Making Us Stupid?" *The Atlantic.com.*
  sponsor
  Atlantic Monthly Group, July/Aug. 2008. Web. 2 Dec. 2008.

26. Article in a newspaper The information you need to create an entry for a printed newspaper article is on the masthead of the newspaper (at the top of the first page) and on the first and last page of the article. For newspaper articles downloaded from a database, the information you need appears on the screen listing the articles that fit your search terms or on the first and last page of the article itself. Articles that appear in online versions of the newspaper usually contain all the information you need at the top of the first screen. Use conventional capitalization of titles even when your original source does not.

a. Printed For an article in a daily newspaper, include the date (day, month, year). If the paper paginates sections separately, include the section number, letter, or name immediately before the page number.

  Bolanos, Enrique. "Facing Down the Sandinistas." *Washington Times*
     date sec. & pg.
  12 May 2005: A20. Print.

If the section number or letter is not part of the page number, add the abbreviation *sec.* and the section name, number, or letter. If the section is named, add the section name before the abbreviation *sec.* If no author is listed, begin the entry with the title of the article. If the article continues on a nonconsecutive page, add a plus sign after the

MLA Works-Cited Entries

24. Article in a scholarly journal
25. Article in a magazine
26. Article in a newspaper
27. Article on microform
28. Review

first page number (*A20+*). If the newspaper's masthead specifies an edition (such as late edition or national edition), include that information after the date.

edition   section

Keller, Julia. "Viral Villainy." *Chicago Tribune* 22 Mar. 2009, final ed., sec. 6:
nonconsecutive pg.
1+. Print.

If the name of the city in which the newspaper is published does not appear in the newspaper's title, include it in brackets after the title.

Willman, David. "NIH Calls Actions of Senior Researcher 'Serious
newspaper   city
Misconduct.'" *Plain Dealer* [Cleveland] 10 Sept. 2006: A15. Print.

For well-known national newspapers (such as the *Christian Science Monitor, USA Today,* and the *Wall Street Journal*), no city or state is needed. If you are unsure whether the newspaper is well known, consult your instructor or a reference librarian.

b. Accessed through a database For a newspaper article accessed through a database, add the database name, change the medium to *Web,* and add the access date.

Bolanos, Enrique. "Facing Down the Sandinistas." *Washington Times*
database medium access date
12 May 2005: A20. *LexisNexis.* Web. 2 Dec. 2008.

c. Online For an online newspaper article, provide the website name and sponsor, and include your date of access.

Woo, Elaine. "Edna Parker Dies at 115; Former Teacher Was World's
website   sponsor
Oldest Person." *LATimes.com.* Los Angeles Times, 28 Nov. 2008.
access date
Web. 2 Dec. 2008.

Example 24a, 271
Example 25a, 272
Example 26a, 273

27. Article on microform Many libraries still store some back issues of periodicals on microform, a photograph of a periodical printed on plastic and viewed through a special microform reader. Your entry for an article stored on microform is the same as for a printed article.

If your source is preserved on microform in a reference source such as *NewsBank,* change the medium of publication to *Microform* and add the title of the reference source and any access numbers (such as fiche and grid numbers) following the medium of publication.

28. Review (printed or online) Begin with the reviewer's name (if provided), followed by the title of the review (if any) and the label *Rev. of* (for *Review of*). Then include the title and author of the work being reviewed. Finally, include the title of the periodical and its publication information. If the review was accessed online, add information as shown in item 24b–c, 25b–c, or 26b–c.

reviewer   title (review)   title (book)

Grover, Jan. "Unreliable Narrator." Rev. of *Love Works Like This: Opening*

author

One's Life to a Child, by Lauren Slater. *Women's Review of Books*

19.10–11 (2002): 40. Print.

29. Editorial Often editorials are unsigned. When that is the case, begin the title of the editorial (if any). Then insert the label *Editorial* and follow with the periodical's publication information.

editorial title

"Expanding the Horizon: OSU President Seeks to Give Students a New

label

View of Their Place in the World." Editorial. *Columbus Dispatch*

12 Mar. 2009: A8. Print.

If the editorial was accessed online, add information as shown in item 23b–c, 24b–c, or 25b–c.

30. Letter to the editor Begin with the author's name, followed by the label *Letter* and the periodical's publication information.

letter author   label

Pritchett, Laura. Letter. *Poets & Writers Magazine* Jan.–Feb. 2004: 7. Print.

If the letter to the editor has a title, add it after the author's name (in quotation marks). If the letter to the editor was accessed online, add information as shown in item 23b–c, 24b–c, or 25b–c.

Other Electronic Sources

While it is usually easy to find the information you need to create a complete entry for a book or an article in a periodical, websites can be a bit trickier. Most of the information you need will appear on the site's home page, usually at the bottom or top of the page, or on the web page you are documenting. Sometimes you may need to look

MLA Works-Cited Entries

26. Article in a newspaper
27. Article on microform
28. Review
29. Editorial
30. Letter to the editor
31. Website
32. Web page

▶▶▶Annotated visual of where to find author, title, publication, and other information, on foldout following p. 393.

further: Click on links such as "About us" or "More information." Frequently, websites will not provide complete information, so provide as much as you can.

31. Website The basic entry for a website looks like this:

Author's surname, First name. *Website Title.* Site sponsor, Publication date

or date last updated. Sponsor. Medium. Access date.

Here is an example of an actual entry:

      editor   title (website)
McGann, Jerome J., ed. *The Complete Writings and Pictures of Dante*

Gabriel Rossetti: A Hypermedia Archive. Institute for Advanced
                                site sponsors
Technology in the Humanities, U of Virginia, and Networked

Infrastructure for Nineteenth-Century Electronic Scholarship.
update medium access date
2008. Web. 5 May 2010.

If no author or editor is listed, begin with the website's title.

32. Web page or short work on a website Add the title of the web page to the entry for a website.

                  page title
Bahri, Deepika. "Yehuda Amichai." *Postcolonial Studies.* Dept. of English,

Emory U. 13 Nov. 2002. Web. 7 Feb. 2007.

Personal websites often do not provide all the information needed to create a complete entry. If the site does not have a title, include the identifier home page or website; if the title includes the author's name, do not restate it.

33. Home page (academic)
a. Course

    instructor   title (course)   title (website)   site sponsor
Gray, David. "Introduction to Ethics." *Dept. of Philosophy,* Carnegie
                       medium access date
Mellon U, Spring 2006. Web. 17 Apr. 2007.

b. Department

    dept.   label
English. Dept. home page. U of California–Santa Barbara. 2005. Web.

20 July 2007.

34. Discussion list posting Treat the subject line (or *thread*) as the title, and include the name of the list, the sponsoring group, and the date of the posting.

subj. line   list name

Tucker, Mieke Koppen. "Grammar Study." *Writing Program Administration*

site sponsor post date

Discussion List. WPA, 7 Oct. 1995. Web. 2 Jan. 2004.

35. Article on a wiki Since wikis are written and edited collaboratively, there is no author to cite. Instead, begin the entry with the article title.

"The Knife of Never Letting Go." *ChildLitWiki.* Mat Berman, 14 Sept. 2008.

Web. 17 Sept. 2008.

36. Blog

a. Blog

blogger   title (blog)   sponsor   update

Vaidhyanathan, Siva. *Sivacracy.net.* Siva Vaidhyanathan, 2010. Web.

access date   medium

12 June 2010.

b. Blog posting

author (post)   title (post)

Bartow, Ann. "Why Are There So Many Academic Books Out There That

Would Be Better as Longish Articles?" *Sivacracy.net.* Siva

date (post)

Vaidhyanathan, 26 Dec. 2006. Web. 30 Dec. 2006.

c. Comment on a blog posting

author (comment)   title of entry commented on

Bailey, Jonathan. "Content Theft / Blog Plagiarism." *Cube Games.*

sponsor   date (comment)

Ryan McCue, 18 Nov. 2004. Web. 19 Nov. 2004.

If the comment's author uses a screen name, use that; if the actual name is available and of interest to readers, provide that as well, following the screen name, in square brackets.

37. *Second Life* If the author/speaker uses an avatar with a different name than the writer's actual name, use the avatar's name, but if the writer's actual name is available and of interest to readers (it may lend credibility, for example), provide it in square brackets following the avatar name.

avatar   actual name
Reuters, Eric [Eric Krangel]. "*Second Life* on *The Daily Show*." *Second*

sponsor/host
Life News Center/Reuters. Linden Lab, 8 Apr. 2007. Web.

10 Feb. 2008.

38. Source published in more than one medium Some sources may include multiple media; for example, a printed book may come with a supplementary website or CD-ROM. In the entry in your list of works cited, follow the entry format for the part of the source that you mainly used, but list all the media you consulted in alphabetical order.

Davis, Robert L., H. Jay Siskin, and Alicia Ramos. *Entrevistas: An*

Introduction to Language and Culture. 2nd ed. New York: McGraw,

list of media
2005. Print, website.

39. Computer software

release   download
title   vendor date   medium   date
PowerResearcher. Atlanta: Uniting Networks, 2004. Digital file. 8 June 2004.

40. Video game

release
game   publisher date
Rock Band 2. Wii. Nintendo, 2008.
platform

Audio and Visual Sources

The information you need to create an entry for most audio and visual sources will appear on the cover, label, or program of the work or in the credits at the end of a film. The person you list in the "author" position—the director, performer, artist, or composer—will vary depending on what you have emphasized in your research project. If you are writing about a director's body of work, put the director's name first; if you are writing about a performance, put the performer's name first. If you are writing about the work itself, put the title of the work first. (This decision should be mirrored in your in-text citation.) However you choose to organize the entry, indicate the role of those whom you list, using abbreviations such as *perf.* (*performer*), *dir.* (*director*), and *cond.* (*conductor*).

As with any other entry, italicize the titles of complete or longer works (such as albums, films, operas, and original works of art) and place quotation marks around the titles of shorter works or works published as part of a larger whole (such as songs on a CD or a single episode of a television show). Publication information includes the name of the distributor, production company, or network, as well as the date on which the audio or visual was created, recorded, or broadcast. The medium will be *Film, DVD, Television, Radio, Podcast*—however you accessed the work. If you found the audio or visual source online, also include the date on which you last accessed it.

41. Motion picture

a. Film

title   director   distributor   release date   medium
King of Kong. Dir. Seth Gordon. PictureHouse Entertainment, 2007. Film.

If other artists besides the director are relevant to your project, list them between the director and the distributor.

performers
King of Kong. Dir. Seth Gordon. Perf. Steve Wiebe and Billy Mitchell.

PictureHouse Entertainment, 2007. Film.

If your project stresses the director, performer, or other contributor, place that information at the beginning of the citation.

Gordon, Seth, dir. *King of Kong.* Perf. Steve Wiebe and Billy Mitchell.

PictureHouse Entertainment, 2007. Film.

b. Video or DVD Include the original release date, when relevant, before the distributor, and include the medium you viewed.

The Lady Eve. Dir. Preston Sturges. Perf. Barbara Stanwyck and Henry
orig. release   distributor   medium
Fonda. 1941. Universal Home Entertainment, 2006. DVD.

c. Internet download Include the date on which you accessed the film.

Juno. Screenplay by Diablo Cody. Dir. Jason Reitman. Perf. Ellen Page,

Michael Cera, Jennifer Garner, Jason Bateman. Fox Searchlight,
access date
2007. iTunes, 2008. Internet download. 19 Jan. 2009.

MLA Works-Cited Entries

39. Computer software
40. Video game
41. **Motion picture**
42. DVD extras
43. Television or radio broadcast

d. Online video clip Cite a video clip on *YouTube* or a similar site as you would a web page.

performer   video clip title   website
Ok Go. "This Too Shall Pass—Rube Goldberg Machine Version." *YouTube.*

site sponsor   medium
YouTube, 2 Mar. 2010. Web. 4 Mar. 2010.
      date posted   date accessed

42. DVD extras Add the title of the extra (in quotation marks).

DVD extra
"Making *Capote:* Concept to Script." *Capote.* Dir. Bennett Miller. Perf.

Philip Seymour Hoffman and Catherine Keener. 2005. Sony Pictures,

2006. DVD.

43. Television or radio broadcast In most cases, begin with the title of the series or episode. Follow that with a list of the relevant contributors and information about the local station that broadcast the program (omit for cable). Because the director may change from episode to episode, other contributors, such as the creator or producer, may be more relevant. Include the date of the program and the medium in which you accessed it. If your project emphasizes an individual, begin with that person's name. Add any supplementary information at the end of the entry.

a. Series

series title
The Office. Creat. and exec. prod. Greg Daniels, Ricky Gervais, and

Stephen Merchant. Perf. Steve Carell, Rainn Wilson, John

                        city of local
           network   station
Krasinski, and Jenna Fischer. NBC. WNBC, New York,
      broadcast dates   call letters
24 Mar. 2005–20 May 2010. Television.
              medium

Bridging the Morphine Gap. Host, Mukti Jain Campion. BBC. Radio 4,

London, 3 Mar. 2008. Radio.

b. Episode

"In Buddy's Eyes." *Desperate Housewives.* Perf. Teri Hatcher, Felicity

Huffman, Marcia Cross, Eva Longoria Parker, and Nicollette

Sheridan. ABC. KNXV, Phoenix, 20 Apr. 2008. Internet download,

supplementary info.
television. *iTunes, 2008.*

c. Single program

Persuasion. By Jane Austen. Adapt. Simon Burke. Perf. Julia Davis and

Rupert Penry-Jones. PBS. WGBH, Boston, 13 Jan. 2008. Television.

d. Podcast For a podcast, replace the original medium of publication with the word *Podcast* and the date on which you accessed the file.

"The Giant Pool of Money." Narr. Ira Glass. *This American Life.* Natl. Public

medium   access date
Radio. WBEZ, Chicago, 27 Sept. 2008. Podcast. 3 Oct. 2008.

44. Musical or other audio recording Begin with whichever part of the entry is most relevant to your project—the name of the composer or performer, or the title of the CD or song. Place the title of shorter works, such as a song, in quotation marks. Italicize the titles of longer works, such as the title of an opera, but not the titles of symphonies identifid only by form, number, and key, such as Brahms's Symphony no. 1.

a. CD, LP, audiobook

Adamo, Mark. *Little Women.* Perf. Stephanie Novacek, Chad Shelton,

Margaret Lloyd, and Stacey Tappan. Houston Grand Opera.

prod. co. & release date
Cond. Patrick Summers. Ondine, 2001. CD.
medium

Bruckner, Anton. Symphony No. 8. Vienna Philharmonic Orchestra. Cond.

Herbert von Karajan. Deutsche Grammophon, 1989. CD.

MLA Works-Cited Entries

42. DVD extras
43. Television or radio broadcast
44. Musical or other audio recording
45. Live performance
46. Musical composition

b. Song or selection from a CD or a chapter from an audiobook

Los Campesinos. "My Year in Lists." *Hold on Now, Youngster.* . . . Arts &

Crafts, 2008. CD.

c. Compressed music file (MP3, MP4)

Los Campesinos. "My Year in Lists." *Hold on Now, Youngster.* . . .

supplementary info.   download date
Arts & Crafts, 2008. *iTunes,* 2008. MP3. 16 Dec. 2008.

d. Online sound file or clip For a sound recording accessed online, combine the format for a web page with the format for a sound recording.

author   selection title
Chaucer, Geoffrey. "'The Miller's Tale': Nicholas Seduces Alisoun."

title of work   website
Perf. Alfred David. *The Canterbury Tales.* "The Criyng and the Soun":

sponsor
The Chaucer Metapage Audio Files. VA Military Inst. Dept. of Eng.

date posted   date accessed
and Fine Arts. 11 Dec. 2006. Web. 20 July 2007.

> Example 32, 276

MLA Works-
Cited Entries

45. Live performance The entry for a performance is similar to that for a film. Instead of the distributor, year of release, and medium of publication, include the group (if any), the venue and city of the performance, the date of the performance you attended, and the word *Performance.* If your project emphasizes the composer, writer, or performer, begin the entry with that information. If the performance is untitled, include a descriptive label.

a. Ensemble

Macbeth. By William Shakespeare. Dir. Christopher Carter Sanderson.

Perf. Natasha Badillo, Ambjorn Elder, and Frances You.

group   venue   city
Gorilla Repertory Theatre Company. Fort Tryon Park, New York.

perf. date
17 May 2002. Performance.

b. Individual

performer   descriptive label
Stinespring, Marjorie M. Piano recital. Chicago State University.

2 Mar. 2004. Performance.

46. Musical composition To document a musical composition itself rather than a specific performance, recording, or published version of it, include the composer and the title of the work (in italics unless the composition is identified only by form, number, and key).

composer   untitled symphony
Schumann, Robert. Symphony no. 1 in B-flat major, op. 38.

47. Lecture, speech, or debate Treat the speaker as the author; place the title in quotation marks (if there is one); and indicate the occasion and sponsoring organization (if relevant), location, date, and mode of delivery. If the lecture, speech, or debate is untitled, replace the title with a brief descriptive label.

speaker   title   sponsor
Capri, Frank. "The Peace Movement of the 1960s." 92nd St. Y,
location   date   medium
New York. 14 Mar. 2010. Lecture.

48. Table For a table included in your paper, place a source note below the table. For a table that you are discussing but that does not appear in your paper, follow the model below:

author   title   label   website
United States. Senate. "Senate Salaries since 1789." Chart. *U.S. Senate.*
sponsor   access date medium
U.S. Senate, 7 June 2004. Web.

49. Work of art For a work of art included in your paper, place source information in the figure caption. For a work that you discuss but that does not appear in your project, include an entry in your list of works cited following the models below.

a. Original work

             date of
artist   title   production medium
Pollock, Jackson. *One Number 31, 1950.* 1950. Acrylic on canvas.
location
Museum of Modern Art, New York.

b. Reproduction of a work of art

Lichtenstein, Roy. *Whaam!* 1963. Acrylic on canvas. Tate Gallery, London.

Responding to Art: Form, Content, and Context. By Robert Bersson.

New York: McGraw, 2004. Print.

50. Comic or cartoon For a cartoon reproduced in your project, provide source information in the caption. For cartoons that you discuss but that do not appear in your project, include an entry in your list of works cited following the models below.

a. Cartoon or comic strip

artist   title   label   publication information
Wright, Larry. "Kit 'n' Carlyle." Comic strip. *Evening Sun* [Norwich, NY]
medium
28 Dec. 2006: 8. Print.

b. Comic book or graphic novel

authors   title
Pekar, Harvey, and Joyce Brabner. *Our Cancer Year.* Illus. Frank Stack.
pub. info.   medium
Philadelphia: Running Press, 1994. Print.

51. Map or chart For a map or chart reproduced in your project, provide source information in the caption. For a map or chart discussed but not included in your project, include an entry in your list of works cited following the model below.

"The Invasion of Sicily: Allied Advance to Messina (23 July–17 August
label
1943." Map. *The West Point Atlas of American Wars.* Ed.

Vincent J. Esposito. Vol. 2. New York: Praeger, 1959. Print.

52. Advertisement For an advertisement reproduced in your project, provide source information in the caption. For an advertisement discussed but not included in your project, include an entry in your list of works cited following the model below.

label
Earthlink Cable Internet. Advertisement. *Metro* 17 Apr. 2007: 11. Print.
date accessed
Infiniti. Advertisement. *Yahoo.com.* Web. 20 Apr. 2007.
date viewed
Domino's Pizza. Advertisement. Comedy Central. 2 Aug. 2006.

Television.

Miscellaneous Sources

53. Government publication If no author is listed, use the name of the governing nation and the government agency or department that produced the document as you would for a work with a corporate author. Abbreviate Government Printing Office as *GPO*.

Example 7, 251

nation   department
United States. War Department. *Advanced Map and Aerial Photograph*

    Reading. Washington: GPO, 1941. Print.

For Congressional documents, include the number and session of Congress and the number and type of document. Common abbreviations in U.S. government documents include the following:

HR	House of Representatives	**Res.**	Resolution
S	Senate	**Doc.**	Document
Sess.	Session	**GPO**	Government Printing Office
Rept.	Report		

MLA Works-Cited Entries

a. **Printed**

    United States. Cong. House. *Combat Bonus Act.* 110th Cong., 2nd sess.

      HR 6760. Washington: GPO, 2008. Print.

b. **Online**

    United States. Cong. House. *Combat Bonus Act.* 110th Cong., 2nd sess.

website   sponsor
      HR 6760. *Thomas.gov.* Library of Congress, 31 July 2008. Web.

access date
      16 Dec. 2008.

54. Legal case

legal case   case number   court   decision yr
Gideon v. Wainwright. 372 US 335. Supreme Court of the US. 1963.
website   sponsor   medium access date
FindLaw. Thomas Reuters, 2010. Web. 16 Dec. 2008.
update

55. Letter (published)

Example 10, 265

a. **Single letter** Cite a single letter as you would a selection from an edited book or anthology, but add the recipient's name, the date the letter was written, and the letter number (if there is one).

author   recipient   date written
Brooks, Phillips. "To Agnes." 24 Sept. 1882. *Children's Letters: A Collection*

Example 9, 264

of Letters Written to Children by Famous Men and Women. Ed.

Elizabeth Colson and Anna Gauseroot Chittenden. New York: Hinds,

1905. 3–4. Print.

Examples 24–26, 271–74

b. Collection of letters Cite as you would an edited book or anthology.

Example 43, 280–81

56. Interview Treat a published interview as you would an article in a periodical. Treat an interview broadcast on radio or television or podcasted as you would a broadcast. In either case, if there is no title, use the label *Interview,* and include the interviewer's name. For an unpublished interview you conducted, include the name of the person interviewed, the label *Personal interview, Telephone interview,* or *Email interview,* and the date on which the interview took place.

MLA Works-
Cited Entries

54. Legal case
55. Letter
    (published)
56. Interview
57. Personal
    correspondence
58. Diary or journal

person
interviewed   label   date
Freund, Deborah. Personal interview. 11 Feb. 2003.

57. Personal correspondence To document personal correspondence, such as a letter or email message you received, include a descriptive label such as *Letter to the author* or *Message to the author,* as well as the medium (*MS* for "manuscript;" *Email*).

a. Letter

letter writer   label   date written
Gould, Stephen Jay. Letter to the author. 13 Nov. 1986. MS.
                                                            medium

b. Email Treat the subject line as the title; include the descriptive label *Message to the author* and the date the email message was sent. Change the medium to *Email.*

email author   subject line   label
Elbow, Peter. "Re: bibliography about resistance." Message to the author.
date sent   medium
12 Apr. 2004. Email.

A mass email or electronic memo should include a label describing recipients, such as *Email to ENG 204 students.*

c. Memorandum Very few institutions send out printed memos anymore, but if you need to document one, treat it as you would an email message, replacing the word *email* with the word *memo* at the end of your entry.

d. Instant message (IM)

> White, Rose. Message to the author. 14 June 2007. Instant Message.

58. Diary or journal

a. Single entry, published Treat an entry in a published diary or journal like an article in an edited book or anthology, but include a descriptive label (*Diary entry*) and the date of composition after the entry title.

Example 10, 250

b. Single entry, unpublished

> writer   title
> Zook, Aaron. "Sketches for *Aesop's Foibles* (new musical)."
> label   entry date medium
> Journal entry. 1 May 2007. MS.

c. Diary or journal, published Treat a complete diary or journal as you would an edited book or anthology.

Example 9, 250

21c   Using MLA Style for Informational Notes

In addition to in-text citations, MLA style allows researchers to include informational notes to provide relevant, but potentially distracting, content or to provide bibliographic information about one or more sources. MLA style recommends using a list of endnotes at the end of the project. To identify informational notes in the text, include a superscript (above-the-line) arabic number that corresponds to the note number in the list of endnotes. Include an entry for each source in your list of works cited.

MLA Works-
Cited Entries

56. Interview
57. Personal
    correspondence
58. Diary or journal

> Beneath the crude humor of *Zap* and similar comics lay insightful commentary on society and its principles, which many readers found to be a refreshing change from mainstream superhero titles.[1] . . . Comics like Tomine's provide a subject or situation that readers can identify with more easily than, say, Superman's battles with Brainiac.[2]

Notes

1. According to Schnakenberg, more than two million copies of *Zap* comics were in print by 1999.

2. For an intriguing argument that the world of classic comic book superheroes is not so different from our own—including a discussion of how comics before World War II commented on then current events—see Wright 1-28.

Sample student research paper, MLA style, 294–305

21d Formatting a Paper in MLA Style

If you are writing for English, composition, or foreign language classes (or if your instructor asks you to), format your project using MLA style. Lydia Nichols's paper, at the end of this chapter, provides a model.

1. Margins and spacing

Set one-inch margins at the top, bottom, and sides of your paper. Indent the first line of each paragraph one-half inch. Double-space the entire paper, including long quotations, the list of works cited, and any endnotes. Indent the first line of each paragraph by half an inch, and do not add an extra space between paragraphs. Use a hanging indent for each entry in the list of works cited: The first line should be flush with the left margin with subsequent lines indented half an inch.

More about ▶▶▶ Choosing a typeface and type size, 219–20

2. Typeface

Choose a standard typeface, such as Times New Roman or Arial, in a readable size (usually 12-point).

3. Header

MLA style requires that each page of your project include a header, consisting of your surname and the page number. Place the header in the upper right-hand corner, a half inch from the upper edge and one inch from the right edge of the page.

➡ **Tech**

Creating a Header

Most word processing programs allow you to insert a header. In Microsoft *Word,* select "Header and Footer" under the View menu. A box for the header will appear at the top of your page, and a box for the footer at the bottom. Any information you type into these boxes will then appear on every page of your manuscript. From the menu bar, you can choose to insert page numbers into the header or footer to paginate your project automatically.

4. Identifying information

No title page is required in MLA style. Instead, include the following identifying information in the upper left-hand corner of the first page of your research project, one inch from the top and left edges of the paper:

- Your name
- Your instructor's name
- The number of the course in which you are submitting the paper
- The date

If you are required to provide a title page, Figure 21.2 provides a model.

5. Title

Center the title of your project and insert it two lines below the date. Do not put quotation marks around your title or italicize it. Drop down two more lines before beginning to type your first paragraph.

More about ▶▶▶
Developing a title, 173

6. Long quotations

Set quotations of prose longer than four lines of your text as a block: Omit the quotation marks and indent the entire quotation one inch from the left margin of your text. When quoting four or more lines of poetry, indent all the lines one inch from the left margin; keep the same indentation and line breaks that were in the original poem; and include the line numbers of the passage quoted. If a line of the poem

More about ▶▶▶
Block quotations, 118, 123
Example block quotation, 248

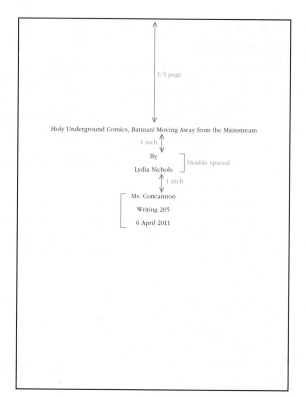

1/3 page

Holy Underground Comics, Batman! Moving Away from the Mainstream

1 inch

By

Lydia Nichols

Double spaced

1 inch

Ms. Concannon

Writing 205

6 April 2011

FIGURE 21.2 A Sample Title Page Note that the title precedes the identifying information from the heading and that the title page does not include a header.

is too long to fit on a single line of your page, indent the continuation by an extra quarter of an inch.

7. Tables and figures

Tables and figures (photographs, cartoons, graphs, and charts) are most effective when they appear as close as possible after the text in which they are first discussed. (If placing figures and tables appropriately is awkward, consider including them in an appendix at the end of your project.) Labeling your tables and figures, both in the text and in your caption, will help readers connect your discussion with the illustration:

- Refer to the visual in your text using the word *table* or the abbreviation *fig.,* and number figures and tables in a separate sequence using arabic numerals (table 1, table 2; fig. 1, fig. 2). MLA style uses lowercase for in-text references to tables and figures unless they begin a sentence: "Table 1 presents 2005 data, and table 2 presents 2009 data."

- Accompany each illustration with the word *Table* or the abbreviation *Fig.,* the appropriate number, and a brief, explanatory title. Customarily, table numbers and titles appear above the table, and figure numbers and titles appear below the figure. They usually use the same margins as the rest of the paper.

- If additional information is needed, provide an explanatory caption after the number and title. (Your text should explain what the figure or table demonstrates. That information should not be repeated in the caption.)

- If you borrow the illustration or borrow information needed to create the illustration, cite your source. Any photographs or drawings you create yourself should identify the subject but do not need a citation. Citations usually appear below the table in a source note or in the figure caption. If you document the illustration in a figure caption or source note, you do not need to include an entry in your list of works cited.

8. Printing and binding

If you are submitting a hard copy of your project, print it using a high-quality printer (make sure it has plenty of ink), on opaque 8½ × 11–inch white paper. Most instructors do not want you to enclose your paper in a binder. Unless your instructor tells you otherwise, staple or paper-clip the pages together in the upper left-hand corner.

9. Portfolios

Many instructors ask students to submit the final draft of the research paper in a portfolio, which may include a research log, an outline, preliminary notes and drafts, a working or annotated bibliography, and a

More about ▶▶▶
Portfolio, 51–52
Research notes, 117
Working bibliography, 52–53
Annotated bibliography, 53–56
Outlining and sample outlines, 162–66

Writing Responsibly

Of Deadlines, Staples, and Paper Clips

Instructors expect students to turn in thoughtful, carefully proofread, and neatly formatted papers on time—usually in class on the due date. Another assumption is that the writer will clip or staple the pages of the paper *before* it is submitted. Do justice to yourself by being fully prepared.

personal statement describing your writing process and what you have learned from the experience (Figure 21.3).

Student Research Project: MLA Style

In the sample student research project that follows, Lydia Nichols explores the world of underground comics. She uses comparison-contrast to support her claim that underground comics are more innovative than their mainstream cousins, and she provides a historical overview to fill in the background her readers lack. Her research draws on a variety of print and online sources, and she uses visuals to support some of her points.

More about ▶▶▶
Gathering information, 60–75
Online research, 76–87
Using visuals as support, 186–87

FIGURE 21.3 Page 1 of Lydia Nichols's Personal Statement Nichols created a visual personal statement to explain how her interest in underground comics developed.

½″ 1″

Header

Header: Author's surname, page number

1″

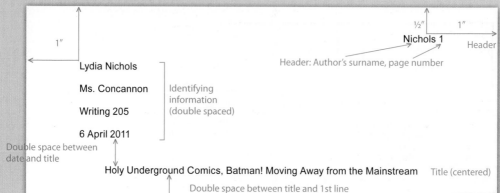

Lydia Nichols

Ms. Concannon

Writing 205

6 April 2011

Identifying information (double spaced)

Double space between date and title

Holy Underground Comics, Batman! Moving Away from the Mainstream Title (centered)

Double space between title and 1st line

½″ When most people think of comic books, predictable images usually

come to mind: caped heroes, maniacal villains, deeds of incredible strength,

and other typical elements of super-powered adventures. Undeniably, characters

like Batman, Superman, and Spider-Man are the most prominent features of

the comic book landscape, in terms of both popularity and revenue (Wright xiv).

However, there is more to comic books than superpowers and secret identities.

Underground comics (also known as *comix*), printed by small publishers or by

individual artists, are very different from what is usually expected in the genre.

While far less well-known than their superhero counterparts, underground comics

often offer an innovative and more sophisticated alternative to mainstream titles.

Almost from the beginning, comic books were associated with superheroes.

The first comic books appeared in the early 1930s, nearly four decades after

comic strips such as *Yellow Boy* began appearing in the major newspapers.

Yet comic books did not gain widespread popularity until June of 1938, when

writer Jerry Siegel and artist Joe Shuster debuted their character Superman in

Action Comics #1 (Daniels 9). Superman was an immediate success, and he

quickly inspired the creation of copycat superheroes in other comic books. The

1″

Funnel introduction: Initiates contrast, moves from familiar to unfamiliar, concludes with thesis

In-text citation—book

Thesis: Establishes topic, purpose, and author's position

Topic sentence: Prepares reader for historical overview

Body: Begins with historical overview

protagonists of these comics each had their own strengths and vulnerabilities, but the stories all shared a basic formula: individuals with extraordinary abilities battling against evil and struggling to maintain a secret identity. These superhero comics, though similar to each other, set the comic book industry on its feet, paving the way to profits and sustained success (Daniels 9). Over the decades and even today, the best-selling comics have typically been in the superhero genre.

While artists and writers over the years have certainly done inventive work in superhero comics, some similarity in mainstream titles was for many years unavoidable. This was due to the creation in 1954 of the Comics Code Authority (CCA), an organization formed by a number of the leading comic publishers to regulate the content of comics (Heller 101). It set very explicit standards, dictating what content was allowed in comic books and what content was expected. Some parts of the code are incredibly specific and controlling:

> The letters of the word "crime" on a comics magazine shall never be appreciably greater in dimension than the other words contained in the title. The word "crime" shall never appear alone on a cover. . . . Restraint in the use of the word "crime" in titles or subtitles shall be exercised.
> (qtd. in "Good Shall Triumph over Evil")

Other rules were more general—vague enough to allow the CCA a free hand in shaping content. One read, "Respect for parents, the moral code, and for honorable behavior shall be fostered" (qtd. in "Good Shall Triumph over Evil"). The CCA also regulated the presentation of criminals and criminal acts, themes of religion and race, and dialogue, especially profanity. While the CCA had no legal authority,

Block indention for long quotes

Indirect source: Author unknown, so title used

Quotation marks for brief quotation

major magazine distributors refused comics that did not have CCA approval. Many comic publishers, such as EC Comics (*Vault of Horror, Tales from the Crypt*), were virtually forced out of business as a result of the CCA, though the banned titles would eventually gain the appreciation of collectors and aspiring comic artists such as Art Spiegelman, author of the graphic novel *Maus* (1986) ("Comic Book Code"). Other publishers, including DC Comics, made their artists abide by CCA rules in order to continue selling to a wide audience. The result was that the comics with the largest distribution were those that conformed to the CCA's strict rules about appropriate language, subjects, and tone ("Good Shall Triumph over Evil").

Website: no page numbers

In the 1960s, in contrast to mainstream CCA-approved superhero comics (fig. 1, left), alternatives (fig. 1, right) began to appear. Robert Crumb's *Zap,* first released in 1968, initiated the "underground comix revolution" (Heller 101). Crumb and other like-minded artists did not submit their comics for CCA approval. Though this limited the distribution of their work, it allowed them artistic freedom. From its first issue, *Zap* satirized mainstream, conservative beliefs and did not shy away from sexual or political content (Heller 101–02). Beneath the crude humor of *Zap* and similar comics lay insightful commentary on society and its principles, which many readers found to be a refreshing change from mainstream superhero titles.[1]

Figure number in text to link discussion to visual

Citation: Placement separates writer's ideas from source information

Content note

To see the contrast between these mainstream and underground comics, compare the two covers in fig. 1. The *Amazing Fantasy* cover (left) includes the Comics Code Authority approval stamp in its upper right corner, while the *Snarf* cover (right) does not. The *Snarf* cover actually pokes fun at covers like the one at left; on the *Amazing Fantasy* cover, superhero Spider-Man dangles from a high

Topic sentence: Claim supported by visual, analysis

Fig. 1. Mainstream versus Underground Comics. Spider-Man (left) extols (and exhibits) his prowess as superhero, while (right) a less conventional comic book "hero" struts his stuff. (Left: Cover from Jack Kirby and Steve Ditko, *Amazing Fantasy* #15. [New York: Marvel Comics, 1962]; right: Cover from Robert Crumb, *Snarf* #6 [Amherst: Kitchen Sink Enterprises, 1976])

building by a thread, proclaiming his "awesome might" to the world, while on the *Snarf* cover, a geeky guy in an unwieldy homemade contraption wants to save the world by fighting "the big companies"—which include oil companies (the "Gas" industry this inventor is trying to boycott) and probably DC Comics, too.

Topic sentence: Claim supported by examples

Underground comics continue to be less well-known than superhero comics, but they are also better-respected among mature readers for their bold and inventive content. Graphic novels, such as Spiegelman's *Maus* and Harvey Pekar's *Our Cancer Year* (1994), have successfully addressed some of the most highly charged and sensitive subjects in modern society. Both of these show the subtlety of and the wide range of topics that underground comics explore. Other common themes of underground comics include sex and sexual identity, politics, and social issues (Daniels 165), as shown in Crumb's work, which is well known for its satirical approach to countercultural topics (Heller).

Illustrations referenced but not reproduced in paper

Refers to entire work: no page number

Topic sentence: Claim supported by example, visual, quotation

Mainstream superhero comics are set on an epic scale—depicting amazing feats, heroic battles between good and evil, and the like—while underground comics tend to focus on everyday life. Adrian Tomine, for example, has been called "a master of pseudorealistic stories" due to his ability to present an ordinary situation as profoundly interesting and complex (Weiner 58; see fig. 2). Comics like Tomine's also provide a subject or situation that readers can identify with more easily than, say, Superman's battles with Brainiac.[2]

Bibliographic note

The quirky perspectives of underground artists would be impossible in mainstream comics because the structure for producing and publishing mainstream comics limits the input of the artists working on them. The modern comic book industry is a huge business, selling not only comics, but also related merchandise such as T-shirts, toys, and video games, not to mention tickets to comic book–inspired movies. Story decisions involving major characters such as Batman or the Hulk have to be made with profits in mind. Because mainstream

Fig. 2. Comic whose characters face realistic challenges—the loss of a loved one, parental guilt—that readers can easily relate to. From Adrian Tomine, *Optic Nerve* #6, p. 22 (Montreal: Drawn and Quarterly, Feb. 1999).

comic publishers often change the creative teams working on their titles (Herndon) and because teams can include dozens of members (McCloud 180), individual artists can have only so much impact on a particular character or story. Most mainstream comics are the result of work done by many different people.

Online article: no page reference

In contrast, the individual artist in the underground realm has almost total control in creating his or her comic book. The creative teams working on underground titles are usually very small, and they rarely change (Herndon). Les Daniels, who has written several books about DC Comics' creations, notes that underground comic artists are not controlled by corporate interests that discourage "daring" material that might not sell (165, 180). This freedom allows for the uninhibited creativity that distinguishes underground comics from their more commercially oriented counterparts.

Underground artists not only push the envelope in terms of content, but they also incorporate experimental visual devices, earning critical praise for breaking away from traditional comic layouts in favor of more artistic perspectives. Artists such as Daniel Clowes argue that comic art can be more evocative than film, especially in the use of nonlinear storytelling techniques (Hignite 18). *New York Times* columnist John Hodgman agrees: Discussing a moment of existential crisis in Kevin Huizenga's *Ganges* #1, he writes, "I have never seen any film or read any prose that gets at that frozen moment when we suddenly feel our mortality, when God is seen or denied, as effectively as a comic panel." Artist Chris Ware manipulates the borders and frames in his comics so extensively that even reading his works can feel like an art to be mastered (see fig. 3). The demands his comics place on the reader create an interaction between viewer and artist that is unheard of in the pages of superhero titles.

While Ware and Clowes demonstrate how the page can be used to create innovative and complicated layouts, other underground artists excel at creating

---

Annotations (margin notes):

- Transition
- Signal phrase
- Information from two passages, same source
- Claim supported by summary, quotation, visual example
- Signal phrase with background; one-page article—no page number

Title identifies illustration

Caption explains visual support of claim

Fig. 3. Cover from Chris Ware's *Jimmy Corrigan: The Smartest Kid on Earth* (New York: Pantheon, 2000). Critically acclaimed *Jimmy Corrigan* comics use visual storytelling techniques, pushing the limitations of comics and forcing the reader to work to achieve understanding.

simple, striking visuals. Unlike mainstream comics, which depict dynamic scenes through loud, flamboyant colors, underground comics often achieve their effects through simplicity. Frequently, they are printed in black and white or with limited colors, with characters rendered in clean, bold lines. The clarity and lack of clutter in such art allows for immediate, striking storytelling (see fig. 2).

Reference to earlier figure

Obviously, most underground comics are not intended for young children. Yet, because of the childish connotations of the term "comic," most adults overlook the fascinating work that underground comic artists do. The association of comics with superheroes and children has made reading comics a source of shame or embarrassment for many adults. As Clowes comments, "I think that the average reader is far more open to a well-designed book than a standard comic book. . . . Very few would feel comfortable reading a standard comic book pamphlet" (qtd. in Hignite 17). Artists such as Scott McCloud have changed this perception of comic books by offering a broader definition of what a comic is. According to McCloud, comics are "juxtaposed pictorial and other images in a deliberate sequence" (12). This definition includes not only what one might find in the latest Spider-Man comic, but also all the experimental work that McCloud and his underground colleagues are creating.

Signal phrase and parenthetical page reference

McCloud and others have succeeded in bringing underground comics to a wider audience. Since the 1980s, comics have been finding their way into gallery and museum exhibitions, where the craftsmanship of the individual comic book artist can be better appreciated (Hignite 18). Major newspapers like the *New York Times* have begun featuring comics in their pages, including serialized graphic novels such as *George Sprott (1894–1975)* and *Watergate Sue*. The market for underground comics has also expanded through internet venues such as *eBay*, where interested readers can find not only new titles, but also classic comics otherwise available only in specialty shops. The internet has also become an outlet for direct distribution through artists' websites, making independent titles not only more accessible to consumers but also more affordable for individual artists to produce and market (Fenty, Houp, and Taylor, par. 1). While underground comics may never sell as well or be as large a part of popular culture as Superman and his ilk, their creators will likely continue to be heroes to anyone seeking courage, creativity, and artistic quality in their comics.

Conclusion: Restatement of thesis—closure

Article by more than one author, paragraph no. cited

Notes   Heading (centered), new page

½″

1. According to Schnakenberg, over 2 million copies of *Zap Comix* were in print by 1999.

2. For an intriguing argument that the world of classic comic book superheroes is not so different from our own—including a discussion of how comics before World War II commented on then-current events—see Wright 1–28.

Content note: Pertinent information not central to project's claim

Bibliographic note

Works Cited Heading (centered), new page; entries alphabetized by author

"The Comic Book Code." *Culture Shock.* PBS, n.d. Web. 17 Mar. 2009. Web page: No author, no date

Daniels, Les. *Comix: A History of Comic Books in America.* New York: Outerbridge
^{½"}and Dienstfrey, 1971. Print.

More than one author: Order of names reversed for first author

Fenty, Sean, Trena Houp, and Laurie Taylor. "Webcomics: The Influence and Journal article: Published only online, paragraph numbers

Continuation of the Comix Revolution." *ImageTexT* 1.2 (2004): 22 pars. Web.

18 Mar. 2009.

Online scholarly project: No authors—alphabetized by title

"'Good Shall Triumph over Evil': The Comic Book Code of 1954." *History Matters:*

The U.S. History Survey Course on the Web. George Mason University, n.d.

Web. 22 Mar. 2009.

Heller, Steven. "Zap Comics." *Print* May/June 2000: 100–05. *Academic Search*

Premier. Web. 26 Mar. 2009.

Herndon, L. Kristen. "Mainstream Culture Is in Trouble, and Superman's Not Journal article: Accessed through database

Gonna Save It. But the Simpsons Might." *Art Papers* 21 (1997): 22–25. *Art*

Index. Web. 10 Mar. 2009.

Hignite, M. Todd. "Avante-Garde and Comics: Serious Cartooning." *Art Papers* 26.1

(2002): 17–19. *Art Index.* Web. 10 Mar. 2009.

Newspaper article: Accessed through database

Hodgman, John. "Comics Chronicle." *New York Times* 4 June 2006, late ed., sec.

7: 18. *LexisNexis.* Web. 19 Mar. 2009.

McCloud, Scott. *Understanding Comics, the Invisible Art.* New York: Harper Book (printed): Popular press

Perennial, 1994. Print.

Specialized reference work: Accessed through database

Schnakenberg, Robert E. "Zap Comix." *St. James Encyclopedia of Popular Culture.*

2002. *Find Articles.* Web. 17 Mar. 2009.

Weiner, Stephen. "Beyond Superheroes: Comics Get Serious." *Library Journal* 7.2

(2002): 55–58. *Academic Search Premier.* Web. 10 Mar. 2009.

Wright, Bradford W. *Comic Book Nation: The Transformation of Youth Culture in

America.* Baltimore: Johns Hopkins UP, 2001. Print.

Book (printed):
Scholarly press

22 Documenting Sources: APA Style

Sixth Edition

Publication Manual

of the American Psychological Association

Developed by the American Psychological Association, APA style is used by researchers in psychology and many other social science disciplines, such as education, social work, and sociology. APA style requires that sources be cited in two ways:

- **Citation.** Provide an in-text citation in the body of your project for each source used.

- **Documentation.** Provide a reference list at the project's end.

Writing Responsibly — Citing and Documenting Sources

When you cite and document sources, you acknowledge any material that you have borrowed from a source, and you join the conversation on your topic by adding your own interpretation. Simultaneously, you give interested readers (including your instructor) a way to join the conversation: Accurate entries in the text and list of references allow your audience to find and read your sources so that they can evaluate your interpretation and learn more about the subject themselves. Accurate entries also demonstrate the care with which you have written your research project and reinforce your reputation as a sound scholar.

22a **Creating APA-Style In-Text Citations**

In-text citations appear in the body of your project. They mark each use you make of a source, regardless of whether you are quoting, paraphrasing, or drawing on an idea. In-text citations should include just enough information for readers to locate the source in your reference list, which appears at the end of the project. They should also alert readers to shifts between *your* ideas and those you have borrowed from a source.

1. Place in-text citations so readers know where borrowed material starts and stops.

When you incorporate a quotation, paraphrase, summary, or idea from a source into your own prose, carefully consider the placement of the in-text citation, keeping the following goals in mind:

More about ▶▶▶
What you *must* cite,
   129–31
What you do not
   need to cite,
   131–32
Signal phrases,
   194–95

- To make clear exactly which material is drawn from the source
- To avoid distracting your reader

You can cite a source in your text in two ways:

- **Signal phrase.** Include the author's name (first initial[s] and surname for the first mention and just the surname for each mention thereafter) and an appropriate verb in your sentence; place the date of publication, in parentheses, immediately following the author's name. For quotations or paraphrases of anything less than the entire argument, place a page reference, in parentheses, at the end of the borrowed passage.

   Psychologist G. H. Edwards (1992) studied the beliefs associated
   with gender.

   A signal phrase often makes it easier for readers to determine where your ideas end and borrowed material begins. It also allows you to integrate the borrowed material into your sentence and to put the source in context by adding your own interpretation and the qualifications of the source author. For these reasons, most of your summaries, paraphrases, and quotations should be introduced by a signal phrase.

- **Parenthetical note.** In parentheses, provide the author's surname, followed by a comma and the year in which the source was published. Place the note immediately after the borrowed material.

Subtypes or subcategories of beliefs emerge from within

gender categories (Edwards, 1992).

Parenthetical notes are most appropriate when citing more than one source or establishing facts.

NOTE The reference list entry is the same, regardless of whether you use a signal phrase or a parenthetical note:

author   pub. date   title
Edwards, G. H. (1992). The structure and content of the male gender role
                                                    publication info.
stereotype: An exploration of subtypes. *Sex Roles, 27,* 553–561.

Example 1, 309
Example 14, 315
Example 10, 314

Provide enough information in your in-text citation for readers to locate the source in the reference list. In most cases, the author's

Quick Reference ➝ **Formatting APA In-Text Citations**

1. One author 309
   a. Signal phrase 309
   b. Parenthetical note 309
   c. Quotation 309
2. Two authors 310
3. Three to five authors 310
4. Six or more authors 311
5. Group or corporate author 311
6. Unnamed (anonymous) author 312
7. Two or more sources in one citation 312
8. Two or more sources by the same author in one citation 313
9. Two or more sources by the same author in the same year 313
10. Two or more authors with the same surname 314
11. Reprinted or republished work 314
12. Sacred or classical source 314
13. Indirect source 314
14. Website or other online source 315
15. Personal communication, interview, or email 316

surname and the date of publication are sufficient. Occasionally, you may need to provide more information. When citing works by authors with the same surname, also include the authors' initials.

2. Adjust in-text citations to different types of sources.

The exact form of an in-text citation depends on the type of source you are citing. The examples that follow cover the most common types. For more unusual sources, study the general principles outlined here and adapt them to your special circumstances, or consult the *Publication Manual of the American Psychological Association,* 6th ed. (available in any library).

1. One author
a. Signal phrase

signal phrase
Plummer (2001) indicates that boys begin pressuring one another to conform in childhood, telling each other to toughen up or to stop acting like a baby.

APA In-Text Citations

1. One author
2. Two authors
3. Three to five authors

b. Parenthetical note

This pressure to conform to recognized masculine norms typically begins at a very young age, and boys may tell each other to toughen up or to stop acting like a baby (Plummer, 2001).

c. Quotation If you are borrowing specific language from your source, include the author's name, the year of publication, and a page reference. When possible, use a combination of signal phrase and parenthetical note to make clear exactly what comes from the source.

> Plummer (2001) argues that an overt pressure to conform to recognized norms of masculinity typically begins at a very young age, with boys discouraging one another from being "soft" or "artistic" (p. 18).

Or put all three pieces of information in parentheses.

> This overt pressure to conform to recognized norms of masculinity typically begins at a very young age, with boys discouraging each other from being "soft" or "artistic" (Plummer, 2001, p. 18).

Example 2, 318

APA In-Text Citations

1. One author
2. **Two authors**
3. **Three to five authors**
4. Six or more authors
5. Group or corporate author

2. Two authors List two authors by surnames in the order listed by the source; be sure to use this same order in your reference list entry. In a signal phrase, spell out the word *and* between the two surnames; in a parenthetical citation, replace the word *and* with an ampersand (&).

> signal phrase (*and* spelled out)
> Carpenter and Readman (2006) define physical disability as "the restriction of activity caused by impairments, for example, the loss of a limb, involuntary movements, loss of speech or sight" (p. 131).

> Medical doctors define the word *disability* as "an individual problem of
> parenthetical note (ampersand)
> disease, incapacity, and impairment" (Carpenter & Readman, 2006, p. 131).

3. Three to five authors When a source has three, four, or five authors, list them all in your first in-text citation of the source.

> The research of Oller, Pearson, and Cobo-Lewis (2007) suggests
>
> that bilingual children may have a smaller vocabulary in each of their
>
> languages than monolingual children have in their sole language.

In subsequent citations, list only the first author, representing the others with the abbreviation *et al.* In APA style, this abbreviation should not be underlined or italicized.

> The bilingual children in the study were all Spanish-English speakers
>
> (Oller et al., 2007).

et al. Abbreviation of the Latin phrase *et alii,* "and others."

NOTE *al.* is an abbreviation, so it requires a period; *et* is a complete word, so it does not. There should be no punctuation between the author's name and *et al.*

4. Six or more authors If the source has six or more authors, use only the surname of the first author plus *et al.* unless confusion will result.

> The researchers note that "there is less direct experimental evidence for
>
> effect of grazing animal species on biodiversity" (Rook et al., 2003, p. 141).

5. Group or corporate author Provide the full name of the group in your parenthetical note or signal phrase. If you are going to cite this source subsequently, use the group's name in a signal phrase and insert an abbreviation of its name in parentheses. In subsequent in-text references, use only the abbreviation.

APA In-Text Citations

2. Two authors
3. Three to five authors
4. Six or more authors
5. Group or corporate author
6. Unnamed (anonymous) author
7. Two or more sources in one citation

> full name
> In 2003 the National Commission on Writing in America's Schools and
> acronym
> Colleges (NCWASC) demanded that "the nation's leaders . . . place
>
> writing squarely in the center of the school agenda, and [that]
>
> policymakers at the state and local levels . . . provide the resources
>
> required to improve writing" (p. 3). The NCWASC also noted that . . .

Alternatively, include the full name in a parenthetical citation, and insert the acronym in square brackets afterward.

APA In-Text Citations

4. Six or more authors
5. Group or corporate author
6. **Unnamed (anonymous) author**
7. **Two or more sources in one citation**
8. Two or more sources by the same author in one citation
9. Two or more sources by the same author in the same year

> If writing is to improve, our society "must place writing squarely in
>
> the center of the school agenda, and policymakers at the state and
>
> local levels must provide the resources required to improve writing"
> full name
> (National Commission on Writing in America's Schools and Colleges
> acronym
> [NCWASC], 2003, p. 3).

6. Unnamed (anonymous) author When no author is named, use the first few words of the reference list entry (usually the title).

> On average, smokers shave about twelve minutes off their life span for
> title
> every cigarette smoked ("A Fistful of Risks," 1996, pp. 82–83).

Set titles of articles or parts of books in quotation marks and titles of books, periodicals, and other longer works in italics.

7. Two or more sources in one citation When the information you are drawing on comes from more than one source, follow the borrowed material with a list of all relevant sources, separated by semicolons. List the sources in alphabetical order, the same order in which they appear in the reference list.

APA In-Text Citations

6. Unnamed (anonymous) author
7. Two or more sources in one citation
8. **Two or more sources by the same author in one citation**
9. **Two or more sources by the same author in the same year**
10. Two or more authors with the same surname
11. Reprinted or republished work

When placed in well-structured rehabilitative programs, juvenile

offenders—even those who commit serious crimes such as murder—

can become more mature thinkers, more involved and loving members

of their families, and more successful workers and learners (Beyer,

2006; Burns & Hoagwood, 2002).

8. Two or more sources by the same author in one citation When citing two or more sources by the same author in a single citation, name the author once but include all publication years, separating them with commas.

Wynn's work explores the ability of human infants to perform

mathematical functions, such as addition and subtraction (1992, 2000).

pub.
date 1   pub.
date 2

Human infants have shown surprising abilities to perform mathematical

functions, such as addition and subtraction (Wynn, 1992, 2000).

pub.
date 1   pub.
date 2

9. Two or more sources by the same author in the same year When your reference list includes two or more publications by the same author in the same year, add a letter following the year, beginning with *a*. (*2012b*). Use these year-and-letter designations in your in-text citations and in your reference list.

❯ Example 6, 319

The brain not only controls the senses of sight and sound, but it also

plays an important role in associating emotions such as fear with

particular situations (Barinaga, 1992b).

source letter assigned

10. Two or more authors with the same surname If your reference list includes works by different authors with the same surname, include the authors' initials to differentiate them.

> Rehabilitation is a viable option for many juvenile offenders, whose
>
> immaturities and disabilities can, with institutional support and
>
> first initial + surname
> guidance, be overcome as the child matures (**M.** Beyer, 2006).

If the source has more than one author, include initials for the first author only.

Example 9, 321

APA In-Text
Citations

11. Reprinted or republished work Include both dates in your in-text citation, with the original date of publication first.

> orig. date
> Danon-Boileau (2005/2006) takes a cross-disciplinary approach to the
> reprint date
> study of language disorders in children.

12. Sacred or classical source Cite sacred texts, such as the Bible, the Talmud, or the Qur'an (Koran), in the body of your research project using standard book titles, chapter numbers, and verse numbers, and indicate the version you used.

> In the Song of Solomon, the female speaker concludes her description
>
> of her lover with this proclamation: "His mouth is sweetness itself,
>
> he is all delight. / Such is my lover, and such my friend, O daughter of
>
> ch.   version
> Jerusalem" (5:16; Revised Standard Version).
> verse

13. Indirect source When you can, avoid quoting from a secondhand source (material you have learned about through its mention in another source). When you cannot locate or translate the original source, mention the original author's name in a signal phrase. In your parenthetical note, include *as cited in* followed by the name of the author of the source in which you found the information, and conclude with the year of that source's publication.

> Choy, Fyer, and Lipsitz (as cited in King, 2008) make the distinction
>
> that people with phobias, unlike those with general anxiety, can identify
>
> specific causes for their feelings of nervousness and dread.

In the reference list, provide only the source you used: For the example above, include a reference list entry for King, not Choy, Fyer, and Lipsitz.

14. Website or other online source Frequently, the information you need to create a complete in-text citation is missing. Electronic sources may lack fixed page numbers. Use page numbers only when they are fixed, as in a PDF file. When paragraph numbers are provided, include those (with the abbreviation *para.*) instead of a page number.

> The internet has also become an outlet for direct distribution of
>
> underground comics through artist websites, making independent
>
> titles more affordable to market (Fenty, Houp, and Taylor para. 1).

When paragraphs are not numbered, include the title of the section and number of the paragraph in which the material you are citing appears. If the author is unnamed, use the first few words of the title.

> Cell-phone use while driving can impair performance as badly as
>
> drinking alcohol does. ("Driven to Distraction," 2006, para. 1).

APA In-Text Citations

12. Sacred or classical source
13. Indirect source
14. **Website or other online source**
15. Personal communication, interview, or email

Examples 25, 26, 328

APA In-Text Citations

If no date is provided, use *n.d.* for *no date.*

Barrett (n.d.) unwittingly reveals the sexism prevalent on college campuses in the early 1960s through his account of a football game.

15. Personal communication, interview, or email For sources such as personal email messages, interviews, and phone calls that your readers cannot retrieve and read, mention the communication in your text or provide a parenthetical note, but do not include an entry in the reference list.

More about ▶▶▶
Interviews, 90–94

Quick Reference ➡ APA Reference List Entries

The scientist himself was much more modest about the development

message author   source type   date
(S. J. Gould, personal communication, November 13, 1986).

22b Preparing an APA-Style Reference List

The reference list, which comes at the end of your research project, lists the sources you have cited in your text. The format of each entry in the list depends in part on the type of source you are citing, such as a printed book, an article in an electronic journal or accessed through a database, or an audio recording.

Books—Printed and Electronic

In a printed book, the information you need to create a reference list entry appears on the title and copyright pages. In an online book or e-book, print and electronic publication information appears at the top or bottom of the first page or is available through a link.

1. One author

▶▶▶Annotated visual of where to find author, title, publication, and other information, on foldout following p. 393

a. Printed The basic entry for a printed book looks like this:

Author's surname, Initial(s). (Year of publication). *Title: Subtitle.* Place of

publication (city, state [abbreviated]): Publisher.

Here is an example of an actual citation:

For books, only first word of title and subtitle (plus names) are capitalized.

Boateng, B. (2011). *The copyright thing doesn't work here: Adinkra*

and Kente cloth and intellectual property in Ghana. Minneapolis:

University of Minnesota Press.

APA Reference List Entries

1. **One author**
2. **Two authors**
3. Three to seven authors
4. Eight or more authors

b. E-book Works published electronically or made accessible online are now frequently tagged with a digital object identifier (DOI). If the e-book you are documenting is tagged with a DOI, use that identifier instead of publication information or URL, and add a description of the source type in brackets after the title. If no DOI has been assigned, replace publication information with the URL from which the electronic file can be obtained.

Carter, J. (2003). *Nasty people: How to stop being hurt by them*

without stooping to their level [Adobe Digital Editions version].

doi: 10.1036/0071410228

If no publication date is available, use *n.d.*

Stokes, R. (n.d.). *E-marketing: The essential guide to online marketing.*

Retrieved from http://www.quirk.bix/emarketingtextbook/download

2. Two authors
List two authors in the order they appear on the title page.

author 1   author 2

Use an ampersand (&) between names.

Tavris, C., & Aronson, E. (2007). *Mistakes were made (but not by me):*

Why we justify foolish beliefs, bad decisions, and hurtful acts.

New York, NY: Harcourt.

→ Tech

Citing Electronic Sources: Digital Object Identifiers (DOIs) and URLs

Because URLs change and links break, the APA now recommends using a digital object identifier (DOI), a permanent identifying code, whenever available; use a URL, or web address, only when no DOI is available. Most electronic books and articles in academic journals now include a DOI. When your citation ends with a DOI or URL, do *not* add a period after it. Break a DOI or URL (if necessary) only after a slash or before a dot or other punctuation mark; do not add a hyphen.

3. Three to seven authors List all their names.

> Oltmanns, T. F., Neale, J. M., & Davison, G. C. (1992). *Case studies in abnormal psychology.* New York, NY: Guilford Press.

Use an ampersand (&) between the last two names.

4. Eight or more authors List the first six authors followed by three ellipsis points and the last author's name.

> Masters, R., Skrapec, C., Muscat, B., Dussich, J. P., Pincu, L., Way, L. B., . . . Gerstenfeld, P. (2010). *Criminal justice: Realities and challenges.* New York, NY: McGraw-Hill.

⟩ More about ▶▶▶
et al., 311

APA Reference List Entries

5. Unnamed (anonymous) author Start the entry with the title followed by the publication date. Alphabetize the entry in the reference list using the first significant word in the title (not an article such as *a, an,* or *the*).

> And still we conquer! The diary of a Nazi Unteroffizier in the German Africa Corps. (1968). University, AL: Confederate Publishing.

6. Two or more books by the same author Arrange the entries in order of publication (from least to most recent).

> Tonkiss, F. (2005). *Space, the city and social theory: Social relations and urban forms.* Malden, MA: Polity.

Tonkiss, F. (2006). *Contemporary economic sociology: Globalization,*

production, inequality. New York, NY: Routledge.

For books written by the same author(s) in the same year, alphabetize entries by title and add a letter following the year, beginning with *a* (*2012a, 2012b*).

Cervone, D., & Shoda, Y. (1999a). Beyond traits in the study of personality

coherence. *Current Directions in Psychological Science, 8,* 27–32.

Cervone, D., & Shoda, Y. (1999b). Social-cognitive theories and the

coherence of personality. In D. Cervone & Y. Shoda (Eds.), *The*

coherence of personality: Social-cognitive bases of consistency,

variability, and organization. New York, NY: Guilford Press.

Works written by a single author should be listed *before* sources written by that same author plus a coauthor, regardless of publication dates.

Multiple sources by an author and various coauthors are alphabetized by surname of the second author.

Clarke-Stewart, A., & Allhusen, V. D. (2005). *What we know about*

childcare. Cambridge, MA: Harvard University Press.

Clarke-Stewart, A., & Brentano, C. (2006). *Divorce: Causes and*

consequences. New Haven, CT: Yale University Press.

7. Two or more authors with the same surname and first initial Differentiate them by including their first names in brackets.

Cohen, A. [Andrew]. (1994). *Assessing language ability in the classroom.*

Boston, MA: Heinle.

Cohen, A. [Anne]. (1973). *Poor Pearl, poor girl! The murdered girl*

stereotype in ballad and nwspaper. Austin: University of Texas Press.

8. Group or corporate author List the sponsoring organization as the author. Use the full name, and alphabetize it in the reference list

---

APA Reference
List Entries

5. Unnamed (anonymous) author

6. Two or more books by the same author

7. Two or more authors with the same surname and first initial

8. Group or corporate author

9. Author and editor or translator

10. Edited book or anthology

No state abbreviation if state is included in name of university press according to the name's first significant word. If the same group or corporation is also listed as the publisher, replace the name of the publisher with the word *Author.*

> Fabian Society, Commission on Life Chances and Child Poverty. (2006).
>
> *Narrowing the gap: The final report of the Fabian Commission on Life*
>
> *Chances and Child Poverty.* London, England: Author.

9. Author and editor or translator If the source originally appeared earlier than the edited or translated version, add the date of original publication at the end of the entry. If the work has an editor, use the abbreviation *Ed.* For a translator, use the abbreviation *Trans.*

> Alvtegen, K. (2010). *Shame* (S. Murray, Trans.) New York, NY: Felony and
>
> Mayhem. (Original work published 2006).

10. Edited book or anthology Put the editor's name in the author position.

> Atzmon, L. (Ed.). (2011). *Visual rhetoric and the eloquence of design.*
>
> Anderson, SC: Parlor Press.

For a book with multiple editors, change the abbreviation from *Ed.* to *Eds.*

11. Selection from an edited book or anthology Begin with the selection's author, followed by the publication date of the book and the selection's title (with no quotation marks or other formatting). Then insert the word *In*, the editors' names, and the title of the book or anthology (italicized). Next include page numbers for the entire selection (even if you used only part of it). Conclude the entry with the publication information for the book in which the selection appeared.

> selection author   selection title
>
> Ray, B. (2010). Tim Burton and the idea of fairy tales. In P. Greenhill &
>
> S. E. Matrix (Eds.), *Fairy tale vilms: Visions of ambiguity*
>
> (pp. 198–218). Logan: Utah State University Press.

APA Reference List Entries

7. Two or more authors with the same surname and first initial
8. Group or corporate author
9. **Author and editor or translator**
10. **Edited book or anthology**
11. **Selection from an edited book or anthology**
12. Edition other than the first
13. Entry in a reference work

12. Edition other than the first Insert the edition number (*2nd ed., 3rd ed.*) or edition name (*Rev. ed.* for "revised edition") after the book's title. (The edition number or name should appear on the title page.)

> Johnson, J. B., & Reynolds, H. T. (2008). *Political science research*
>
> *methods* (6th ed.). Washington, DC: CQ Press.

13. Entry in a reference work Format as you would a selection from an edited book. For signed articles, include the author's name. (Articles in reference works often carry the author's initials only, so you may need to cross-reference the initials with a list of contributors in the front or back of the book.) If an article is unsigned, begin with its title.

Example 11, 321

a. Printed

> Treffert, D. A. (2000). Savant syndrome. In A. E. Kazdin (Ed.), *Encyclopedia*
>
> *of psychology* (pp. 144–148). New York, NY: Oxford.

b. Online

> Major depression. (2009). In *Medline Plus encyclopedia*. Retrieved
>
> URL
>
> from http://www.nlm.nih.gov/medlineplus/ency/article/000945.htm

14. Multivolume work

> Tomasello, M. (Ed.). (1998–2003). *The new psychology of language:*
>
> *Cognitive and functional approaches to language structure* (Vols.
>
> 1–2). Mahwah, NJ: Erlbaum.

15. Republished book

> Huxley, E. (2006). *Red strangers*. New York, NY: Penguin Group. (Original
>
> work published 1939)

16. Sacred or classical source No entry in the reference list is needed for a sacred source, such as the Bible, the Talmud, or the Qu'ran (Koran), or for a classical source, such as Plato's *Republic*.

17. Dissertation or thesis Indicate whether the work is a doctoral dissertation or a master's thesis. If the dissertation or thesis was accessed through a database service, include the name of the database from which it was obtained and provide any identifying number. If it was obtained from a university or personal website, include the URL.

a. Published

Song, L. Z. (2003). *Relations between optimism, stress and health in*

Chinese and American students (Doctoral dissertation). Available

from ProQuest Dissertations and Theses database. (UMI No.

AA13107041)

b. Unpublished

Lillie, A. S. (2008). *MusicBox: Navigating the space of your music* (Master's

thesis, Massachusetts Institute of Technology). Retrieved from http://

thesis.flyingpudding.com/documents/anita_FINAL_THESIS.pdf

c. Abstracted in DAI

Luster, L. (1992). *Schooling, survival and struggle: Black women and the*

GED (Unpublished doctoral dissertation). Stanford University,

Stanford, CA.

Periodicals—Printed and Electronic

A periodical is a publication issued at regular intervals—newspapers are generally published every day, magazines every week or month, and scholarly journals four times a year. For periodicals, include not only the title of the article (no quotation marks or italics) but also the title of the periodical (in italics, all important words capitalized). The type of publication information you include depends on the type of periodical you are citing.

18. Article in a scholarly journal The information needed to create a reference list entry for a printed journal article appears on the cover or table of contents of the journal and on the first and last page of the article. For articles downloaded from a database, the information appears either on the screen listing the articles that fit your search terms

APA Reference List Entries

16. Sacred or classical source
17. Dissertation or thesis
18. **Article in a scholarly journal**
19. Special issue of a journal
20. Article in a magazine

▶▶▶ Annotated visual of where to find author, title, publication, and other information, on foldout following p. 393

More about ▶▶▶
Searching databases, 61–66

APA Reference List Entries

or on the first (and last) page of the downloaded file. For articles that appear in journals that are published solely online, the needed information may be on the website's home page, in the journal's table of contents, or on the first page of the article.

a. Printed The basic citation for an article in a printed journal looks like this:

Author's surname, Initial(s). (date of publication). Article title. *Title of Journal, vol no.*(issue no.), pages.

Here is an example of an actual citation:

author   date   article title   journal title   vol.
May, V. (2011). Self, belonging, and social change. *Sociology, 64,*
pgs.
363–378.

If the article is published in a journal that starts each issue with page 1, provide the issue number after the volume number (not italicized, in parentheses).

Sui, C. (2007). Giving indigenous people a voice. *Taiwan Review, 57*(8), 40.

> **More about ▶▶▶**
> Formatting author information: examples 318–23

> **More about ▶▶▶**
> DOIs, 318

b. Online or accessed through a database More and more, researchers access journal articles electronically, either through online journals or through databases that provide access to articles in PDF or HTML format. Articles accessed electronically now frequently include a digital object identifier (DOI). The DOI is a permanent code that does not change from library to library or database to database. The DOI makes URLs unnecessary. Whenever a DOI is provided, include it at the end of your reference list entry. The basic citation for an article in an online journal or accessed through an online database that has a DOI is the same as for a printed journal article except that the DOI appears at the end of the citation:

Rozin, P. (2007). Exploring the landscape of modern academic psychology: Finding and filling the holes. *American Psychologist, 62,* 754–766.
DOI
doi: 10.1037/1091-7527.25.4.468

For an article in an online journal that does *not* include a DOI, replace the DOI with the phrase *Retrieved from* followed by the URL for the journal's home page.

Janyam, K. (2011). The influence of job satisfaction on mental health

of factory workers. *Internet Journal of Mental Health 7.*

URL (permalink)
Retrieved from http://www.ispub.com/journal/the_internet_journal_

of_mental_health.html

19. Special issue of a journal

special issue title
Leong, F. (Ed.). (2009). History of racial and ethnic minority psychology

label
[Special issue]. *Cultural Diversity and Ethnic Minority Psychology, 15.*

20. Article in a magazine

a. Printed or accessed through a database Provide the full publication date of the issue (year, month, and day; or year and month). If the volume and issue number of the magazine are available, include that information as you would for a journal article.

Gladwell, M. (2007, November 12). Dangerous minds. *The New Yorker,*

36–45.

Pelusi, N. (2009, January/February). The appeal of the bad boy.

Psychology Today, 42(1), 58–59.

b. Online Include the URL for the magazine's home page.

Chamberlin, J. (2009, July/August). Strong families, safe children. *Monitor*

on Psychology, 40(7). Retrieved from http://www.apa.org/monitor

If the magazine is available in a printed edition but the article is only available online, include the phrase *Supplemental material* in brackets after the article's title.

Daniller, A. (2007, December). Psychology research done right

[Supplemental material]. *GradPSYCH*. Retrieved from http://

gradpsych.apags.org

21. Article in a newspaper
The information you need to create a reference list entry for a printed newspaper article is on the masthead of the newspaper (at the top of the first page) and on the first and last

page of the article. For newspaper articles downloaded from a database, the information you need appears on the search results screen, the full record of the article, or the article itself. For articles that appear in online versions of the newspaper, the information you need is usually at the top of the first page of the article.

a. Printed or accessed through a database

author   pub. date   title
Rarback, S. (2010, January 26). Eating well the best medicine.

newspaper   sec./pg. no.
Miami Herald, p. E2.

If the title of a newspaper does not include its place of publication, supply the city and state, in square brackets, following the title.

Jalonick, M. C. (2010, March 20). USDA called lax on organics. *The Courier-*
sec./pg. no.
Journal [Louisville, KY], p. A43

If the pages of the article are not continuous, provide all page numbers, with a comma after each.

Borrelli, C. (2011, May 30). The tortured cartoonist. *The Chicago Tribune*

pp. 1, 4.

To cite a newspaper article downloaded from a database, follow the model for a printed newspaper article, but omit the page numbers, and change the comma after the newspaper's title to a period.

b. Online Follow the format for a printed newspaper article, but omit the page reference and include the words *Retrieved from* and the URL for the newspaper's home page.

Harris, G. (2011, June 15). FDA unveils new rules for sun lotions. *The*

Sacramento Bee. Retrieved from http://www.sacbee.com/

22. Review (printed or online) Follow the model for the type of periodical in which the review appeared. In the author position, insert the name of the author of the review; if the review is titled, insert that title in the title position (no italics or quotation marks); add in brackets the label *Review of the book* (or *Review of the film,* and so forth) followed by the title and author of the reviewed work. End with publication information for the periodical in which the review appeared.

review author   review title
Balk, D. E. (2007). Diamonds and mummies are forever [Review of

reviewed work
the book *Remember me: A lively tour of the new American way of*

death, by L. T. Cullen]. *Death Studies, 31*(10), 941–947. doi:

10.1080/07481180701603436

Examples 18–21, 323–26

If the review is untitled, substitute the label *Review of the book*, the book's title, and the book's author in brackets.

Schredl, M. (2008). [Review of the book *The dream experience: A*

systematic exploration] by Milton Kramer. *Dreaming, 18*(4), 280–286.

23. Letter to the editor (printed or online) Follow the model for the type of periodical in which the letter appeared, and insert the label *Letter to the editor* in brackets following the letter's title.

letter author   letter title   label
Richmond, A. (2009, May). Miracle drug? [Letter to the editor]. *The Atlantic,*

303(4), 14.

If the letter is untitled, put the label *Letter to the editor,* in brackets, in the title position.

24. Abstract It is always better to read and cite an article itself. However, if your research relied only on the abstract, or summary, cite only the abstract to avoid misrepresenting your source and your research.

Loverock, D. S. (2007). Object superiority as a function of object coherence

and task difficulty [Abstract]. *American Journal of Psychology, 120,*

565–591.

Bruce, A. S., Ray, W., & Carlson, R. A. (2007). Understanding cognitive

failures: What's dissociation got to do with it? *American Journal of*

Psychology, 120, 553–563. Abstract retrieved from http://ajp

.press.illinois.edu/index.html

APA Reference
List Entries

21. Article in a newspaper
22. Review (printed or online)
23. Letter to the editor (printed or online)
24. Abstract
25. Website
26. Web page

▶▶▶Annotated visual of where to find author, title, publication, and other information, on foldout following p. 393

Other Electronic Sources

While it is usually easy to find the information you need to create a complete citation for a book or an article in a periodical, websites can be a bit trickier. Most of the information you need will appear on the site's home page, usually at the bottom or top of that page, or on the web page you are citing. Sometimes, however, you may need to look further. Click on links with titles such as "About us" or "More information." Frequently, websites do not provide complete information, so include as much information in your entry as you can.

25. Website When mentioning an entire website, you do not usually have to include an entry in your reference list. However, if you quote, paraphrase, or summarize content from the site, include it, following this model:

Gilbert, R. (2001). *Shake your shyness*. Retrieved from http://

shakeyourshyness.com

The website *Psychology Matters* provides information that anyone

can access on everything from money issues to trauma (http://

psychologymatters.apa.org).

26. Web page Provide the title of the page (with no formatting) and the URL for the specific page you are citing.

web page title

American Psychological Association. (2008). Getting a good night's sleep

with the help of psychology. In *Psychology matters*. Retrieved from

URL for web page
http://www.psychologymatters.org/insomnia.html

If the website is untitled, add a description.

The Writing Center, University of North Carolina. (2007). Handouts and

links: Sociology. Retrieved from http://www.unc.edu/depts/wcweb/

handouts/sociology.html

→ Tech

Checking URLs and DOIs

DOIs. If your selection includes a DOI number, you can check it by visiting <crossref.org> and inserting the DOI into the search box.

URLs. Just before submitting your paper, test all the URLs; sometimes web addresses change or content is taken down. If the URL you provided no longer works, search for the work online by title or keyword; you may find it "cached" on the Web even though the owner of the original site has taken the work down. Then use the URL for the cached version in your bibliographic entry.

---

27. Discussion list posting Treat the subject line (or *thread*) as the title, and include the label *Discussion list post* (in brackets).

date posted   subj. line   label
Arendes, L. (2008, July 9). Objectivity [Discussion list post]. Retrieved from
URL
news://sci.psychology.research

28. Article on a wiki Cite a wiki as you would a web page. Because wikis are written and edited collaboratively, there is no author to cite; begin with the article's title. Always include a retrieval date and direct URL. If the date of the most recent update is not noted, include the abbreviation *n.d.* (*no date*) in its place. Always include a retrieval date and direct URL.

International relations. (n.d.). Retrieved April 22, 2008, from Political

Science Wiki: http://polisci.wikidot.com/international-relations

29. Blog Include a screen name if the author's name is not provided.

a. Blog posting

post author   post date   post title
Dean, J. (2009, January 1). Gratitude enhanced by focusing on end

of pleasurable experience [Web log post]. Retrieved from
URL (post)
www.spring.org.uk/2009_01_01_blogarchive.php

More about ▶▶▶
Reliability, 102–05

b. Comment on a blog posting

comment author   date posted   thread title
HLVictoria. (2004, January 11). Re: Sociology of weblogs [Web log
                                                                  URL
comment]. Retrieved from http://blog.niceperson.org/2003/02/11/

sociology-of-weblogs/#comment-62

30. Computer software Provide an entry for computer software only if it is unfamiliar to your readers and it is necessary to a computation you have made.

title   label
Power Researcher [Computer software]. Atlanta, GA: Uniting Networks.

31. Presentation slides The sixth edition of the *Publication Manual of the APA* does not provide an example of an entry for presentation slides, but based on other examples such an entry might look like the one below:

Doyle, T. (2009). *Privacy, free expression, and compromising images*
                     label
[PowerPoint slides]. Retrieved from http://library.hunter.cuny

.edu/pdf/Privacyfreeexpression.ppt

Audio and Visual Sources

The information you need to create an entry for most audio and visual sources will appear on the cover, label, or program of the work or in the credits at the end of a film or television show. As with other citations, italicize the titles of longer works, such as albums and films, and do not format the titles of shorter works such as single songs or single episodes of television programs.

32. Motion picture

                                              release   title
Howard, R. (Director), & Grazer, B. (Producer). (2001). *A beautiful mind*
                                      distributor
[Motion picture]. United States: Warner Bros.

33. Online video or video blog (vlog)

ATTC Network. (2007, July 12). Michael–Clinical psychologist [Video file].

Retrieved from http://www.youtube.com/watch?v=4OAYT5P6xaQ

34. Television or radio broadcast
a. Series

> Hanson, H., Josephson, B. & Nathan, S. (Executive producers). (2011).
>
> > *Bones* [Television series]. Los Angeles, CA: Fox.

b. Episode

> Toynton, I. (Director). (2011). The change in the game [Television series
>
> > episode]. In Hanson, H., Josephson, B., Nathan, S., & Toynton, I.
> >
> > (Executive producers), *Bones*. Los Angeles, CA: Fox

c. Podcast

> Mitchell, N. (Producer). (2008, March 15). The psyche on death row. *All in*
>
> > *the mind.* [Audio podcast]. Retrieved from http://www.abc.net.au/rn/
> >
> > allinthemind/default.htm

35. Musical or other audio recording
a. CD, LP, or audiobook

> Gore, A. (Writer), & Patton, W. (Narrator). (2007). *The assault on reason*
>
> > [CD]. New York, NY: Penguin Audio.

b. Selection or song on a CD, LP, or audiobook

> writers   © date   performers
> Dilly, D., & Wilkin, M. (1959). The long black veil [Recorded by H. Dickens &
>
> > A. Gerrard]. On *Pioneering women of bluegrass* [CD]. Washington,
> >
> >   recording date
> > DC: Smithsonian/Folkways Records. (1996)

36. Lecture, speech, or conference presentation

> Robinson, G. E. (2008, May 6). *Preventing violence against women.*
>
> > Paper presented at the annual meeting of the American Psychiatric
> >
> > Association, Washington, DC.

APA Reference
List Entries

32. Motion picture
33. Online video
    or video blog
    (vlog)
34. **Television or
    radio broadcast**
35. **Musical or other
    audio recording**
36. **Lecture, speech,
    or conference
    presentation**
37. Map
38. Government
    publication

Miscellaneous Sources

37. Map

U.S. Census Bureau, Geography Division (Cartographer). (2001).

Mean center of population for the United States: 1790 to 2000

[Demographic map]. Retrieved from http://www.census.gov/geo/

www/cenpop/meanctr.pdf

38. Government publication
a. Printed

Example 8, 320–21

U.S. Department of Health and Human Services, National Institutes of

Health, National Institute of Mental Health. (2008). *Bipolar disorder*

(NIH Publication No. 3679). Washington, DC: Government Printing

Office.

U.S. Department of Health and Human Services. (2005). *Steps to a*

healthier US. Washington, DC: Author.

b. Online

U.S. General Accounting Office. (1993, September 21). *North American*

Free Trade Agreement: A focus on the substantive issues

(Publication No. GAO/T-GGD-93-44). Retrieved from http://www

.gpoaccess.gov/gaoreports/search.html

39. Report (nongovernmental)

American Psychological Association, Task Force on Gender Identity and

Gender Variance. (2008). *Report of the Task Force on Gender*

Identity and Gender Variance. Retrieved from http://www.apa.org/pi/

lgbc/transgender/2008TaskForceReport.pdf

40. Data set

U.S. Department of Justice, Federal Bureau of Investigation. (2007,

September). *2006 Crime in the United States* [Data set]. Retrieved

from http://www.data.gov/raw/310

41. Fact sheet, brochure, pamphlet

Department of Health and Human Services, Centers for Disease Control

and Prevention. (2005, May 3). Basic information about SARS

[Fact sheet]. Retrieved from http://www.cdc.gov/ncidod/SARS/

factsheet.htm

42. Conference proceedings Cite conference proceedings either as an edited book or as the special issue of a journal, depending on how they were published.

43. Legal source (printed or online)

case title   *U.S. Reports*   decision
(abbreviated)   vol.   no.   date
Lynn v. Alabama, 493 U.S. 945 (1989). Retrieved from Open Jurist website:

http://openjurist.org/493/us/945/lynn-v-alabama

44. Interview (published or broadcast)

interview subject   broadcast date
Cameron, J. (2009, December 18). James Cameron, a king with a soft

touch. Interview by M. Norris [Digital download]. National Public

Radio, Washington, DC. Retrieved from http://www.npr.org

45. Personal communication (email, letter, interview) Cite personal communications that are not available to the public in the body of your research project, but do not include an entry in the reference list.

APA Reference List Entries

22c Using APA Style for Informational Notes

▶▶▶Sample content note, 341

In addition to in-text citations, APA style allows researchers to include informational notes. These notes may provide supplementary information, acknowledge any help the writer received, or call attention to possible conflicts of interest.

To add supplementary information, include a superscript (above-the-line) Arabic number in the text and at the beginning of the note (either at the bottom of the page for a footnote or in a list of notes at the end of the project).

22d Formatting a Paper in APA Style

The appearance of your paper reflects the care you have taken in writing it. For most writing projects in the social sciences, format your project using APA style. The following section explains how to format a student paper, and Heather DeGroot's paper at the end of this chapter provides a model.

▶▶▶Student research project (APA style): "The Power of Wardrobe," Heather DeGroot, 243–305

1. Margins and spacing

- Set one-inch margins at the top, bottom, left-, and right-hand sides of your paper.
- Indent the first line of each paragraph half an inch.
- Indent quotations of forty or more words as a block, half an inch from the left margin.
- Double-space the entire paper.
- Use a hanging indent for each reference list entry: The first line should be flush with the left margin, with subsequent lines indented half an inch.

▶▶▶Sample reference list, 349–76

More about ▶▶▶ Applying the principles of design, 377–93

2. Typeface, header, and page number

Use a standard typeface such as Times New Roman or Arial in a readable size (usually 12-point). Include a header, or *running head*, consisting of the first two or three words of the title (no more than fifty characters) in the upper left-hand corner of the page, half an inch from the upper edge. Include the page number half an inch from the top and one inch from the right edge of the page. Use your word processor's header feature to insert the header and to number the pages automatically.

3. Title page

- Insert the title, typed in upper- and lowercase letters, centered on the top half of the page.
- Insert a blank line, and then type your name.
- Include the course number, the name of the instructor to whom the project will be submitted, and the date of submission, centered on separate lines.
- If you need to acknowledge help you received—for example, in conducting your research or interpreting your results—include a note on the title page, four lines below the identifying information.

More about ▶▶▶
Developing a title, 173
Reconsidering your title, 207–08

A sample title page appears on p. 337.

4. Abstract

The abstract, 150–250 words long, usually includes a one-sentence summary of the most important points in each section of the project:

- Introduction: Problem you are investigating
- Methods: Number and characteristics of participants and your research methods
- Results: Your outcomes
- Conclusions: Implications of your results

More about ▶▶▶
Organizing, 157–69
Introductions, 174–75
Methods, 50–51
Conclusions, 176–77
Social scientific research structure, 238–39

The abstract follows the title page and appears on its own page, headed with the word *Abstract* centered at the top of the page.

5. Tables and figures

- Refer to tables and figures in the text, using the word *Table* or *Figure* followed by the number of the table or figure in sequence. (The first figure is Figure 1; the second table is Table 2.) Discuss the significance of tables and figures in the text, but do not repeat the information that appears in the table or figure itself.

▶▶▶Sample figure caption, APA style, 343

- Include a caption with each figure, using the word *Figure* with the number assigned in the text. The caption, which follows the figure, should describe the figure briefly but not repeat the information in your text. If you borrowed the figure or the data to create your figure, include the source information at the end of your caption.

Writing Responsibly

Of Deadlines and Paper Clips

Instructors expect students to turn in thoughtful, carefully proofread, and neatly formatted papers on time—usually in class on the due date. Another expectation is that the writer will clip (or staple) the pages of the paper *before* the paper is submitted. Do justice to yourself by being fully prepared.

- Include the word *Table* and the table number (no italics) on one line, and, on the next line, the table title (in italics). The table itself should appear below the table number and title. If you borrowed the table or the data to create it, include source information in a note below the table.

- Unless your instructor tells you otherwise, place each table on a new page, after the reference list or endnotes (if any). Figures (photographs, graphs, charts, and so on) should appear, each on a new page, following the tables.

6. Reference list

- Center the heading "References" at the top of the page.

- Use a hanging indent for each reference list entry: The first line should be flush with the left margin and subsequent lines indented half an inch.

- Alphabetize entries by the surname of the author or, if no author is listed, by the first important word in the title (ignoring *A, An,* or *The*).

7. Printing, paper, and binding

Print your project using a high-quality printer (make sure it has plenty of ink), on opaque, 8½ × 11–inch white paper. Most instructors do not want you to enclose your paper in a binder, but if you are in doubt, ask. If you do not use a binder, paper-clip the pages together.

More about ▶▶▶
Writing in the social, physical, and natural sciences, 241–42

Student Research Project: APA Style

In the sample student research project that follows, Heather DeGroot examines the influence that gender stereotypes can have on behavior. Her paper follows the format of an APA-style research report.

The Power of Wardrobe:

Male Stereotype Influences

Title, centered, upper half of page

Heather DeGroot

Author's name

James Madison University

Institutional affiliation

Psychology 220

Dr. Lawrence

May 2, 2011

Other identifying information for class purposes (double spaced)

Abstract   Heading (centered), new page

This study explores the potential influence of stereotypical appearances on male subjects' stated opinions regarding entertainment perceived as "feminine." Results are based on responses from 26 undergraduate males. Data were analyzed using one-way variance tests and Tukey HSD post hoc tests. The findings show that participants were more likely to give a favorable rating to a "chick-flick" in the presence of a counterstereotypical male ($M = 8.67$, $SD = 1.53$) than in the presence of a stereotypical male ($M = 5.31$, $SD = 1.97$) or control proctor ($M = 5.20$, $SD = 1.99$). Results suggest that participants may have experienced gender role conflict.

Abstract: Summary of problem, methods, results, discussion

¶ indent: The Power of Wardrobe: Male Stereotype Influences   Title: Centered
5 spaces or ½″

⟵⟶ Stereotypes—expectations placed upon people because of their gender,

race, or religion—may be discouraged in their most overt forms, but they continue

to flourish in the media. In contemporary American culture, this sort of bias places   Text: Double
                                                                                            spaced
an exaggerated emphasis on physical appearance. Such attitudes are not isolated

features of media programming; rather, they influence many interactions in everyday

life—especially among adolescents and young adults, for whom clothing, personal   Summary of
                                                                                       whole source, so
image, and identity tend to be inextricably bound (Sontag, Peteu, & Lee, 1999).   no page number

        Impressions of other people can be classified into two categories: stereoypes   Introduction
                                                                                             (funnel): Back-
and individuating information (Kunda & Thagard, 1996). Stereotypes focus on social   ground, defini-
                                                                                             tions, hypothesis
categories, while individuating information is the focus of other factors, including

personality, actions of the individual, and so forth. The stereotype effect, as defined

Signal phrase   by Monica Biernat (2003), is "a finding that individual members (comparable in all
with parenthet-
ical citation   ways except their category membership) are judged in a direction consistent with
for date, page
number   group-level expectations or stereotypes" (p. 1019). Under such circumstances,

people are judged more by the category in which one can group them than by their

qualities or skills as individuals. However, according to Kunda and Thagard (1996),

the division of these types of judgment is not always clear. This was the influence

for their impression formation theory, in which stereotypes, traits, and behaviors

are all constrained by positive and negative associations. In their research, they

found that appearance was crucial in this process.

        The influential power of stereotypes is particularly interesting when gender

        1″   boundaries are crossed. In a 2003 study, researchers found that while membership

                1″

in a socioeconomic class or "power position" tended to give participants a biased

or predetermined opinion about the beliefs and behaviors (such as work ethic)

by which a person in another category lived, gender exerted at least as great an

influence on the manner in which people were categorized (Vescio, Snyder, &

Butz). Men in power positions were likely to be viewed differently than females in

the same positions (Mansfield, 2006).

Would these findings remain consistent if only one gender were used in the

study? That is to say, can we identify intragender roles or stereotypes that similarly

affect perception and beliefs about individuals? A study by G. H. Edwards (1992)

found that beliefs regarding men and women transcend gender, for subtypes

or categories emerge within each sex; for example, among American men one

might be perceived as businessman, athlete, family man, or loser. Typically,

such seeming variations represent varying degrees of a supposed normative

"masculinity," rather than truly distinct expressions of a male gender role. Rudman

and Fairchild (2004) write that "for men, a lifetime of experience observing one's

peers being teased or ostracized for 'effeminate' behavior may evoke strong

normative pressures toward highly masculine self-presentations" (p. 160). Plummer

(2001) indicates that boys begin pressuring one another to conform in childhood,

telling each other to toughen up or to stop acting like a baby.

The purpose of this study is to observe whether male participants are likely

to be influenced by a stereotypically "male" opinion. Are college-aged males more

swayed by the "jock" or "cool guy on campus" than by those with an "average Joe"

or a "metrosexual" appearance? Hypothetically, male participants should more

---

Date of publication in text, so omitted from parenthetical citation

Paraphrase of whole source, so no page number included

Direct quotation from PDF; page number included

Hypothesis

likely be swayed by the opinions of the stereotypical male than by those of the

control group ("average Joe") or the experimental group (counterstereotypical).

Methods   *First-level heading (centered, bold)*

Participants *Second-level heading (left, bold)*

Twenty-six undergraduate males from a large Southeastern university,

(mean age = 19) participated in this study in order to fill a course requirement in

their general psychology classes.

Procedure

The participants were randomly assigned to one of three conditions in

the study: the stereotypically "male" proctor group, the counterstereotypical

proctor group, and the control group. The proctor was the same person in each

condition, but his appearance was different in each. In the stereotypically male

proctor condition, the proctor wore an outfit consisting of team sports apparel:

Methods: How study was conducted

a baseball cap, a basketball jersey, shorts, and sneakers (Figure 1a). In the

counterstereotypical condition, he wore a long-sleeved, light pink button-down

shirt (tucked in), creased khaki pants, and dress shoes (Figure 1b). In the control

condition, the proctor wore a short-sleeved blue button-down shirt (not tucked in),

khaki shorts, and sneakers (Figure 1c).

The participants in each condition were told at the beginning of the

experiment that they were participating in a memory-recall task. They were to

identify what they could remember from a clip from the movie *Pretty Woman*

Content note: Additional information, endnote

(Marshall, 1990),[1] a stereotypical "chick-flick." During the ten-minute film clip, which

was constant for each of the three conditions, the proctor read scripted lines such as "Oh! I love this part!" and "I'm seriously such a sap, but this film is just so good!" The script was a constant in each of the three conditions.

After the clip was viewed by all, the proctor then handed out a questionnaire to conduct the "memory-recall task." The questionnaire contained diversion questions such as "What color is the dress that Vivian (Julia Roberts's character) wears in the scene?" and "What game do Edward and Vivian play after the performance?" At the end of the questionnaire, the participants rated the movie on an opinion scale from 1 to 10, with 10 being the highest overall liking.

After the experiment was over, participants in each condition were debriefed as a group and were dismissed from the study.

Results

A one-way analysis of variance (ANOVA) was conducted on the data in order to determine whether males are more influenced by a stereotypically "male" proctor in comparison to the counterstereotypical and control-group proctors. The analysis demonstrated that at least one group was significantly different from the others, $F(2, 23) = 4.08$, $p < .05$. Tukey HSD post hoc tests were performed to measure the difference between the groups individually. The Tukey HSD revealed that the participants were more likely to give a favorable movie rating under the influence of the counterstereotypically masculine proctor ($M = 8.67$, $SD = 1.53$) than the stereotypically masculine proctor ($M = 5.31$, $SD = 1.97$) or the control proctor ($M = 5.20$, $SD = 1.99$) (see Figure 2).

There were no significant differences in movie ratings between those in the stereotypically masculine proctor's group and those in the control proctor's. These

Results: Summarizes data and research findings; includes figure

(a)   (b)   (c)

Figure 1. Male proctor in three conditions: (a) stereotypical,

(b) counterstereotypical, and (c) control.

DeGroot's instructor requested that figures be integrated into the body rather than placed after the reference list.

Figure caption: Label *(Figure)* and number in italics; caption below illustration

Figure 2. Tukey HSD post hoc test results for the three groups: Group with the

stereotypical proctor, group with the counterstereotypical proctor, and control group.

results were contrary to the study's initial hypothesis, and they suggest that male participants are more likely to defy gender roles in the presence of a counter-stereotypical proctor than in the presence of a stereotypically masculine proctor.

Discussion

The study elicited something beyond stereotypical responses from the participants. In fact, the participants may have experienced gender role conflict. Instead of scoring favorably when the masculine male proctor said he enjoyed the film, the participants instead scored the film lower than initially expected. The presence of a highly or moderately "masculine" male, though he made favorable comments in each condition, may have caused the participants to adhere more rigidly to socialized male gender roles and thus rate the movie lower than subjects in the atypically "masculine" proctor group, who did not feel the pressure to assert masculinity in their rating of *Pretty Woman* (McCreary et al., 1996).

Certain irregularities in the study provoked questions that might be investigated in future research. Due to factors beyond the researcher's control, each condition had a different number of participants. The counterstereotypical condition, which had significant findings, had the smallest number of participants; as a result, those scores are subject to greater statistical variation due to strong individual opinion. However, one might also question whether the number of males present influences a subject's tendency to admit to a counterstereotypical opinion or value judgment. If the study were to be replicated to find for stereotype differences alone, it would be crucial for the number of participants in each condition to be the same. On the other hand, a separate study might use multiple

Discussion: Author's interpretation of data, conclusions, concerns, and questions for further study

Citations of six or more authors: First author plus *et al.*

viewing groups of varying individual sizes to determine the effect of group size in gender-stereotype-determined valuations.

Another issue to consider is the effect of the fictional nature of the film to which the male viewers were asked to react. A recent study reported in *Business Week* suggested that men are more willing to show empathy when they know the stories eliciting their emotional response are fictional. Jennifer Argo, one of the authors of the study, is quoted as saying that fictional works provide "an excuse to relax gender stereotypes" (as cited in Coplan, 2008, p. 17). This factor was not considered in the study reported here.

References   Heading (centered), new page; references
alphabetized by author single spaced with
double space between entries

Biernat, M. (2003). Toward a broader view of social stereotyping. *American
←——→Psychologist, 58,* 1019–1027. doi: 10.1037/0003-066X.58.12.1019
5 spaces or ½"

Coplan, J. H. (2008, January 28). When it's all right for guys to cry. *Business Week,
4068,* 17.

Edwards, G. H. (1992). The structure and content of the male gender role
stereotype: An exploration of subtypes. *Sex Roles: A Journal of Research,
27,* 533–551. doi: 10.1007/BF00290008

Kunda, Z., & Thagard, P. (1996). Forming impressions from stereotypes, traits, and
behaviors: A parallel-constraint-satisfaction theory. *Psychological Review,
103,* 284–308. doi: 10.1037/0033-295X.103.2.284

Mansfield, H. C. (2006). *Manliness.* New Haven, CT: Yale University Press.

Marshall, G. (Director). (1990). *Pretty woman* [DVD]. USA: Touchstone Pictures.

McCreary, D. R., Wong, F. Y., Wiener, W., Carpenter, K. M., Engle, A., & Nelson,
P. (1996). The relationship between masculine gender role stress and
psychological adjustment: A question of construct validity? *Sex Roles: A
Journal of Research, 34,* 507–516. doi: 10.1007/BF01545029

Plummer, D. C. (2001). The quest for modern manhood: Masculine stereotypes,
peer culture and the social significance of homophobia. *Journal of
Adolescence, 24,* 15–23. doi: 10.1006/jado.2000.0370

Rudman, L. A., & Fairchild, K. (2004). Reactions to counterstereotypic behavior: The
role of backlash in cultural stereotype maintenance. *Journal of Personality and
Social Psychology, 87,* 157–176. doi: 10.1037/0022-3514.87.2.157

Sontag, M. S., Peteu, M., & Lee, J. (1999). *Clothing in the self-system of
adolescents: Relationships among values, proximity of clothing to self,*

Journal article:
Accessed
through data-
base, DOI
included

Magazine
article: print
version

Book: Scholarly
press

Film: Medium in
brackets

Journal article:
Online; PDF
accessed—
page numbers
included

clothing interest, anticipated outcomes and perceived quality of life. Retrieved
from Michigan State University Extension Web site:
http://web1.msue.msu.edu/msue/imp/modrr/rr556098.html

Vescio, T. K., Snyder, M., & Butz, D. A. (2003). Power in stereotypically masculine
domains: A social influence strategy X stereotype match model. *Journal
of Personality and Social Psychology, 85,* 1062. doi: 10.1037/0022-
3514.85.6.1062

Article on
website: URL
included

Notes   Heading (centered), new page

1. This romantic comedy starring Julia Roberts and Richard Gere (dir. Garry Marshall) was extremely popular, grossing nearly $464 million worldwide, according to the site Box Office Mojo (www.boxofficemojo.com/movies/?id=prettywoman.htm). Nevertheless, participants had not seen the film before participating in this experiment.

Content note: Relevant information not central to argument

348

23 Documenting Sources: *Chicago* Style

The Chicago
Manual of
Style
16 SIXTEENTH EDITION

The Essential Guide for
Writers, Editors, and Publishers

Written by editors at the University of Chicago Press, the *Chicago Manual of Style,* 16th ed., provides advice to help writers and editors produce clear and consistent copy for their readers. Many writers in the humanities and social sciences (in history, economics, and philosophy, for example) follow the guidelines provided by the *Chicago Manual* for citing and documenting sources.

Editors at the University of Chicago Press recognize that readers from different disciplines may have different expectations about how in-text citations and bibliography entries should look, so the *Chicago Manual* provides an author-date system similar to that of the American Psychological Association (APA) and the Council of Science Editors (CSE) for writers in the sciences. It also provides a note and bibliography system for writers in the humanities and social sciences. If your readers (including your instructor) expect you to use the author-date system, consult the *Chicago Manual* itself or follow the style detailed in the APA and CSE chapters in this book.

This chapter includes examples of the most common types of *Chicago*-style in-text citations and bibliography entries. For more information or for examples of less common types of sources, consult the *Chicago Manual* itself. You can also subscribe to the *Chicago Manual* online.

> **More about ▶▶▶**
> Popular academic documentation styles per discipline, 235
> MLA style, 243–305
> APA style, 306–48
> CSE style, 377–93

349

Writing
Responsibly   Citing and Documenting Sources

When you cite and document sources, you acknowledge any material from which you have quoted, paraphrased, summarized, or drawn information, and you join the conversation on your topic by adding your own interpretation. Simultaneously, you give interested readers (including your instructor) a way to join the conversation.

Accurate entries in the text and bibliography allow your audience to find and read your sources so that they can evaluate your interpretation and learn more about the subject themselves. Accurate entries also demonstrate the care with which you have written your research project, which reinforces your credibility, or *ethos*.

More about ▶▶▶
Entering conversations and supporting your claims, 182–92

23a Creating *Chicago*-Style Notes and Bibliography Entries

The note system offered by the *Chicago Manual* allows you to include full bibliographic information in a footnote or endnote or to use an abbreviated footnote or endnote with a bibliography. The University of Chicago Press recommends using abbreviated notes with a bibliography.

Examples of the *complete* form of notes and bibliography entries for different types of sources appear in the next section. An *abbreviated* note typically includes enough information for readers to recognize the work and find it in the bibliography. It usually includes the author's surname, a shortened version of the title that includes the title's key words in the same order as they appear on the title page, and the page number you are citing. Here is an example of an abbreviated note and a bibliography entry for the same book:

NOTE (ABBREVIATED)   1. Vancouver, *Voyage of Discovery*, 283.

BIBLIOGRAPHY   Vancouver, George. *A Voyage of Discovery* to the North Pacific Ocean and Round the World, 1791–1795. Edited by W. Kaye Lamb. London: Hakluyt Society, 1984.

A complete bibliographic note or bibliography entry includes three parts: the author's name, the title of the work, and the publication information (print, electronic, or both). The information you include in each of these parts will differ depending on the type of source you are citing. There are many models, and every variation cannot be covered, so be prepared to adapt a model to your special circumstances.

Books—Printed and Electronic

In a printed book, the information you need to create a note and bibliography entry (with the exception of the page numbers) is on the title and copyright pages, at the beginning of the book. In an online

▶▶▶ Student research project (*Chicago* style): "Exploration and Empire," Abrams Conrad, 369–376

Reference ➔ *Chicago*-Style Notes and Bibliography Entries

Chicago Note & Bibliography Entries

▶▶▶Annotated visual of where to find author, title, publication, and other information, on foldout following p. 393

or e-book, print and electronic publication information often appears at the top or bottom of the first screen or is available through a link.

1. One author

a. Printed The basic note for a printed book looks like this:

> Ref. No. Author's first name Surname, *Title: Subtitle* (Place of
>
> Publication: Publisher, Date of publication), Page(s).

Here is an example of an actual note:

> 1. Michael Novak, *The Universal Hunger for Liberty: Why the Clash*
>
> *of Civilizations Is Not Inevitable* (New York: Basic Books, 2004), 96–98.

The basic bibliography entry for a printed book looks like this:

> Author's surname, First name. *Title: Subtitle.* Place of publication:
>
> Publisher, date of publication.

Here is an example of an actual bibliography entry:

> Novak, Michael. *The Universal Hunger for Liberty: Why the Clash of*
>
> *Civilizations Is Not Inevitable.* New York: Basic Books, 2004.

The *Chicago Manual* allows for either full publishers' names (the name minus words like *Incorporated* or *Publishers*) or abbreviated versions (*Basic* instead of *Basic Books,* for example). Be consistent within your research project. This chapter uses full names.

b. Database

> 2. W. E. B. Du Bois, *The Souls of Black Folk* (Chicago: A. C. McClurg
>
> & Co., 1903; Bartleby.com, 1999), chap. 1, http://www.bartleby. com/114/.

> Du Bois, W. E. B. *The Souls of Black Folk.* Chicago: A. C. McClurg & Co.,
>
> 1903. Bartleby.com, 1999. http://www.bartleby.com/114/.

If the online book is *not* available in print or is not yet in final form and might change by the time your readers seek it out, provide your access date in parentheses following the URL.

c. E-book

3. Charles C. Mann, *1491: New Revelations of the Americas before Columbus* (New York: Knopf Publishing Group, 2006), Adobe Reader e-book, chap. 3

Mann, Charles C. *1491: New Revelations of the Americas before Columbus*. New York: Knopf Publishing Group, 2006. Adobe Reader e-book.

2. Two or three authors

4. Peter Bernstein and Annalyn Swan, *All the Money in the World* (New York: Random House, 2008), 122.

5. Cynthia Kuhn, Scott Swartzwelder, and Wilkie Wilson, *Buzzed: The Straight Facts about the Most Used and Abused Drugs from Alcohol to Ecstasy,* 3rd ed. (New York: W. W. Norton & Co., 2008), 225.

Bernstein, Peter, and Annalyn Swan. *All the Money in the World*. New York: Random House, 2008.

Kuhn, Cynthia, Scott Swartzwelder, and Wilkie Wilson. *Buzzed: The Straight Facts about the Most Used and Abused Drugs from Alcohol to Ecstasy*. 3rd ed. New York: W. W. Norton & Co., 2008.

3. More than three authors

6. Peter M. Senge et al., *The Necessary Revolution: How Individuals and Organizations Are Working Together to Create a Sustainable World* (New York: Random House, 2008), 83.

→ Tech

Guidelines for Formatting URLs

As you format notes and bibliography entries for online sources, you will find that not all URLs fit on one line. The *Chicago Manual* recommends breaking a URL (if necessary) after a slash (/) or double slash (//) or before a dot or other punctuation.

Chicago Note & Bibliography Entries

1. One author
2. Two or three authors
3. More than three authors
4. Unnamed (anonymous) author
5. Two or more works by the same author

Place surname first only for first author

1st author plus *et al.* ("and others" in Latin) in note

Chicago Note & Bibliography Entries

Senge, Peter M., Bryan Smith, Nina Kruschwitz, Joe Laur, and

Sarah Schley. *The Necessary Revolution: How Individuals and*

Organizations Are Working Together to Create a Sustainable World.

New York: Random House, 2008.

4. Unnamed (anonymous) author If no author is listed, begin with the title.

7. *Terrorist Hunter: The Extraordinary Story of a Woman Who Went*

Undercover to Infiltrate the Radical Islamic Groups Operating in America

(New York: Ecco-HarperCollins, 2003), 82.

Terrorist Hunter: The Extraordinary Story of a Woman Who Went

Undercover to Infiltrate the Radical Islamic Groups Operating in

America. New York: Ecco-HarperCollins, 2003.

5. Two or more works by the same author Your note will be the same as for any book by one or more authors. In your bibliography, alphabetize the entries by the first important word in the title, and replace the author's name with three dashes in entries after the first.

Foer, Jonathan Safran. *Eating Animals.* New York: Little, Brown, 2009.

———. *Extremely Loud and Incredibly Close: A Novel.* Boston: Houghton

Mifflin, 2005.

6. Group or corporate author

group as author

8. Blackfoot Gallery Committee, *The Story of the Blackfoot People:*

Nitsitapiisinni (Richmond Hill, ON: Firefly Books, 2002), 15.

group as author

Blackfoot Gallery Committee. *The Story of the Blackfoot People:*

Nitsitapiisinni. Richmond Hill, ON: Firefly Books, 2002.

7. Editor (no author)

> 9. Susan E. Cook, ed., *Genocide in Cambodia and Rwanda: New Perspectives* (New Haven, CT: Yale Center for International and Area Studies, 2004), 79.

> Cook, Susan E., ed. *Genocide in Cambodia and Rwanda: New Perspectives*. New Haven, CT: Yale Center for International and Area Studies, 2004.

When the abbreviation *ed.* appears after a name, it means *editor,* so for more than one editor, change the abbreviation *ed.* to *eds.*

8. Author and editor or translator

> 10. John Locke, *The Second Treatise of Government*, ed. Thomas P. Peardon (Indianapolis: Oxford University Press, 1990), 124.

> 11. Stefan Chwin, *Death in Danzig*, trans. Philip Boehm (New York: Harcourt, 2004), 24.

> Locke, John. *The Second Treatise of Government*. Edited by Thomas P. Peardon. Indianapolis: Oxford University Press, 1990.

> Chwin, Stefan. *Death in Danzig*. Translated by Philip Boehm. New York: Harcourt, 2004.

9. Selection from an edited book or anthology

> selection author · selection title · title of book in which selection appears
> 12. Rebecca Arnold, "Fashion," in *Feminist Visual Culture,* ed. Fiona Carson and Claire Pajaczkowska (New York: Routledge, 2001), 212.

> Arnold, Rebecca. "Fashion." In *Feminist Visual Culture*, edited by Fiona Carson and Claire Pajaczkowska, 207–22. New York: Routledge, 2001.
> selection pgs.

s.v. Abbreviation of the Latin phrase *sub verbo,* "under the word"

10. Edition other than the first

13. James A. Herrick, *The History and Theory of Rhetoric: An Introduction*, 3rd ed. (Boston: Allyn & Bacon, 2005), 50.

Herrick, James A. *The History and Theory of Rhetoric: An Introduction*. 3rd ed. Boston: Allyn & Bacon, 2005.

11. Introduction, preface, foreword, or afterword by a different writer

14. Mario Andretti, label foreword to *Race to Win: How to Become a Complete Champion,* by Derek Daly (Minneapolis: Motorbooks, 2008).

Andretti, Mario. Foreword to *Race to Win: How to Become a Complete Champion,* by Derek Daly, 7–8. Minneapolis: Motorbooks, 2008.

12. Entry in an encyclopedia or dictionary For a well-known reference work such as the *American Heritage Dictionary* or the *Encyclopedia Britannica,* a bibliography entry is not necessary.

a. Printed

15. *The American Heritage Dictionary*, 2nd college ed., s.v. "plagiarism."

b. Online Unless a "last updated" date appears on the site, include an access date before the URL.

16. *Dictionary.com*, s.v. "plagiarism," accessed July 14, 2010, http://dictionary.reference.com/browse/plagiarism.

13. Multivolume work

vol. title

17. Robert Caro, *The Years of Lyndon Johnson,* vol. 3, *Master of the Senate* (New York: Alfred A. Knopf, 2002), 4.

Vols. published in different years with different titles

18. George Brown Tindall and David E. Shi, *America: A Narrative History,* 8th ed. (New York: W. W. Norton, 2003), 2:123.

vol. pg.

Vols. published in same year with same title

Caro, Robert. *The Years of Lyndon Johnson.* Vol. 3, *The Master of the Senate.* New York: Alfred A. Knopf, 2002.

Tindall, George Brown, and David E. Shi. *America: A Narrative History,* 8th ed. 2 vols. New York: W. W. Norton, 2003.

Chicago Note & Bibliography Entries

12. Entry in an encyclopedia or dictionary
13. Multivolume work
14. **Book in a series**
15. **Sacred text**
16. **Dissertation**
17. Article in a scholarly journal
18. Article in a magazine

14. Book in a series

book title

19. Oleg V. Khlevnyuk, ed. *The History of the Gulag: From Collectivization to the Great Terror,* Annals of Communism (New Haven, CT: Yale University Press, 2004), 186–87.

series title

Khlevnyuk, Oleg V., ed. *The History of the Gulag: From Collectivization to the Great Terror.* Annals of Communism. New Haven, CT: Yale University Press, 2004.

15. Sacred text

book   lines   version

20. 1 Kings 3:23–26 (King James Version).

verse

21. Qur'an 17:1–2.

Sacred texts are usually not included in the bibliography.

16. Dissertation

For an unpublished dissertation or thesis, place the title in quotation marks. Titles of published dissertations or theses are italicized. Include the type of document (*PhD diss., MA thesis*), the university where it was submitted, and the date of submission.

22. Jessica Davis Powers, *"Patrons, Houses and Viewers in Pompeii: Reconsidering the House of the Gilded Cupids"* (PhD diss., University of Michigan, 2006), Proquest (AAI 3208535) 43–57.

❯ Example 1, 352

Powers, Jessica Davis. *"Patrons, Houses and Viewers in Pompeii:*

Reconsidering the House of the Gilded Cupids." PhD diss., University

of Michigan, 2006.

❯ ▶▶▶Annotated
visual of where to
find author, title,
publication, and
other information,
on foldout following
p. 393

Periodicals—Printed and Electronic

A periodical is a publication issued at regular intervals—newspapers are generally published every day, magazines every week or month, and scholarly journals four times a year. For periodicals, include not only the title of the article (in quotation marks) but also the title of the periodical (in italics). The type of publication information you include depends on the type of periodical you are citing.

17. Article in a scholarly journal The information you need to create a note and bibliography entry for a printed journal article appears on the cover or title page of the journal and on the first and last page of the article. For articles downloaded from a database, the information appears on the screen listing the articles that fit your search terms on the full record of the article, or on the first and last page of the file you download. For articles that appear in journals published solely online, you will find the publication information on the website's home page, in the journal's table of contents, or on the first page of the article.

Chicago Note
& Bibliography
Entries

15. Sacred text

16. Dissertation

**17. Article in a
scholarly
journal**

18. Article in a
magazine

19. Article in a
newspaper
(signed)

a. Printed The basic note for an article in a printed journal looks like this:

> Ref. No. Author's first name Surname, "Title of Article," *Title of*
>
> *Journal* Vol. number, Issue number (Year of publication): Pages.

Months (May) or seasons (Winter) may be included before the year of publication, but they are not required. If a journal is paginated by volume—for example, if issue 1 ends on page 175 and issue 2 begins on page 176—the issue number may be omitted. Here are examples of notes and bibliography entries of journals with and without issue numbers.

Paginated by Issue (Issue Number Included)

> 23. Bill McCarron, "Basilisk Puns in *Harry Potter and the Chamber*
>
>   vol. no.
> *of Secrets," Notes on Contemporary Literature* 36, no. 1 (2006): 2.
>
>   issue no.

McCarron, Bill. "Basilisk Puns in *Harry Potter and the Chamber of Secrets*."

Notes on Contemporary Literature 36, no. 1 (2006): 2.

Chicago Note & Bibliography Entries

Paginated by Volume (No Issue Number)

24. Jason Phillips, "The Grape Vine Telegraph: Rumors and

vol. no.

Confederate Persistence," *Journal of Southern History* 72 (2006): 770.

Phillips, Jason. "The Grape Vine Telegraph: Rumors and Confederate

Persistence." *Journal of Southern History* 72 (2006): 753–88.

b. Accessed through a database Most researchers locate journal articles through subscription databases available through their college library. Frequently, articles indexed in such databases are also available in HTML or PDF format through the database. If the article you are citing is available in PDF format, include the page numbers you are citing in your note and the page range in your bibliography entry. If the article is available only in HTML format, add a subhead or paragraph number to your note if this will help readers locate the passage you are citing. To cite an article accessed through a subscription database, add the URL of the database's home page at the end of your entry. More and more academic journals are also adding digital object identifiers (DOIs); if the article you are citing includes a DOI, add it before the name of the database.

25. Michael J. Furlong and Sandra L. Christenson, "Engaging

Students at School and with Learning: A Relevant Construct for *All*

DOI

Students," *Psychology in the Schools* 45, no. 5 (May 2008), doi: 10.1002/

database

pits.20302, EBSCOHost (AN31581251)

More about ▶▶▶
DOIs, 360

Furlong, Michael J., and Sandra L. Christenson. "Engaging Students at

School and with Learning: A Relevant Construct for *All* Students."

Psychology in the Schools 45, no. 5 (May 2008). doi: 10.1002/

pits.20302, EBSCOHost (AN31581251)

c. Online Online journals may not provide page numbers. Provide a subheading or paragraph number (if your audience will need it to locate the passage you are citing), and include the DOI (if there is one) and the URL for the article (if there is not).

26. Jeremy Adelman, "An Age of Imperial Revolutions," *American Historical Review* 113, no. 2 (April 2008), doi: 10.1086/ahr.113.2.319, http://www.journals.uchicago.edu/doi/full/10.1086/ahr.113.2.319.

Adelman, Jeremy. "An Age of Imperial Revolutions." *American Historical Review* 113, no. 2 (April 2008). doi: 10.1086/ahr.113.2.319, http://www.journals.uchicago.edu/doi/full/10.1086/ahr.113.2.319.

18. Article in a magazine Omit volume and issue numbers, and replace the parentheses around the publication date (month and year; or month, day, and year) with commas.

a. Printed

27. Marian Smith Holmes, "The Freedom Riders," *Smithsonian,* February 2009, 72.

Holmes, Marian Smith. "The Freedom Riders." *Smithsonian,* February 2009, 70–75.

b. Accessed through a database

28. Jesse Ellison, "The Refugees Who Saved Lewiston," *Newsweek,* January 17, 2009, 69, LexisNexis Academic.

Ellison, Jesse. "The Refugees Who Saved Lewiston." *Newsweek,* January 17, 2009, 69. LexisNexis Academic.

c. Online

29. Mike Madden, "What's Love Got to Do with It?," *Salon,* January 28, 2009, http://www.salon.com/news/feature/2009/01/28/stimulus/.

Madden, Mike. "What's Love Got to Do with It?" *Salon*, January 28, 2009.

http://www.salon.com/news/feature/2009/01/28/stimulus/.

19. Article in a newspaper (signed) Because page numbers may differ from edition to edition, omit them and use section letters or numbers (if available) instead. A bibliography entry may be omitted.

a. Printed

30. John M. Broder, "Geography Is Dividing Democrats over Energy,"

edition name   section no.
New York Times, January 26, 2009, national edition, sec. 1.

Broder, John M. "Geography Is Dividing Democrats over Energy." *New York*

Times, January 26, 2009, national edition, sec. 1.

If the city in which the newspaper is published is not identified on the newspaper's masthead, add it in italics; if it might be unfamiliar to readers, add the state, also.

31. Jim Kenneally, "When Brockton Was Home to a Marathon,"

Brockton (MA) Enterprise, April 20, 2006, sec. 1.

Kenneally, Jim. "When Brockton Was Home to a Marathon." *Brockton (MA)*

Enterprise, April 20, 2006, sec. 1.

For well-known national newspapers (such as the *Christian Science Monitor, USA Today,* and the *Wall Street Journal*), no city or state is needed. If you are unsure whether the newspaper is well known, consult your instructor or a reference librarian.

b. Accessed through a database

32. John M. Broder, "Geography Is Dividing Democrats over

Energy," *New York Times,* January 26, 2009, late edition, sec. A,

database
LexisNexis Academic.

Broder, John M. "Geography Is Dividing Democrats over Energy." *New York Times,* January 26, 2009, late edition, sec. A. LexisNexis Academic.

c. Online

33. Steve Chapman, "Moderating the Terror War," *Chicago Tribune,* January 25, 2009, URL http://www.chicagotribune.com/news/columnists/chi-oped0125chapmanjan25,0,1998584.column.

Chapman, Steve. "Moderating the Terror War." *Chicago Tribune,* January 25, 2009. http://www.chicagotribune.com/news/columnists/chi-oped0125chapmanjan25,0,1998584.column.

20. Article or editorial in a newspaper (unsigned) When no author is named, place the newspaper's title in the author position in your bibliography. (*Chicago* style does not require a bibliography entry for unsigned newspaper articles or editorials, but your instructor might.)

34. *Los Angeles Times,* "Health before Ideology," January 27, 2009, sec. A.

Los Angeles Times. "Health before Ideology," January 27, 2009, sec. A.

21. Review

35. Ben Brantley, review of *Romeo and Juliet,* by William Shakespeare, directed by Michael Greif, Delacorte Theater, New York, *New York Times,* June 25, 2007, sec. E.

Brantley, Ben. Review of *Romeo and Juliet,* by William Shakespeare, directed by Michael Greif, Delacorte Theater, New York. *New York Times,* June 25, 2007, sec. E.

22. Letter to the editor Omit the letter's title, page numbers, and the edition name or number.

36. John A. Beck, letter to the editor, *Los Angeles Times,* March 16, 2010.

Beck, John A. Letter to the editor. *Los Angeles Times,* March 16, 2010.

Other Electronic Sources

Although it is usually easy to find citation information for books and articles in periodicals, websites can be a bit trickier. Most of the information you need will appear at the bottom or top of the web page or on the site's home page. Sometimes, however, you may need to look further. Click on links such as "About us" or "More information." Frequently, websites will not provide complete information; include as much information as you can. If no author is listed, place the site's sponsor in the "author" position. If key information is missing, include a phrase describing the site, in case the URL changes.

23. Website The basic note for a website looks like this:

Ref. No. *Website Title*, Author, Sponsoring Organization, last update or access date if last update not provided, URL.

Here is an example of an actual note:

37. *Victorian England: An Introduction,* Christine Roth, University of Wisconsin–Oshkosh, Department of English, accessed August 1, 2010, http://www.english.uwosh.edu/roth/VictorianEngland.htm.

The bibliography entry for the note above looks like this:

Roth, Christine. *Victorian England: An Introduction.* University of Wisconsin–Oshkosh, Department of English. Accessed August 1, 2010. http://www.english.uwosh.edu/roth/VictorianEngland.htm.

Include an access date only when the publication date or last update is not indicated. *Chicago* style does not require an entry in the bibliography for web content, but if your instructor does, follow the example above.

Chicago Note & Bibliography Entries

24. Web page or wiki article When referring to a specific page or article on a website or wiki, place that page's title in quotation marks. For a wiki article, begin with the article's title.

38. "Lewis and Clark County History Project," Montana History Wiki, Montana Historical Society, last modified September 24, 2007, http://montanahistorywiki.pbwiki.com/Lewis+and+Clark+County+History+Project.

Montana History Wiki, Montana Historical Society. "Lewis and Clark County History Project." Last modified September 24, 2007. http://montanahistorywiki.pbwiki.com/FinePage?RevisionsFor=Lewis+and+Clark+County+History+Project.

25. Discussion list or blog posting A blog post need not be included in the bibliography.

blog author   post title   blog title
39. Francis Heaney, "The Tie Project, Days 164–173," *Heaneyland*
post date
(blog), July 28, 2007, http://www.yarnivore.com/francis/archives/001900.html#more.

Heaney, Francis. *Heaneyland* (blog). http://www.yarnivore.com/francis/archives/001900.html#more.

26. CD-ROM If there is more than one version or edition of the CD-ROM add that information after the title.

40. *History through Art: The 20th Century* (San Jose, CA: Fogware Publishing, 2000). CD-ROM, chap. 1.

History through Art: The 20th Century. San Jose, CA: Fogware Publishing, 2000. CD-ROM.

Audio and Visual Sources

The information you need for creating notes and bibliography entries for most audio and visual sources will appear on the cover, label, or program, or in the credits at the end of a film or a television show. Begin with the author, director, conductor, or performer, or begin your citation with the name of the work, depending on what your project emphasizes. The *Chicago Manual* provides few models of audio-visual sources. Those below are based on the principles explained in *Chicago*.

27. Motion picture (film, video, DVD)

41. *Juno,* directed by Jason Reitman, written by Diablo Cody (2007; Los Angeles: Fox Searchlight Home Entertainment, 2008).

Juno. Directed by Jason Reitman, written by Diablo Cody, 2007. Los Angeles: Fox Searchlight Home Entertainment, 2008.

28. Music or other audio recording

42. Johannes Brahms, *Piano Concerto no. 1 in D minor, op. 15,* Berliner Philharmoniker, dir. Claudio Abbado, 1986, Philips Classics Productions, BMG D153907, compact disc.

Brahms, Johannes. *Piano Concerto no. 1 in D minor, op. 15.* Berliner Philharmoniker. Dir. Claudio Abbado. 1986. Philips Classics Productions. BMG D153907, compact disc.

29. Podcast

43. Melvyn Bragg, host, "The Indian Mutiny," *In Our Time,* BBC Radio 4, Podcast audio, 45:00, February 18, 2010, http://www.bbc.co.uk/programmes/b00qprnj.

More about ▶▶▶
Figure captions
(*Chicago* style),
368, 371

Bragg, Melvyn, host. "The Indian Mutiny." *In Our Time,* BBC Radio 4,

February 18, 2010. Podcast audio, 45:00. http://www.bbc.co.uk/

programmes/b00qprnj.

30. Performance

44. Lauren Ambrose, *Romeo and Juliet,* dir. Michael Greif, Delacorte

Theatre, New York, July 1, 2007.

Ambrose, Lauren. *Romeo and Juliet.* Directed by Michael Greif. Delacorte

Theatre, New York, July 1, 2007.

Chicago Note
& Bibliography
Entries

28. Music or other
audio recording
29. Podcast
30. Performance
31. Work of art
**32. Government
publication**
33. Interview
34. Personal
communication

31. Work of art If a reproduction of the work appears in your project, identify the work in a figure caption. If you discuss the work but do not show it, cite it in your notes but do not provide an entry in your bibliography. If the reproduction is taken from a book, follow the model for a selection from an edited book or anthology.

45. Alexander Calder, *Two Acrobats,* 1929, wire sculpture, Menil

Collection, Houston.

Miscellaneous Sources—Printed and Electronic

32. Government publication For documents published by the U.S. Government Printing Office (or GPO), including the publisher is optional. If you omit the publisher, change the colon after the location to a period (Washington, DC.).

46. U.S. Department of Education, Office of Innovation and

Improvement, *Charter High Schools: Closing the Achievement Gap*

(Washington, DC: U.S. Government Printing Office, 2006).

Or (Washington, DC, 2006).

U.S. Department of Education, Office of Innovation and Improvement.

Charter High Schools: Closing the Achievement Gap.

Washington, DC: U.S. Government Printing Office, 2006.

33. Interview (Published or Broadcast)
a. Printed or broadcast

47. Barack Obama, interview by Maria Bartiromo, *Closing Bell,*

CNBC, March 27, 2008.

Obama, Barack. Interview by Maria Bartiromo. *Closing Bell.* CNBC,

March 27, 2008.

b. Online

48. Barack Obama, interview by Maria Bartiromo, *Closing Bell,*

CNBC, March 27, 2008, http://www.cnbc.com/id/23832520.

Obama, Barack. Interview by Maria Bartiromo. *Closing Bell.* CNBC,

March 27, 2008. http://www.cnbc.com/id/23832520.

34. Personal communication   Unless your instructor requires it, no bibliography entry is required.

a. Letter

49. Evan Marks, letter to the author, August 13, 2005.

b. Email

50. Amy E. Robillard, email message to the author, March 14, 2007.

35. Indirect source   If you do not have access to the original source, mention the author you are citing in your text and include an entry in the bibliography that names both the original source and the source from which you borrowed the material.

Theophrastus (quoted in Gleitman) offers a witty description of the

garrulous (talkative, rambling) man. . . .

Theophrastus. *The Characters of Theophrastus.* Edited by J. M. Edmonds and G. E. V. Austen. London: Blackie and Sons, 1904, 48. Quoted in Gleitman, Henry. *Psychology.* 5th ed. New York: W. W. Norton, 2000, 553.

→ Tech

Creating Footnotes and Endnotes

Most word processing programs, including Microsoft *Word* and Google *Docs,* allow you to insert footnotes and endnotes easily. This automated system for inserting footnotes will automatically renumber all the notes in your project if you add or delete one. However, the software for managing notes may not provide many formatting options, so check with your instructor in advance to make sure the software's default format is acceptable.

More about ▶▶▶
Designing an
academic research
essay, 227–29

23b Using *Chicago* Style for Tables and Figures

The *Chicago Manual* recommends that you number tables and figures in a separate sequence (*Table 1, Table 2, Figure 1, Figure 2*) both in the text and in the table title or figure caption. Tables and figures should be placed as close as possible after the text reference. For tables, provide a brief identifying title and place it above the table. For figures, provide a caption that includes any information about the figure that readers will need to identify it, such as the title of a work of art, the artist's name, the work's location, and a brief description. If the figure, table, or information used to create these illustrations comes from another source, provide a source note. Source notes for tables generally appear below the table, while source information for figures appears at the end of the figure caption.

23c Formatting a Paper in *Chicago* Style

The *Chicago Manual* provides detailed instructions about manuscript preparation for authors submitting their work for publication, but it does not offer formatting instructions for college projects. Follow the formatting instructions provided in *Chicago* chapter 17 or chapter 19 (MLA style), or consult your instructor.

Writing Responsibly

Of Deadlines and Paper Clips

Instructors expect students to turn in thoughtful, carefully proofread, and neatly formatted papers on time—usually in class on the due date. They also expect writers to clip (or staple) the pages of the paper *before* the paper is submitted. Do justice to yourself by being fully prepared: Do not hand in a stack of loose sheets or expect your instructor to supply a paper clip.

The *Chicago Manual* recommends numbering bibliographic notes consecutively throughout the paper, using superscript (above-the-line) numbers in the body of the paper:

> While acknowledging that not all scholars agree, Mann observes, "If Monte Verde is correct, as most believe, people were thriving from Alaska to Chile while much of northern Europe was still empty of mankind and its works."[8]

Type the heading "Notes" at the top of a new page following the end of the text, and type the notes below the heading. (You may need to insert a page break if your word processor has automatically created endnotes on the last page of your paper.)

To begin your list of works cited, type the heading "Bibliography" or "Works Cited" at the top of a new page. (Ask your instructor which heading is preferred.) Entries should be set with a hanging indent: Position the first line of each entry flush with the left margin, and indent subsequent lines by half an inch. Entries should be alphabetized by the author's surname.

Student Research Project: *Chicago* Style

The following excerpts are taken from a research project written by Abrams Conrad for a history course at American University. His formatting has been modified to show both abbreviated notes with a list of works cited and full notes without one.

More about ▶▶▶
Using abbreviated notes, 350, 352

If your instructor requires a title page, see the model on p. 234

Abrams Conrad

History 235

Professor Burke

December 15, 2011

Identifying information (double spaced)

Descriptive title

Exploration and Empire: James Cook and the Pacific Northwest   Title (centered)

Exploration of the Pacific Northwest begins and ends with Captain James Cook, the first British explorer to reach the area, map it, and study its peoples and with those who had sailed and trained under his command. While others sailed to the Pacific Northwest, their motivation was largely for trade. Cook's voyage and those of his successors were motivated as much by a desire to understand the region and its peoples as by the desire for financial gain.

Thesis at end of first paragraph to guide reader

In the late 1770s, the Pacific Northwest was the globe's last temperate coast to be explored and mapped, primarily due to its remoteness from Europe. To get there, ships had to sail around Cape Horn at the tip of South America. Cook's third voyage, begun in 1778, was undertaken to discover a Northwest Passage, an inland waterway connecting the Pacific Ocean with the Atlantic that would shorten the sailing time from Europe to Asia. The Admiralty had instructed him "to search for, and to explore, such Rivers or Inlets as may appear to be of a considerable extent and pointing towards Hudsons or Baffins Bay."[1] While his findings were negative—he all but eliminated the possibility of an inland passage—he was the first Briton to make contact with the area and truly to study the geography and culture of the region.

Quotation integrated into text; source in endnote

Cook made anchor in Nootka Sound for most of April 1778 and then ventured north along the Canadian coast, searching for a waterway northeast, until he put in at Prince William Sound.[2] He made a detailed survey of the coast, a portion of which is shown in Figure 1.

Summary in text with bibliographic endnote

Figure callout in text

Cook's third voyage was also politically strategic: to thwart Spanish and Russian claims to the Pacific Northwest.[3] With the Spanish in the south and moving north, and the Russians in the north and moving south, the northwest coast, or "New Albion," was a place where the British could establish a claim and perhaps eventually a colony.[4]

Transition

Another reason for Cook's exploration of the Northwest was the man himself. Cook was the quintessential explorer; he "never missed an opportunity to chart a reef or an island," wrote Ernest Dodge of the Peabody Museum in Salem, Massachusetts.[5] Cook stood out because he was so

Signal phrase with background information

1"

1"

370

Figure 1. A chart of the northwest coast of America and the northeast coast of Asia, explored in the years 1778 and 1779. Prepared by Lieut. Henry Roberts, under the immediate inspection of Capt. Cook. (1794), David Rumsey Map Coll.

Figure identified in caption

methodical. He was exact in his measurements and never missed an opportunity to learn or write about indigenous peoples.

Cook's explorations of the Pacific Northwest ended with his death in the Hawaiian Islands in early 1779, but his explorations of the Pacific Northwest had direct consequences for traders. James King, who took over command of the expedition after Cook's death, received 800 Spanish dollars in return for twenty sea otter pelts he brought back from the Pacific Northwest—and those were the ragged ones; King received 120 dollars each for pelts in pristine condition, an immense amount of money at that time.[6] It is doubtful the price ever went that high again,[7] but this sum put the region on the map for traders and spawned a new series of voyages.

Claim in topic sentence; supporting facts in balance of ¶

Note numbers placed at natural pause

What made Cook so important to the Pacific Northwest were the explorations of the area by those who had sailed with him. In this regard, it is interesting to compare the results of those who sailed under Cook with those who did not. Some of the first voyages to the area after Cook's death were the trading voyages of James Hanna, James Strange, and John Meares. Hanna sailed from

Claim in topic sentence; supported by comparison in next 4 ¶s

Example 1

Macao to Nootka Sound (in what is now British Columbia) in 1784–86.[8] His voyage produced few results except those of trade, collecting more than 500 skins.[9] Strange sailed from India; his mission was to proceed to the Northwest, trade at Nootka Sound and Alaska, make discoveries, and sail through the Bering Strait and Arctic Ocean, as far north as the North Pole.[10] While his instructions stated discovery as the primary goal, his investors looked upon trade as the focus of the expedition, and Strange ended up doing neither very well. He brought back barely 600 skins, not enough to offset the costs of the voyage, and though he tried to put together another trip, he was unsuccessful.[11]

John Meares led a voyage in 1785 to the Gulf of Alaska, where he anticipated better trading and finer pelts; he proved ignorant both of Russian control over the area and of the harsh Alaskan climate.[12] Meares lost twenty-three men to disease.[13] He also got his ship stuck in the ice and was released only with warm weather and the help of George Dixon and Nathanial Portlock (both had sailed with Cook), who provided aid if he promised to leave at once.[14] While Meares showed some bad judgment, he was ultimately successful in trade in the Northwest, but he was not committed to exploration of the coast or the discovery and naming of locations.[15] Meares himself refers to his voyages as "commercial" and describes people and geography in terms of "extension of our particular commerce."[16] Compare Meares's voyages with those of Portlock, Dixon, and Vancouver, all students of Cook.

In May 1785, the King George's Sound Company sent Nathanial Portlock out on a mission to control the region where furs came from. Portlock, who had been to the Northwest with Cook, sailed from London in September 1785 with two ships, the *King George* and the *Queen Charlotte,* captained by George Dixon, another Cook disciple.[17] They became the first men to drop anchor in Hawaii, specifically Kealakekua Bay, since Cook's death. Their primary goal was to collect furs and trade them in Macao or Canton on the Chinese coast. While they did return with a surplus, they made no real killing.[18] Their journals, published in 1789, heavily advocated advancement of the fur trade, but their voyage became known for its geographical results.[19] They discovered the Queen Charlotte Islands off what is now British Columbia, and their accounts of the local people ultimately proved more important than whatever furs they sold.[20] In their accounts, Cook's influence is easily seen. Both made detailed observations, were meticulous in their calculations, and proved to be just as interested in who sold them goods as in the goods themselves.

Example 2

Example 3

Transition sentence

Example 4

Example 5

Example 6

It is in the voyage of George Vancouver where Cook's influence is clearest. Sailing from England in 1791, Vancouver's voyage was one part discovery, one part trade, and one part diplomacy. He was to chart the coast from Nootka Sound to Cook Sound for traders, investigate the possibility of an inland northwest passage,[21] retrieve the territory taken by the Spanish around Nootka Sound, and, in the winter months, survey all of the Hawaiian Islands.[22] Arriving in the Strait of Juan de Fuca in late April 1792, Vancouver immediately began his survey of the coast north of California, accomplishing much during the summer of 1792. He missed the Columbia River, much to his dismay, but he mapped and named Puget Sound.[23] His survey finally revealed most of the hazards of the Northwest coastline and negated the idea of an inland northwest passage and a large inland sea.[24] In late August, he met with the Spanish to negotiate the restitution of Nootka Sound. Reaching an impasse, he sent his executive officer back to England requesting instructions and sailed for Hawaii, where he surveyed the Islands.[25] There, in February 1794 (in contrast with Cook), he concluded a treaty with the Hawaiian king, actually gaining control of the islands for England, though the treaty was not ratified in London.[26]

When comparing the voyages of Hanna, Strange, and Meares with those of Portlock, Dixon, and Vancouver, a glaring difference stands out: While all the voyages shared similar objectives, the *approach* to those objectives was vastly different. Hanna, Strange, and Meares were concerned with trade, pure and simple; Cook's men were also concerned with trade, but as Dodge writes, "[t]he drilling of the Master was notable."[27] The men who had served under Cook considered it their duty both to fulfill their trade objectives and to explore, chart, discover, and explain as much of the region as they could. The missions to the Pacific Northwest that were motivated by trade alone yielded only temporary results. The geographic information gained from the exploratory expeditions of Cook's men paid dividends for years to come. Not only did they provide information for those who followed, both traders and scholars, but they also contributed to the British goal of empire building. Empire is not just geography or territory. It is also about having gone somewhere, mapped it, and named the places. In the Pacific, where the British played a major role in discovery, there are British names in every corner of the sea.[28] Cook and his men were letting it be known worldwide that they had been there. Seeing all those vastly different places, all with British names, added to the inquisitive and the imperialistic mindset of the British. It is at least part of the reason they were so ready to go to war over places so distant.

Conclusion: Provides summary and explains significance of research

Notes

Short form of notes used with list of works cited

1. Cook, *The Journals,* 220–24.

2. Ibid., 230.

"Ibid." (abbreviation of *ibidem,* Latin for "in the same place") used when source cited in note immediately above

3. Rose, "Captain Cook," 102–9.

4. Schwantes, *The Pacific Northwest,* 41.

5. Dodge, *Beyond the Capes,* 15.

6. Schwantes, *The Pacific Northwest,* 43.

7. Ibid.

8. Blumenthal, *The Early Exploration,* 3.

9. Dodge, *Beyond the Capes,* 43–44.

10. Gough, "India-Based Expeditions," 219.

11. Ibid., 217–19.

12. Ibid., 220.

Two citations in same footnote separated with a semicolon

13. Ibid.

14. Blumenthal, *The Early Exploration,* 4; *Oxford Dictionary of National Biography,* s.v. "Meares, John," accessed April 28, 2009, http://www.oxforddnb.com/subscribed.

Reference work: no entry in bibliography, full entry here; use "s.v." *sub verbo,* "under the word" (Latin)

15. Blumenthal, *The Early Exploration,* 3.

16. Ibid., 3, 10.

17. Dodge, *Beyond the Capes,* 44.

18. Ibid., 43–58.

19. *Oxford Dictionary of National Biography,* s.v. "Portlock, Nathanial," accessed April 28, 2009, http://www.oxforddnb.com/subscribed.

20. Dodge, *Beyond the Capes,* 53.

21. Ibid., 135–55.

22. Vancouver, *Voyage of Discovery,* 283–88.

23. Ibid.

24. Ibid., 288.

25. Dodge, *Beyond the Capes,* 135–55.

26. Ibid.

27. Ibid., 43.

28. Dobbie, "Pacific Place Names," 258–65.

Works Cited

Blumenthal, Richard W., ed. *The Early Exploration of Inland Washington Waters: Journals and Logs from Six Expeditions, 1786–1792.* Jefferson, NC: McFarland, 2004.

Cook, James. *The Journals of Captain James Cook on His Voyages of Discovery.* Edited by J. C. Beaglehole. Vol. 3. Cambridge: Cambridge University Press, 1967.

Dobbie, Elliot V. K. "Pacific Place Names and the History of Discovery." *American Speech* 36 (1961): 258–65.

Dodge, Ernest S. *Beyond the Capes: Pacific Exploration from Captain Cook to the* Challenger, *1776–1877.* Boston: Little, Brown, 1971.

Gough, Barry M. "India-Based Expeditions of Trade and Discovery in the North Pacific in the Late Eighteenth Century." *Geographical Journal* 155 (July 1989): 215–23, JSTOR.

Rose, J. Holland. "Captain Cook and the Founding of British Power in the Pacific." *Geographical Journal* 73 (February 1929): 102–22, JSTOR.

Schwantes, Carlos A. *The Pacific Northwest: An Interpretive History.* Lincoln: University of Nebraska Press, 1989.

Vancouver, George. *A Voyage of Discovery to the North Pacific Ocean and Round the World, 1791–1795: With an Introduction and Appendices.* Edited by W. Kaye Lamb. Vol. 1. London: Hakluyt Society, 1984.

Annotations (left margin):

- Entries arranged alphabetically
- Book: Editor, no author
- Book: Editor and author; one volume from multi-volume work
- Book (printed): Popular press
- Journal article: Accessed through a database, URL of database home page provided
- Book (printed): Scholarly press

24 Documenting Sources: CSE Style

Writers in the sciences customarily use formatting and documentation guidelines from *Scientific Style and Format: The CSE Manual for Authors, Editors, and Publishers* (7th ed.) published by the Council of Science Editors (CSE). CSE style requires that sources be cited briefly in the text and documented in a reference list at the end of the project. The goal of providing in-text citations and a list of references is to allow readers to locate and read the sources for themselves and to distinguish the writer's ideas from those borrowed from sources.

24a Creating CSE-Style In-Text Citations

More about ▶▶▶
Popular academic documentation styles per discipline, 235
MLA style, 243–305 (ch. 21)
APA style, 306–348 (ch. 22)
Chicago style, 349–376 (ch. 23)

In-text citations, which appear in the body of your paper, identify any material borrowed from a source, whether it is a quotation, paraphrase, summary, or idea. The CSE offers three formats for citing sources in the body of the project:

- name-year
- citation-sequence
- citation-name

The ***name-year system*** requires you to include the last name of the author and the year of publication in parentheses whenever the source is cited:

Advances have clarified the role of betalains and carotenoids in

author   date

determining the color of flowers (Groteworld 2006).

Signal phrase The author's last name plus an appropriate verb (194)

If you use the author's name in a ***signal phrase,*** include just the year of publication in parentheses:

author

Christoffel (2007) argues that public health officers adopted the strategies

date

they did because they were facing a crisis.

More about ▶▶▶
Signal phrases, 194–95

The name-year system tells readers immediately who wrote the source and how current it is, which is particularly crucial in the sciences. This system involves many rules for creating in-text citations (for example, how to create in-text citations for several authors, with organizations as authors, and so on), which can make it difficult to apply the rules consistently.

The ***citation-sequence*** and ***citation-name systems*** use a superscript number (the same number for a source each time it is cited) to refer the reader to a list of references at the end of the project.

Some testing of the River Invertebrate Prediction and Classification System

(RIVPACS) had already been conducted.[1] Biologists in Great Britain then

used environmental data to establish community type,[2] and two studies

developed predictive models for testing the effects of habitat-specific

sampling.[3,4] These did not, however, account for the earlier RIVPACS

research.[1]

Place reference numbers after punctuation marks. When drawing information from multiple sources, include multiple citations, separated by commas.

When using the citation-sequence system, arrange the sources in your reference list in order of first mention in your research report and then number them. (The first work cited is number 1, the second work cited is number 2, and so on.) When using the citation-name system, alphabetize sources and then number them. (The first work alphabetically is number 1, the second work alphabetically is number 2, and so on.)

Tech

Creating Superscript Numbers

The footnoting function in your word processing program will not work for inserting reference numbers for the citation-sequence or citation-name systems because it will only insert the reference marks in sequence (*1, 2, 3, . . .*), whereas the CSE system requires that you use the same super-script number for a source each time you cite it. Instead, insert superscript numbers manually, without using your word processing program's foot-note function, and type your list of references separately. (Use the Help Directory function to learn about in-serting superscript numbers.)

The citation-sequence and citation-name systems need no rules about how to form in-text citations, but they do require readers to turn to the reference list to see the name of the author and the source's date of publication. Since the word processor's footnoting system can-not be used, numbering (and renumbering) of notes must be done by hand. To avoid the confusion that can arise during revision and edit-ing, consider using a simplified author-date system while drafting the research project and inserting the numbers for the citation-sequence or citation-name system in the final draft.

Check with your instructor about which system to use, and use it consistently. If your instructor does not have a preference, consider the advantages and drawbacks of each system before making your choice.

24b Preparing a CSE-Style Reference List

A research report or project in CSE style ends with a list of cited ref-erences. How you format those references depends on the type of source and the system you use.

Books—Printed and Electronic

In a printed book, you can find most or all of the information you need to create a reference list entry on the copyright and title pages at the beginning of the book. In an online or e-book, print and elec-tronic publication information often appears at the top or bottom of the first page or is available through a link.

▶▶▶Annotated vi-sual of where to find author and publica-tion information, on foldouts following this chapter.

Quick Reference → A List of CSE-Style Reference List Examples

Books—Printed and Electronic

Periodicals—Printed and Electronic

Miscellaneous Sources—Printed and Electronic

CSE Reference List Entries

No punctuation between surname and initials and no period or space between initials

Lines after the first align with the author's name, not the reference number.

▶▶▶Annotated visual of where to find author, title, and publication information, on foldouts following this chapter.

1. One author

a. Printed The basic format for a printed book looks like this:

Name-year system

> Author's surname First and Middle Initials. Date of publication. Title: subtitle. Place of publication: Publisher.

Citation-sequence and citation-name systems

> Ref. No. Author's surname First and Middle Initials. Title: subtitle. Place of publication: Publisher; date of publication.

NOTE Book titles are neither italicized nor underlined in CSE style.

Here are examples of actual reference list entries:

Name-year system

> Field RI. 2007. Health care regulation in America: complexity, confrontation, and compromise. New York: Oxford University Press.

Citation-sequence and citation-name systems

1. Field RI. Health care regulation in America: complexity, confrontation, and compromise. New York: Oxford University Press; 2007.

b. Online

Name-year system

Stroup A. 1990. A company of scientists: botany, patronage, and community at the seventeenth-century Parisian Royal Academy of

print publication information

Sciences [Internet]. Berkeley (CA): University of California Press [cited

access date   *URL (permalink)*

2007 Mar 10]. Available from: http://ark.cdlib.org/ark:/13030/ft587006gh/

Citation-sequence and citation-name systems

2. Stroup A. A company of scientists: botany, patronage, and community at the seventeenth-century Parisian Royal Academy of Sciences [Internet]. Berkeley (CA): University of California Press; 1990. Available from: http://ark.cdlib.org/ark:/13030/ft587006gh/

2. Two or more authors

Name-year system

Jamieson BGM, Dallai R, Afzelius BA. 1999. Insects: their spermatozoa and phylogeny. Enfield (NH): Science Publishers.

Citation-sequence and citation-name systems

3. Jamieson BGM, Dallai R, Afzelius BA. Insects: their spermatozoa and phylogeny. Enfield (NH): Science Publishers; 1999.

If the source has more than ten authors, list the first ten; after the tenth author, insert the words *and others.*

CSE Reference List Entries

1. One author
2. **Two or more authors**
3. Group or corporate author
4. Edited book

Follow the order of authors on the title page. No *and* before last author.

3. Group or corporate author

Name-year system

Institute of Medicine Committee on the Use of Complementary and Alternative Medicine by the American Public. 2005. Complementary and alternative medicine in the United States. Washington, DC: National Academies Press.

Citation-sequence and citation-name systems

4. Institute of Medicine Committee on the Use of Complementary and Alternative Medicine by the American Public. Complementary and alternative medicine in the United States. Washington, DC: National Academies Press; 2005.

4. Edited book

Name-year system

Whelan CT, Mason NJ, editors. 2005. Electron scattering: from atoms, molecules, nuclei, and bulk matter. New York: Kluwer Academic/Plenum.

Citation-sequence and citation-name systems

5. Whelan CT, Mason NJ, editors. Electron scattering: from atoms, molecules, nuclei, and bulk matter. New York: Kluwer Academic/Plenum; 2005.

5. Selection from an edited book or conference proceedings

Name-year system

selection author   selection title
Berkenkotter C. 2000. Scientific writing and scientific thinking: writing the
    book title
scientific habit of mind. In: Goggin MD, editor. Inventing a discipline: rhetoric scholarship in honor of Richard E. Young. Urbana (IL): National
    selection pages
Council of Teachers of English. p. 270–284.

Citation-sequence and citation-name systems

6. Berkenkotter C. Scientific writing and scientific thinking: writing the scientific habit of mind. In: Goggin MD, editor. Inventing a discipline: rhetoric scholarship in honor of Richard E. Young. Urbana (IL): National Council of Teachers of English; 2000. p. 270–284.

To cite a paper published in the proceedings of a conference, add the number and name of the conference, the date of the conference, and the location of the conference (separated by semicolons and ending with a period) after the title of the book and before the publication information.

48th Annual American Society for Cell Biology Conference; 2008

Dec 13–17; San Francisco, CA.

6. Dissertation For dissertations published by University Microfilms International (UMI), include the access number.

Name-year system

Song LZ. 2003. Relations between optimism, stress and health in Chinese and American students [dissertation]. Tucson (AZ): University of Arizona.

access information   location   access no.
Available from: UMI, Ann Arbor, MI; AAI3107041.

Citation-sequence and citation-name systems

7. Song LZ. Relations between optimism, stress and health in Chinese and American students [dissertation]. Tucson (AZ): University of Arizona; 2003. Available from: UMI, Ann Arbor, MI; AAI3107041.

If the location of the college is not listed on the title page of the dissertation, place square brackets around this information: [Tucson (AZ)].

Periodicals—Printed and Electronic

The information needed to document a printed journal article is on the cover or table of contents of the journal and the first and last page

CSE Reference List Entries

4. Edited book
5. Selection from an edited book or conference proceedings
6. Dissertation
7. Article in a scholarly journal
8. Article in a magazine

> **More about ▶▶▶**
> Formatting author information: Examples 380–82

▶▶▶Annotated visual of where to find author and publication information, on foldouts following this chapter.

of the article. For articles downloaded from a database, the information you need appears on the screen listing the articles that fit your search terms, on the full record of the article, or on the first (and last) page of the file you download. For journal articles published online, the information you need appears on the website's home page, on that issue's web page, or on the first screen of the article.

CSE Reference List Entries

Journal titles: Omit punctuation, articles (*an, the*), and prepositions (*of, on, in*), and abbreviate most words longer than 5 letters (except 1-word titles like *Science* and *Nature*).

DOI Digital object identifier, a permanent identifier assigned to electronic articles (360)

7. Article in a scholarly journal

a. Printed The basic citation for an article in a scholarly journal looks like this:

Name-year system

Author's surname First and Middle Initials. Year of publication. Title: subtitle.

Abbreviated Journal Title. Vol. number(Issue number):page numbers.

Citation-sequence and citation-name systems

Ref. No. Author's surname First and Middle Initials. Title:subtitle. Abbreviated

Journal Title. Year of publication;Vol. number(Issue number):page

numbers.

Here is an actual citation of each type:

Name-year system

Cox L. 2007. The community health center perspective. Behav Healthc.

27(3):20–21.

Citation-sequence and citation-name systems

8. Cox L. The community health center perspective. Behav Healthc.

2007;27(3):20–21.

b. Accessed through a database Most researchers locate journal articles through subscription databases available through their college library. Frequently, articles indexed in such databases are available in HTML or PDF format through a link from the database. As yet, the CSE does not provide a model for an article accessed through an online database, but since most library databases are by subscription, readers will probably find the URL of the database's home page more useful than a direct link to the article itself. If a DOI is available, include it.

Name-year system

Borrok D, Fein JB, Tischler M, O'Loughlin E, Meyer H, Liss M,

access date

Kemner KM. 2004 [cited 2004 Aug 7]. The effect of acidic solutions and

growth conditions on the adsorptive properties of bacterial surfaces. Chem

medium   database

Geol [Internet]. 209(1–2):107–119. In Science Direct. Available from:

URL (database home page)   DOI

http://www.sciencedirect.com doi:10.1016/j.chemgeo.2004.04.025

> No period after
> URL or DOI

Citation-sequence and citation-name systems

9. Borrok D, Fein JB, Tischler M, O'Loughlin E, Meyer H, Liss M,

Kemner KM. The effect of acidic solutions and growth conditions

on the adsorptive properties of bacterial surfaces. Chem Geol [Internet].

2004 [cited 2004 Aug 7]; 209(1–2):107–119. Available from: http://www

.sciencedirect.com doi:10.1016/j.chemgeo.2004.04.025

c. Online Omit page numbers for online articles. When a subscription is not required to access the article, provide a direct permalink URL to the article; otherwise, provide the URL to the journal's home page. If a DOI is provided, include it.

Name-year system

Patten SB, Williams HVA, Lavorato DH, Eliasziw M. 2009. Allergies and

major depression: a longitudinal community study. Biopsychosoc Med

URL (permalink)

[Internet]. [cited 2009 Feb 5];3(3). Available from: http://www.bpsmedicine

DOI

.com/content/3/1/3 doi:10.1186/1751-0759-3-3

> No period after
> URL or DOI

Citation-sequence and citation-name systems

10. Patten SB, Williams HVA, Lavorato DH, Eliasziw M. Allergies and major

depression: a longitudinal community study. Biopsychosoc Med

[Internet]. 2009 [cited 2009 Feb 5];3(3). Available from: http://www

.bpsmedicine.com/content/3/1/3 doi:10.1186/1751-0759-3-3

CSE Reference
List Entries

5. Selection from
   an edited book
   or conference
   proceedings
6. Dissertation
7. **Article in a
   scholarly
   journal**
8. Article in a
   magazine
9. Article in a
   newspaper

8. Article in a magazine

a. Printed

Name-year system

Gladwell M. 2006 Oct 16. The formula. New Yorker:138–149.

Citation-sequence and citation-name systems

11. Gladwell M. The formula. New Yorker 2006 Oct 16:138–149.

b. Accessed through a database

Name-year system

Gladwell M. 2006 Oct 16 [cited 2008 Apr 23]. The formula. New Yorker

[Internet]:138–149. Available from: http:www.ebscohost.com/

Citation-sequence and citation-name systems

12. Gladwell M. The formula. New Yorker [Internet]. 2006 Oct 16 [cited

2008 Apr 23]:138–149. Available from: http://www.ebscohost.com/

c. Online

Name-year system

Coghlan A. 2007 May 16 [cited 2007 May 19]. Bipolar children—is the

US overdiagnosing? NewScientist.com [Internet] Available from:

URL (permalink)
http://www.newscientist.com/channel/health/mg19426043.900-bipolar-

children--is-the-us-overdiagnosing.html/

Citation-sequence and citation-name systems

13. Coghlan A. Bipolar children—is the US overdiagnosing? NewScientist

.com [Internet]. 2007 May 16 [cited 2007 May 19]. Available from:

http://www.newscientist.com/channel/health/mg19426043.900-bipolar-

children--is-the-us-overdiagnosing.html/

9. Article in a newspaper

a. Printed

Name-year system

LaFraniere S. 2009 Feb 6. Scientists point to possible link between dam

edition   section   col. no.
and China quake. New York Times (Late Ed.). Sect. A:1 (col. 3).
1st pg.

Citation-sequence and citation-name systems

14. LaFraniere S. Scientists point to possible link between dam and China

quake. New York Times (Late Ed.). 2009 Feb 6;Sect. A:1 (col. 3).

b. Accessed through a database

Name-year system

LaFraniere S. 2009 Feb 6 [cited 2009 Feb 28]. Scientists point to possible

link between dam and China quake. New York Times [Internet]. Sect. A:1.

Available from: http://www.lexisnexis.com/

Citation-sequence and citation-name systems

15. LaFraniere S. Scientists point to possible link between dam and China

quake. New York Times [Internet]. 2009 Feb 6 [cited 2009 Feb 28];

Sect. A:1. Available from: http://www.lexisnexis.com/

c. Online

Name-year system

LaFee S. 2006 May 17. Light can hold fatal attraction for many nocturnal

animals. San Diego Union-Tribune [Internet] [cited 2006 May 20] [about

length
11 paragraphs]. Available from: http://www.signonsandiego.com/news/

science/

CSE Reference
List Entries

7. Article in a
   scholarly journal
8. Article in a
   magazine
9. **Article in a**
   newspaper
10. Website
11. Web page

Include permalink
URL if available; if not,
use URL of home page.

Citation-sequence and citation-name systems

16. LaFee S. Light can hold fatal attraction for many nocturnal animals.

San Diego Union-Tribune [Internet]. 2006 May 17 [cited 2006 May 20]

[about 11 paragraphs]. Available from: http://www.signonsandiego.com/

news/science/

Miscellaneous Sources—Printed and Electronic

▶▶▶Annotated visual of where to find author, title, and publication information, on foldouts following this chapter.

The information needed to document a website or web page usually appears at the top or bottom of the home page or web page. You may also need to look for a link to a page labeled "About us" or "Contact us." Frequently, information needed for a complete reference list entry is missing, in which case provide as much information as you can.

10. Website

CSE Reference
List Entries

Name-year system

In the name-year system, a sample reference entry for a website looks like this:

Author. Title of website [Medium (internet)]. Publication date [Access date].

Available from: URL (home page)

Here is an example of an actual entry:

MIT news [Internet]. 2009 Feb 9 [cited 2009 Mar 10]. Available from: http://

web.mit.edu/newsoffice/index.html/

The site has no author, so the reference list entry begins with the name of the site's sponsor.

Citation-sequence and citation-name systems

When referencing an entire website, the only difference between the name-year system and the citation-sequence and citation-name systems is that the citation-sequence and citation-name entries add a reference number at the beginning of the entry.

11. Web page When documenting a web page or a document on a website, provide the URL for the web page, not the site's home page.

Name-year system

article author · article title
Schorow S. 2009 Feb 5 [cited 2009 Mar 10]. Aliens at sea: anthropologist
· website
Helmreich studies researchers studying ocean microbes. MIT News
· URL (web page)
[Internet]. Available from: http://web.mit.edu/newsoffice/2009/alien-

ocean-0205.html

Citation-sequence and citation-name systems

17. Schorow S. Aliens at sea: anthropologist Helmreich studies

    researchers studying ocean microbes. MIT News [Internet] 2009 Feb 5

    [cited 2009 Mar 10]. Available from: http://web.mit.edu/newsoffice/2009/

    alien-ocean-0205.html

12. Discussion list or blog posting

Name-year system

date/time posted
Hall A. 2004 Aug 5, 11:33 am [cited 2005 Jan 30]. Biology of deep Gulf
· disc. list · medium
of Mexico shipwrecks. In: FISH-SCI [Internet discussion list]. [Lulea

(Sweden): National Higher Research and Education Network] [about

4 paragraphs]. Available from: http://segate.sunet.se/archives/

fish-sci.html

Citation-sequence and citation-name systems

18. Hall A. Biology of deep Gulf of Mexico shipwrecks. In: FISH-SCI

    [Internet discussion list]. [Lulea (Sweden): National Higher Research

    and Education Network] 2004 Aug 5, 11:33 am [cited 2005 Jan 30]

    [about 4 paragraphs]. Available from: http://segate.sunet.se/archives/

    fish-sci.html

CSE Reference List Entries

9. Article in a newspaper
10. Website
11. **Web page**
12. **Discussion list or blog posting**
13. Email message
14. Technical report or government document

13. Email message

Name-year system

email author   date/time sent   subject line
Martin SP. 2005 Nov 18, 3:31 pm. Revised results [Email]. Message to:
email recipient   length
Lydia Jimenez [cited 2005 Nov 20] [about 2 screens].

Citation-sequence and citation-name systems

19. Martin SP. Revised results [Email]. Message to: Lydia Jimenez.

2005 Nov 18, 3:31 pm [cited 2005 Nov 20] [about 2 screens].

14. Technical report or government document If no author is listed, use the name of the governing nation and the government agency that produced the document, and include any identifying number.

Name-year system

Department of Health and Human Services (US). 1985 May. Women's

health. Report of the Public Health Service Task Force on Women's Health

Issues. PHS:85-50206.

Citation-sequence and citation-name systems

20. Department of Health and Human Services (US). Women's health.

Report of the Public Health Service Task Force on Women's Health

Issues; 1985 May. PHS:85-50206.

CSE Reference List Entries

11. Web page
12. Discussion list or blog posting
13. Email message
14. Technical report or government document

Writing
Responsibly   **Of Deadlines and Paper Clips**

Instructors expect students to turn in thoughtful, carefully proofread, and neatly formatted papers on time—usually in class on the due date. They also expect writers to clip or staple the pages of the paper *before* the paper is submitted. Do justice to yourself by being fully prepared.

24c Formatting a CSE-Style Research Project

The CSE does not specify a format for the body of a college research report, but most scientific reports include the following sections:

- Abstract
- Introduction
- Methods
- Results
- Discussion
- References

More about ▶▶▶
Writing an abstract, 240
Formatting college papers, 288–92
Formatting a paper in APA style, 334–336

Ask your instructor for formatting guidelines, refer to the general formatting guidelines provided in Chapter 19, or follow the formatting guidelines for APA style on pages 334–336.

Start a new page for your reference list, and title it "References."

Name-Year System List entries in alphabetical order by author's surname. If no author is listed, alphabetize by the first main word of the title (omitting articles such as *the, a,* and *an*). Do not number the entries.

Citation-Sequence System Number your entries in order of their appearance in your paper. Each work should appear in your reference list only once, even if it is cited more than once in your project. Double-check to make sure that the numbers in your reference list match the numbers in your text.

Citation-Name System Alphabetize the entries in your reference list first (by the author's surname or the first main word of the title if no author is listed). Then number them. Each work should appear in your reference list only once, even if it is cited more than once in your project. Double-check to make sure that the numbers in your reference list match the numbers in your text.

Student Research Project: CSE-Style Reference List

The sample reference list below is taken from a laboratory report by Alicia Keefe, University of Maryland. Keefe fulfilled her responsibility to the writers from whom she borrowed information and ideas by supplying a complete citation for each source. She fulfilled her responsibility to her reader by formatting the entries using the name-year system in CSE style, in keeping with her reader's expectations.

References

Geiger P. 2002. Introduction to *Drosophila melanogaster.* Tucson (AZ): University of Arizona, General Biology Program for Teachers, Biology Department [Internet] [cited 2008 Apr 30]. Available from: http://biology.arizona.edu/sciconn/lessons2/geiger/intro.htm

Hoikkala A, Aspi J. 1993 [cited 2008 Apr 28]. Criteria of female mate choice in *Drosophila littoralis, D. montana,* and *D. ezoana.* Evolution [Internet]. 47(3):768–778. Available from: http://web.ebscohost.com

Ives JD. 1921. Cross-over values in the fruit fly, *Drosophila ampelophila,* when the linked factors enter in different ways. Am Naturalist. 6:571–573.

Mader, S. 2005. Lab manual. 9th ed. New York: McGraw-Hill.

Marcillac F, Bousquet F, Alabouvette J, Savarit F, Ferveur JF. 2005 [cited 2008 Apr 28]. A mutation with major effects on *Drosophila melanogaster* sex pheromones. Genetics [Internet]. 171(4):1617–1628. Available from: http://web.ebscohost.com doi:10.1534/genetics.104.033159

Service PM. 1991. Laboratory evolution of longevity and reproductive fitness components in male fruit flies: mating ability. Evolution. 47:387–399.

Web page: Date cited and URL of web page provided

Journal article: accessed through a database, no DOI; URL of database home page provided

Journal article: Printed, title of journal abbreviated

Journal article: accessed through a database, with DOI

Journal article: printed, one-word journal title not abbreviated

Representing Indirect Sources

As the Citation Project researchers studied researched papers produced at a variety of U.S. colleges, they noticed how few of the student writers successfully handled indirect sources. When a source was quoting from, paraphrasing, or summarizing another source, very few of the students acknowledged both sources. Instead, they tended simply to cite the source in which they found the information, which misleads their readers about who was speaking. The following example shows how the problem occurs:

First draft

Paraphrase of
passage in source

Quotation from source

Parenthetical note

> Non-traditional high school students in the GED Options Pathway program shouldn't be labeled "GED kids"; they should be judged on their individual accomplishments. "This is supposed to be the land of the free, and equal opportunity, and all that stuff" (Peterson).

Peterson, who is cited in the sample above, is the writer of the newspaper story in which the quotation appears. However, Peterson doesn't speak the sentence in quotation marks. That sentence does appear in her story, but it is being spoken by someone whom Peterson is quoting. It appears in the following passage in Peterson's story:

Passage from Source

Quoted passage

> The program does use the Graduate Equivalency Degree, or GED, as a tool. The students all have to pass the test's five sections, but when they complete the program they earn a regular high school diploma. This is an important point for Robbins, and she stresses that her students will get to graduate with their classes.
>
> "In fact, I'm trying to get everybody to quit calling them those GED kids," she said. "Number one, they've labeled them. That irritates me. This is supposed to be land of the free and equal opportunity and all that stuff. Don't label my kids. Let them prove what they can do. Let the test scores speak."

When you are borrowing material that your source has also borrowed, your citations should accurately indicate who is speaking and should also indicate where you found the material. This can be accomplished in a parenthetical citation, a signal phrase, or a combination of the two:

Parenthetical citation: *Name the speaker; then write "qtd. in" (quoted in); then name the author of the source*

> Students in the GED Options Pathway program shouldn't be labeled "GED kids"; they should be judged on their individual accomplishments. "This is supposed to be the land of the free, and equal opportunity, and all that stuff" (Robbins, qtd. in Peterson).

Paraphrase of passage in source

Quotation from source

In-text citation

Signal phrase: *Name both speaker and source in your text*

> Erica Peterson reports Anastasia Robbins' beliefs: Students in the GED Options Pathway program shouldn't be labeled "GED kids"; they should be judged on their individual accomplishments. "This is supposed to be the land of the free, and equal opportunity, and all that stuff."

Signal phrase identifies source and speaker

Paraphrase of passage in source

Quotation

Combination of signal phrase and parenthetical note:

> Anastasia Robbins believes that students in the GED Options Pathway program shouldn't be labeled "GED kids"; they should be judged on their individual accomplishments. "This is supposed to be the land of the free, and equal opportunity, and all that stuff" (qtd. in Peterson).

Signal phrase identifies the speaker

Paraphrase of passage in source

Quotation

Parenthetical note identifies the source

Source: Peterson, Erica. "W.Va. Program Gives High-Risk Students an Option." Charleston *Gazette-Mail* 24 Apr. 2011. Web. 24 Apr. 2011.

Book (Printed)

author   title   publication information   medium

Morrison, Toni. *A Mercy*. New York: Knopf, 2008. Print.

place of   publisher publication
publication   date

title →

A Mercy

author →

Toni Morrison

publisher

ALFRED A. KNOPF   NEW YORK • TORONTO 2009

Title page   place of publication

THIS IS A BORZOI BOOK
PUBLISHED BY ALFRED A. KNOPF
AND ALFRED A. KNOPF CANADA

Copyright © 2008 by Toni Morrison ← publication date
All rights reserved.
...ed in the United States by Alfred A. Knopf,
...on of Random House, Inc., New York, and
...y Random House of Canada Limited, Toronto.
www.aaknopf.com
www.randomhouse.ca

...ooks, and the colophon are registered trademarks of
Random House, Inc.
...f Canada and colophon are trademarks.

...of Congress Cataloging-in-Publication Data
Morrison, Toni.
...rcy : a novel / by Toni Morrison.—1st ed.
p.   cm.
ISBN 978-0-307-26423-7
...a girls—Fiction.   2. Interracial adoption—Fiction.   3.
Racism—Fiction.   I. Title.
PS3563.O8749M47 2008
813'.54—dc22   2008021067

...d Archives Canada Cataloguing-in-Publication
Morrison, Toni.
A mercy / Toni Morrison.
ISBN 978-0-676-97830-8
I. Title.
...7 2008   813'.54   C2008-902500-8

...of fiction. Names, characters, places, and incidents
...e product of the author's imagination or are used
...ny resemblance to actual persons, living or dead,
...ents, or locales is entirely coincidental.

...afactured in the United States of America
Published November 14, 2008
Reprinted Five Times
Seventh Printing, January 2009

Copyright page

Look for the information you need to document a printed book on the book's title page and copyright page. If more than one location for the publisher is listed on the title page, use the first. (For more about documenting a book, see pp. 262–70.)

Documenting a Source: APA

Book (Printed)

authors   publication date   title and subtitle

Tavris, C., & Aronson, E. (2007). *Mistakes were made (but not by me): Why we justify*

publication information

foolish beliefs, bad decisions, and hurtful acts. Orlando, FL: Harcourt.

place of   publisher
publication

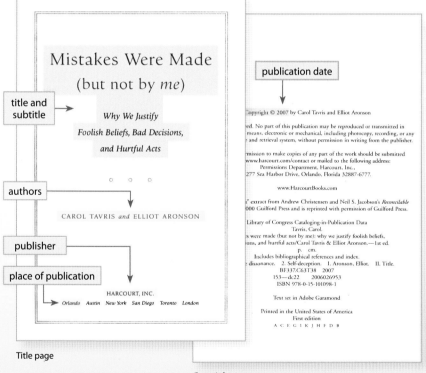

Mistakes Were Made
(but not by *me*)

title and subtitle →

Why We Justify
Foolish Beliefs, Bad Decisions,
and Hurtful Acts

o   o   o

authors

CAROL TAVRIS and ELLIOT ARONSON

publisher

place of publication

HARCOURT, INC.

→ Orlando   Austin   New York   San Diego   Toronto   London

Title page

publication date

Copyright © 2007 by Carol Tavris and Elliot Aronson

...ed. No part of this publication may be reproduced or transmitted in
... means, electronic or mechanical, including photocopy, recording, or any
... and retrieval system, without permission in writing from the publisher.

...rmission to make copies of any part of the work should be submitted
...www.harcourt.com/contact or mailed to the following address:
     Permissions Department, Harcourt, Inc.,
...277 Sea Harbor Drive, Orlando, Florida 32887-6777.

www.HarcourtBooks.com

..." extract from Andrew Christensen and Neil S. Jacobson's *Reconcilable*
...000 Guilford Press and is reprinted with permission of Guilford Press.

...Library of Congress Cataloging-in-Publication Data
     Tavris, Carol.
...s were made (but not by me): why we justify foolish beliefs,
...ons, and hurtful acts/Carol Tavris & Elliot Aronson.—1st ed.
       p.   cm.
    Includes bibliographical references and index.
...e dissonance.   2. Self-deception.   I. Aronson, Elliot.   II. Title.
       BE337.C63T38   2007
     153—dc22   2006026953
      ISBN 978-0-15-101098-1

Text set in Adobe Garamond

Printed in the United States of America
First edition
A C E G I K J H F D B

Copyright page

Look for the information you need to document a printed book on the book's title page and copyright page. If more than one location for the publisher is listed on the title page, use the first or the publisher's home office location (if indicated). (For more about documenting a book, see pp. 304–13.)

Short Work on a **Website**

author   web page title   website title   sponsor/publisher

Kukkonen, Karin. "The Rhetoric of Comics." *Project Narrative Weblog*. Ohio State University,

medium   access date

College of the Humanities, 4 Nov. 2008. Web. 2 Dec. 2008.

©date/last update

Web page

Frequently, the information you need to create a complete entry in the list of works cited is missing or difficult to find on web pages. Look at the top or bottom of the web page or home page or for a link to an "About" or "Contact Us" page. If no sponsor or publisher is listed, use *n.p.*; if no publication date is available, use *n.d.* (For more about documenting online sources, see pp. 273-75.)

Journal Article from an Online Database

authors   article title and subtitle

Cantor, Nancy, and Steve Schomberg. "What We Want Students to Learn: Cultivating Playfulness

journal title   issue   pages   database

and Responsibility in a Liberal Education." *Change* 34.6 (2002): 47-49. *Academic Search*

medium   access date   volume   year

Premier. Web. 2 Dec. 2008.

database

article full text (HTML)

article title

authors

article full text (PDF)

journal title, date of publication, volume, issue, article starting page number

Database screen: full record for article

Look for the information you need to document an article you accessed through an online database on the search results screen, the full record of the article, or the first and last pages of the article itself. The access date is the date you last consulted the source; record this date in your notes. (For more about documenting an article accessed through an online database, see p. 271.)

APA Style

Journal Article (Printed)

author   year   article title and subtitle

Fancher, R. E. 2009. Scientific cousins: The relationship between Charles Darwin and Francis Galton.

        publication information

American Psychologist 64, 84–92.

journal title   volume   pages

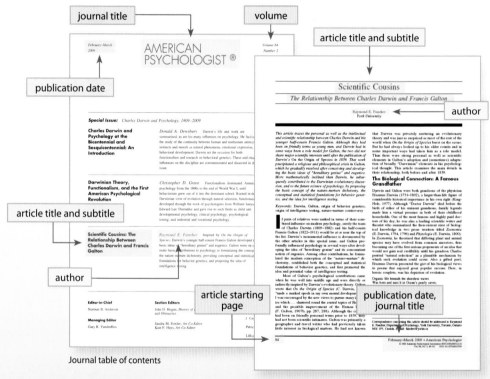

journal title

volume

article title and subtitle

publication date

author

article title and subtitle

author

article starting page

publication date, journal title

Journal table of contents

First page of article

Look for the information you need to document a journal article on the cover or table of contents of the journal and on the first and last pages of the article. (Turn to the last page of the article for the last page number.) If each issue of the journal begins with page 1, include the issue number, in parentheses, after the volume number. (For more about documenting an article from a printed or online periodical, see pp. 321–25.)

MLA Style

Journal Article (Printed)

authors · article title and subtitle
Cantor, Nancy, and Steve Schomberg. "What We Want Students to Learn: Cultivating Playfulness
journal title · issue · pages
and Responsibility in a Liberal Education." *Change* 34.6 (2002): 47-49. Print.
volume · year · medium

Journal table of contents

First page of article

Look for the information you need to document a journal article on the cover or table of contents of the journal and on the first and last pages of the article. (Turn to the last page of the article for the last page number.) (For more about documenting an article from a printed or online periodical, see pp. 268–70.)

Journal Article from an Online Database

author   year   article title and subtitle

Fancher, R. E. (2009). Scientific cousins: The relationship between Charles Darwin and Francis Galton.

           publication information   digital object identifier

American Psychologist 64, 84–92. doi:10.1037/a0013339

        journal title   volume pages

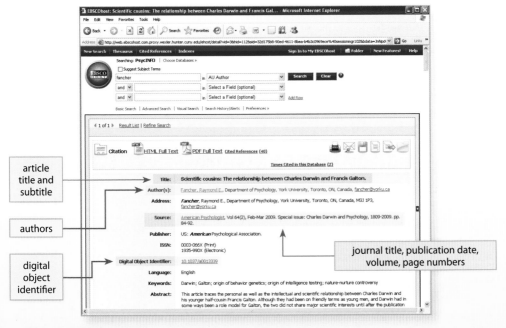

Database screen

Look for the information you need to document an article you accessed through an online database on the search results screen, the full record of the article, or the first and last pages of the article itself. Include a digital object identifier (DOI) if one is provided. No access date is needed. (For more about documenting an article accessed through an online database, see pp. 322–25.)

Short Work on a Website

corporate author/publisher   ©date/last update   web page title and subtitle
American Psychological Association. (2005). The fast and the furious: Psychologists figure out who

                                                                retrieval statement
gets road rage and find ways to calm them down. Retrieved March 31, 2009, from

                URL for web page   retrieval date
http://www.psychologymatters.org/roadrage.html

Web page

Frequently, the information you need to create a complete entry in the reference list is missing or difficult to find on web pages. Look at the top or bottom of the web page or home page or for a link to an "About" or "Contact Us" page. If no author is cited, move the title to the author position. If the web page is untitled, add a description (in brackets) in place of the title. If the page was created and published by the same group, omit the publisher name from the retrieval statement (as here); if not, add the publisher's name before the URL (*Retrieved from APA website:*). (For more about documenting online sources, see pp. 328–31.)

Appendix

Resources in the Disciplines

This appendix contains an annotated list of research resources in a variety of academic disciplines. The resources are grouped into four broad categories—Humanities, Social Sciences, Natural Sciences and Mathematics, and Professional Disciplines—that cover most of the academic disciplines. Each broad category is then subcategorized for user convenience. A list of associations and organizations concludes each category.

General Databases

Many libraries subscribe to these databases, which are excellent starting points for research.

EBSCOhost <search.ebscohost.com/> Subscription-based service including multiple subject-specific databases from which searchers can select.

JSTOR <www.jstor.org/> Full-text database of more than 1,000 journals in the humanities, social sciences, and sciences.

OCLC FirstSearch <firstsearch.oclc.org/> WorldCat. Subscription-based service including multiple subject-specific databases from which searchers can select.

General Web Index

Information You Can Trust. <http://ipl.org/div/subject/>. Internet Public Library and Librarians' Internet Index combined resources. This website has listings for virtually all disciplines.

Humanities

General

Wilson Humanities Index: 1974–date. Wilson. Available through Ovid. Check your library for a subscription. Bibliographic database that cites articles from the most popular English-language scholarly journals and periodicals and many other specialized magazines.

Library of Congress Humanities and Social Sciences Division: Databases and E-resources <openlibrary.org/a/OL419954A/Library_of_Congress._Humanities_and_Social_Sciences_Division> Information about the 70,000-volume general reference collection, online catalogs, subscription databases, CD-ROMs, bibliographies and guides, and internet resources.

Project Muse <muse.jhu.edu/> Johns Hopkins UP. Check your library for a subscription. Full-text articles in the humanities and social sciences.

Voice of the Shuttle <vos.ucsb.edu/> Online database of resources in the humanities and some social sciences.

Art

Artcyclopedia <www.artcyclopedia.com/> Searchable online encyclopedia organized by artist, artwork, museum, medium, subject, nationality, movement, and gender.

Art Index Retrospective: 1929–1984. Wilson. Check your library for a subscription. An extensive multi-language index of art history texts.

Grove Art Dictionary Online <www.oxfordartonline.com/public/> Oxford UP. Contains 45,000 articles on every aspect of the visual arts from prehistory to the present day. Compiled over 15 years, it represents the work of more than 6,800 international scholars.

Heilbrunn Timeline of Art History <www.metmuseum.org/toah/> Overview of the history of art as illustrated and represented in the Metropolitan Museum of Art's collection.

Film

The Film Encyclopedia: The Complete Guide to Film and the Film Industry. Ephraim Katz (New York: Collins, 2008). A single-volume reference with entries on such categories as major figures in film, film organizations, terminology, theories, and industry advances.

The Library of Congress: Motion Picture and Television Reading Room <www.loc.gov/rr/mopic/> Access to and information about the field provided by the Motion Picture, Broadcasting, and Recorded Sound Division of the Library of Congress.

Motion Picture Association of America <www.mpaa.org> General guide to the American motion picture, home video, and television industries.

The New Biographical Dictionary of Film. David Thomson (New York: Knopf, 2002). Contains 1,300 entries from film critic Thomson. Not comprehensive; rather, it draws on Thomson's opinions and critiques about artists.

History

Dictionary of American History, 2nd ed. rev., vol. 1. Ed. James Truslow Adams and R. V. Coleman (New York: Scribner's, 1940). Contains more than 6,000 articles covering a wide range of military, political, social, and economic subjects.

Encyclopedia of African-American Culture and History: The Black Experience in the Americas. 6 vols. Ed. Colin A. Palmer (New York: Cengage, 2005). Also available as e-book. Covers the African-American experience from 1619 to 2005.

Princeton's Guide to History Web Sites <www.princeton.edu/~pressman/hiswebs.htm> Comprehensive guide to general web resources in history.

Languages

Cambridge Encyclopedia of Language, 2nd ed. David Crystal (New York: Cambridge UP, 1997). General study of language covering words, speech, writing, and thought.

MLA Bibliography (New York: Modern Language Association). Available through EBSCO, ProQuest, Cengage/Gale, OCLC. The core resource for languages and literatures; virtually all libraries subscribe to this database.

Literature

Academy of American Poets <www.poets.org/audio> Includes more than 150 sound files of recited poetry.

Bibliographic Guide to the Study of the Literature of the USA, 5th ed. Clarence Louis Frank Gohdes (Durham, NC: Duke UP, 1984). Extensive list of books and articles on the literature of the United States.

Cambridge Bibliography of English Literature, 3rd ed. Ed. Joanne Shattock (New York: Cambridge UP, 2000). Extensive list of books and articles in English literature.

MLA Bibliography (New York: Modern Language Association). Available through EBSCO, ProQuest, Cengage/Gale, OCLC. The core resource for languages and literatures; virtually all libraries subscribe to this database.

Music

Music Online: American Song <amso.alexanderstreet.com/> Check your library for a subscription. Database of American music, with an emphasis on history. More than 58,000 tracks compiled.

The Garland Encyclopedia of World Music Online <glnd.alexanderstreet.com/> Comprehensive online resource devoted to music research on all the world's peoples; includes 9,000 pages of information, essays, and images.

Grove Dictionary of Music and Musicians, 2nd ed. Charles Newell Boyd (New York: Oxford UP, 2001). Largest single reference work on Western music. Included in Oxford Music Online (see next entry).

Oxford Music Online <www.oxfordmusiconline.com/> Includes the *Oxford Dictionary of Music, Grove Music Online* (biographies), and the *Oxford Companion to Music.*

Philosophy

Cambridge Dictionary of Philosophy, 2nd ed. Ed. Robert Audi (New York: Cambridge UP, 1999). Short reference work on philosophy, including coverage of specific philosophers and concepts.

Oxford Companion to Philosophy, new ed. Ed. Ted Honderich (New York: Oxford UP, 2005). Encyclopedia of philosophers, branches of philosophy, and concepts; also includes timeline and visual representations, or "maps," of the field.

Routledge Encyclopedia of Philosophy Online <www.rep.routledge.com> Online resource for philosophy and its related disciplines.

Stanford Encyclopedia of Philosophy <plato.stanford.edu/> Regularly updated and maintained by field experts.

Religion

Encyclopedia of Religion. 15 vols. Ed. Lindsay Jones (Detroit: Macmillan Reference, 2005). Comprehensive reference on religion worldwide across its recorded history.

Encyclopedia of Religion and Society. William H. Swatos Jr. and Peter Kivisto (Walnut Creek, CA: AltaMira Press/Sage, 1998). Broad reference tool in the study of religion and society. Also available online at <hirr.hartsem.edu/ency/acss.htm>.

Theater

The Cambridge Guide to Theater. Martin Banham (New York: Cambridge UP, 1995). Comprehensive guide to the history and current practice of theater throughout the world.

Literary Resources—Theater and Drama <andromeda.rutgers.edu/~jlynch/Lit/theatre.html> Lists several theater, drama, and performance arts resource sites.

Associations and Organizations in the Humanities

Academy of Motion Picture Arts and Sciences
American Comparative Literature Association
American Philosophical Practitioners Association
American Psychological Association
American Society for the History of Rhetoric <www.ashr.org/Resources.html>
American Society of Composers, Authors, and Publishers <www.ascap.com/index.aspx>
Association of Art Historians
Modern Language Association
Theater Development Fund
World History Association
Yahoo! Listing of Religious Organizations <dir.yahoo.com/society_and_culture/religion_and_spirituality/organizations/>

Social Sciences

General

International Bibliography of the Social Sciences <www.lse.ac.uk/collections/IBSS/> Online bibliography for social science and interdisciplinary research produced by the Library at the London School of Economics and Political Science.

Project Muse <muse.jhu.edu/> Johns Hopkins UP. Full-text articles in the humanities and social sciences.

Voice of the Shuttle <vos.ucsb.edu/> Online database of resources on the humanities and some social sciences.

Anthropology

AnthroSource <www.aaanet.org/publications/anthrosource/> American Anthropological Association. Check your library for a subscription. Online database of full-text anthropology resources.

Encyclopedia of Anthropology. Ed. H. James Birx (Walnut Creek, CA: Sage, 2005). Covers physical and biological anthropology, archaeology, cultural and social anthropology, linguistics, and applied anthropology.

Communications

Communication and Mass Media Complete. Accessible through EBSCO (see General Databases). Check your library for a subscription. Database that indexes articles from more than 690 journals (including full text for 380), all in the fields of communications and mass media.

Communication Studies: A SAGE Full-Text Database Check your library for a subscription. Includes full-text articles from SAGE journals in communication.

Criminal Justice

Abstracts Database: National Criminal Justice Reference Service (NCJRS) <www.ncjrs.gov/ App/AbstractDB/AbstractDBSearch.aspx> Federally sponsored database that provides information regarding criminal justice in the United States.

Criminal Justice Abstracts: 1968–present (Thousand Oaks, CA: Sage Publications). Available through ProQuest. Check your library for a subscription. Criminology database covering scholarly and professional works on topics such as "crime trends, crime prevention and deterrence, juvenile delinquency, . . . police, courts, punishment and sentencing."

Economics

American Economic Association Online <www.aeaweb.org/index.php> Collection of information for research in economics. Includes URLs for associations and publications along with contents, abstracts, data files, and full-text links to many economics periodicals and journals.

The Concise Encyclopedia of Economics <www.econlib.org/library/CEECategory.html> Ed. David R. Henderson (Liberty Fund, 2008). A wealth of economic analysis by 150 leading economists.

Education

Bibliographic Guide to Education (Boston: G. K. Hall, 2001). Recent education publications cataloged by Teachers College and Columbia University, supplemented with publications in the field of education cataloged by the Research Libraries of the New York Public Library.

Education Full Text. Wilson. Check your library for a subscription. Bibliographic database that indexes more than 770 education-related English-language periodicals and yearbooks published in the United States and elsewhere, more than 400 of which are peer reviewed.

ERIC: Education Resources Information Center: 1966–present <www.eric.ed.gov/> Check your library for a subscription. Searchable database of full-text and bibliographic resources focused on education.

Geography

A Dictionary of Geography. Susan Mayhew (New York: Oxford UP, 1997). More than 6,000 concise entries for words and terms encountered in both human and physical geography.

The Library of Congress Geography and Map Reading Room <www.loc.gov/rr/geogmap/> Cartographic and geographic information for all parts of the world.

Political Science

Encyclopedia of Government and Politics. Ed. Mary Hawkesworth and Maurice Kogan (New York: Routledge, 2003). Provides a systematic account of politics and political studies, assesses both traditional and contemporary approaches, and projects the paths of future research.

FactCheck.org, A Project of the Annenberg Public Policy Center <www.factcheck.org/> Monitors the factual accuracy of statements by major U.S. political players in TV ads, debates, speeches, interviews, and news releases.

Information Sources in Political Science, 5th ed. Ed. Stephen Green and Douglas Ernest (Santa Barbara, CA: ABC-CLIO, 2005). Comprehensive bibliography of American and international politics covering print and electronic materials published in English, primarily in the United States and the United Kingdom.

U.S. Government Made Easy <www.usa.gov/> Topics and links related to American government.

Psychology

Bibliographic Guide to Psychology (Detroit: G. K. Hall, 2003). Psychology publications cataloged by the Library of Congress and the Research Libraries of the New York Public Library.

PsycARTICLES. American Psychological Association Databases, 1894–present. <www.apa.org/pubs/databases/psycarticles/index.aspx> Check your library for a subscription. Database containing full-text articles from 80 psychology journals published by the American Psychological Association and several other psychology associations.

Sociology

Sociology: A Guide to Reference and Information Sources, 3rd ed. Stephen H. Aby, James Nalen, and Lori Fielding (Santa Barbara, CA: Greenwood, 2005). Descriptions of approximately 610 major reference sources in sociology, its subdisciplines, and the related social sciences.

The Socio Web, Your Independent Guide to Sociological Resources on the Internet <www.socioweb.com/> Independent guide to sociological resources available on the internet.

Women's Studies

WSSLINKS. Woman & Gender Studies Section of the Association of College & Research Libraries. <www.libr.org/wss/wsslinks/> Collects and organizes links to resources on women's studies.

Women's Studies Encyclopedia. Ed. Helen Tierney (Santa Barbara, CA: Greenwood, 1999). Information about women from all fields and disciplines of study in such areas as violence against women, women in public life, and women in specific countries and regions.

Associations and Organizations in the Social Sciences

American Anthropological Association
American Educational Research Association
American Political Science Association
American Sociological Association
Association of American Geographers
International Association of Business Communicators
International Political Science Association <www.ipsa.org/site/>

League of Women Voters <www.lwv.org//AM/Template.cfm?Section=Home>
National Association for Business Economics
National Communication Association
National Education Association
National Women's Studies Association

Natural Sciences and Mathematics

General

Science Reference Center. Found in *EBSCOhost* (see "General Databases"). Indexes full-text reference works and periodicals in the sciences.

Web of Science. ISI Web of Knowledge. Thomson Reuters. Check your library for a subscription. Includes the *Science Citation Index Expanded* and covers 150 disciplines.

Astronomy and Astrophysics

Encyclopedia of Astronomy and Astrophysics <eaa.crcpress.com/> Ed. Paul Murdin. Taylor & Francis Group. Contains more than 2,700 articles covering a broad range of topics in astronomy and astrophysics.

University of Buffalo's Astronomy and Astrophysics: Internet Resources, SUNY, Buffalo. <library.buffalo.edu/asl/guides/astronomy.html> Contains selected astronomy resources freely available on the internet.

Biology

Oxford Dictionary of Biology, 6th ed. Ed. Robert Hine (New York: Oxford UP, 2008). Comprehensive coverage of biology, biophysics, and biochemistry, including biographical entries on key scientists.

The University of Wisconsin-Madison Library's Biology Resources Guide <www.library.wisc.edu/guides/biology/> Comprehensive listing of useful links for biology research.

Chemistry

American Chemical Society Publications <pubs.acs.org/> Comprehensive collection of the most-cited peer-reviewed journals in the chemical and related sciences.

TOXNET <toxnet.nlm.nih.gov/> Databases on toxicology and environmental health created and supported by the Division of Specialized Information Services, National Library of Medicine.

Ecology and Environmental Science

The Dictionary of Ecology and Environmental Science. Ed. Henry W. Art (New York: Holt, 1993). More than 8,000 entries, with definitions, for terms and concepts from environmental biology, chemistry, geology, and physics.

TOXNET. See entry under "Chemistry."

The University of Connecticut's Guide to Resources for Environmental Science <www.lib.uconn.edu/research/bysubject/environm.htm> Comprehensive list of useful links for research in ecology and environmental science.

Geology

Encyclopedia of Geology. Richard C. Selley and Ian R. Plimmer (Philadelphia: Elsevier, 2004). Covers all aspects of geology and new investigative techniques pertaining to earth history, earth materials, surface processes, regional geology, economic geology, engineering geology, petroleum geology, geochemical and mineral exploration, and the history of geology.

Geology.com <geology.com/> Current information about geology in an accessible format.

Health and Medicine

The Gale Encyclopedia of Nursing and Allied Health, 2nd ed. Ed. Jacqueline L. Longe (Farmington Hills, MI: Gale Cengage, 2006). Covers a wide range of subjects related to nursing and the allied health professions including diseases and disorders, tests and procedures, equipment and tools, human biology and body systems, nursing and allied health professions, and current health issues.

Lippincott's Nursing Center <www.nursingcenter.com/home/index.asp> Information from more than 50 nursing journals.

Miller-Keane Encyclopedia and Dictionary of Medicine, Nursing, and Allied Health, rev. reprint 7th ed. Ed. Benjamin Miller, Clare Brackman Keane, and Marie O'Toole (Philadelphia: Saunders, 2005). Provides medical definitions and covers topics across the health care spectrum.

Mathematics

CRC Concise Encyclopedia of Mathematics, 2nd ed. Ed. Eric W. Weisstein (Boca Raton, FL: Chapman & Hall/CRC, 2002). Contains mathematical definitions, formulas, figures, tabulations, and references.

Wolfram MathWorld <mathworld.wolfram.com/> Collaboratively created clearinghouse for researcher-contributed new mathematical discoveries. An educational resource.

Physics

McGraw-Hill Dictionary of Physics, 3rd ed. (New York: McGraw-Hill, 2003). Defines words and phrases encountered in physics.

Physics and Astronomy Online <www.physlink.com/> Comprehensive physics and astronomy research and reference website.

Associations and Organizations in the Natural Sciences and Mathematics

American Association of Physicists in Medicine
American Astronomical Society
American College of Sports Medicine
American Mathematical Society
American Medical Association
American Physical Society
Association for Environmental Health and Sciences
Biology News Net
Geological Organizations and Agencies <geology.com/groups.htm>
International Council of Nurses
International Organization for Chemical Sciences in Development <www.iocd.org/index.shtml>
World Health Organization <www.who.int/en/>

Professional Disciplines

Business

Encyclopedia of Business, 2nd ed. Ed. Jane A. Malonis and Gale Group (Farmington Hills, MI: Gale, 1999). Essays by business school professors, members of the business community, and business writers covering 700 business topics including internal business functions such as finance, human resources, and marketing and external elements that affect businesses, such as technology, environmental concerns, and federal laws.

Rutgers Business Research Guide <libguides.rutgers.edu/business> Descriptions of databases and hundreds of reference books on a variety of business and management topics.

Law

American Legal Systems: A Resource and Reference Guide. Tony M. Fine (New York: Yeshiva University, Benjamin N. Cardozo School of Law, 1997). Overview of the American legal system and the interrelationships between and among its institutions and legal authorities.

Center for International Environmental Law

Lexis/Nexis Academic <www.lexisnexis.com/hottopics/lnacademic/?> Sometimes accessible through college libraries. Indexes approximately 6,000 news, business, and legal resources. Includes case citations from 1789 to present.

Library of Congress Guide to Law Online <www.loc.gov/law/help/guide.php> Annotated guide to sources of information on government and law prepared by the Public Services Division of the Law Library of Congress.

Associations and Organizations in the Professional Disciplines

Academy of International Business <aib.msu.edu/resources/Professionalorgs.asp>
American Association for Justice <www.justice.org/cps/rde/xchg/justice/hs.xsl/default.htm>
American Bar Association
American Civil Liberties Union
American Society of International Law
Business and Professional Women's Foundation <www.bpwfoundation.org/i4a/pages/index.cfm?pageid=1>
Business Professionals of America
International Academy of Business and Economics <www.iabe.com/domains/iabex/Default.aspx>

Credits

Text Credits

405

Chapter 19: Fig. 19.1: http://www .Johnadamslibrary.org. *Courtesy of the John Adams Library at the Boston Public Library* **Fig. 19.4 (left):** http://www.moca.org/museum/ exhibitiondetail.php?id=352. Basquiat painting © 2011 The Estate of Jean-Michel Basquiat/ADAGP, Paris/ARS, New York. Reprinted by permission. Reproduction, including downloading of Basquiat works is prohibited by copyright laws and international conventions without the express written permission of Artists Rights Society (ARS), New York. Screenshot reprinted by permission of the Museum of Contemporary Art. **Fig 19.4 (right):** http://www.c-span.org. © 2011 National Cable Satellite Corporation **Fig 19.6:** From CNN, Sunday, June 26, 2011 © 2011 CNN. All rights reserved. Used by permission and protected by the Copyright Laws of the United States. The printing, copying, redistribution, or retransmission of this Content without express written permission is prohibited." **Fig 19.7:**

Lindsey C. Bohl, "Courting the Youth Vote in 2008: The Obama Effect." From The Vanderbilt Undergraduate Research Journal. Reprinted by permission of the Vanderbilt Undergraduate Research Journal.

Chapter 20: p. 234: Classification under the Linnaean System from http://eapbiofield.wikispaces.com/ Margaret%27s+PR+Exam+Page. Illustration credit: Peter Halasz.

Photo Credits

Page 1: © John Norris/Corbis; **p. 9:** PM Images/Getty Images; **p. 10:** © Michael Newman/PhotoEdit; **p. 23:** © Mascarucci/Corbis; **p. 25:** © Tetra Images/Corbis; **p. 45:** Courtesy Da Vinci's Notebook; **p. F2:** Fancy Photography/Veer; **p. F3:** Comstock/ PictureQuest; **p. 60:** Ingram Publishing; **p. 76:** Bildarchiv Preussischer Kulturbesitz/Art Resource, NY; **p. 88:** Erich Lessing/Art Resource, NY; **p. 111:** Franklin D. Roosevelt Presidential Library and Museum; **p. 113:** Bildarchiv Preussischer Kulturbesitz/ Art Resource; **p. 127 T:** Courtesy of Louis Bloomfield; **p. 127 C:** Courtesy of Harold Garner, Virginia Bioinformatics Institute at Virginia Tech; **p. 127 B:** Adrian Dennis/AFP/Getty Images; **p. 150:** © Sarah Hadley/ Alamy; **p. 157R:** Lenora Gim/Getty Images; **p. 157L:** Radious/Superstock; **p. 170:** © Car Culture/Corbis; **p. 182:** © GraphicallyMinded/Alamy; **p. 189:** "Jacket Cover" from JIMMY CORRIGAN: THE SMARTEST KID ON EARTH by Chris Ware, © 2000 by Mr. Chris Ware. Used by permission of Pantheon Books, a division of Random House, Inc.; **p. 193:** © Bloomimage/Corbis; **p. 203:** © Natali Garyachaya/Alamy; **p. 216:** WPA Poster Collection, Library of Congress, Prints & Photographs Division; **p. 238:** © Corbis; **p. 297L:** SPIDERMAN: TM & © 2013 Marvel Characters, Inc. Used with permission; **p. 297 R:** Copyright © Robert Crumb, 2011. Used by permission, Agence Littéraire Lora Fountain & Associates, Paris, France; **p. 301:** "Jacket Cover" from JIMMY CORRIGAN: THE SMARTEST KID ON EARTH by Chris Ware, © 2000 by Mr. Chris Ware. Used by permission of Pantheon Books, a division of Random House, Inc.; **p. 343 (all):** Photographs courtesy of Jane Carter; **p. 371:** The David Rumsey Map Collection, www.davidrumsey.com.

Index